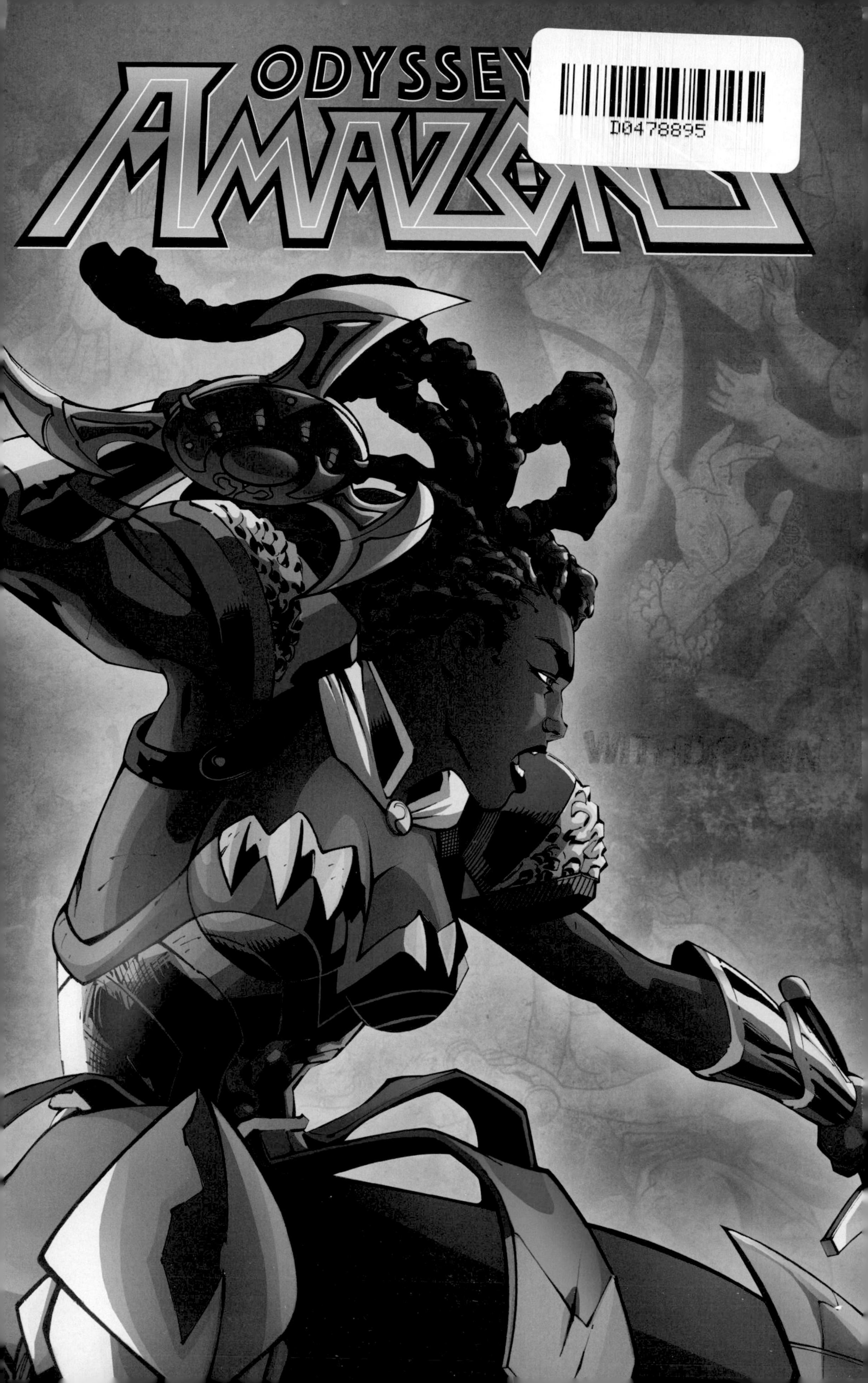
ODYSSEY
AMAZONS

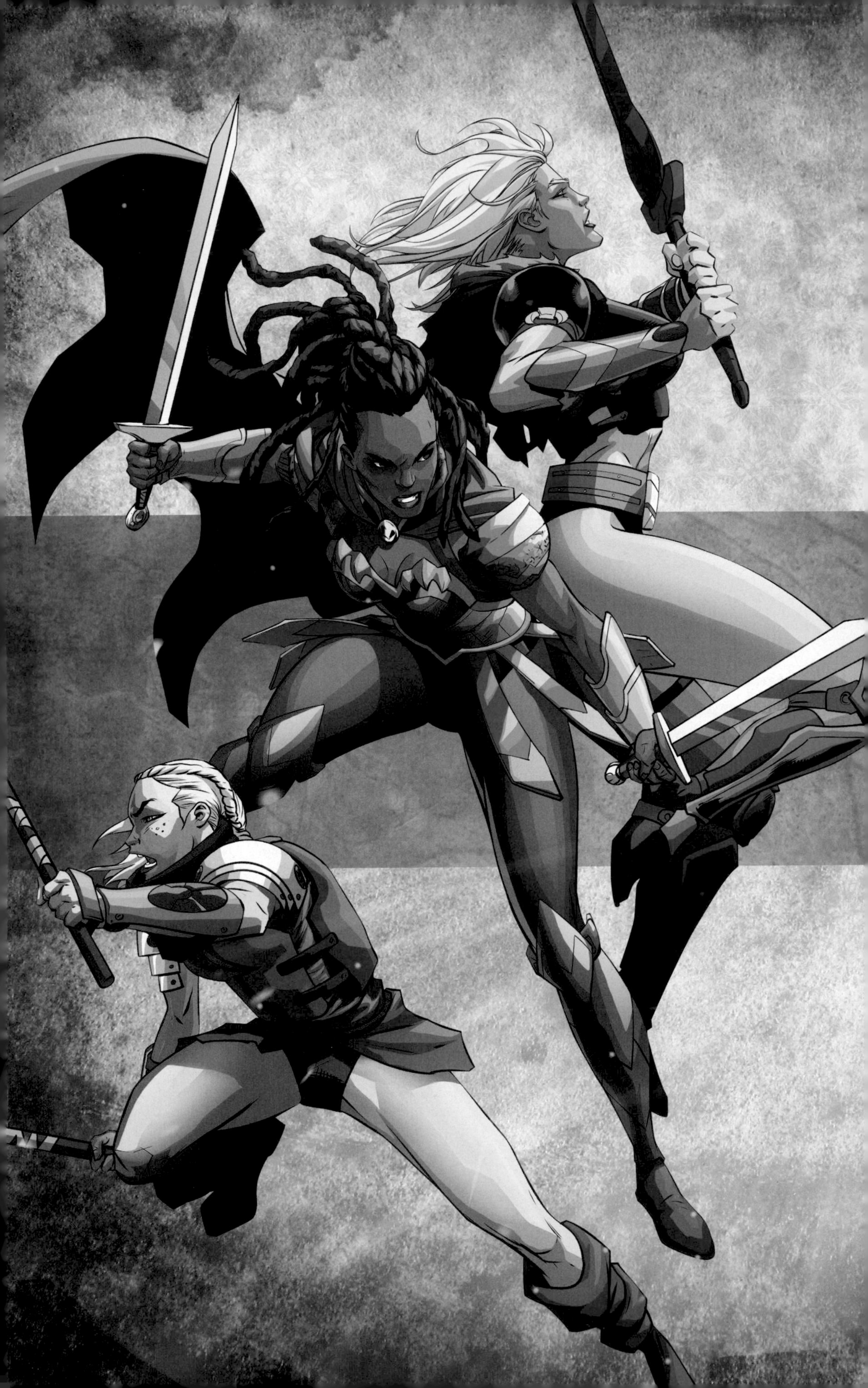

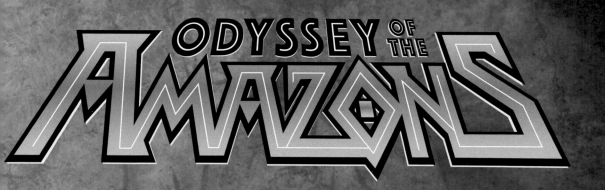

ODYSSEY OF THE AMAZONS

Story and Script by KEVIN GREVIOUX

Designs and Pencils by RYAN BENJAMIN

Inks by DON HO • RICHARD FRIEND • RYAN BENJAMIN

Colors by TONY WASHINGTON • TONY AVIÑA • RYAN BENJAMIN

Letters by SAIDA TEMOFONTE

Cover Art by RYAN BENJAMIN

WONDER WOMAN CREATED BY WILLIAM MOULTON MARSTON

JIM CHADWICK Editor – Original Series
JESSICA CHEN Associate Editor – Original Series
JEB WOODARD Group Editor – Collected Editions
SCOTT NYBAKKEN Editor – Collected Edition
STEVE COOK Design Director – Books
SHANNON STEWART Publication Design

BOB HARRAS Senior VP – Editor-in-Chief, DC Comics
PAT McCALLUM Executive Editor, DC Comics

DIANE NELSON President
DAN DiDIO Publisher
JIM LEE Publisher
GEOFF JOHNS President & Chief Creative Officer
AMIT DESAI Executive VP – Business & Marketing Strategy,
Direct to Consumer & Global Franchise Management
SAM ADES Senior VP & General Manager, Digital Services
BOBBIE CHASE VP & Executive Editor, Young Reader & Talent Development
MARK CHIARELLO Senior VP – Art, Design & Collected Editions
JOHN CUNNINGHAM Senior VP – Sales & Trade Marketing
ANNE DePIES Senior VP – Business Strategy, Finance & Administration
DON FALLETTI VP – Manufacturing Operations
LAWRENCE GANEM VP – Editorial Administration & Talent Relations
ALISON GILL Senior VP – Manufacturing & Operations
HANK KANALZ Senior VP – Editorial Strategy & Administration
JAY KOGAN VP – Legal Affairs
JACK MAHAN VP – Business Affairs
NICK J. NAPOLITANO VP – Manufacturing Administration
EDDIE SCANNELL VP – Consumer Marketing
COURTNEY SIMMONS Senior VP – Publicity & Communications
JIM (SKI) SOKOLOWSKI VP – Comic Book Specialty Sales & Trade Marketing
NANCY SPEARS VP – Mass, Book, Digital Sales & Trade Marketing
MICHELE R. WELLS VP – Content Strategy

ODYSSEY OF THE AMAZONS

DC Comics
2900 West Alameda Ave.
Burbank, CA 91505
Printed by LSC Communications, Kendallville, IN, USA. 10/27/17.
First Printing.
ISBN: 978-1-4012-7447-4

Library of Congress Cataloging-in-Publication Data is available.

PEFC Certified

Printed on paper from
sustainably managed
forests, controlled
sources

PEFC/29-31-337   www.pefc.org

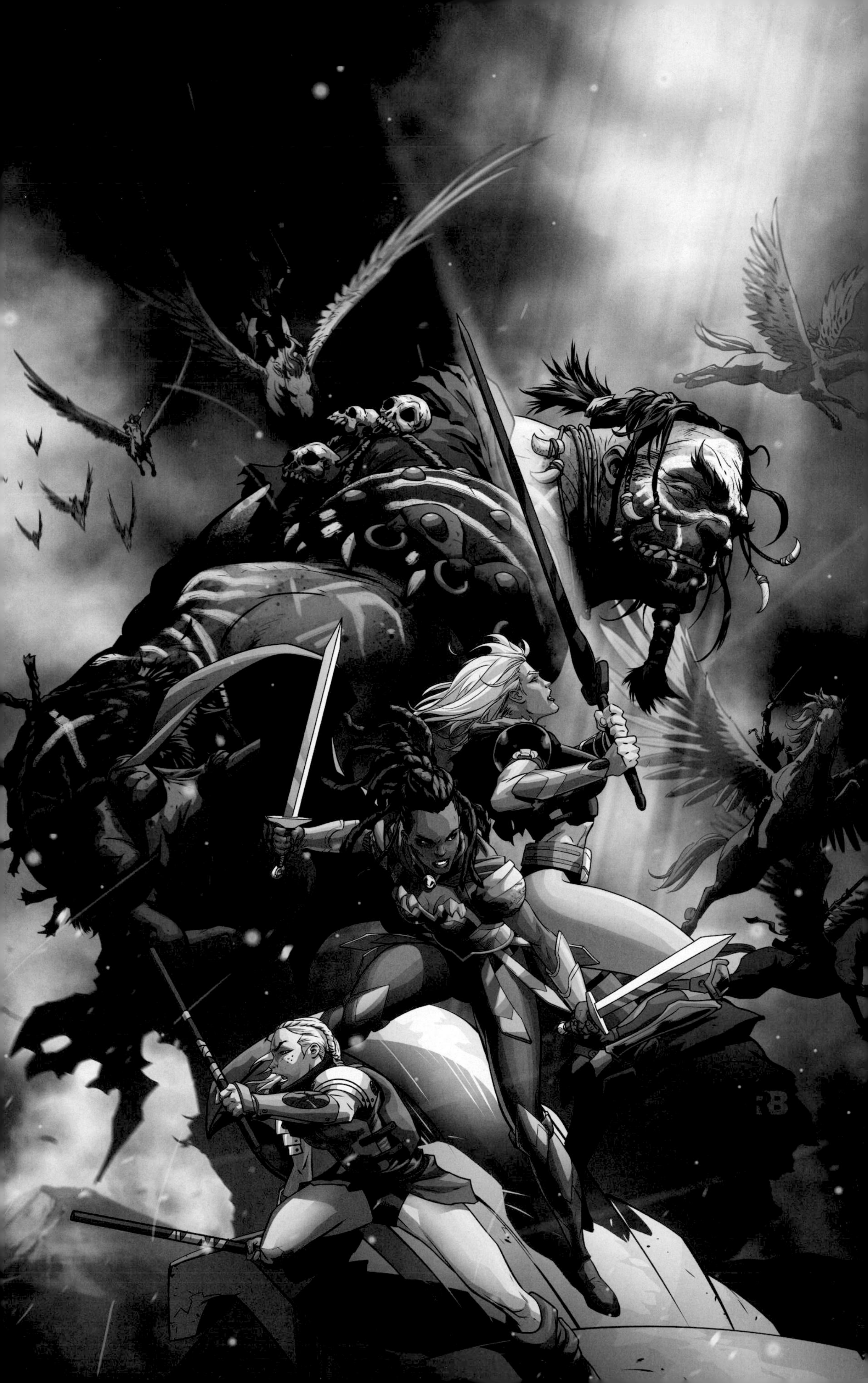

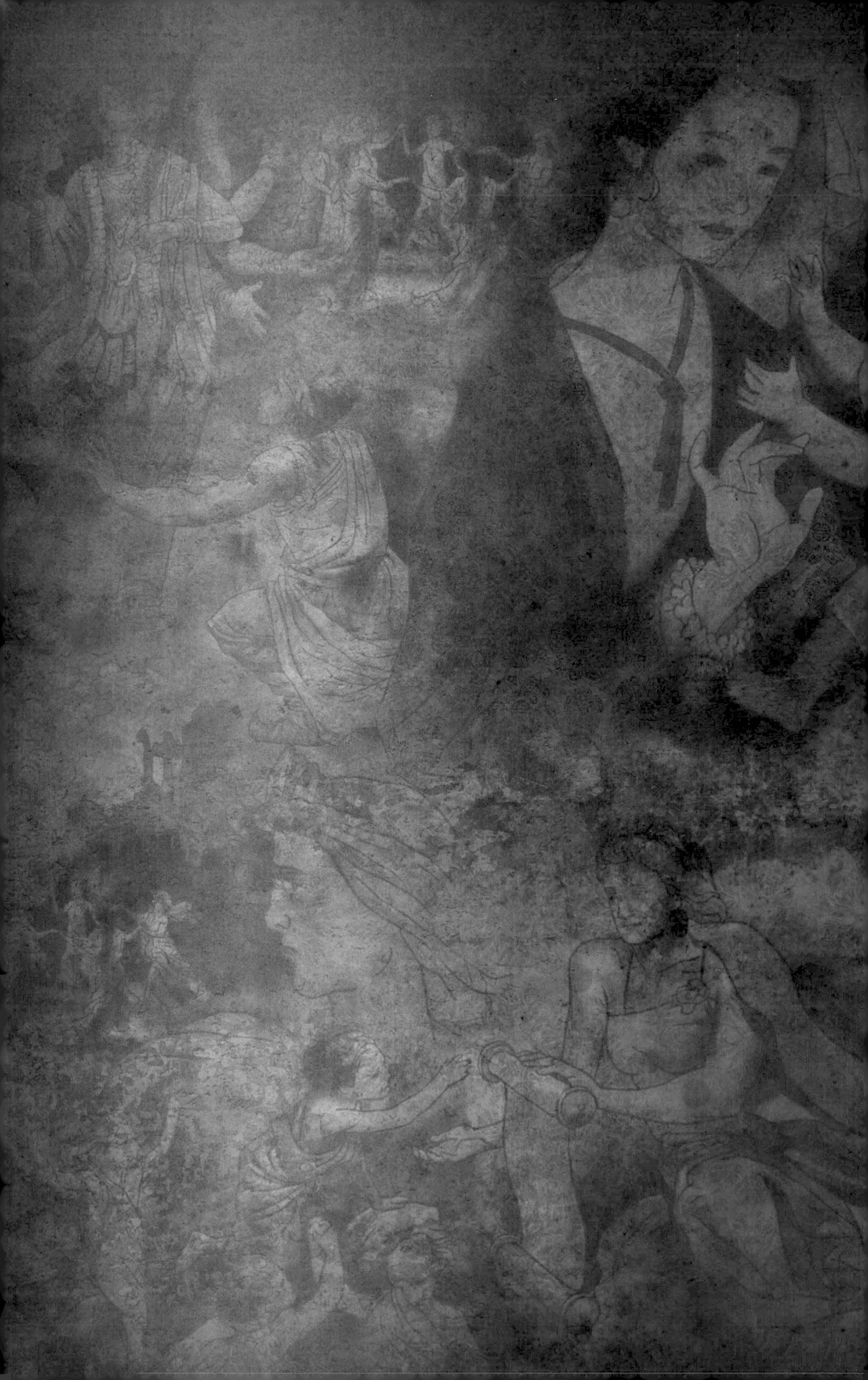

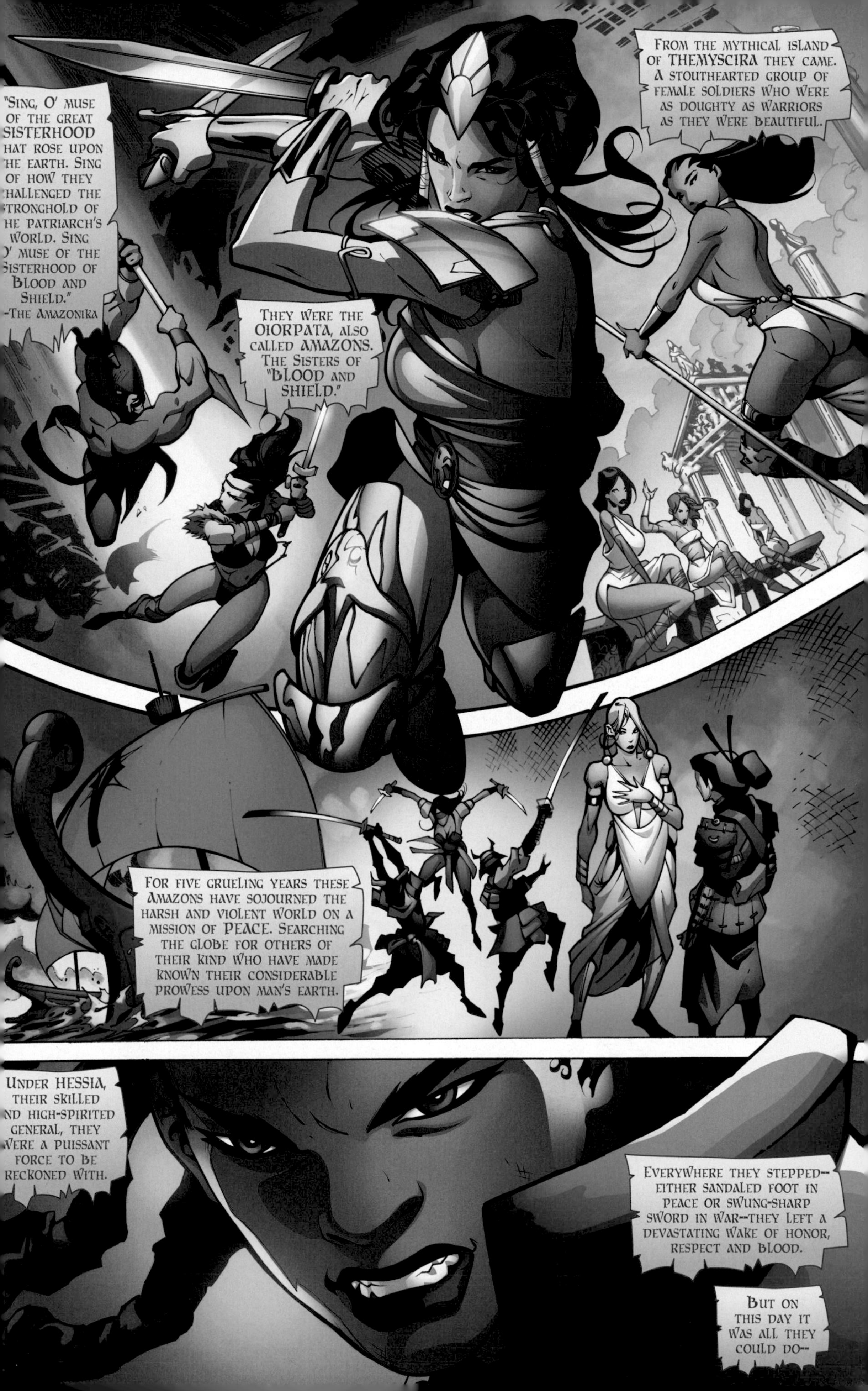
"SING, O' MUSE OF THE GREAT SISTERHOOD HAT ROSE UPON HE EARTH. SING OF HOW THEY CHALLENGED THE STRONGHOLD OF HE PATRIARCH'S WORLD. SING O' MUSE OF THE SISTERHOOD OF BLOOD AND SHIELD." --THE AMAZONIKA
FROM THE MYTHICAL ISLAND OF THEMYSCIRA THEY CAME. A STOUTHEARTED GROUP OF FEMALE SOLDIERS WHO WERE AS DOUGHTY AS WARRIORS AS THEY WERE BEAUTIFUL.
THEY WERE THE OIORPATA, ALSO CALLED AMAZONS. THE SISTERS OF "BLOOD AND SHIELD."
FOR FIVE GRUELING YEARS THESE AMAZONS HAVE SOJOURNED THE HARSH AND VIOLENT WORLD ON A MISSION OF PEACE. SEARCHING THE GLOBE FOR OTHERS OF THEIR KIND WHO HAVE MADE KNOWN THEIR CONSIDERABLE PROWESS UPON MAN'S EARTH.
UNDER HESSIA, THEIR SKILLED ND HIGH-SPIRITED GENERAL, THEY WERE A PUISSANT FORCE TO BE RECKONED WITH.
EVERYWHERE THEY STEPPED--EITHER SANDALED FOOT IN PEACE OR SWUNG-SHARP SWORD IN WAR--THEY LEFT A DEVASTATING WAKE OF HONOR, RESPECT AND BLOOD.
BUT ON THIS DAY IT WAS ALL THEY COULD DO--

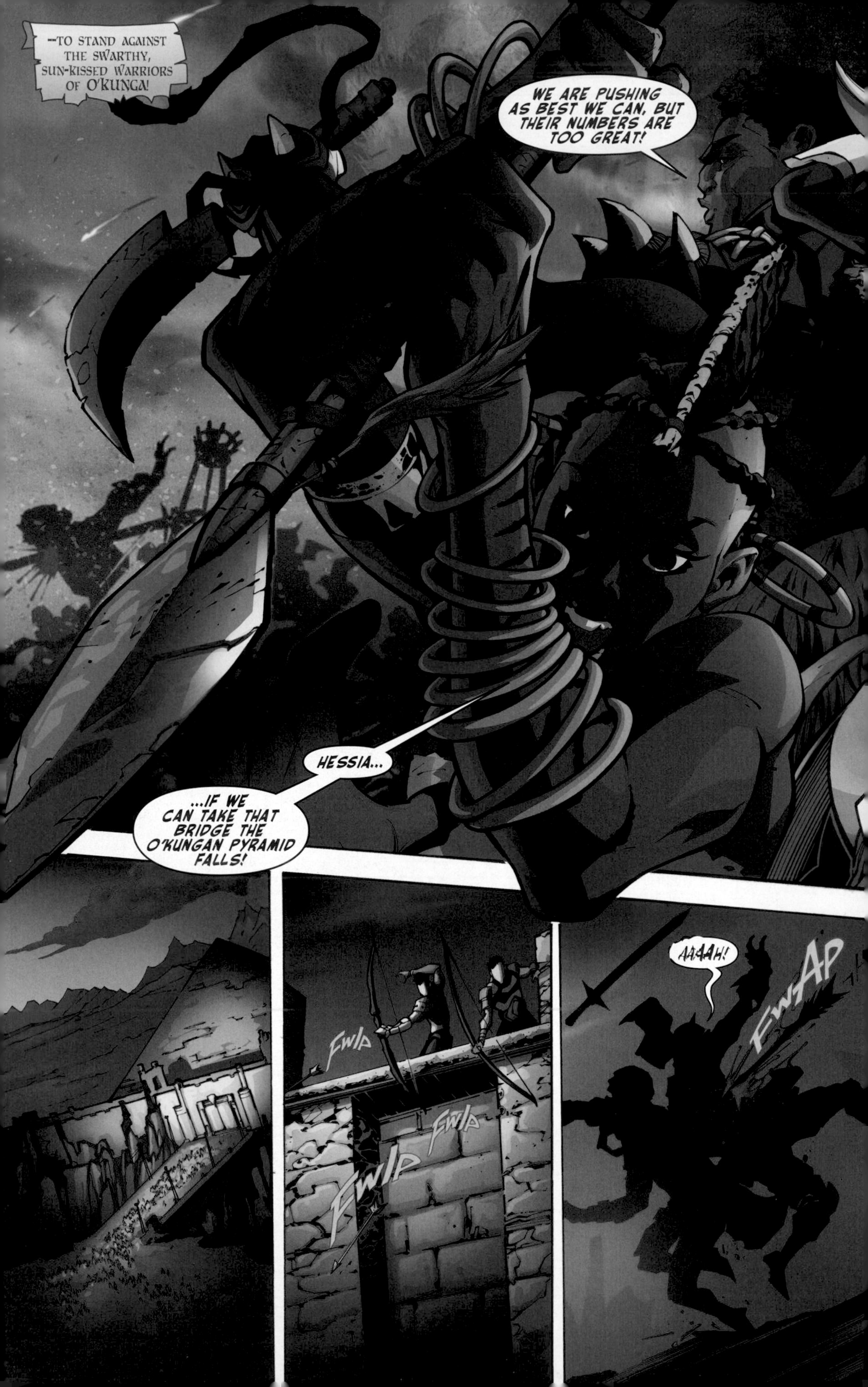
--TO STAND AGAINST THE SWARTHY, SUN-KISSED WARRIORS OF O'KUNGA!
WE ARE PUSHING AS BEST WE CAN, BUT THEIR NUMBERS ARE TOO GREAT!
HESSIA...
...IF WE CAN TAKE THAT BRIDGE THE O'KUNGAN PYRAMID FALLS!
FWIP
FWIP
FWIP
AAAAH!
FWAP

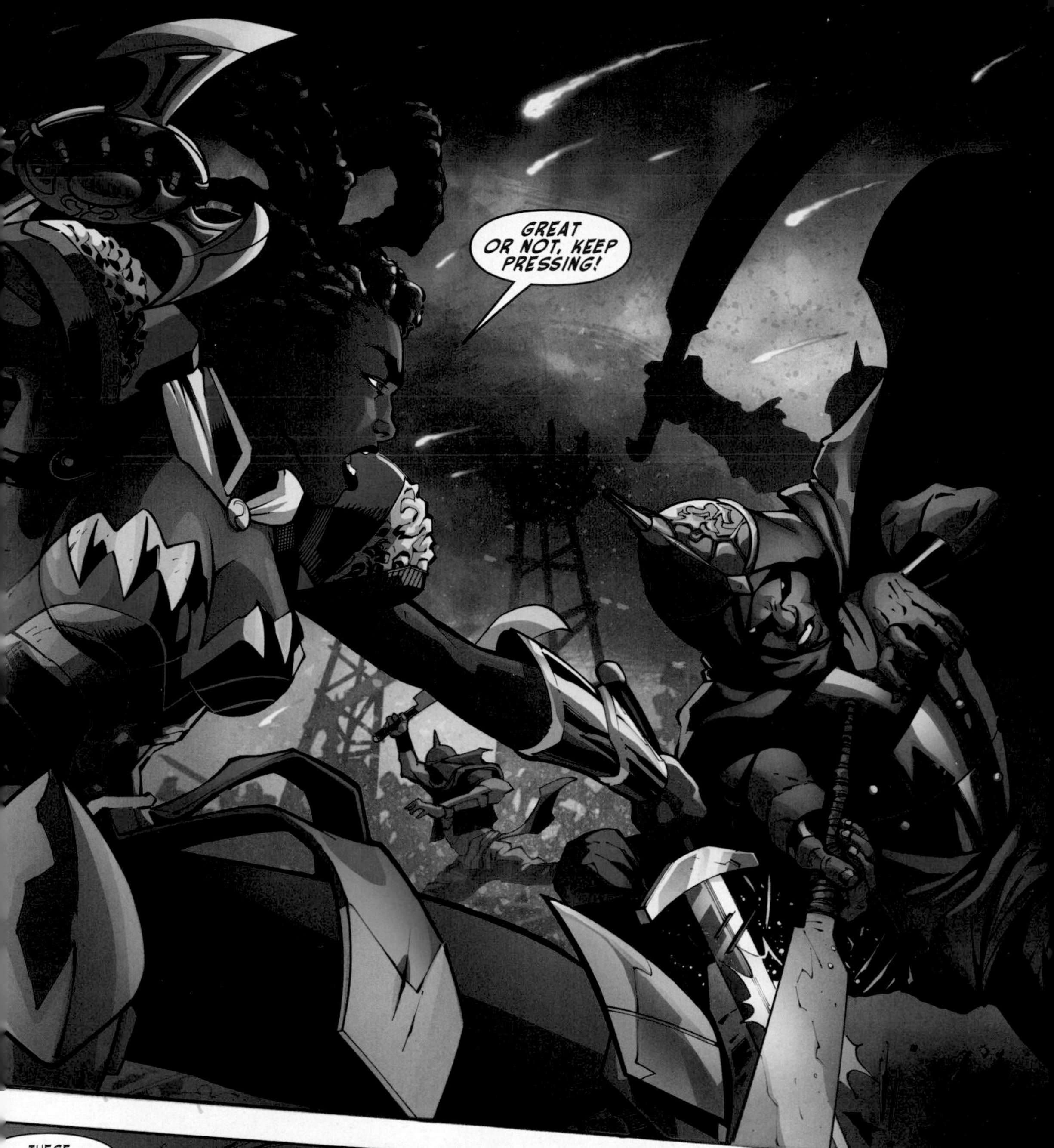
GREAT OR NOT, KEEP PRESSING!

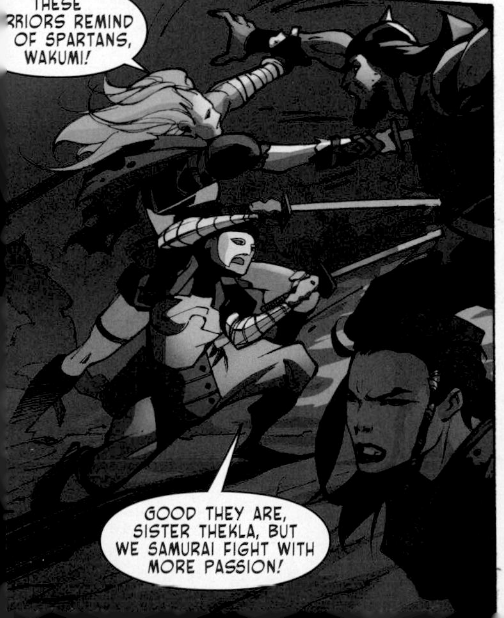
THESE RRIORS REMIND OF SPARTANS, WAKUMI!
GOOD THEY ARE, SISTER THEKLA, BUT WE SAMURAI FIGHT WITH MORE PASSION!

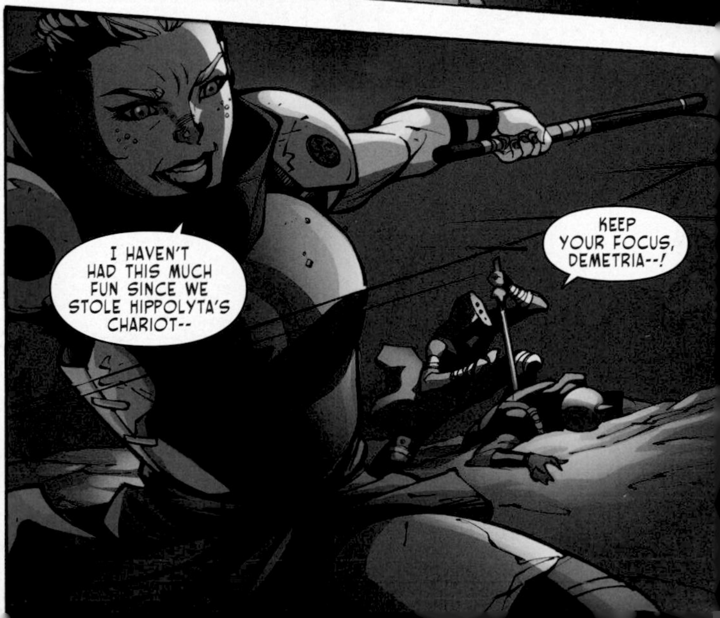
I HAVEN'T HAD THIS MUCH FUN SINCE WE STOLE HIPPOLYTA'S CHARIOT--
KEEP YOUR FOCUS, DEMETRIA--!

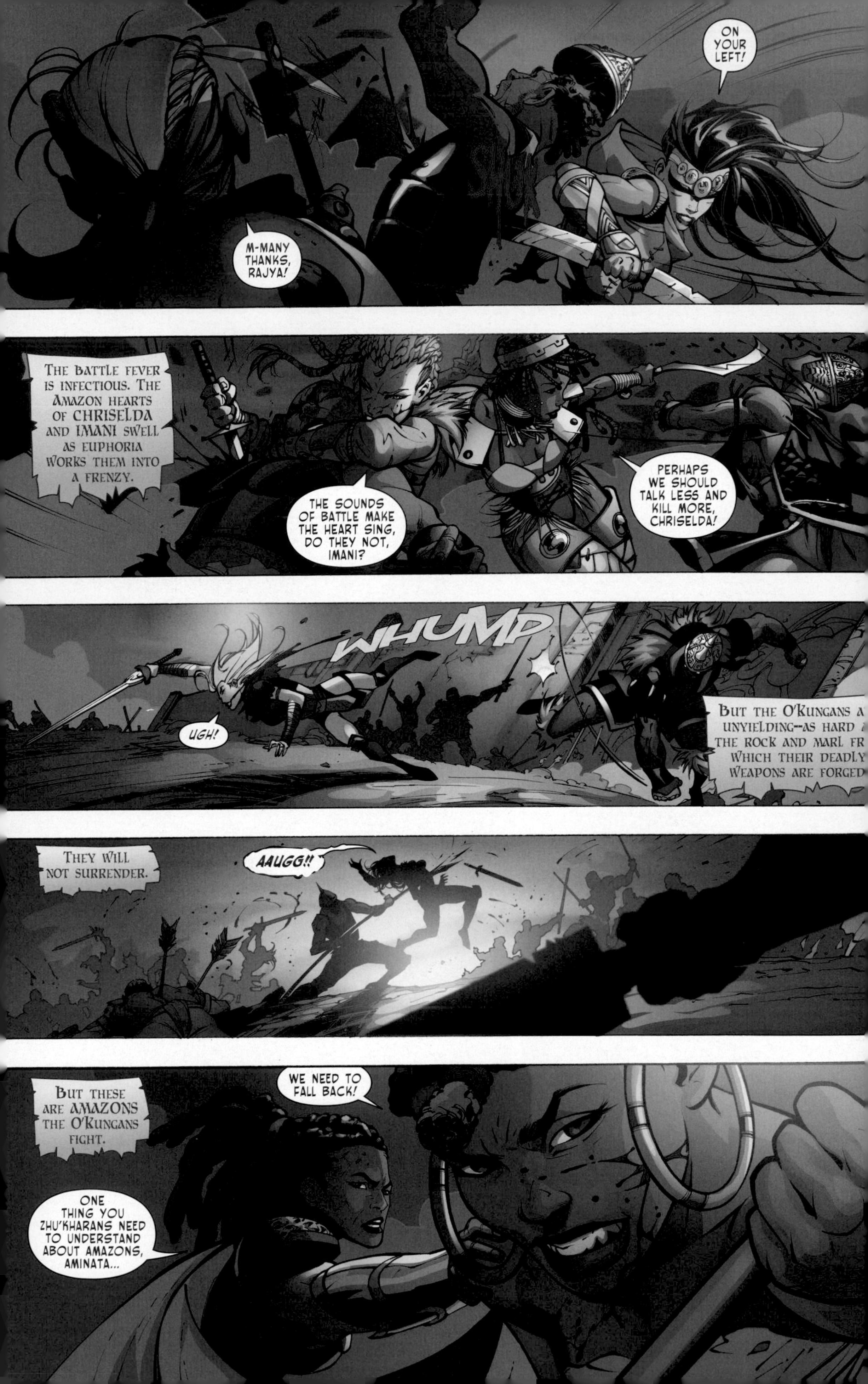
ON YOUR LEFT!
M-MANY THANKS, RAJYA!
THE BATTLE FEVER IS INFECTIOUS. THE AMAZON HEARTS OF CHRISELDA AND IMANI SWELL AS EUPHORIA WORKS THEM INTO A FRENZY.
THE SOUNDS OF BATTLE MAKE THE HEART SING, DO THEY NOT, IMANI?
PERHAPS WE SHOULD TALK LESS AND KILL MORE, CHRISELDA!
WHUMP
UGH!
BUT THE O'KUNGANS A UNYIELDING--AS HARD THE ROCK AND MARL FR WHICH THEIR DEADLY WEAPONS ARE FORGED
THEY WILL NOT SURRENDER.
AAUGG!!
BUT THESE ARE AMAZONS THE O'KUNGANS FIGHT.
WE NEED TO FALL BACK!
ONE THING YOU ZHU'KHARANS NEED TO UNDERSTAND ABOUT AMAZONS, AMINATA...

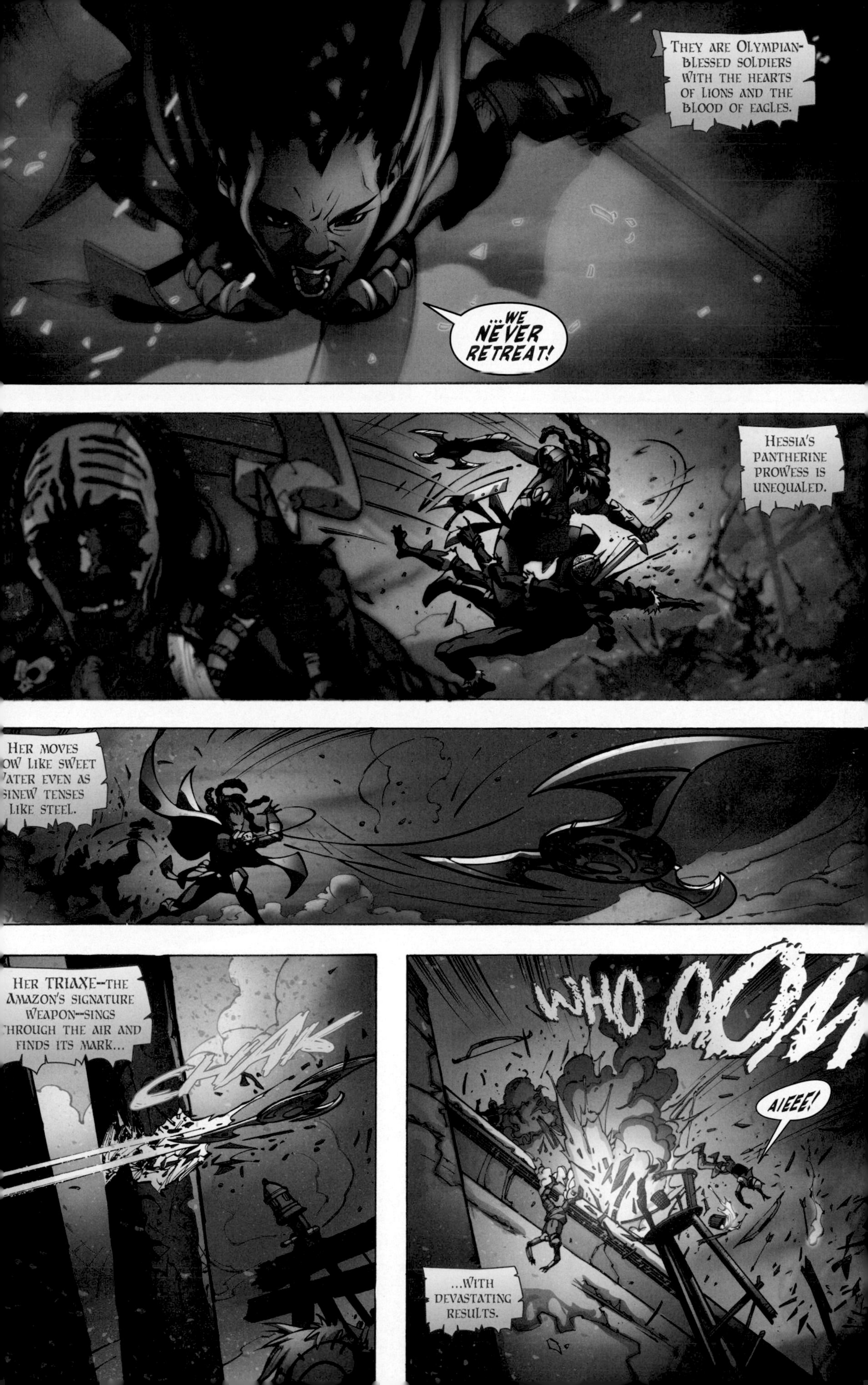
They are Olympian-blessed soldiers with the hearts of lions and the blood of eagles.
...we never retreat!
Hessia's pantherine prowess is unequaled.
Her moves ow like sweet water even as sinew tenses like steel.
Her TRIAXE--the Amazon's signature weapon--sings through the air and finds its mark...
WHOOOM
AIEEE!
...with devastating results.

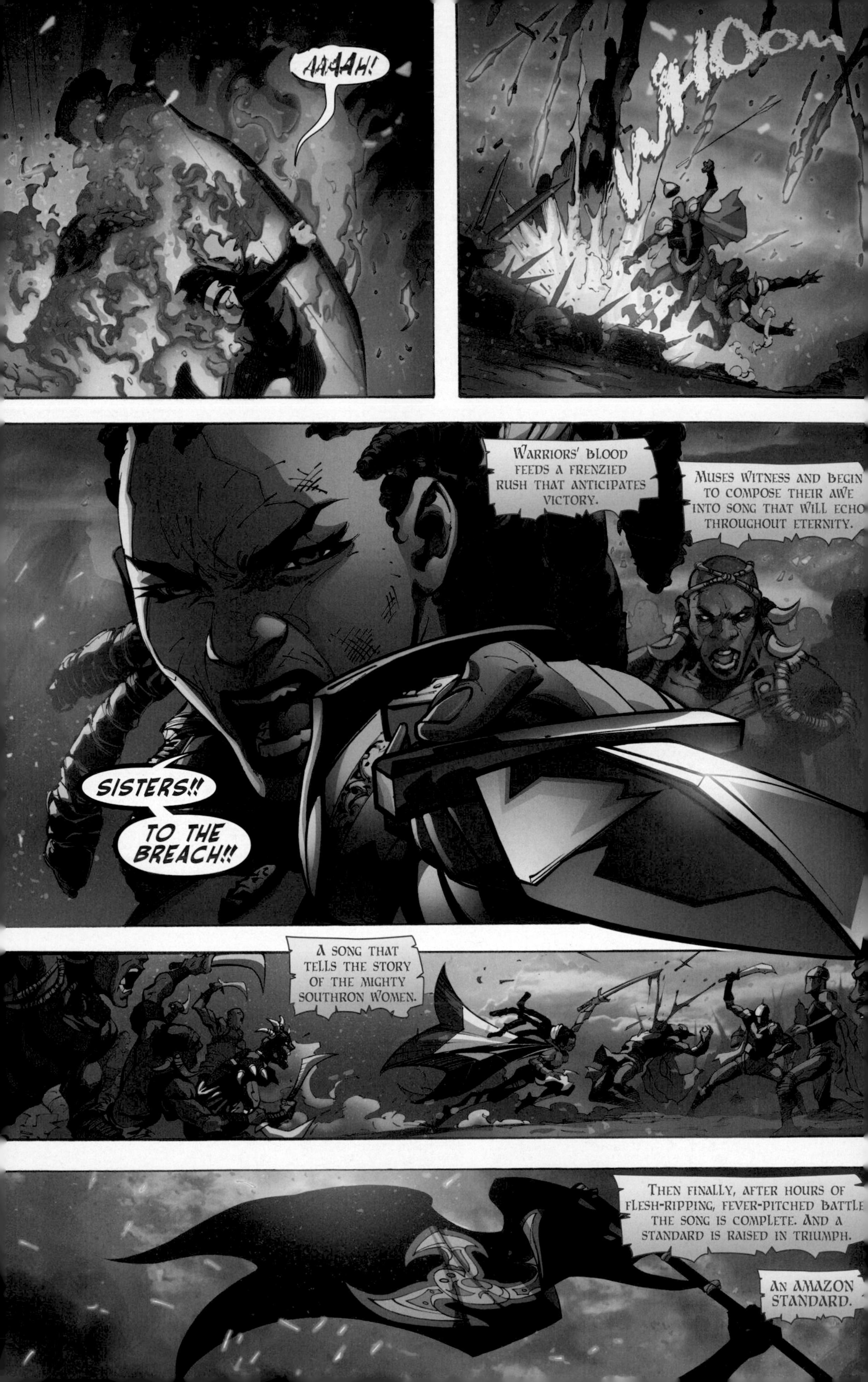
AAAAH!
WHOOM
Warriors' blood feeds a frenzied rush that anticipates victory.
Muses witness and begin to compose their awe into song that will echo throughout eternity.
SISTERS!!
TO THE BREACH!!
A song that tells the story of the mighty Southron women.
Then finally, after hours of flesh-ripping, fever-pitched battle the song is complete. And a standard is raised in triumph.
An Amazon standard.

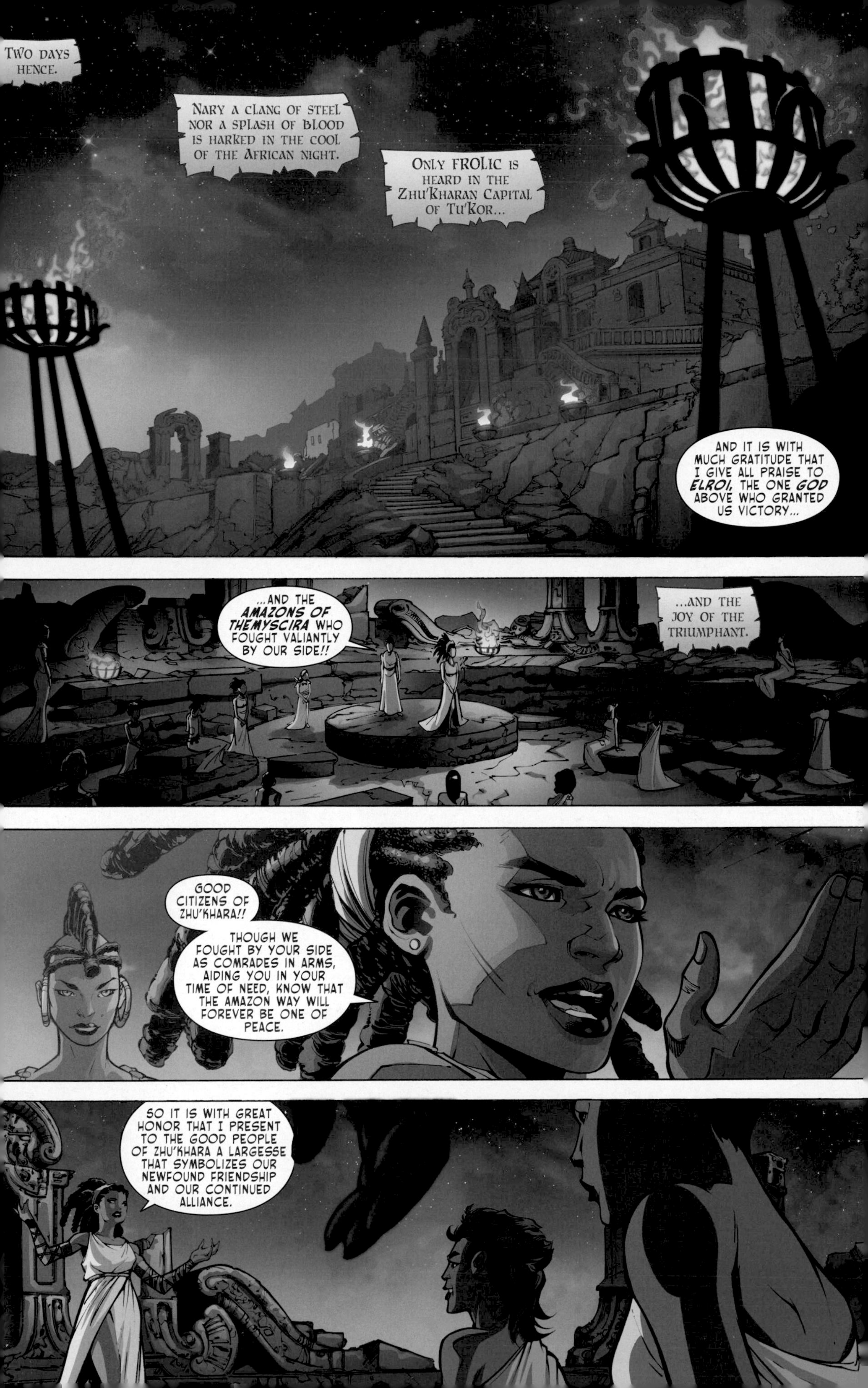
TWO DAYS HENCE.
NARY A CLANG OF STEEL NOR A SPLASH OF BLOOD IS HARKED IN THE COOL OF THE AFRICAN NIGHT.
ONLY FROLIC IS HEARD IN THE ZHU'KHARAN CAPITAL OF TU'KOR...
AND IT IS WITH MUCH GRATITUDE THAT I GIVE ALL PRAISE TO ELROI, THE ONE GOD ABOVE WHO GRANTED US VICTORY...
...AND THE AMAZONS OF THEMYSCIRA WHO FOUGHT VALIANTLY BY OUR SIDE!!
...AND THE JOY OF THE TRIUMPHANT.
GOOD CITIZENS OF ZHU'KHARA!!
THOUGH WE FOUGHT BY YOUR SIDE AS COMRADES IN ARMS, AIDING YOU IN YOUR TIME OF NEED, KNOW THAT THE AMAZON WAY WILL FOREVER BE ONE OF PEACE.
SO IT IS WITH GREAT HONOR THAT I PRESENT TO THE GOOD PEOPLE OF ZHU'KHARA A LARGESSE THAT SYMBOLIZES OUR NEWFOUND FRIENDSHIP AND OUR CONTINUED ALLIANCE.

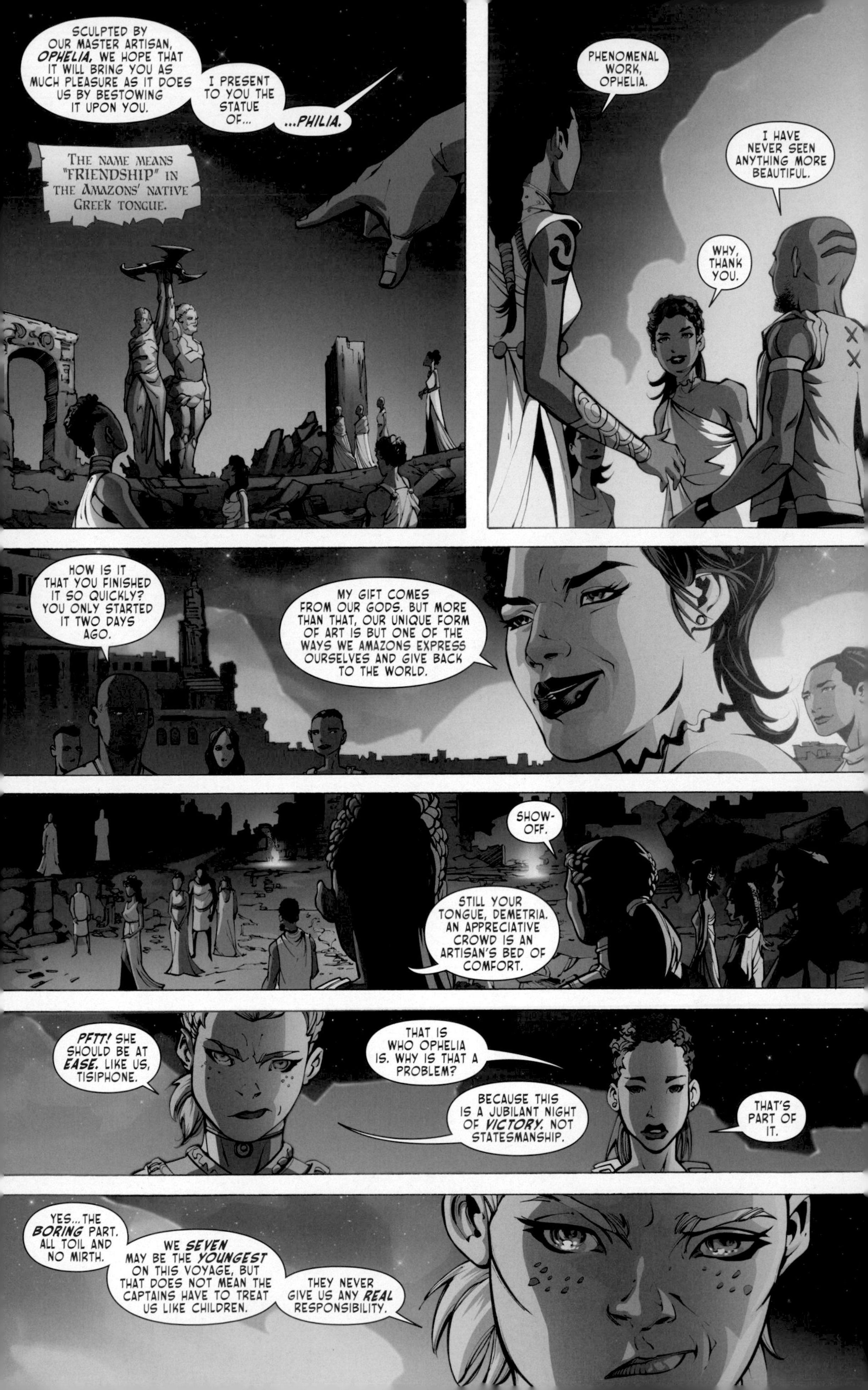
SCULPTED BY OUR MASTER ARTISAN, OPHELIA, WE HOPE THAT IT WILL BRING YOU AS MUCH PLEASURE AS IT DOES US BY BESTOWING IT UPON YOU.
I PRESENT TO YOU THE STATUE OF...
...PHILIA.
THE NAME MEANS "FRIENDSHIP" IN THE AMAZONS' NATIVE GREEK TONGUE.
PHENOMENAL WORK, OPHELIA.
I HAVE NEVER SEEN ANYTHING MORE BEAUTIFUL.
WHY, THANK YOU.
HOW IS IT THAT YOU FINISHED IT SO QUICKLY? YOU ONLY STARTED IT TWO DAYS AGO.
MY GIFT COMES FROM OUR GODS. BUT MORE THAN THAT, OUR UNIQUE FORM OF ART IS BUT ONE OF THE WAYS WE AMAZONS EXPRESS OURSELVES AND GIVE BACK TO THE WORLD.
SHOW-OFF.
STILL YOUR TONGUE, DEMETRIA. AN APPRECIATIVE CROWD IS AN ARTISAN'S BED OF COMFORT.
PFTT! SHE SHOULD BE AT EASE. LIKE US, TISIPHONE.
THAT IS WHO OPHELIA IS. WHY IS THAT A PROBLEM?
BECAUSE THIS IS A JUBILANT NIGHT OF VICTORY. NOT STATESMANSHIP.
THAT'S PART OF IT.
YES...THE BORING PART. ALL TOIL AND NO MIRTH.
WE SEVEN MAY BE THE YOUNGEST ON THIS VOYAGE, BUT THAT DOES NOT MEAN THE CAPTAINS HAVE TO TREAT US LIKE CHILDREN.
THEY NEVER GIVE US ANY REAL RESPONSIBILITY.

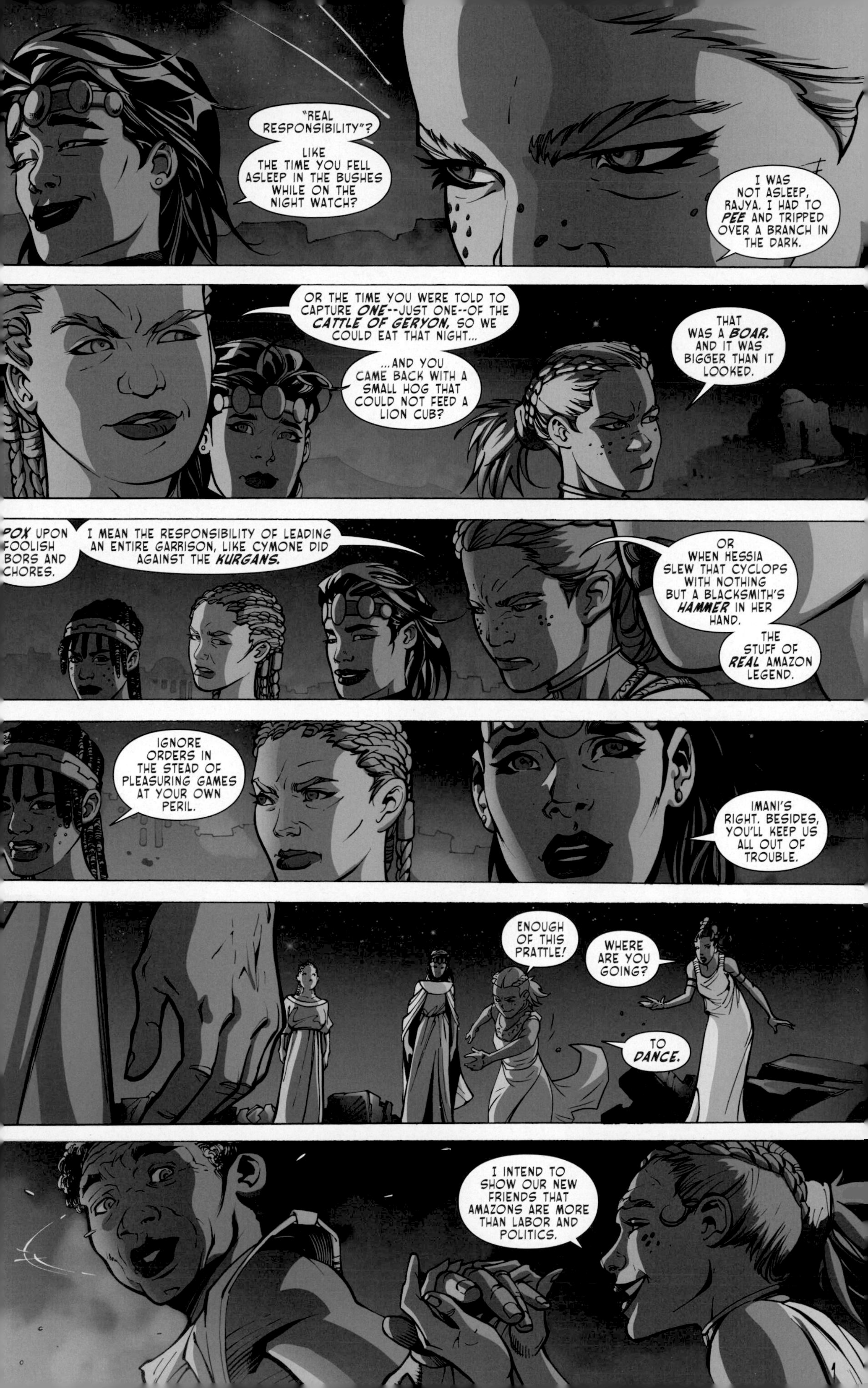
"REAL RESPONSIBILITY"?
LIKE THE TIME YOU FELL ASLEEP IN THE BUSHES WHILE ON THE NIGHT WATCH?
I WAS NOT ASLEEP, RAJYA. I HAD TO PEE AND TRIPPED OVER A BRANCH IN THE DARK.
OR THE TIME YOU WERE TOLD TO CAPTURE ONE--JUST ONE--OF THE CATTLE OF GERYON, SO WE COULD EAT THAT NIGHT...
...AND YOU CAME BACK WITH A SMALL HOG THAT COULD NOT FEED A LION CUB?
THAT WAS A BOAR. AND IT WAS BIGGER THAN IT LOOKED.
POX UPON FOOLISH BORS AND CHORES.
I MEAN THE RESPONSIBILITY OF LEADING AN ENTIRE GARRISON, LIKE CYMONE DID AGAINST THE KURGANS.
OR WHEN HESSIA SLEW THAT CYCLOPS WITH NOTHING BUT A BLACKSMITH'S HAMMER IN HER HAND.
THE STUFF OF REAL AMAZON LEGEND.
IGNORE ORDERS IN THE STEAD OF PLEASURING GAMES AT YOUR OWN PERIL.
IMANI'S RIGHT. BESIDES, YOU'LL KEEP US ALL OUT OF TROUBLE.
ENOUGH OF THIS PRATTLE!
WHERE ARE YOU GOING?
TO DANCE.
I INTEND TO SHOW OUR NEW FRIENDS THAT AMAZONS ARE MORE THAN LABOR AND POLITICS.

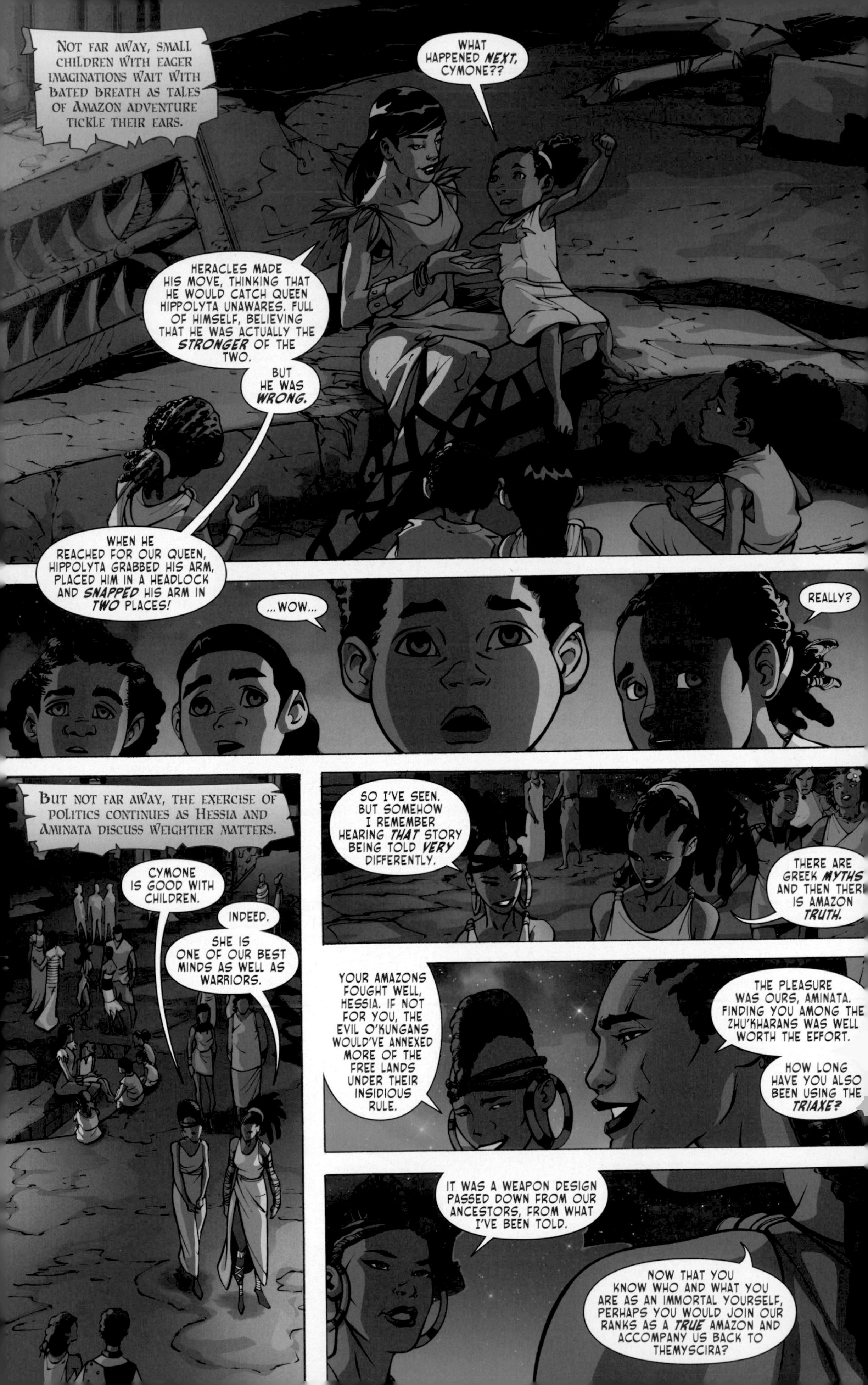

NOT FAR AWAY, SMALL CHILDREN WITH EAGER IMAGINATIONS WAIT WITH BATED BREATH AS TALES OF AMAZON ADVENTURE TICKLE THEIR EARS.
WHAT HAPPENED NEXT, CYMONE??
HERACLES MADE HIS MOVE, THINKING THAT HE WOULD CATCH QUEEN HIPPOLYTA UNAWARES. FULL OF HIMSELF, BELIEVING THAT HE WAS ACTUALLY THE STRONGER OF THE TWO.
BUT HE WAS WRONG.
WHEN HE REACHED FOR OUR QUEEN, HIPPOLYTA GRABBED HIS ARM, PLACED HIM IN A HEADLOCK AND SNAPPED HIS ARM IN TWO PLACES!
...WOW...
REALLY?
BUT NOT FAR AWAY, THE EXERCISE OF POLITICS CONTINUES AS HESSIA AND AMINATA DISCUSS WEIGHTIER MATTERS.
CYMONE IS GOOD WITH CHILDREN.
INDEED.
SHE IS ONE OF OUR BEST MINDS AS WELL AS WARRIORS.
SO I'VE SEEN. BUT SOMEHOW I REMEMBER HEARING THAT STORY BEING TOLD VERY DIFFERENTLY.
THERE ARE GREEK MYTHS AND THEN THERE IS AMAZON TRUTH.
YOUR AMAZONS FOUGHT WELL, HESSIA. IF NOT FOR YOU, THE EVIL O'KUNGANS WOULD'VE ANNEXED MORE OF THE FREE LANDS UNDER THEIR INSIDIOUS RULE.
THE PLEASURE WAS OURS, AMINATA. FINDING YOU AMONG THE ZHU'KHARANS WAS WELL WORTH THE EFFORT.
HOW LONG HAVE YOU ALSO BEEN USING THE TRIAXE?
IT WAS A WEAPON DESIGN PASSED DOWN FROM OUR ANCESTORS, FROM WHAT I'VE BEEN TOLD.
NOW THAT YOU KNOW WHO AND WHAT YOU ARE AS AN IMMORTAL YOURSELF, PERHAPS YOU WOULD JOIN OUR RANKS AS A TRUE AMAZON AND ACCOMPANY US BACK TO THEMYSCIRA?

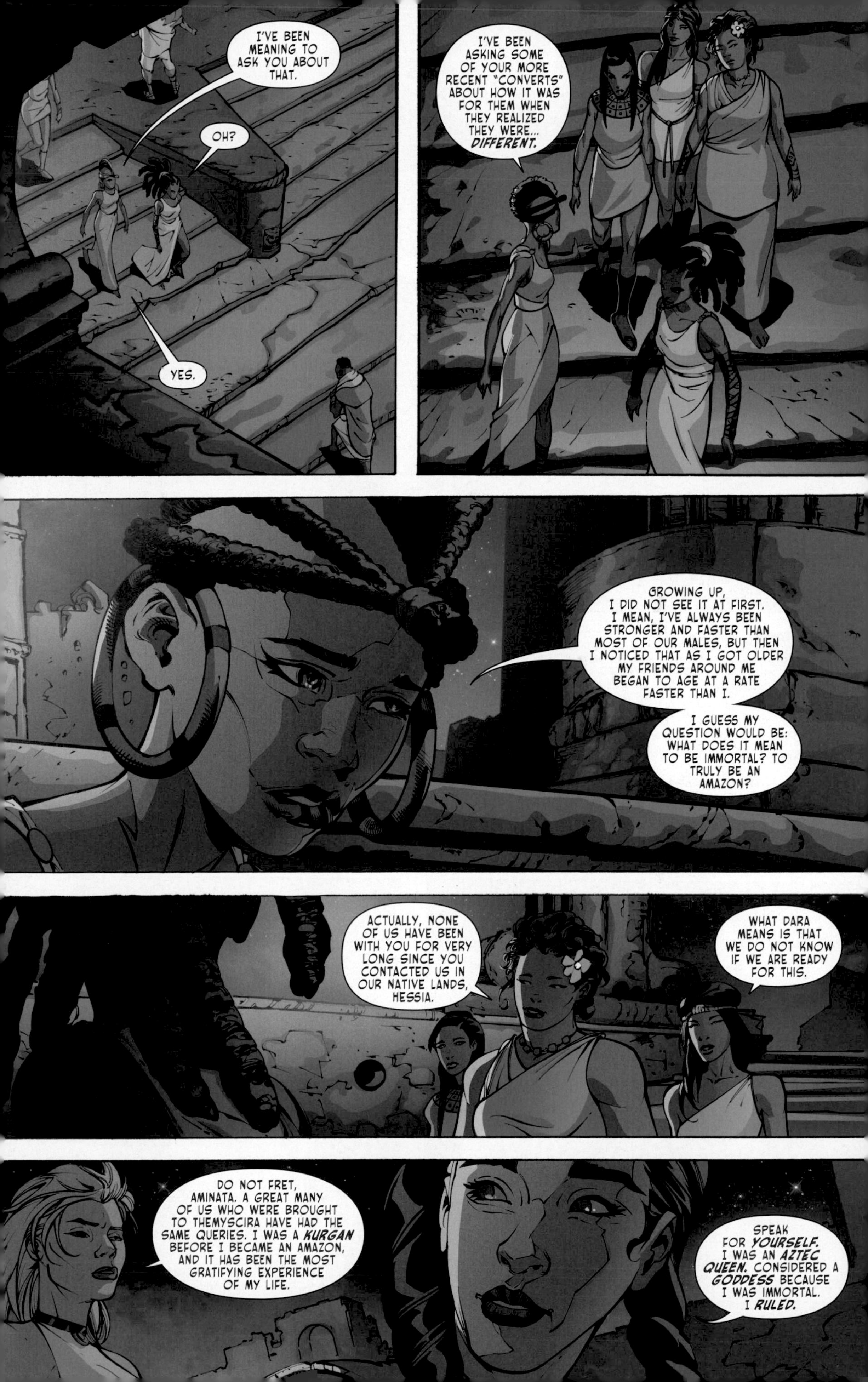

I'VE BEEN MEANING TO ASK YOU ABOUT THAT.
OH?
YES.
I'VE BEEN ASKING SOME OF YOUR MORE RECENT "CONVERTS" ABOUT HOW IT WAS FOR THEM WHEN THEY REALIZED THEY WERE... DIFFERENT.
GROWING UP, I DID NOT SEE IT AT FIRST. I MEAN, I'VE ALWAYS BEEN STRONGER AND FASTER THAN MOST OF OUR MALES, BUT THEN I NOTICED THAT AS I GOT OLDER MY FRIENDS AROUND ME BEGAN TO AGE AT A RATE FASTER THAN I.
I GUESS MY QUESTION WOULD BE: WHAT DOES IT MEAN TO BE IMMORTAL? TO TRULY BE AN AMAZON?
ACTUALLY, NONE OF US HAVE BEEN WITH YOU FOR VERY LONG SINCE YOU CONTACTED US IN OUR NATIVE LANDS, HESSIA.
WHAT DARA MEANS IS THAT WE DO NOT KNOW IF WE ARE READY FOR THIS.
DO NOT FRET, AMINATA. A GREAT MANY OF US WHO WERE BROUGHT TO THEMYSCIRA HAVE HAD THE SAME QUERIES. I WAS A KURGAN BEFORE I BECAME AN AMAZON, AND IT HAS BEEN THE MOST GRATIFYING EXPERIENCE OF MY LIFE.
SPEAK FOR YOURSELF. I WAS AN AZTEC QUEEN. CONSIDERED A GODDESS BECAUSE I WAS IMMORTAL. I RULED.

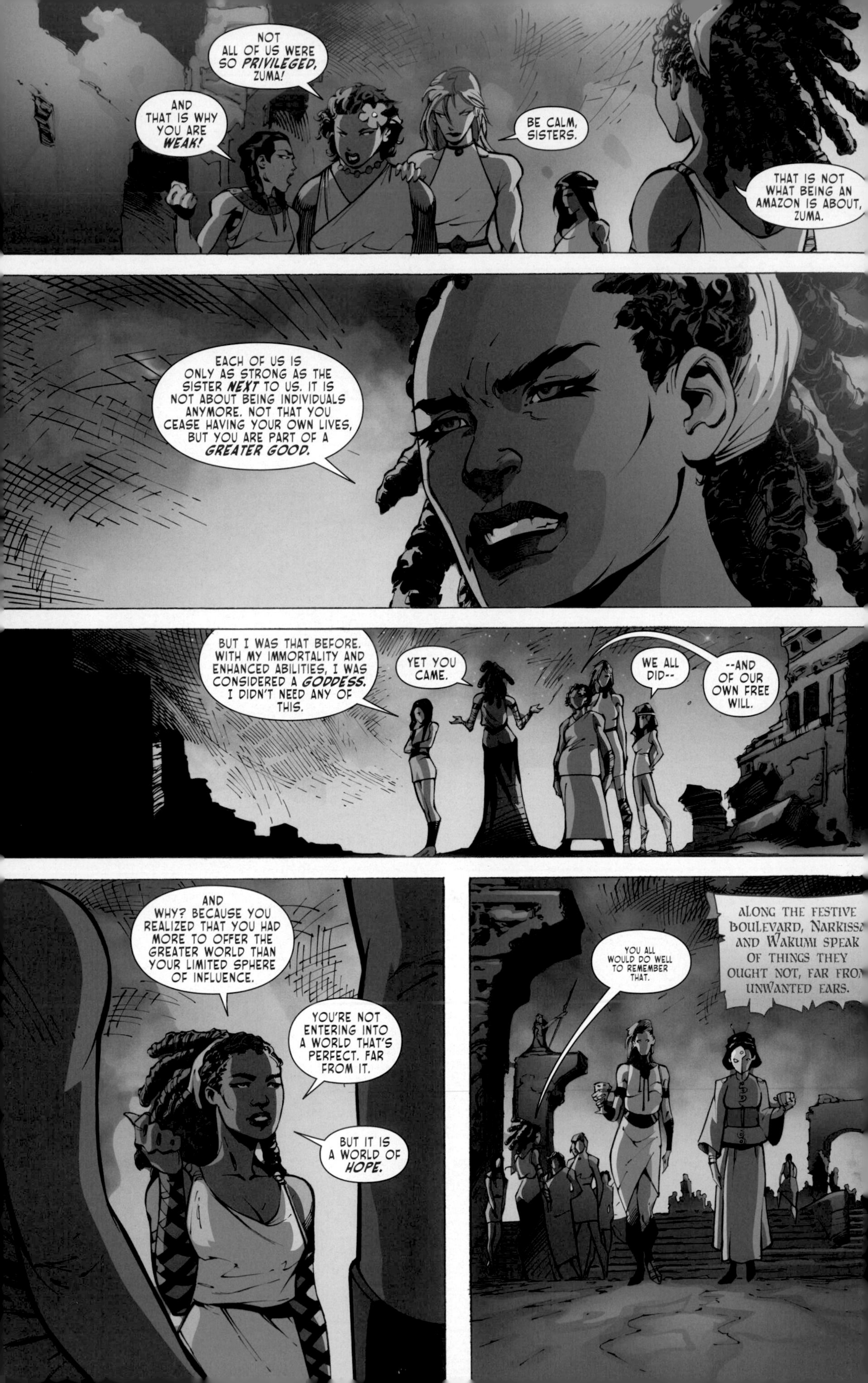
NOT ALL OF US WERE SO PRIVILEGED, ZUMA!
AND THAT IS WHY YOU ARE WEAK!
BE CALM, SISTERS.
THAT IS NOT WHAT BEING AN AMAZON IS ABOUT, ZUMA.
EACH OF US IS ONLY AS STRONG AS THE SISTER NEXT TO US. IT IS NOT ABOUT BEING INDIVIDUALS ANYMORE. NOT THAT YOU CEASE HAVING YOUR OWN LIVES, BUT YOU ARE PART OF A GREATER GOOD.
BUT I WAS THAT BEFORE. WITH MY IMMORTALITY AND ENHANCED ABILITIES, I WAS CONSIDERED A GODDESS. I DIDN'T NEED ANY OF THIS.
YET YOU CAME.
WE ALL DID--
--AND OF OUR OWN FREE WILL.
AND WHY? BECAUSE YOU REALIZED THAT YOU HAD MORE TO OFFER THE GREATER WORLD THAN YOUR LIMITED SPHERE OF INFLUENCE.
YOU'RE NOT ENTERING INTO A WORLD THAT'S PERFECT. FAR FROM IT.
BUT IT IS A WORLD OF HOPE.
YOU ALL WOULD DO WELL TO REMEMBER THAT.
ALONG THE FESTIVE BOULEVARD, NARKISSA AND WAKUMI SPEAK OF THINGS THEY OUGHT NOT, FAR FROM UNWANTED EARS.

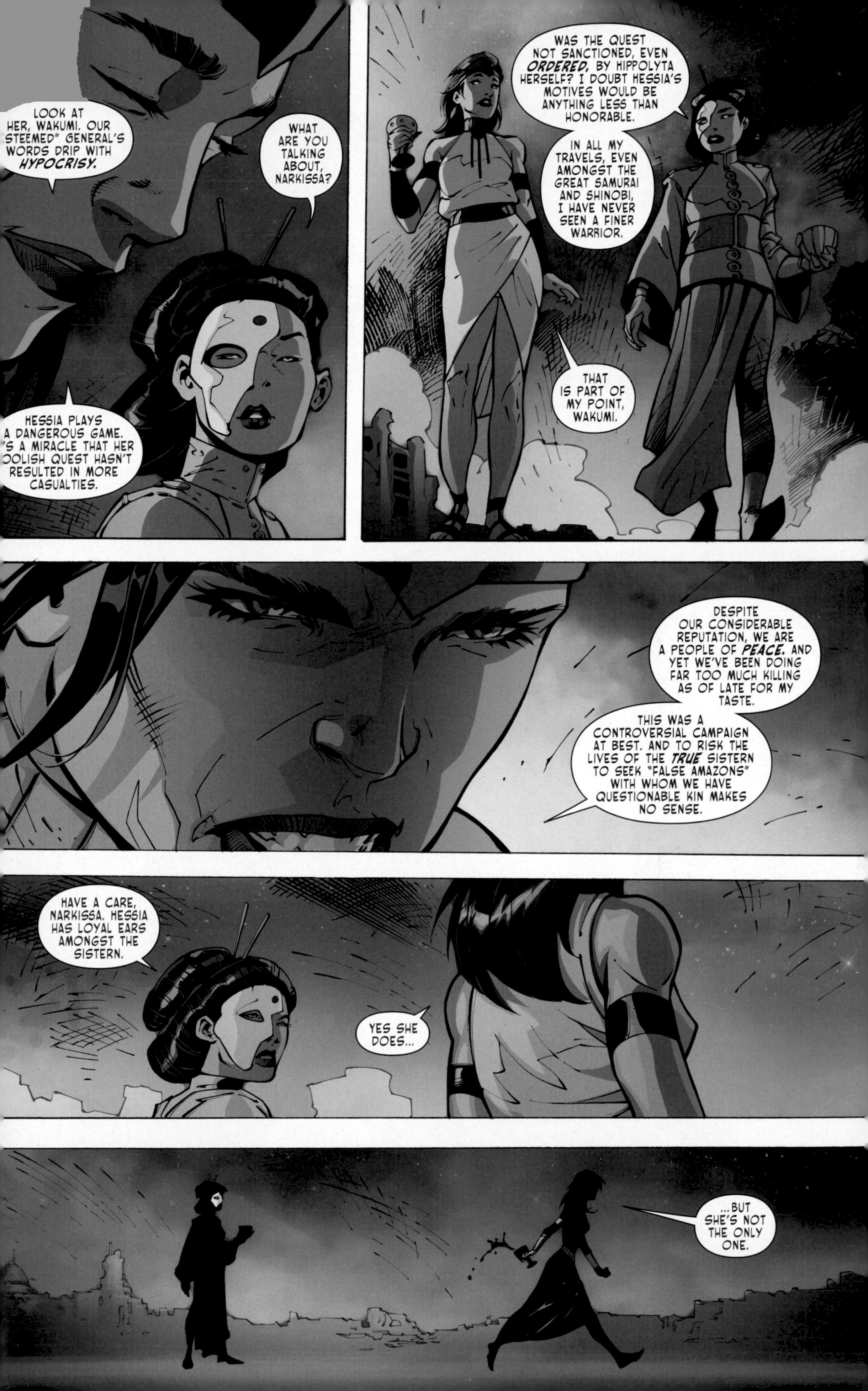
LOOK AT HER, WAKUMI. OUR "ESTEEMED" GENERAL'S WORDS DRIP WITH HYPOCRISY.
WHAT ARE YOU TALKING ABOUT, NARKISSA?
HESSIA PLAYS A DANGEROUS GAME. IT'S A MIRACLE THAT HER FOOLISH QUEST HASN'T RESULTED IN MORE CASUALTIES.
WAS THE QUEST NOT SANCTIONED, EVEN ORDERED, BY HIPPOLYTA HERSELF? I DOUBT HESSIA'S MOTIVES WOULD BE ANYTHING LESS THAN HONORABLE.
IN ALL MY TRAVELS, EVEN AMONGST THE GREAT SAMURAI AND SHINOBI, I HAVE NEVER SEEN A FINER WARRIOR.
THAT IS PART OF MY POINT, WAKUMI.
DESPITE OUR CONSIDERABLE REPUTATION, WE ARE A PEOPLE OF PEACE. AND YET WE'VE BEEN DOING FAR TOO MUCH KILLING AS OF LATE FOR MY TASTE.
THIS WAS A CONTROVERSIAL CAMPAIGN AT BEST. AND TO RISK THE LIVES OF THE TRUE SISTERN TO SEEK "FALSE AMAZONS" WITH WHOM WE HAVE QUESTIONABLE KIN MAKES NO SENSE.
HAVE A CARE, NARKISSA. HESSIA HAS LOYAL EARS AMONGST THE SISTERN.
YES SHE DOES...
...BUT SHE'S NOT THE ONLY ONE.

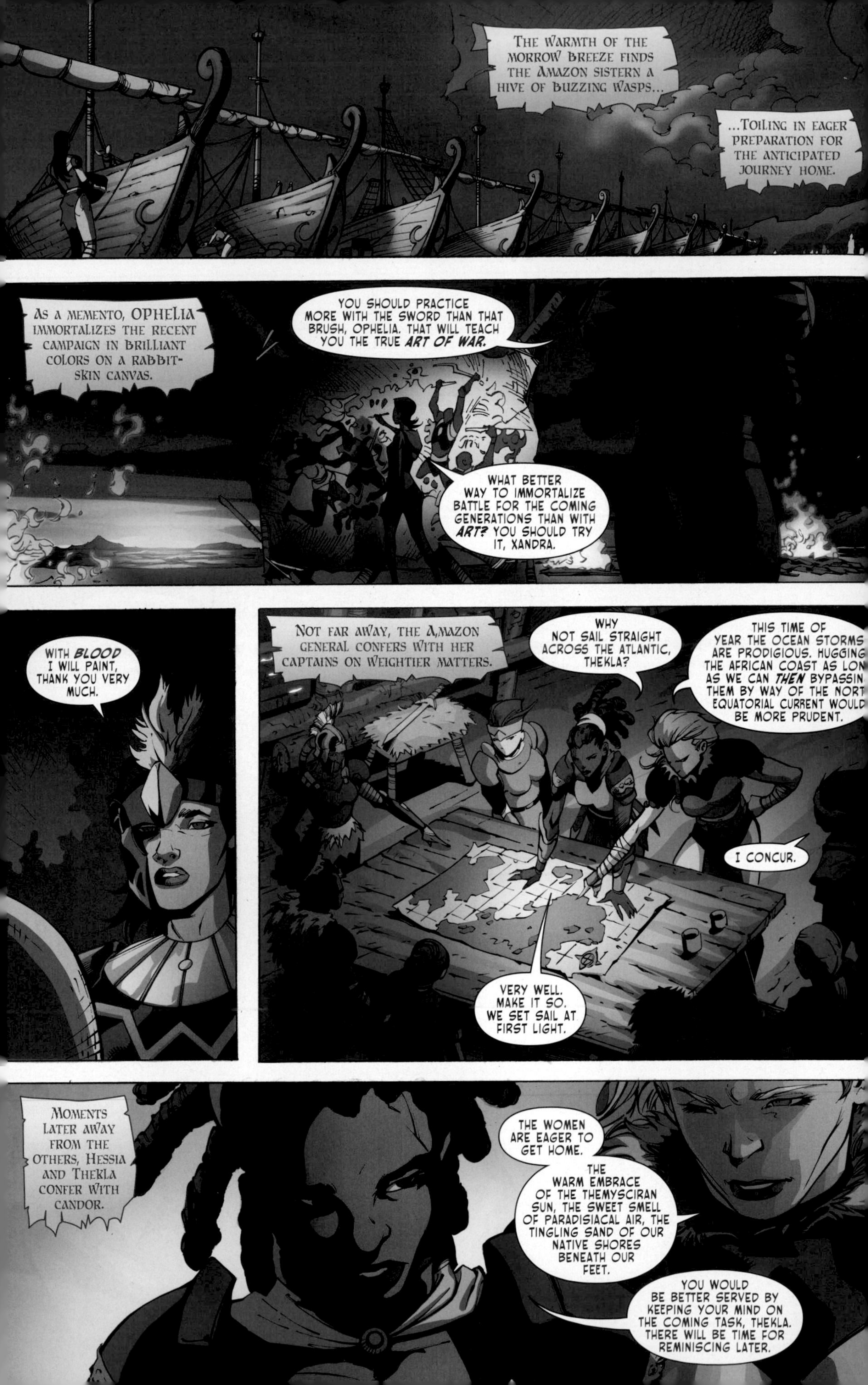
THE WARMTH OF THE MORROW BREEZE FINDS THE AMAZON SISTERN A HIVE OF BUZZING WASPS...
...TOILING IN EAGER PREPARATION FOR THE ANTICIPATED JOURNEY HOME.
AS A MEMENTO, OPHELIA IMMORTALIZES THE RECENT CAMPAIGN IN BRILLIANT COLORS ON A RABBIT-SKIN CANVAS.
YOU SHOULD PRACTICE MORE WITH THE SWORD THAN THAT BRUSH, OPHELIA. THAT WILL TEACH YOU THE TRUE ART OF WAR.
WHAT BETTER WAY TO IMMORTALIZE BATTLE FOR THE COMING GENERATIONS THAN WITH ART? YOU SHOULD TRY IT, XANDRA.
WITH BLOOD I WILL PAINT, THANK YOU VERY MUCH.
NOT FAR AWAY, THE AMAZON GENERAL CONFERS WITH HER CAPTAINS ON WEIGHTIER MATTERS.
WHY NOT SAIL STRAIGHT ACROSS THE ATLANTIC, THEKLA?
THIS TIME OF YEAR THE OCEAN STORMS ARE PRODIGIOUS. HUGGING THE AFRICAN COAST AS LON AS WE CAN THEN BYPASSIN THEM BY WAY OF THE NORT EQUATORIAL CURRENT WOULD BE MORE PRUDENT.
I CONCUR.
VERY WELL. MAKE IT SO. WE SET SAIL AT FIRST LIGHT.
MOMENTS LATER AWAY FROM THE OTHERS, HESSIA AND THEKLA CONFER WITH CANDOR.
THE WOMEN ARE EAGER TO GET HOME.
THE WARM EMBRACE OF THE THEMYSCIRAN SUN, THE SWEET SMELL OF PARADISIACAL AIR, THE TINGLING SAND OF OUR NATIVE SHORES BENEATH OUR FEET.
YOU WOULD BE BETTER SERVED BY KEEPING YOUR MIND ON THE COMING TASK, THEKLA. THERE WILL BE TIME FOR REMINISCING LATER.

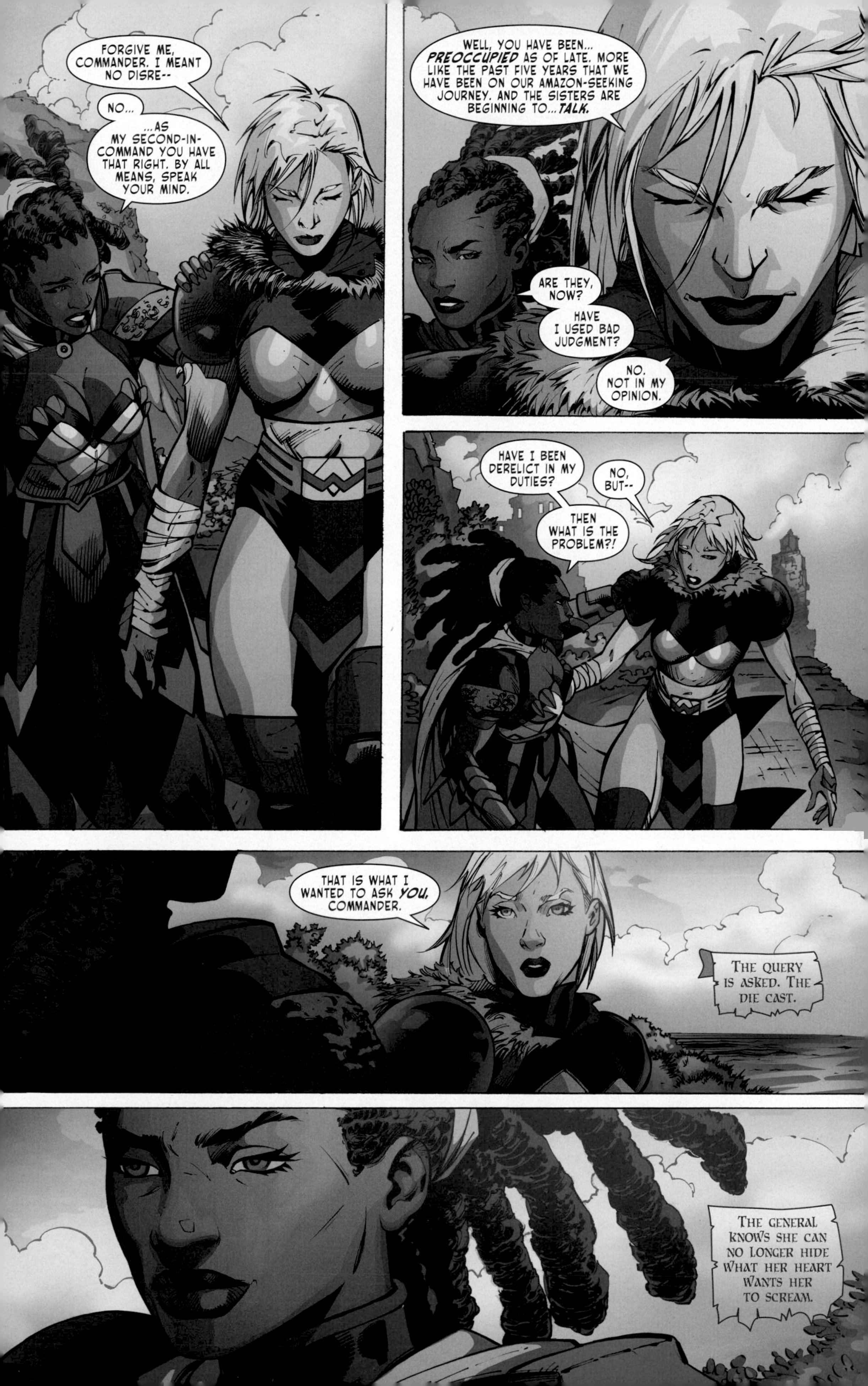
FORGIVE ME, COMMANDER. I MEANT NO DISRE--
NO...
...AS MY SECOND-IN-COMMAND YOU HAVE THAT RIGHT. BY ALL MEANS, SPEAK YOUR MIND.
WELL, YOU HAVE BEEN... PREOCCUPIED AS OF LATE. MORE LIKE THE PAST FIVE YEARS THAT WE HAVE BEEN ON OUR AMAZON-SEEKING JOURNEY. AND THE SISTERS ARE BEGINNING TO...TALK.
ARE THEY, NOW?
HAVE I USED BAD JUDGMENT?
NO. NOT IN MY OPINION.
HAVE I BEEN DERELICT IN MY DUTIES?
NO, BUT--
THEN WHAT IS THE PROBLEM?!
THAT IS WHAT I WANTED TO ASK YOU, COMMANDER.
THE QUERY IS ASKED. THE DIE CAST.
THE GENERAL KNOWS SHE CAN NO LONGER HIDE WHAT HER HEART WANTS HER TO SCREAM.

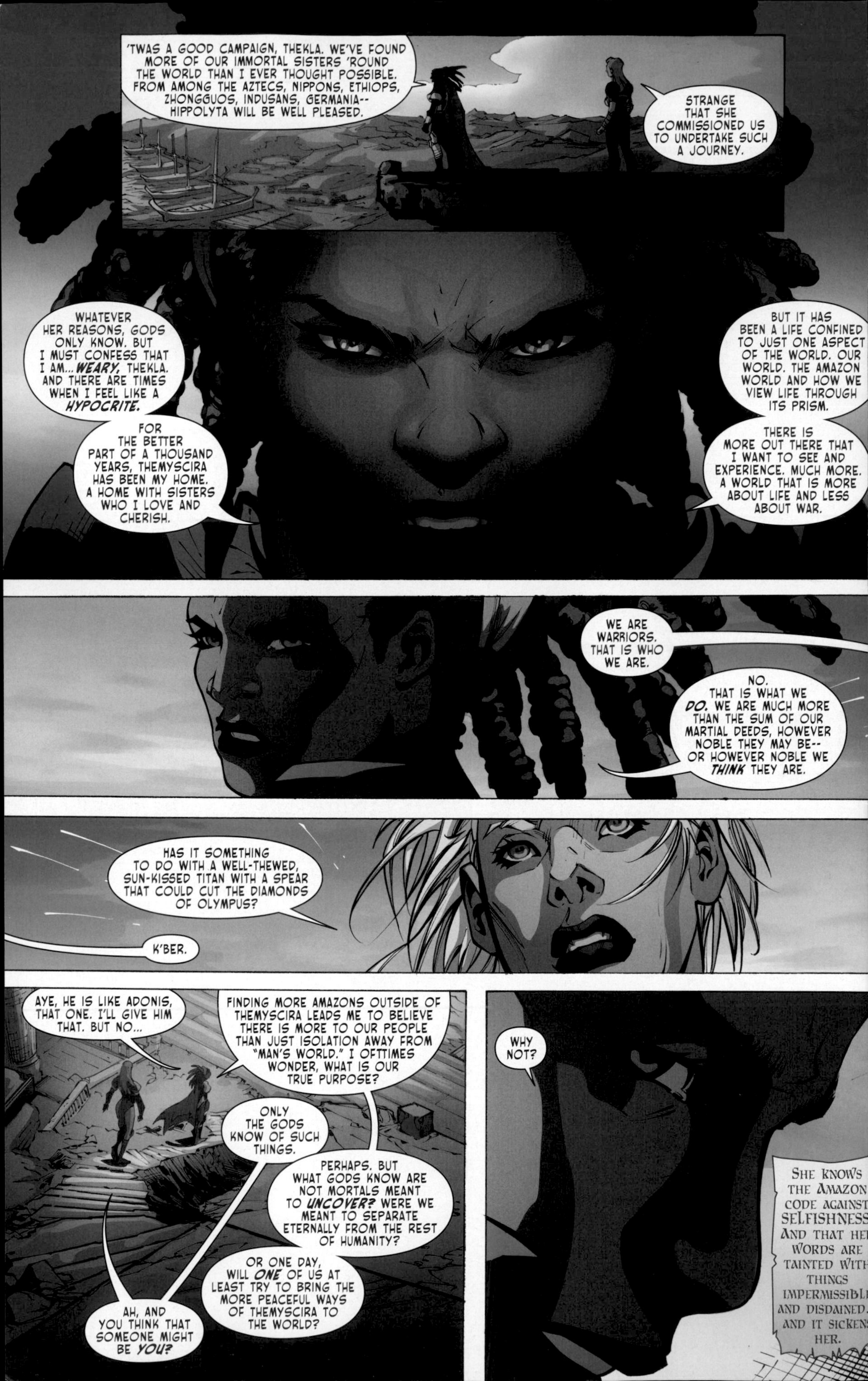
'TWAS A GOOD CAMPAIGN, THEKLA. WE'VE FOUND MORE OF OUR IMMORTAL SISTERS 'ROUND THE WORLD THAN I EVER THOUGHT POSSIBLE. FROM AMONG THE AZTECS, NIPPONS, ETHIOPS, ZHONGGUOS, INDUSANS, GERMANIA-- HIPPOLYTA WILL BE WELL PLEASED.
STRANGE THAT SHE COMMISSIONED US TO UNDERTAKE SUCH A JOURNEY.
WHATEVER HER REASONS, GODS ONLY KNOW. BUT I MUST CONFESS THAT I AM...WEARY, THEKLA. AND THERE ARE TIMES WHEN I FEEL LIKE A HYPOCRITE.
FOR THE BETTER PART OF A THOUSAND YEARS, THEMYSCIRA HAS BEEN MY HOME. A HOME WITH SISTERS WHO I LOVE AND CHERISH.
BUT IT HAS BEEN A LIFE CONFINED TO JUST ONE ASPECT OF THE WORLD. OUR WORLD. THE AMAZON WORLD AND HOW WE VIEW LIFE THROUGH ITS PRISM.
THERE IS MORE OUT THERE THAT I WANT TO SEE AND EXPERIENCE. MUCH MORE. A WORLD THAT IS MORE ABOUT LIFE AND LESS ABOUT WAR.
WE ARE WARRIORS. THAT IS WHO WE ARE.
NO. THAT IS WHAT WE DO. WE ARE MUCH MORE THAN THE SUM OF OUR MARTIAL DEEDS, HOWEVER NOBLE THEY MAY BE-- OR HOWEVER NOBLE WE THINK THEY ARE.
HAS IT SOMETHING TO DO WITH A WELL-THEWED, SUN-KISSED TITAN WITH A SPEAR THAT COULD CUT THE DIAMONDS OF OLYMPUS?
K'BER.
AYE, HE IS LIKE ADONIS, THAT ONE. I'LL GIVE HIM THAT. BUT NO...
FINDING MORE AMAZONS OUTSIDE OF THEMYSCIRA LEADS ME TO BELIEVE THERE IS MORE TO OUR PEOPLE THAN JUST ISOLATION AWAY FROM "MAN'S WORLD." I OFTTIMES WONDER, WHAT IS OUR TRUE PURPOSE?
ONLY THE GODS KNOW OF SUCH THINGS.
PERHAPS. BUT WHAT GODS KNOW ARE NOT MORTALS MEANT TO UNCOVER? WERE WE MEANT TO SEPARATE ETERNALLY FROM THE REST OF HUMANITY?
OR ONE DAY, WILL ONE OF US AT LEAST TRY TO BRING THE MORE PEACEFUL WAYS OF THEMYSCIRA TO THE WORLD?
AH, AND YOU THINK THAT SOMEONE MIGHT BE YOU?
WHY NOT?
SHE KNOWS THE AMAZON CODE AGAINST SELFISHNESS AND THAT HER WORDS ARE TAINTED WITH THINGS IMPERMISSIBLE AND DISDAINED, AND IT SICKENS HER.

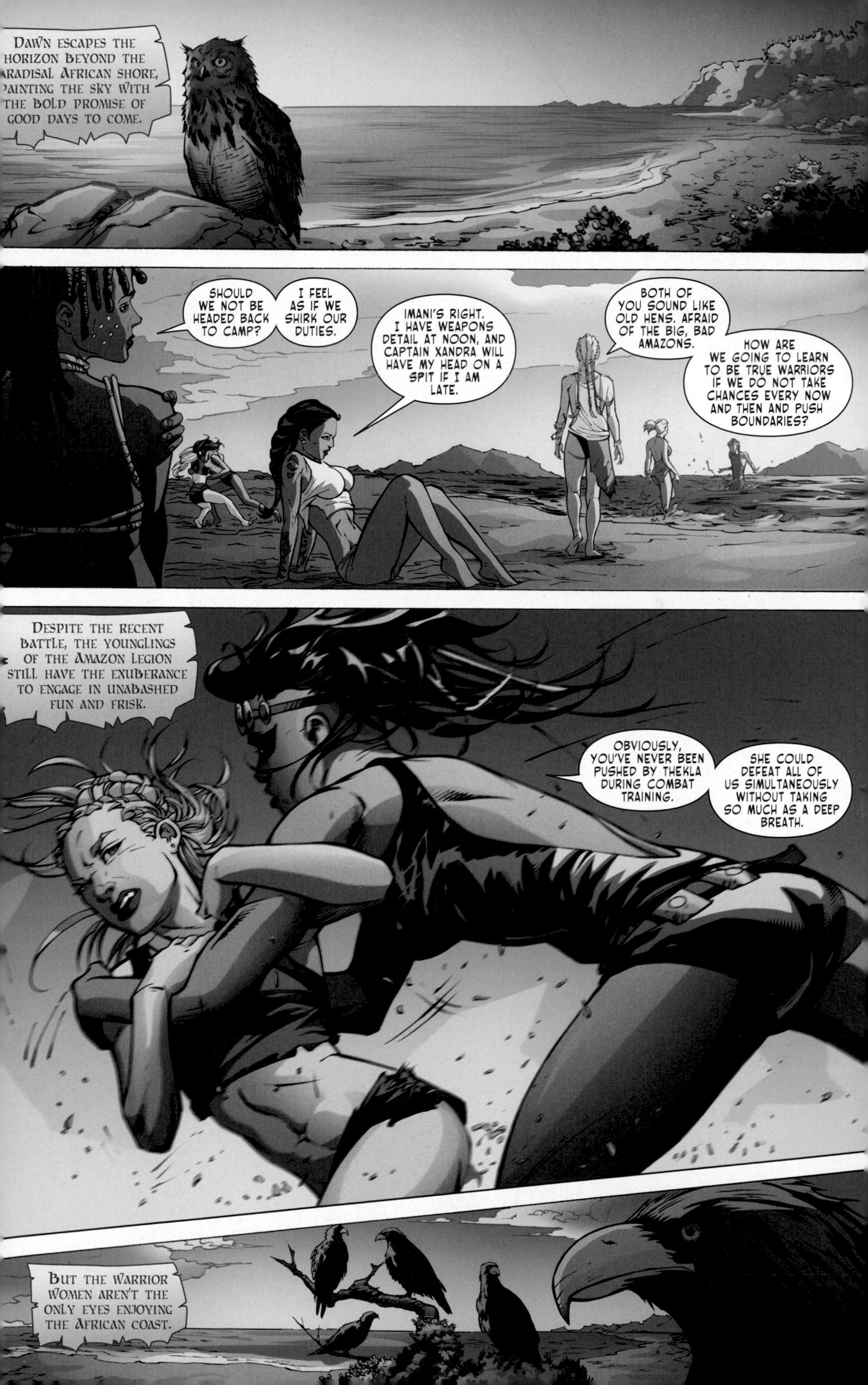

DAWN ESCAPES THE HORIZON BEYOND THE ARADISAL AFRICAN SHORE, PAINTING THE SKY WITH THE BOLD PROMISE OF GOOD DAYS TO COME.
SHOULD WE NOT BE HEADED BACK TO CAMP?
I FEEL AS IF WE SHIRK OUR DUTIES.
IMANI'S RIGHT. I HAVE WEAPONS DETAIL AT NOON, AND CAPTAIN XANDRA WILL HAVE MY HEAD ON A SPIT IF I AM LATE.
BOTH OF YOU SOUND LIKE OLD HENS. AFRAID OF THE BIG, BAD AMAZONS.
HOW ARE WE GOING TO LEARN TO BE TRUE WARRIORS IF WE DO NOT TAKE CHANCES EVERY NOW AND THEN AND PUSH BOUNDARIES?
DESPITE THE RECENT BATTLE, THE YOUNGLINGS OF THE AMAZON LEGION STILL HAVE THE EXUBERANCE TO ENGAGE IN UNABASHED FUN AND FRISK.
OBVIOUSLY, YOU'VE NEVER BEEN PUSHED BY THEKLA DURING COMBAT TRAINING.
SHE COULD DEFEAT ALL OF US SIMULTANEOUSLY WITHOUT TAKING SO MUCH AS A DEEP BREATH.
BUT THE WARRIOR WOMEN AREN'T THE ONLY EYES ENJOYING THE AFRICAN COAST.

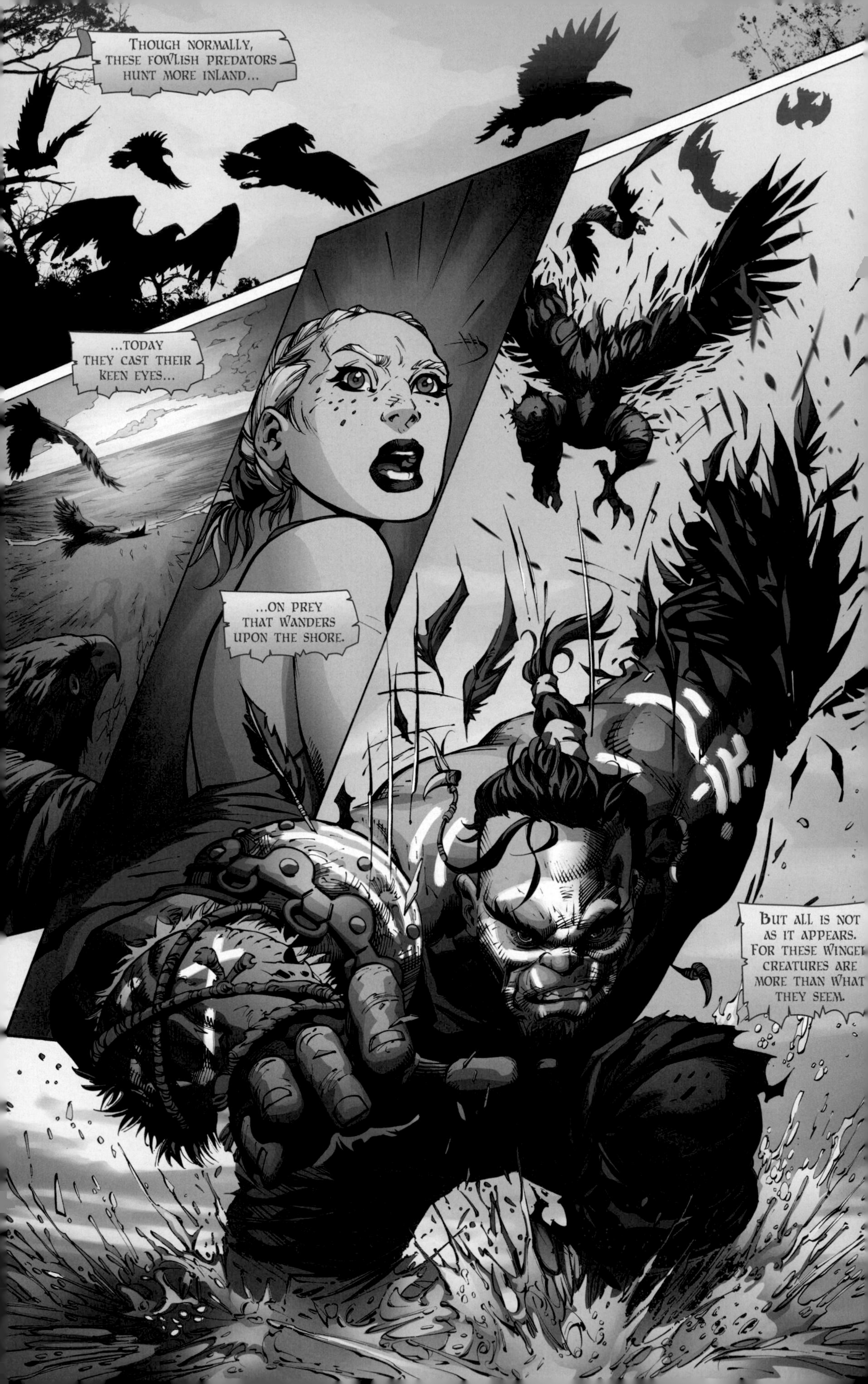
THOUGH NORMALLY, THESE FOWLISH PREDATORS HUNT MORE INLAND...
...TODAY THEY CAST THEIR KEEN EYES...
...ON PREY THAT WANDERS UPON THE SHORE.
BUT ALL IS NOT AS IT APPEARS. FOR THESE WINGET CREATURES ARE MORE THAN WHAT THEY SEEM.

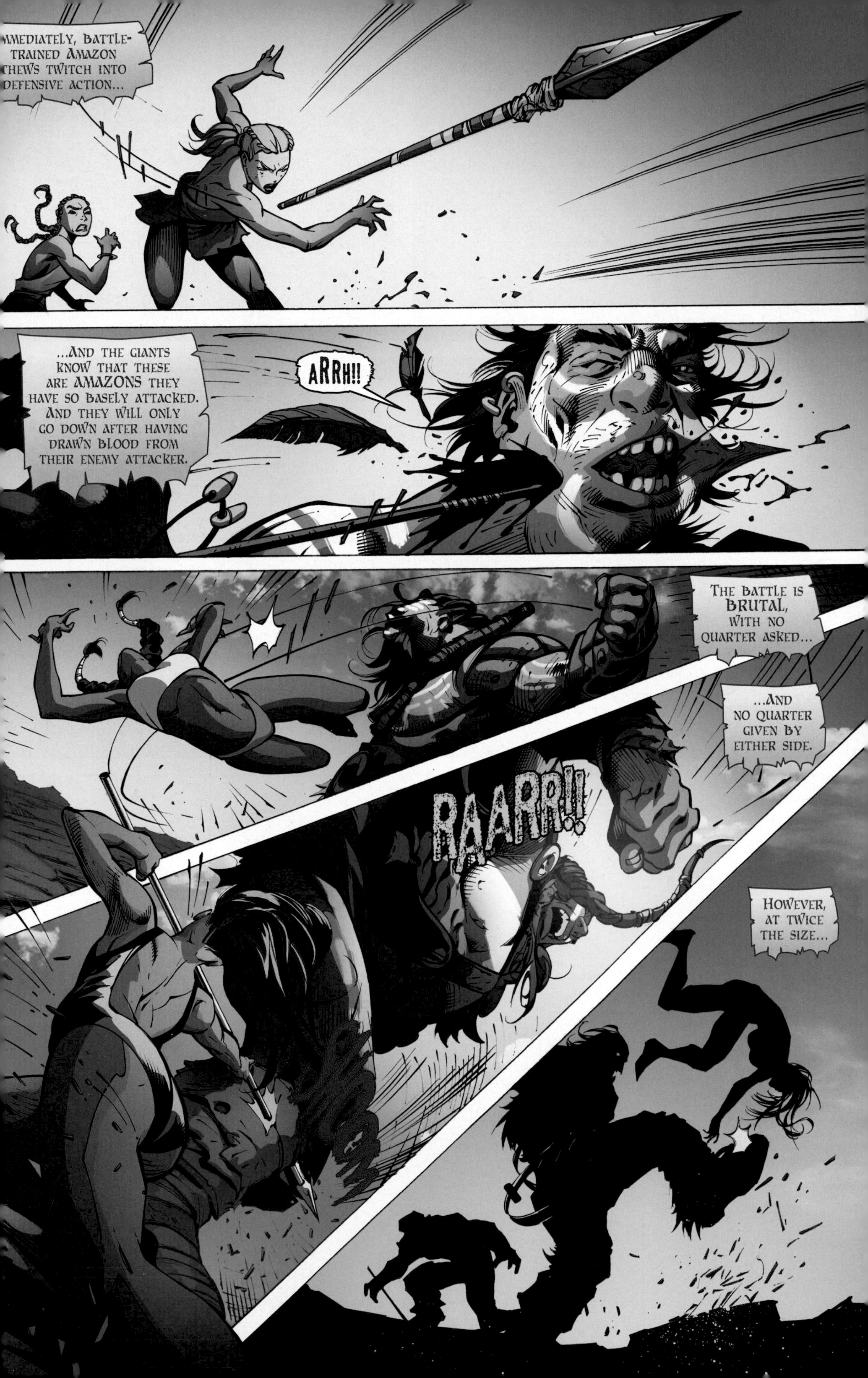
MMEDIATELY, BATTLE-TRAINED AMAZON THEWS TWITCH INTO DEFENSIVE ACTION...
...AND THE GIANTS KNOW THAT THESE ARE AMAZONS THEY HAVE SO BASELY ATTACKED. AND THEY WILL ONLY GO DOWN AFTER HAVING DRAWN BLOOD FROM THEIR ENEMY ATTACKER.
ARRH!!
THE BATTLE IS BRUTAL, WITH NO QUARTER ASKED...
...AND NO QUARTER GIVEN BY EITHER SIDE.
RAARR!!
HOWEVER, AT TWICE THE SIZE...

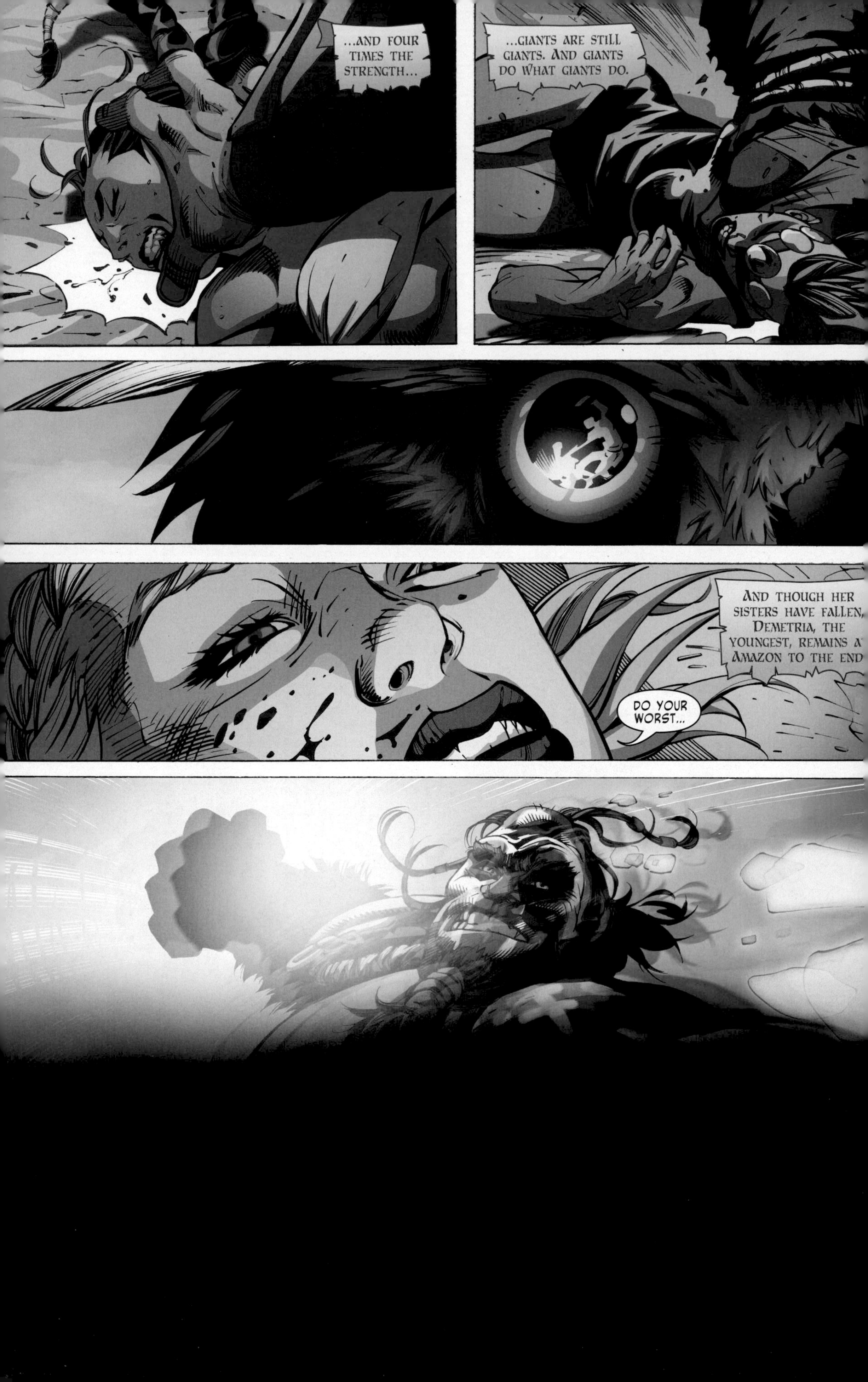
...AND FOUR TIMES THE STRENGTH...
...GIANTS ARE STILL GIANTS. AND GIANTS DO WHAT GIANTS DO.
AND THOUGH HER SISTERS HAVE FALLEN, DEMETRIA, THE YOUNGEST, REMAINS A AMAZON TO THE END
DO YOUR WORST...

THE FOLLOWING DAWN BRINGS TO LIGHT A GRUESOME DISCOVERY AS SISTERS GATHER AROUND THE REMNANTS OF A MYSTERIOUS STRUGGLE.

GIANT FOOTPRINTS...

CYCLOPS? AFRICAN GIANTS?

IT'S CLEAR THERE WAS A FIGHT. THE DISTRIBUTION OF THE WEIGHT ON THE BACK FOOT INDICATES THAT SOME OF OUR SISTERS WERE IN DEFENSIVE POSITIONS. THROWING SOMETHING.

BUT THE PRINTS SEEM CONCENTRATED IN THIS AREA.

THAT'S THE OTHER PROBLEM...THERE ARE NO OTHER FOOTPRINTS.

PERHAPS THE TIDE WASHED THEM AWAY.

THE TIDE DOESN'T REACH THIS FAR, AND THERE'S NO INDICATION THAT THEY WERE CARRIED INLAND NOR OUT TO SEA TO A WAITING SHIP.

SO WHAT ARE YOU SAYING? THAT THEY JUST *DISAPPEARED?*

HESSIA. LOOK AT *THIS.*

WHAT IS IT? A WOODEN LASH?

MORE LIKE A *NECKLACE.*

STRANGE SYMBOL.

IT'S CALLED A *RUNE.* FOUND MOSTLY IN THE FAR NORTH AMONG THE VIKINGS.

I HAVE ENCOUNTERED THESE VIKINGS BEFORE ON A SAMURAI EXCURSION TO THE WEST.

FIERCE WARRIORS, INDEED.

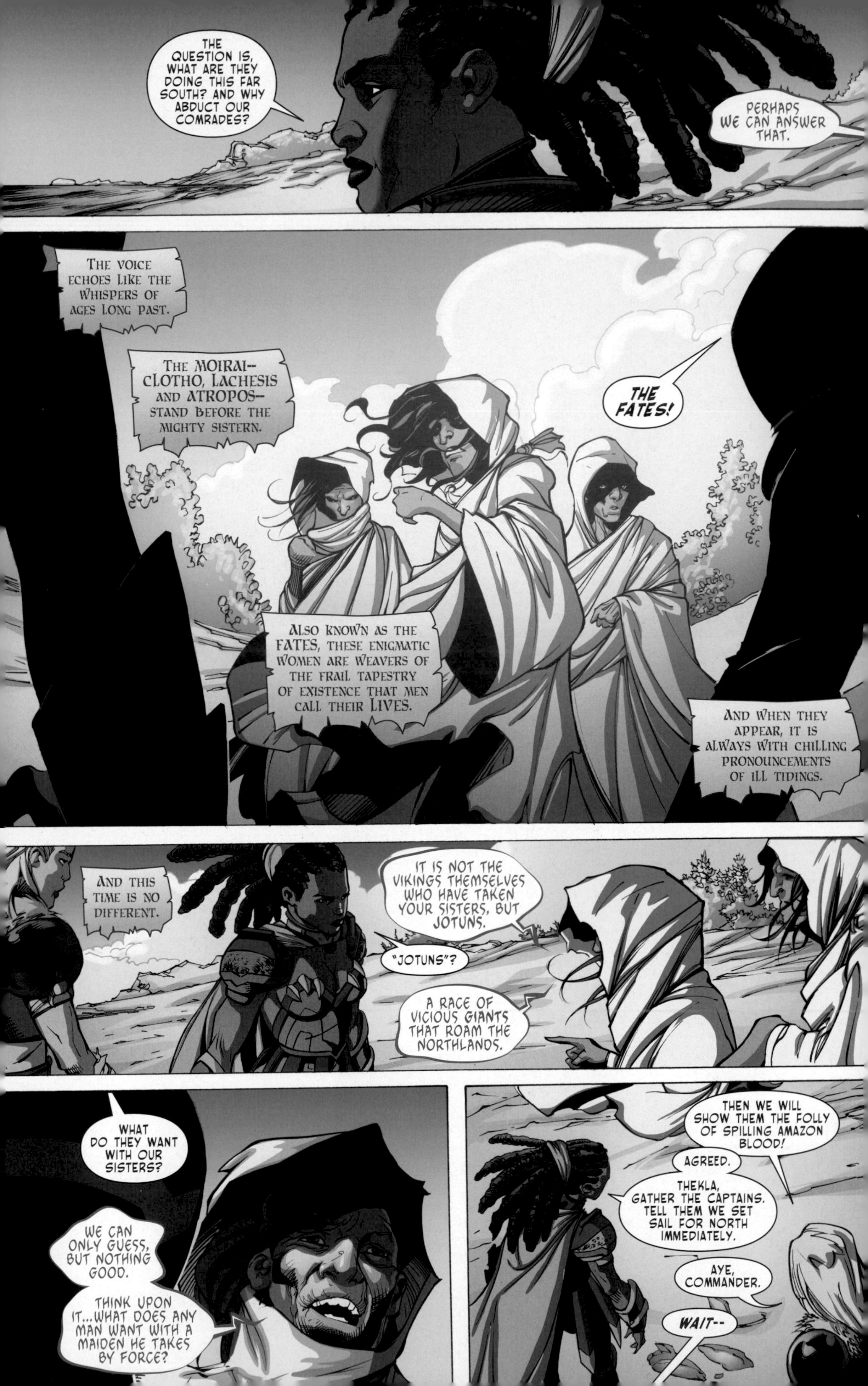
THE QUESTION IS, WHAT ARE THEY DOING THIS FAR SOUTH? AND WHY ABDUCT OUR COMRADES?
PERHAPS WE CAN ANSWER THAT.
The voice echoes like the whispers of ages long past.
The MOIRAI-- CLOTHO, LACHESIS and ATROPOS-- stand before the mighty sistern.
THE FATES!
Also known as the FATES, these enigmatic women are weavers of the frail tapestry of existence that men call their LIVES.
And when they appear, it is always with chilling pronouncements of ill tidings.
And this time is no different.
IT IS NOT THE VIKINGS THEMSELVES WHO HAVE TAKEN YOUR SISTERS, BUT JOTUNS.
"JOTUNS"?
A RACE OF VICIOUS GIANTS THAT ROAM THE NORTHLANDS.
WHAT DO THEY WANT WITH OUR SISTERS?
WE CAN ONLY GUESS, BUT NOTHING GOOD.
THINK UPON IT...WHAT DOES ANY MAN WANT WITH A MAIDEN HE TAKES BY FORCE?
THEN WE WILL SHOW THEM THE FOLLY OF SPILLING AMAZON BLOOD!
AGREED.
THEKLA, GATHER THE CAPTAINS. TELL THEM WE SET SAIL FOR NORTH IMMEDIATELY.
AYE, COMMANDER.
WAIT--

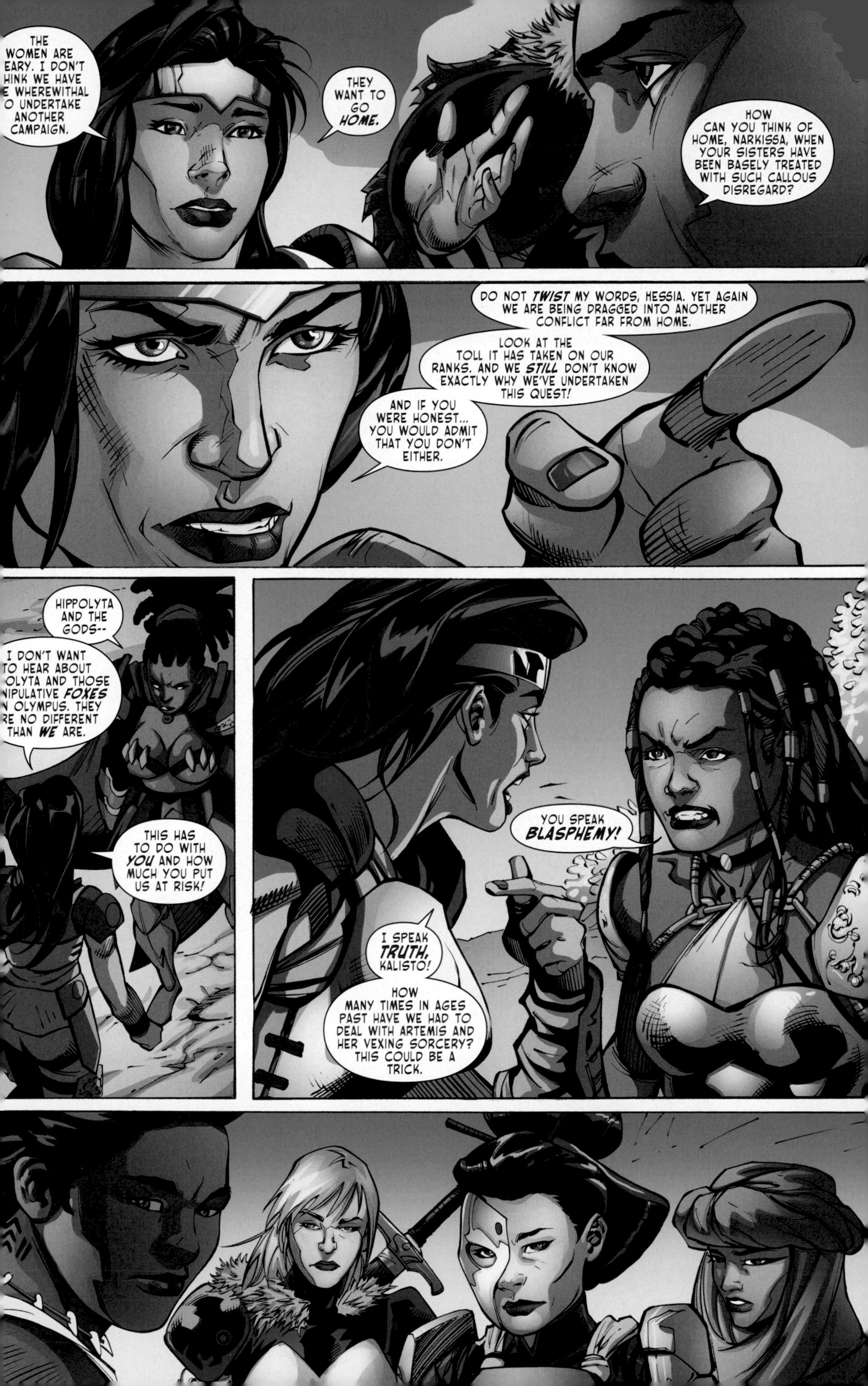
THE WOMEN ARE EARY. I DON'T HINK WE HAVE E WHEREWITHAL O UNDERTAKE ANOTHER CAMPAIGN.
THEY WANT TO GO *HOME.*
HOW CAN YOU THINK OF HOME, NARKISSA, WHEN YOUR SISTERS HAVE BEEN BASELY TREATED WITH SUCH CALLOUS DISREGARD?
DO NOT *TWIST* MY WORDS, HESSIA. YET AGAIN WE ARE BEING DRAGGED INTO ANOTHER CONFLICT FAR FROM HOME.
LOOK AT THE TOLL IT HAS TAKEN ON OUR RANKS. AND WE *STILL* DON'T KNOW EXACTLY WHY WE'VE UNDERTAKEN THIS QUEST!
AND IF YOU WERE HONEST... YOU WOULD ADMIT THAT YOU DON'T EITHER.
HIPPOLYTA AND THE GODS--
I DON'T WANT TO HEAR ABOUT OLYTA AND THOSE NIPULATIVE *FOXES* N OLYMPUS. THEY RE NO DIFFERENT THAN *WE* ARE.
THIS HAS TO DO WITH *YOU* AND HOW MUCH YOU PUT US AT RISK!
YOU SPEAK *BLASPHEMY!*
I SPEAK *TRUTH,* KALISTO!
HOW MANY TIMES IN AGES PAST HAVE WE HAD TO DEAL WITH ARTEMIS AND HER VEXING SORCERY? THIS COULD BE A TRICK.

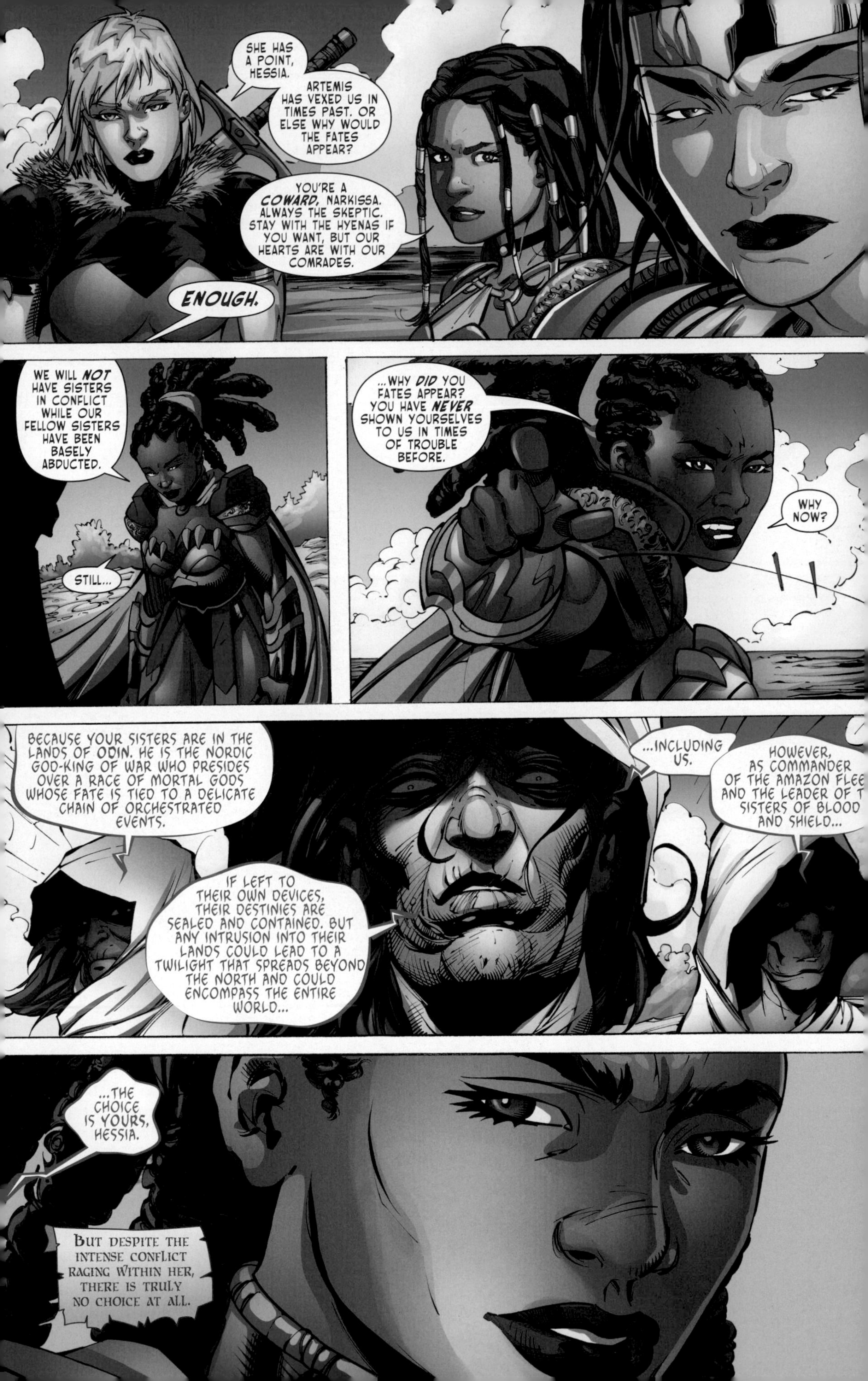
SHE HAS A POINT, HESSIA.
ARTEMIS HAS VEXED US IN TIMES PAST. OR ELSE WHY WOULD THE FATES APPEAR?
YOU'RE A COWARD, NARKISSA. ALWAYS THE SKEPTIC. STAY WITH THE HYENAS IF YOU WANT, BUT OUR HEARTS ARE WITH OUR COMRADES.
ENOUGH.
WE WILL NOT HAVE SISTERS IN CONFLICT WHILE OUR FELLOW SISTERS HAVE BEEN BASELY ABDUCTED.
STILL...
...WHY DID YOU FATES APPEAR? YOU HAVE NEVER SHOWN YOURSELVES TO US IN TIMES OF TROUBLE BEFORE.
WHY NOW?
BECAUSE YOUR SISTERS ARE IN THE LANDS OF ODIN. HE IS THE NORDIC GOD-KING OF WAR WHO PRESIDES OVER A RACE OF MORTAL GODS WHOSE FATE IS TIED TO A DELICATE CHAIN OF ORCHESTRATED EVENTS.
IF LEFT TO THEIR OWN DEVICES, THEIR DESTINIES ARE SEALED AND CONTAINED. BUT ANY INTRUSION INTO THEIR LANDS COULD LEAD TO A TWILIGHT THAT SPREADS BEYOND THE NORTH AND COULD ENCOMPASS THE ENTIRE WORLD...
...INCLUDING US.
HOWEVER, AS COMMANDER OF THE AMAZON FLEE AND THE LEADER OF T SISTERS OF BLOOD AND SHIELD...
...THE CHOICE IS YOURS, HESSIA.
BUT DESPITE THE INTENSE CONFLICT RAGING WITHIN HER, THERE IS TRULY NO CHOICE AT ALL.

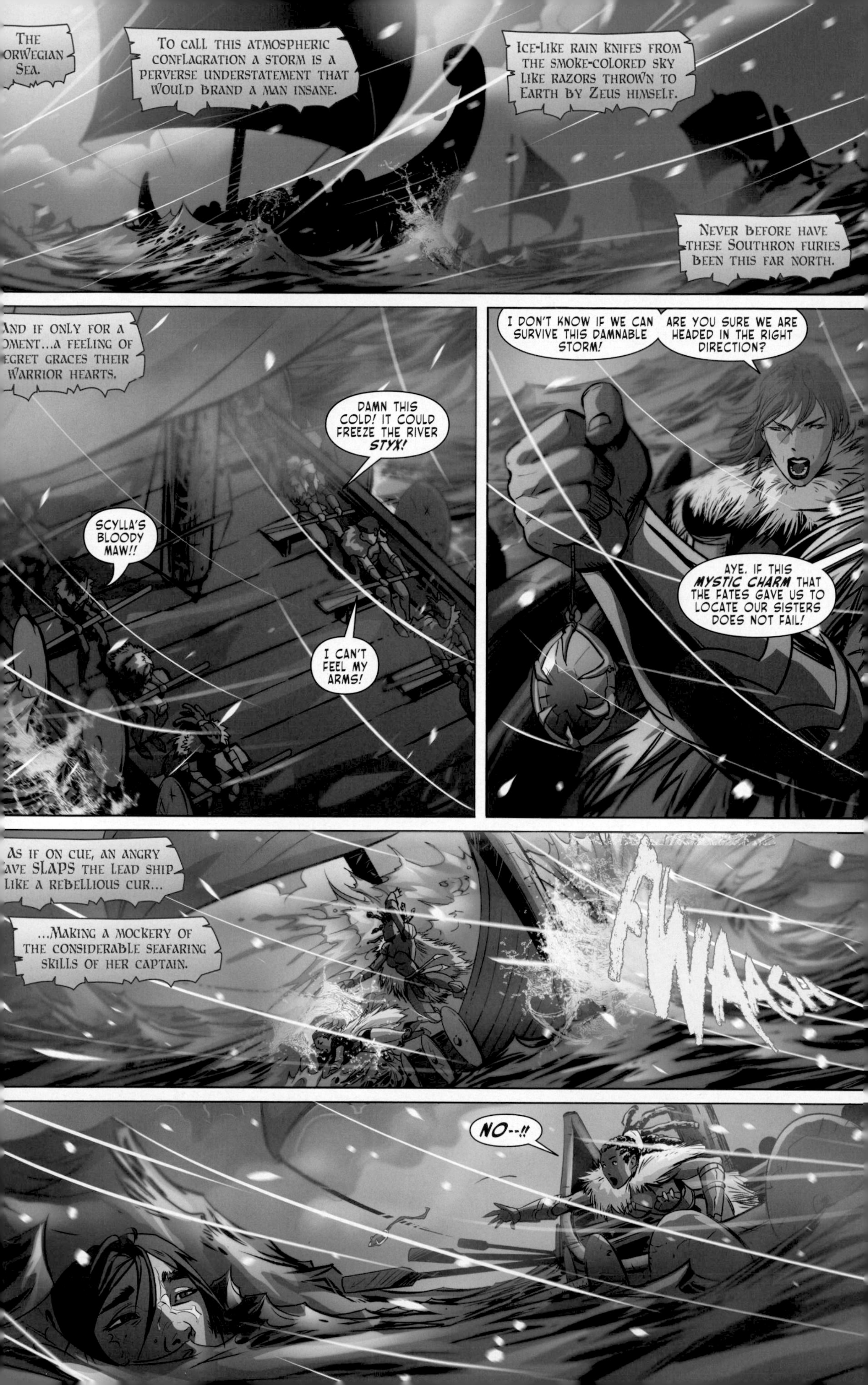

THE NORWEGIAN SEA.
TO CALL THIS ATMOSPHERIC CONFLAGRATION A STORM IS A PERVERSE UNDERSTATEMENT THAT WOULD BRAND A MAN INSANE.
ICE-LIKE RAIN KNIFES FROM THE SMOKE-COLORED SKY LIKE RAZORS THROWN TO EARTH BY ZEUS HIMSELF.
NEVER BEFORE HAVE THESE SOUTHRON FURIES BEEN THIS FAR NORTH.
AND IF ONLY FOR A MOMENT...A FEELING OF REGRET GRACES THEIR WARRIOR HEARTS.
DAMN THIS COLD! IT COULD FREEZE THE RIVER STYX!
SCYLLA'S BLOODY MAW!!
I CAN'T FEEL MY ARMS!
I DON'T KNOW IF WE CAN SURVIVE THIS DAMNABLE STORM!
ARE YOU SURE WE ARE HEADED IN THE RIGHT DIRECTION?
AYE. IF THIS MYSTIC CHARM THAT THE FATES GAVE US TO LOCATE OUR SISTERS DOES NOT FAIL!
AS IF ON CUE, AN ANGRY WAVE SLAPS THE LEAD SHIP LIKE A REBELLIOUS CUR...
...MAKING A MOCKERY OF THE CONSIDERABLE SEAFARING SKILLS OF HER CAPTAIN.
FWAASH
NO--!!

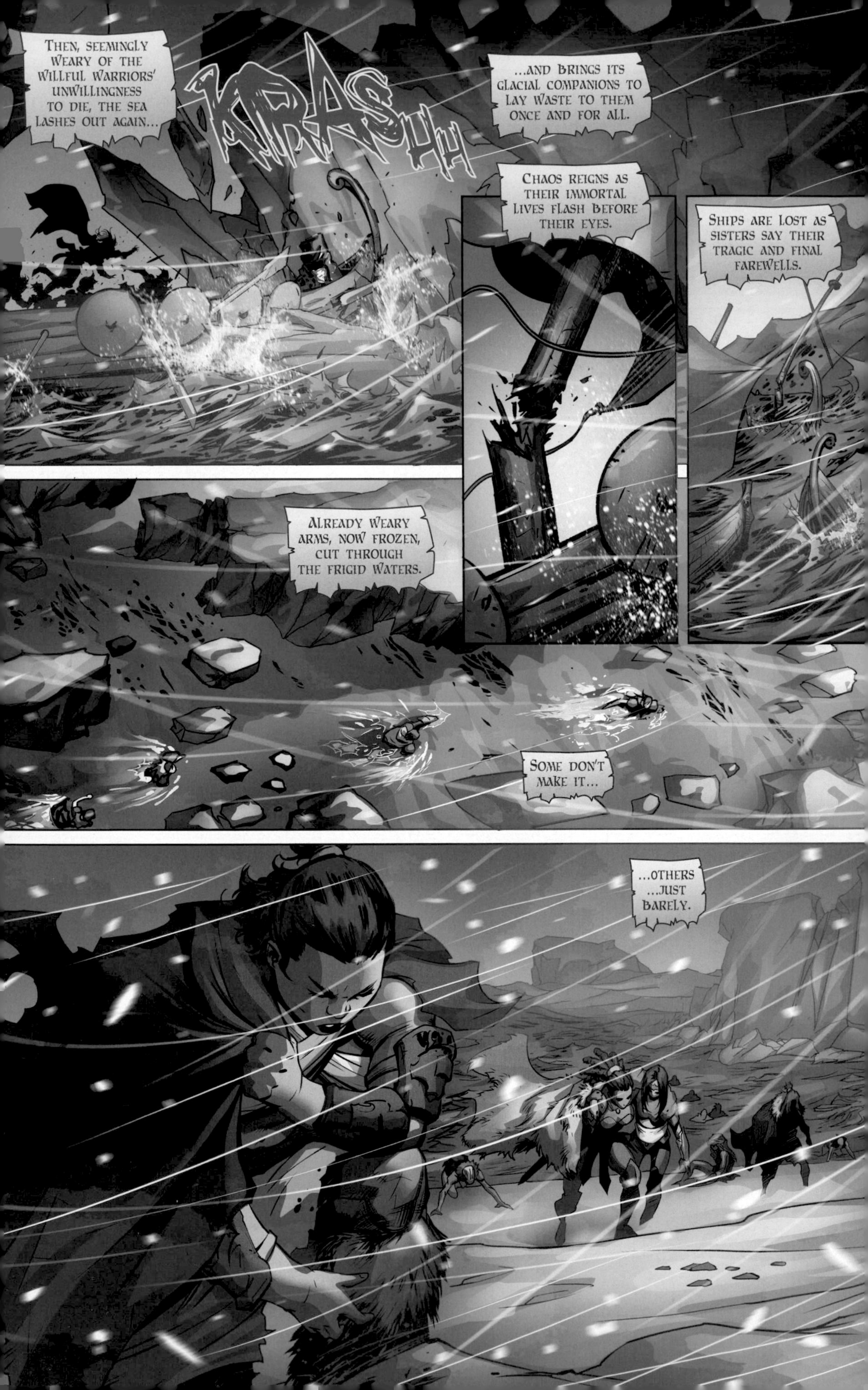
Then, seemingly weary of the willful warriors' unwillingness to die, the sea lashes out again...
KRASHH
...and brings its glacial companions to lay waste to them once and for all.
Chaos reigns as their immortal lives flash before their eyes.
Ships are lost as sisters say their tragic and final farewells.
Already weary arms, now frozen, cut through the frigid waters.
Some don't make it...
...others ...just barely.

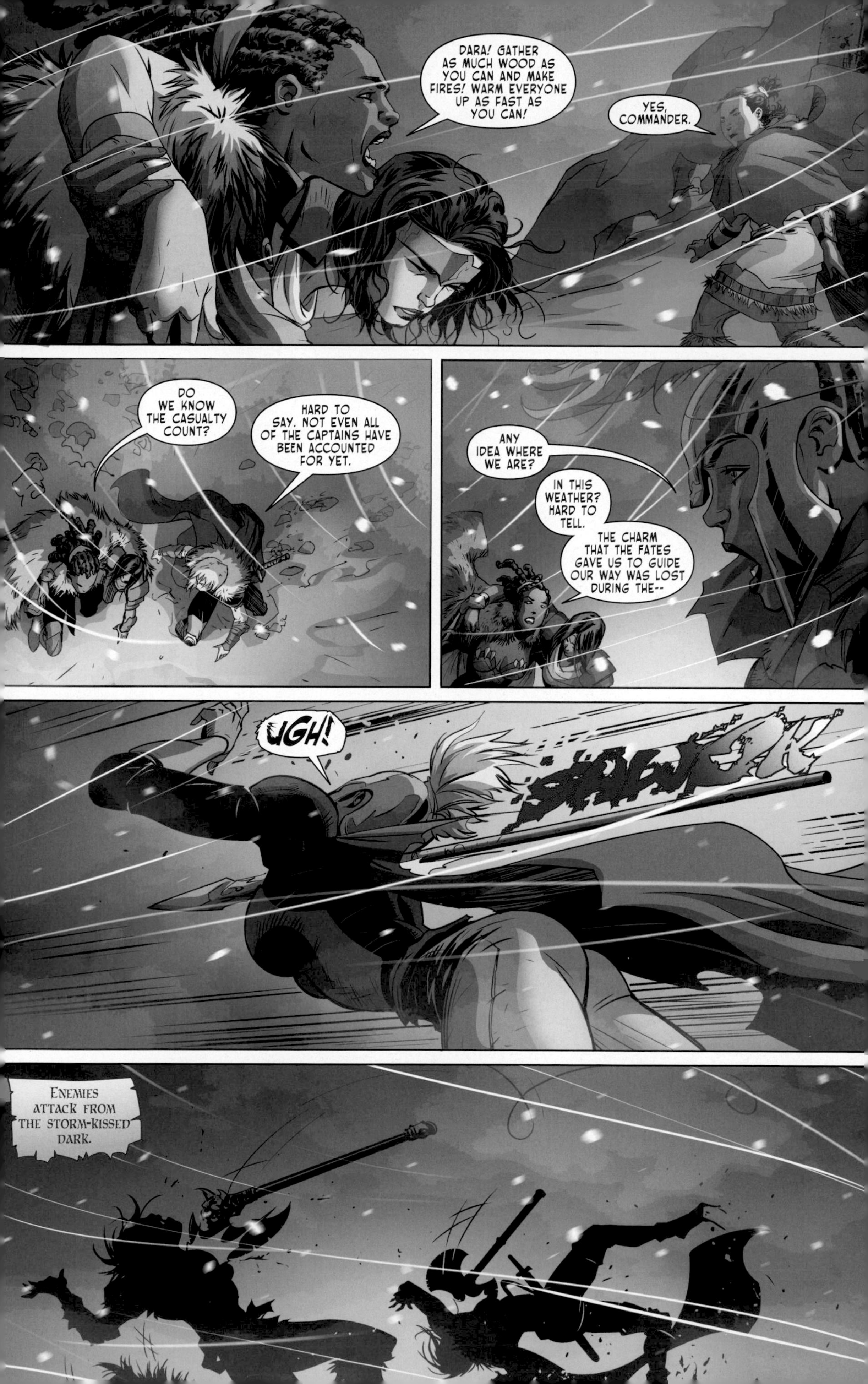
DARA! GATHER AS MUCH WOOD AS YOU CAN AND MAKE FIRES! WARM EVERYONE UP AS FAST AS YOU CAN!
YES, COMMANDER.
DO WE KNOW THE CASUALTY COUNT?
HARD TO SAY. NOT EVEN ALL OF THE CAPTAINS HAVE BEEN ACCOUNTED FOR YET.
ANY IDEA WHERE WE ARE?
IN THIS WEATHER? HARD TO TELL.
THE CHARM THAT THE FATES GAVE US TO GUIDE OUR WAY WAS LOST DURING THE--
UGH!
Enemies attack from the storm-kissed dark.

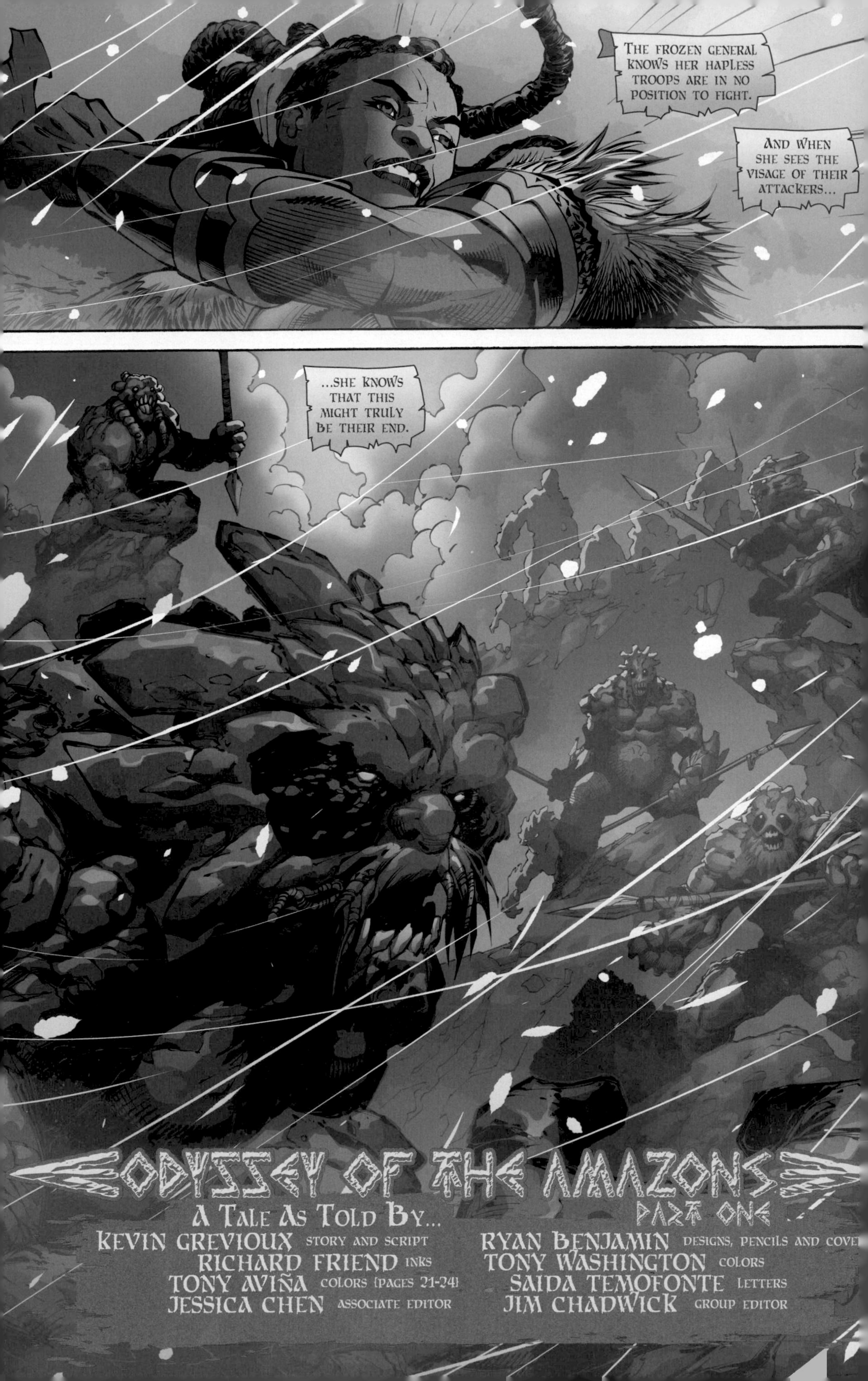
THE FROZEN GENERAL KNOWS HER HAPLESS TROOPS ARE IN NO POSITION TO FIGHT.
AND WHEN SHE SEES THE VISAGE OF THEIR ATTACKERS...
...SHE KNOWS THAT THIS MIGHT TRULY BE THEIR END.
ODYSSEY OF THE AMAZONS
PART ONE
A TALE AS TOLD BY...
KEVIN GREVIOUX STORY AND SCRIPT
RYAN BENJAMIN DESIGNS, PENCILS AND COVE
RICHARD FRIEND INKS
TONY WASHINGTON COLORS
TONY AVIÑA COLORS [PAGES 21-24]
SAIDA TEMOFONTE LETTERS
JESSICA CHEN ASSOCIATE EDITOR
JIM CHADWICK GROUP EDITOR

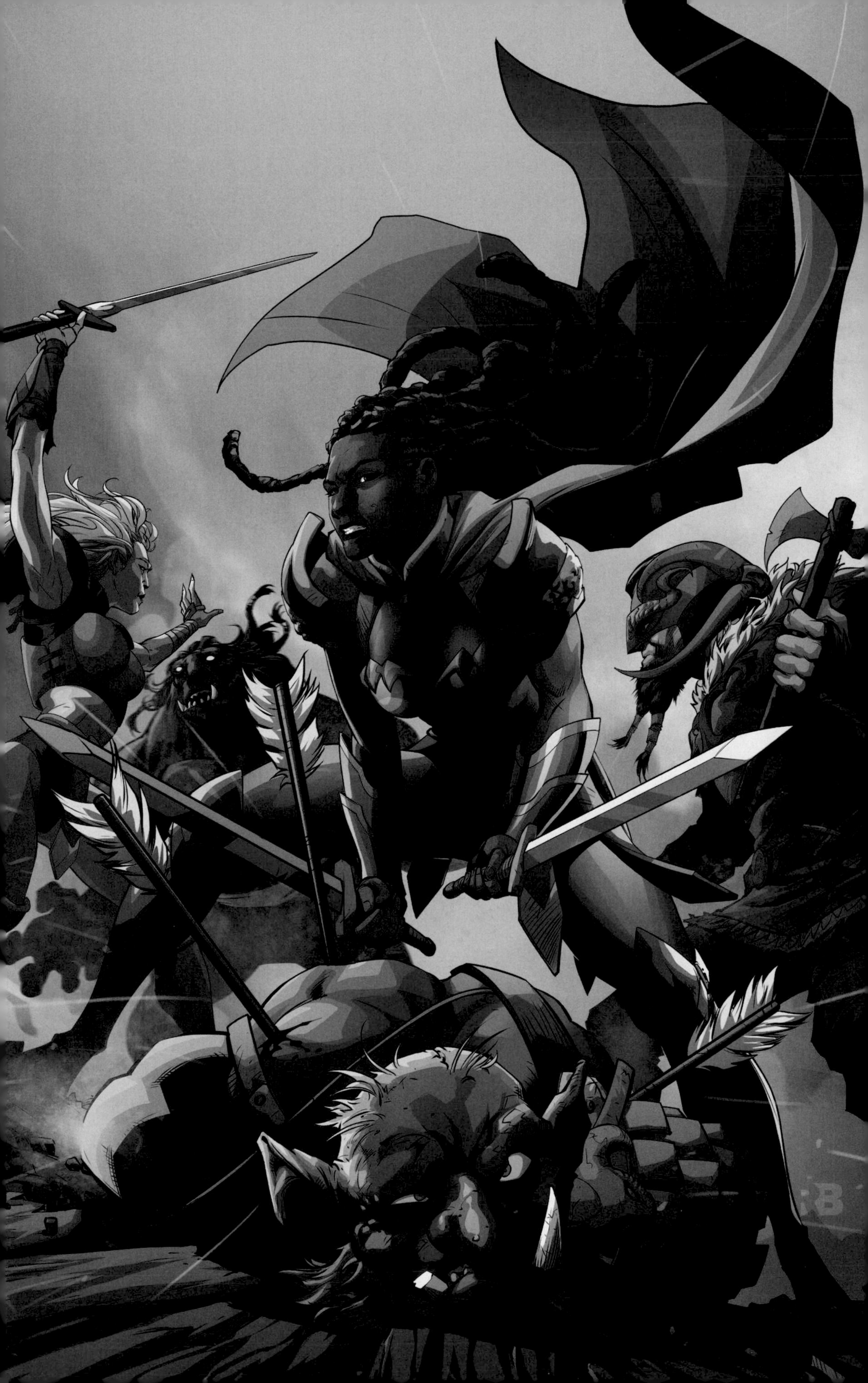

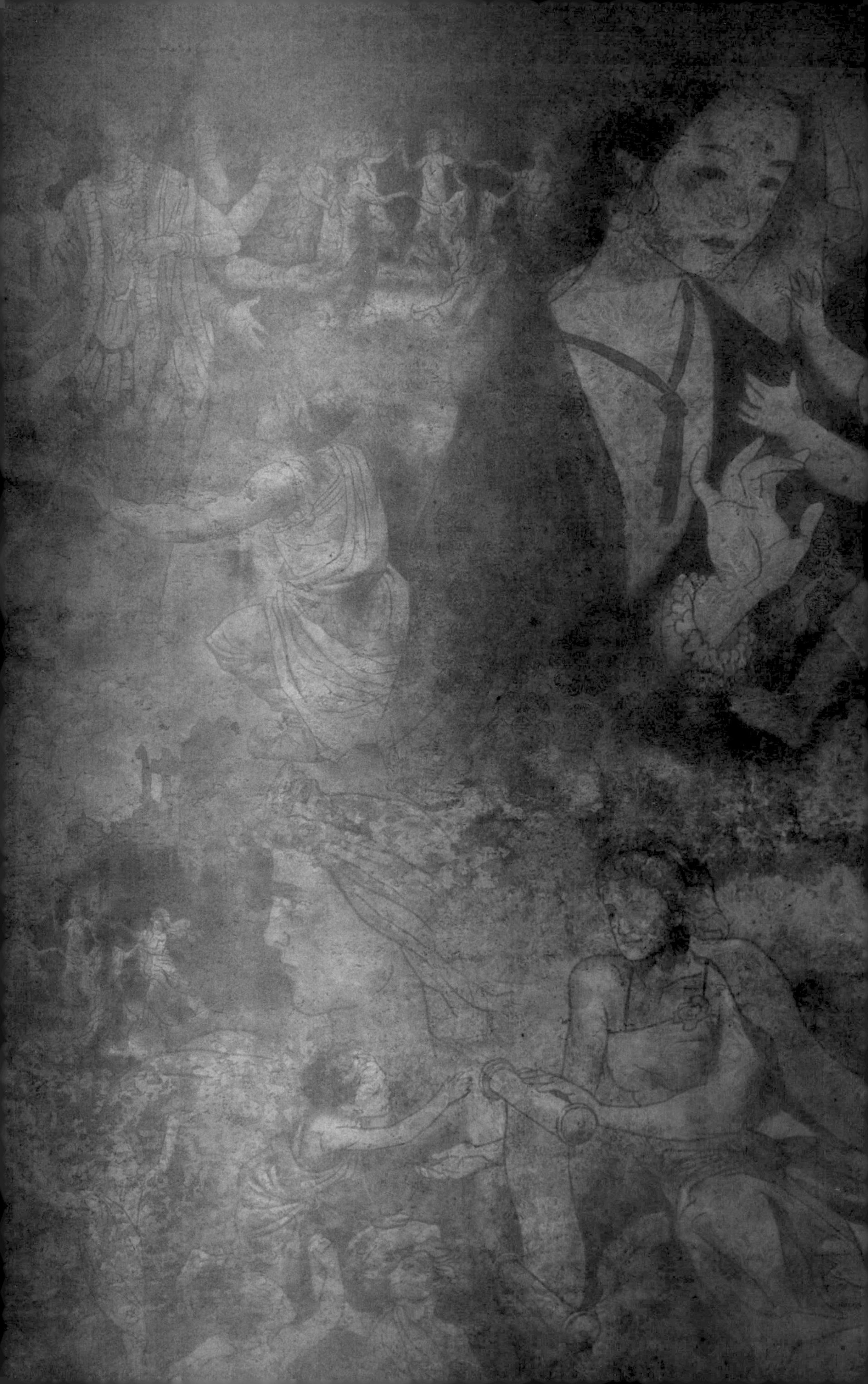

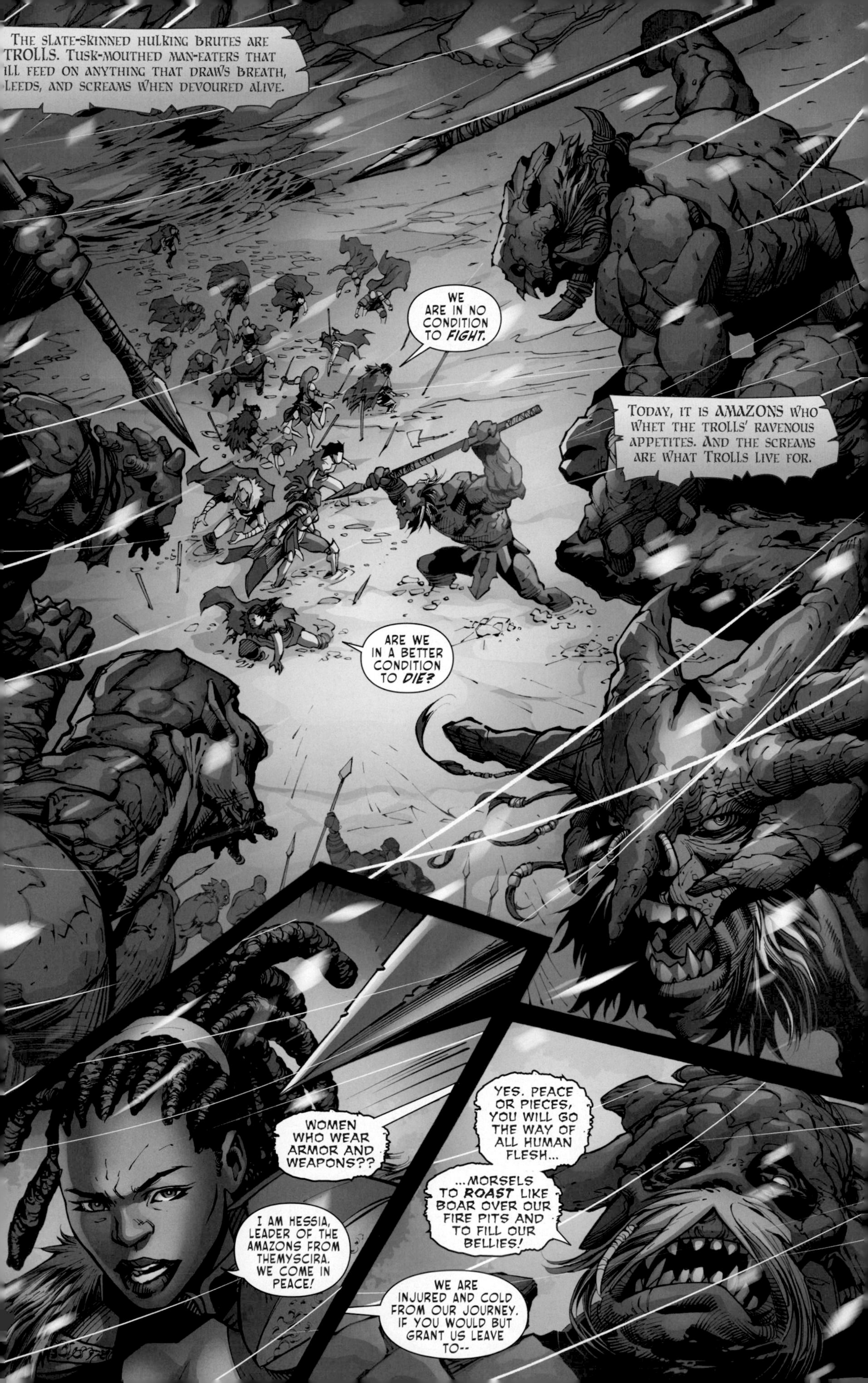
THE SLATE-SKINNED HULKING BRUTES ARE TROLLS. TUSK-MOUTHED MAN-EATERS THAT ILL FEED ON ANYTHING THAT DRAWS BREATH, LEEDS, AND SCREAMS WHEN DEVOURED ALIVE.
WE ARE IN NO CONDITION TO FIGHT.
TODAY, IT IS AMAZONS WHO WHET THE TROLLS' RAVENOUS APPETITES. AND THE SCREAMS ARE WHAT TROLLS LIVE FOR.
ARE WE IN A BETTER CONDITION TO DIE?
WOMEN WHO WEAR ARMOR AND WEAPONS??
I AM HESSIA, LEADER OF THE AMAZONS FROM THEMYSCIRA. WE COME IN PEACE!
YES. PEACE OR PIECES, YOU WILL GO THE WAY OF ALL HUMAN FLESH...
...MORSELS TO ROAST LIKE BOAR OVER OUR FIRE PITS AND TO FILL OUR BELLIES!
WE ARE INJURED AND COLD FROM OUR JOURNEY. IF YOU WOULD BUT GRANT US LEAVE TO--

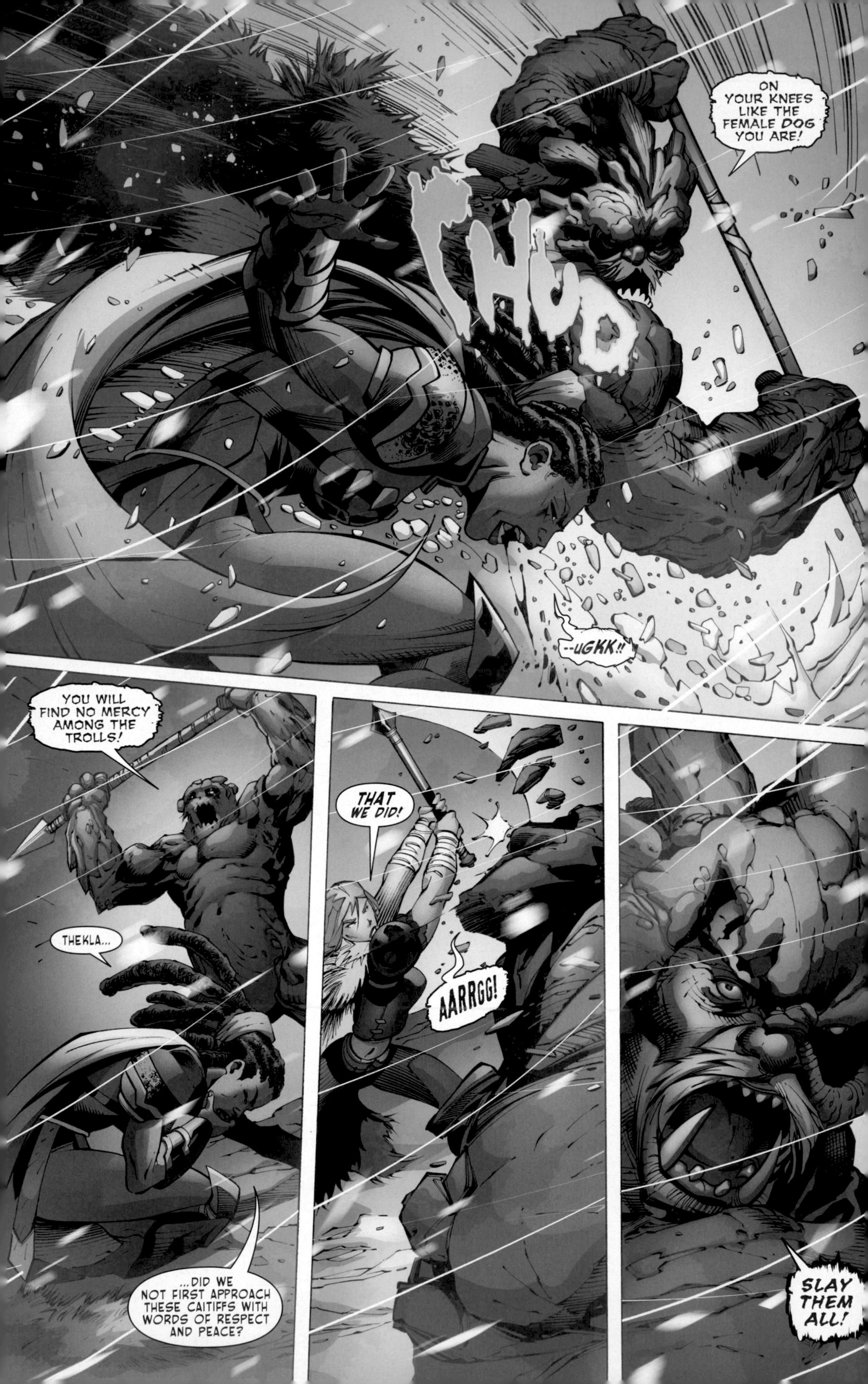
ON YOUR KNEES LIKE THE FEMALE DOG YOU ARE!
CHUD
--UGKK!!
YOU WILL FIND NO MERCY AMONG THE TROLLS!
THEKLA...
...DID WE NOT FIRST APPROACH THESE CAITIFFS WITH WORDS OF RESPECT AND PEACE?
THAT WE DID!
AARRGG!
SLAY THEM ALL!

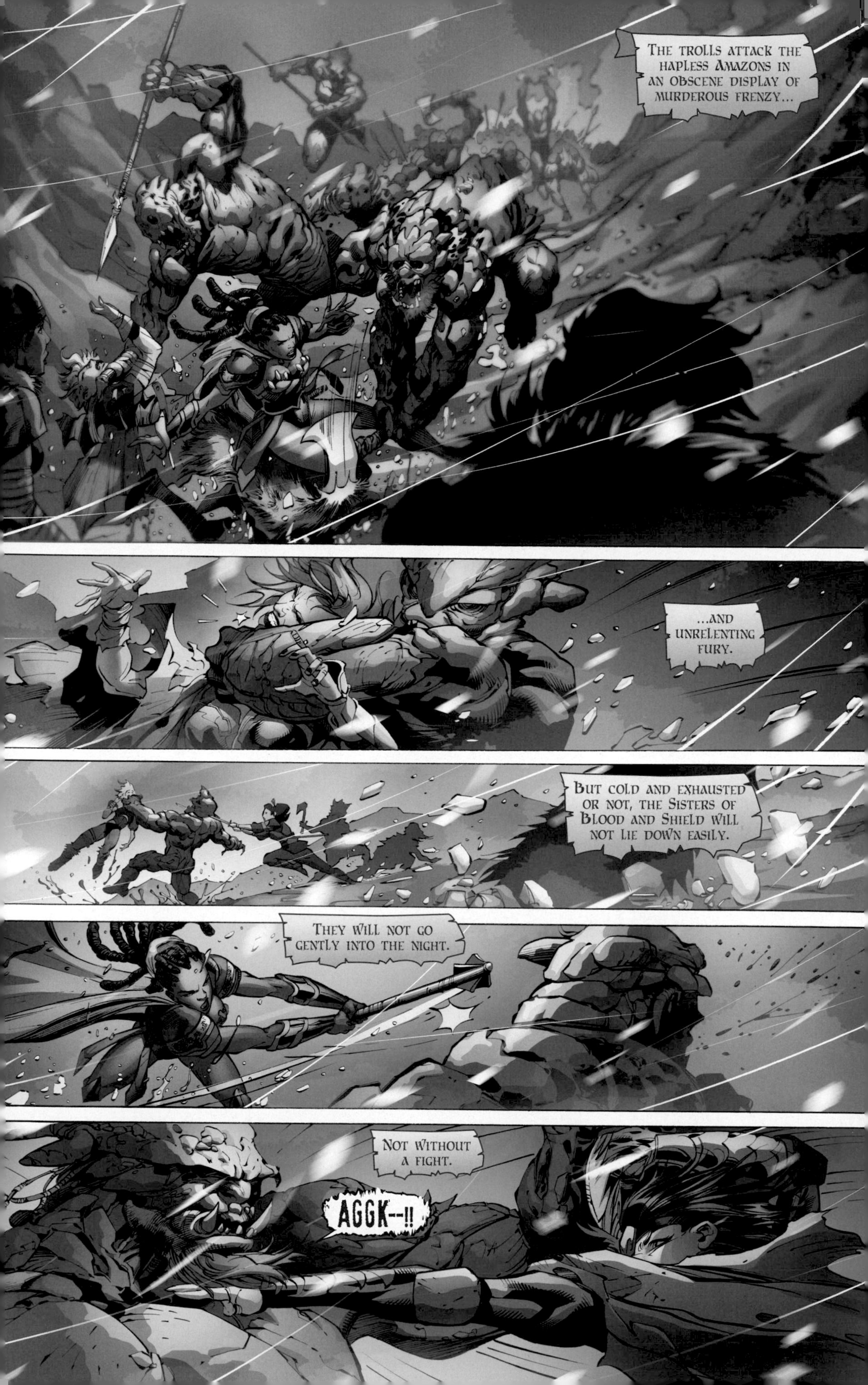
THE TROLLS ATTACK THE HAPLESS AMAZONS IN AN OBSCENE DISPLAY OF MURDEROUS FRENZY...
...AND UNRELENTING FURY.
BUT COLD AND EXHAUSTED OR NOT, THE SISTERS OF BLOOD AND SHIELD WILL NOT LIE DOWN EASILY.
THEY WILL NOT GO GENTLY INTO THE NIGHT.
NOT WITHOUT A FIGHT.
AGGK--!!

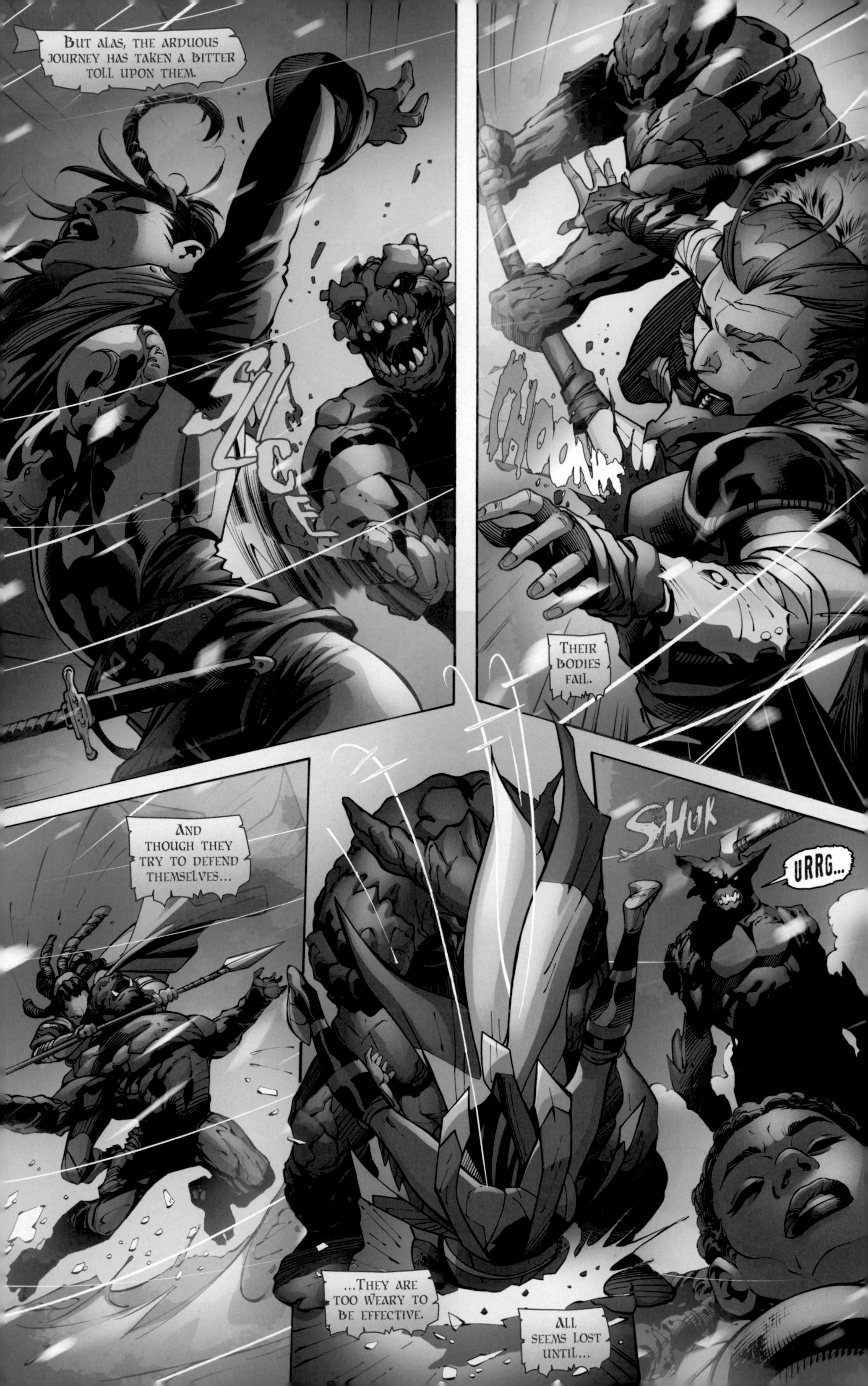
But alas, the arduous journey has taken a bitter toll upon them.
SLICE
CHOOM
Their bodies fail.
And though they try to defend themselves...
SHUK
URRG...
...They are too weary to be effective.
All seems lost until...

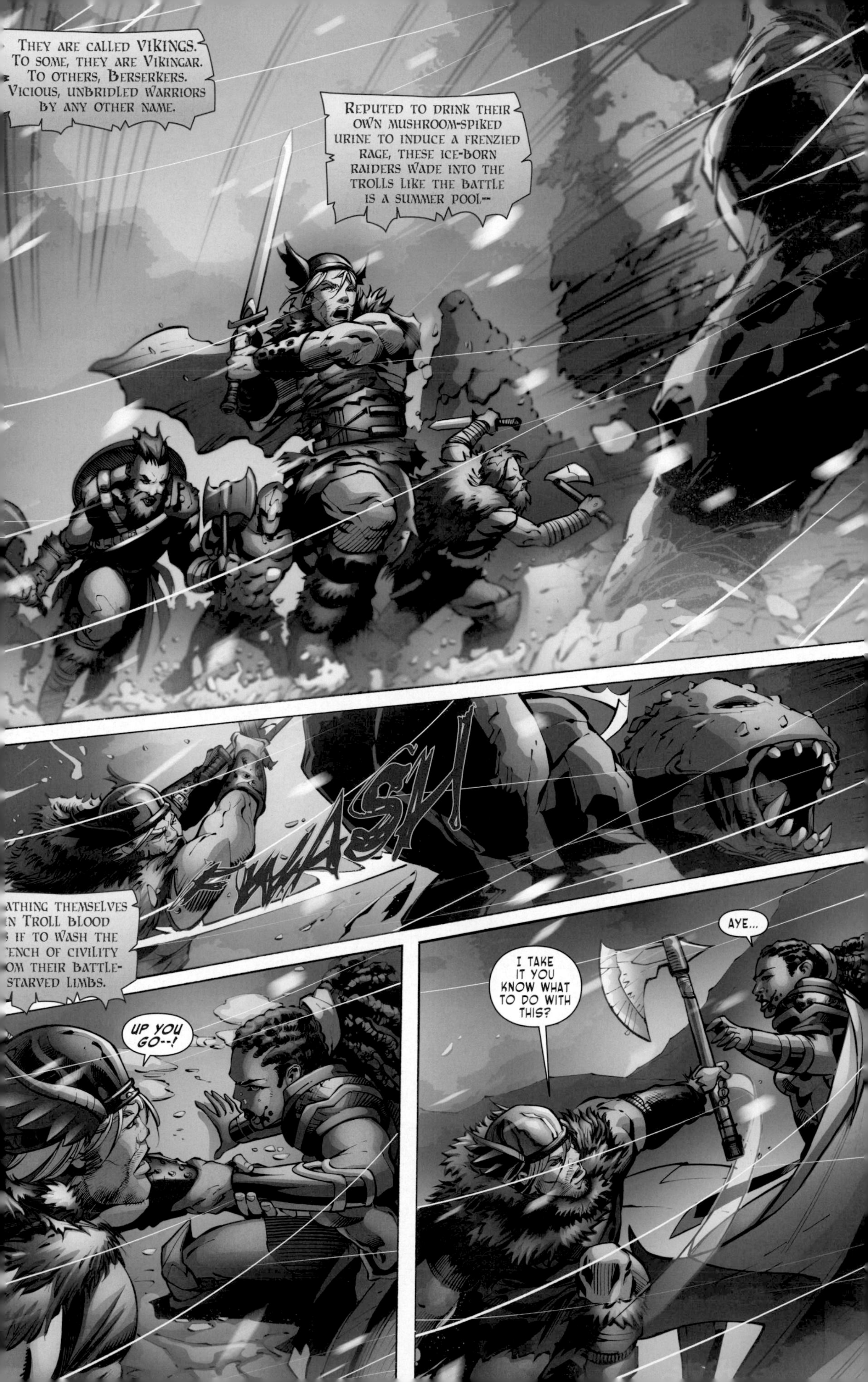
THEY ARE CALLED VIKINGS. TO SOME, THEY ARE VIKINGAR. TO OTHERS, BERSERKERS. VICIOUS, UNBRIDLED WARRIORS BY ANY OTHER NAME.
REPUTED TO DRINK THEIR OWN MUSHROOM-SPIKED URINE TO INDUCE A FRENZIED RAGE, THESE ICE-BORN RAIDERS WADE INTO THE TROLLS LIKE THE BATTLE IS A SUMMER POOL--
ATHING THEMSELVES IN TROLL BLOOD IF TO WASH THE ENCH OF CIVILITY OM THEIR BATTLE-STARVED LIMBS.
UP YOU GO--!
AYE...
I TAKE IT YOU KNOW WHAT TO DO WITH THIS?

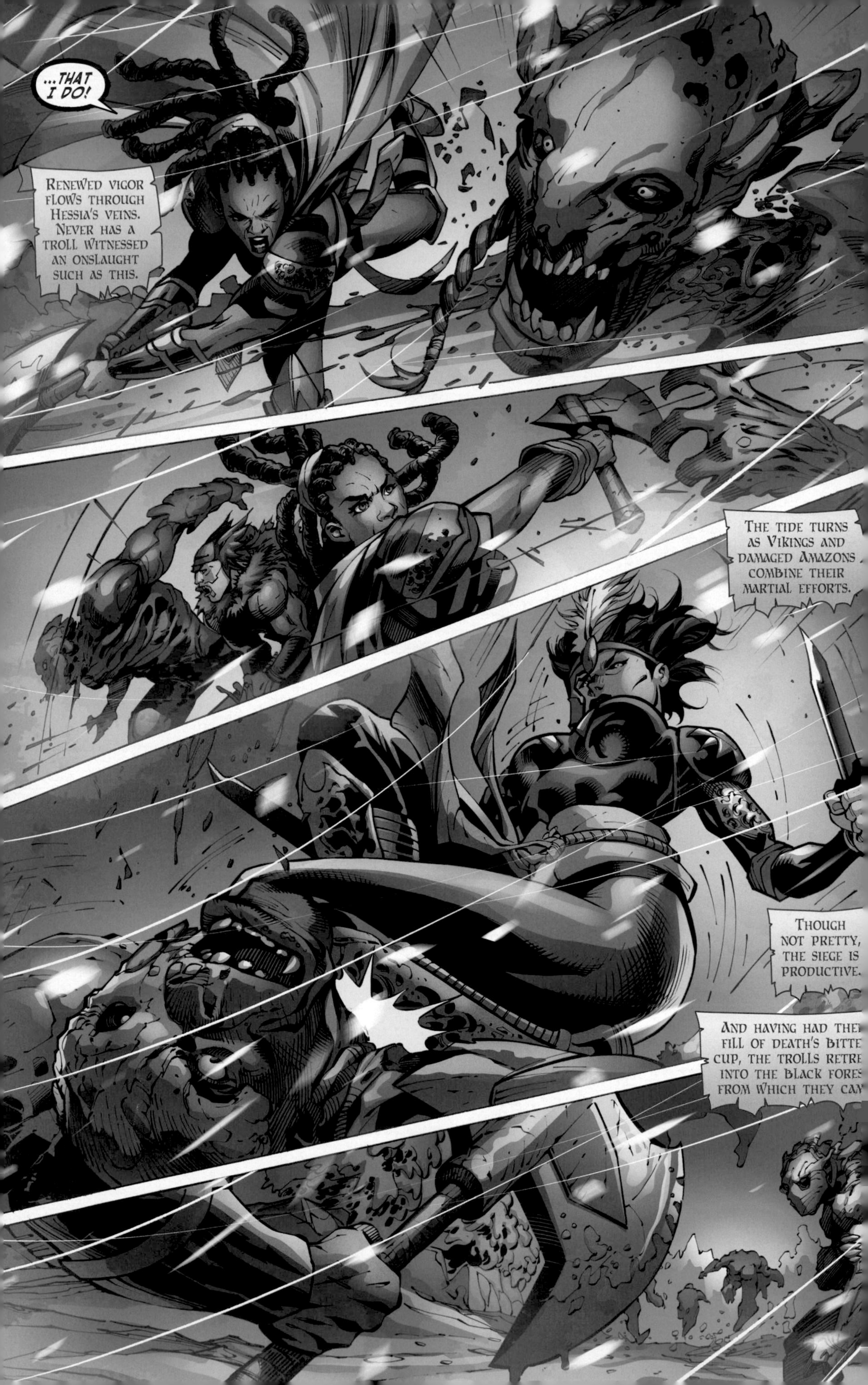
...THAT I DO!
Renewed vigor flows through Hessia's veins. Never has a troll witnessed an onslaught such as this.
The tide turns as Vikings and damaged Amazons combine their martial efforts.
Though not pretty, the siege is productive.
And having had the fill of death's bitte cup, the trolls retre into the black fores from which they ca

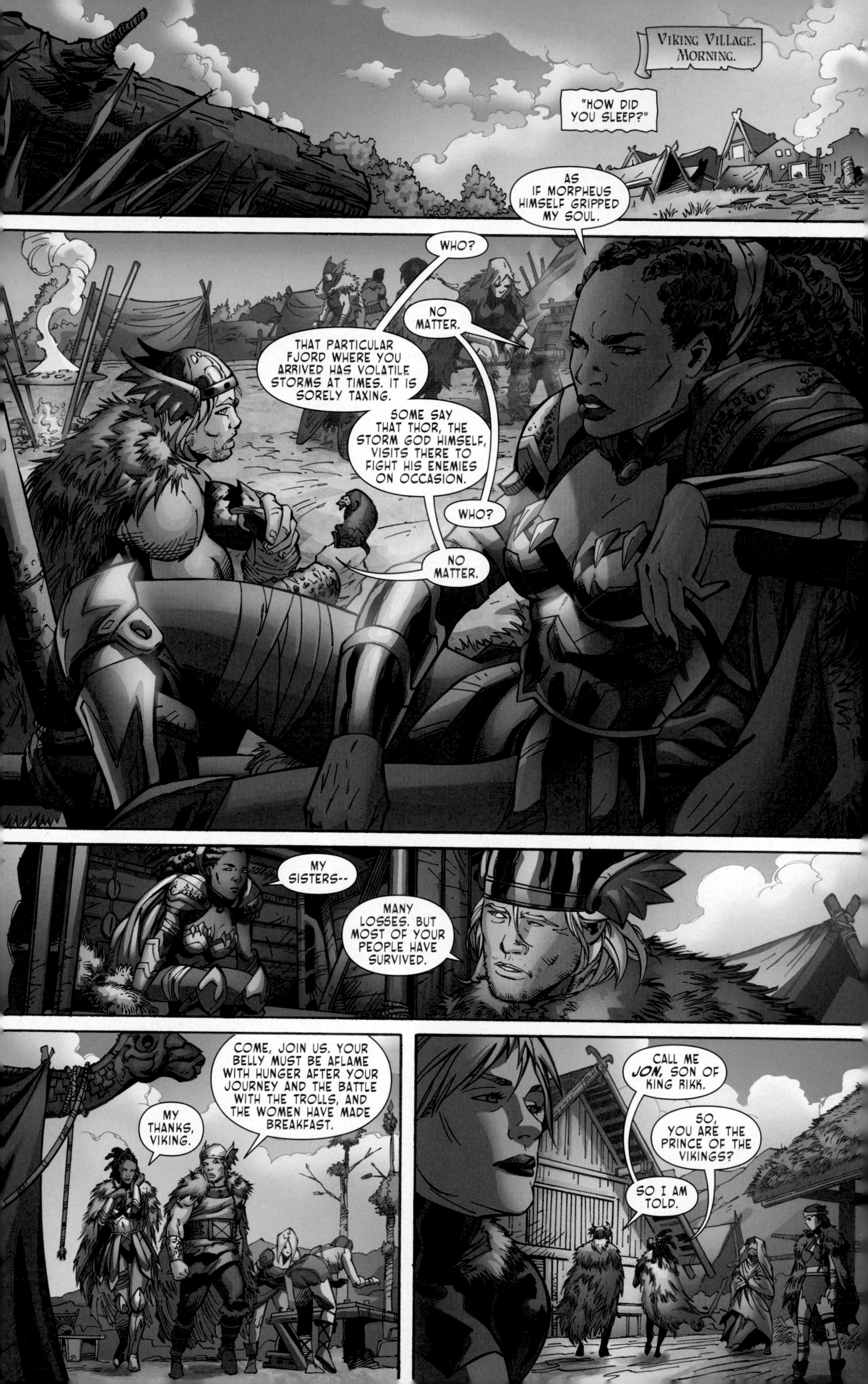
VIKING VILLAGE. MORNING.
"HOW DID YOU SLEEP?"
AS IF MORPHEUS HIMSELF GRIPPED MY SOUL.
WHO?
NO MATTER.
THAT PARTICULAR FJORD WHERE YOU ARRIVED HAS VOLATILE STORMS AT TIMES. IT IS SORELY TAXING.
SOME SAY THAT THOR, THE STORM GOD HIMSELF, VISITS THERE TO FIGHT HIS ENEMIES ON OCCASION.
WHO?
NO MATTER.
MY SISTERS--
MANY LOSSES. BUT MOST OF YOUR PEOPLE HAVE SURVIVED.
COME, JOIN US. YOUR BELLY MUST BE AFLAME WITH HUNGER AFTER YOUR JOURNEY AND THE BATTLE WITH THE TROLLS, AND THE WOMEN HAVE MADE BREAKFAST.
MY THANKS, VIKING.
CALL ME JON, SON OF KING RIKK.
SO, YOU ARE THE PRINCE OF THE VIKINGS?
SO I AM TOLD.

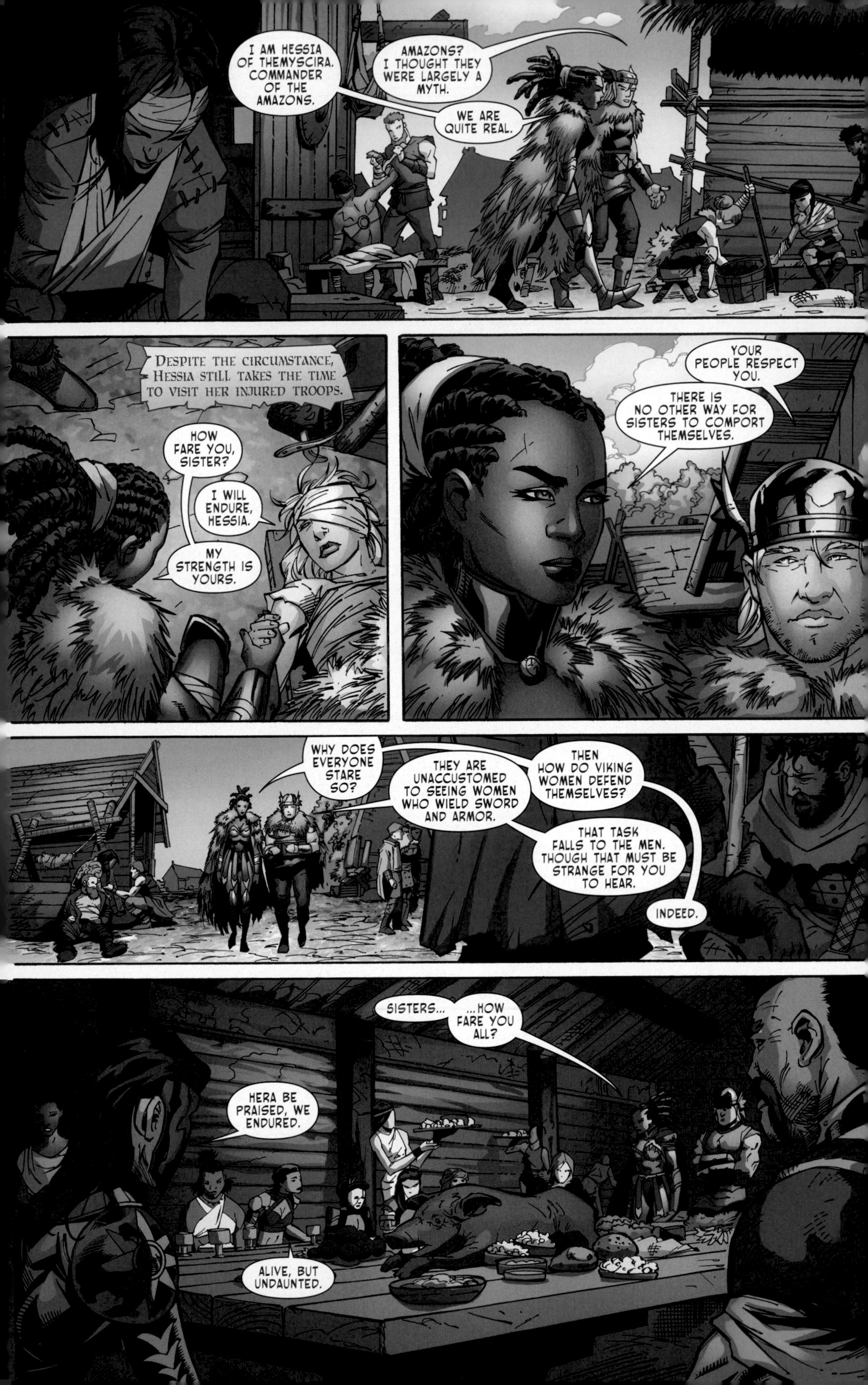
I AM HESSIA OF THEMYSCIRA. COMMANDER OF THE AMAZONS.
AMAZONS? I THOUGHT THEY WERE LARGELY A MYTH.
WE ARE QUITE REAL.
DESPITE THE CIRCUMSTANCE, HESSIA STILL TAKES THE TIME TO VISIT HER INJURED TROOPS.
HOW FARE YOU, SISTER?
I WILL ENDURE, HESSIA.
MY STRENGTH IS YOURS.
YOUR PEOPLE RESPECT YOU.
THERE IS NO OTHER WAY FOR SISTERS TO COMPORT THEMSELVES.
WHY DOES EVERYONE STARE SO?
THEY ARE UNACCUSTOMED TO SEEING WOMEN WHO WIELD SWORD AND ARMOR.
THEN HOW DO VIKING WOMEN DEFEND THEMSELVES?
THAT TASK FALLS TO THE MEN. THOUGH THAT MUST BE STRANGE FOR YOU TO HEAR.
INDEED.
SISTERS...
...HOW FARE YOU ALL?
HERA BE PRAISED, WE ENDURED.
ALIVE, BUT UNDAUNTED.

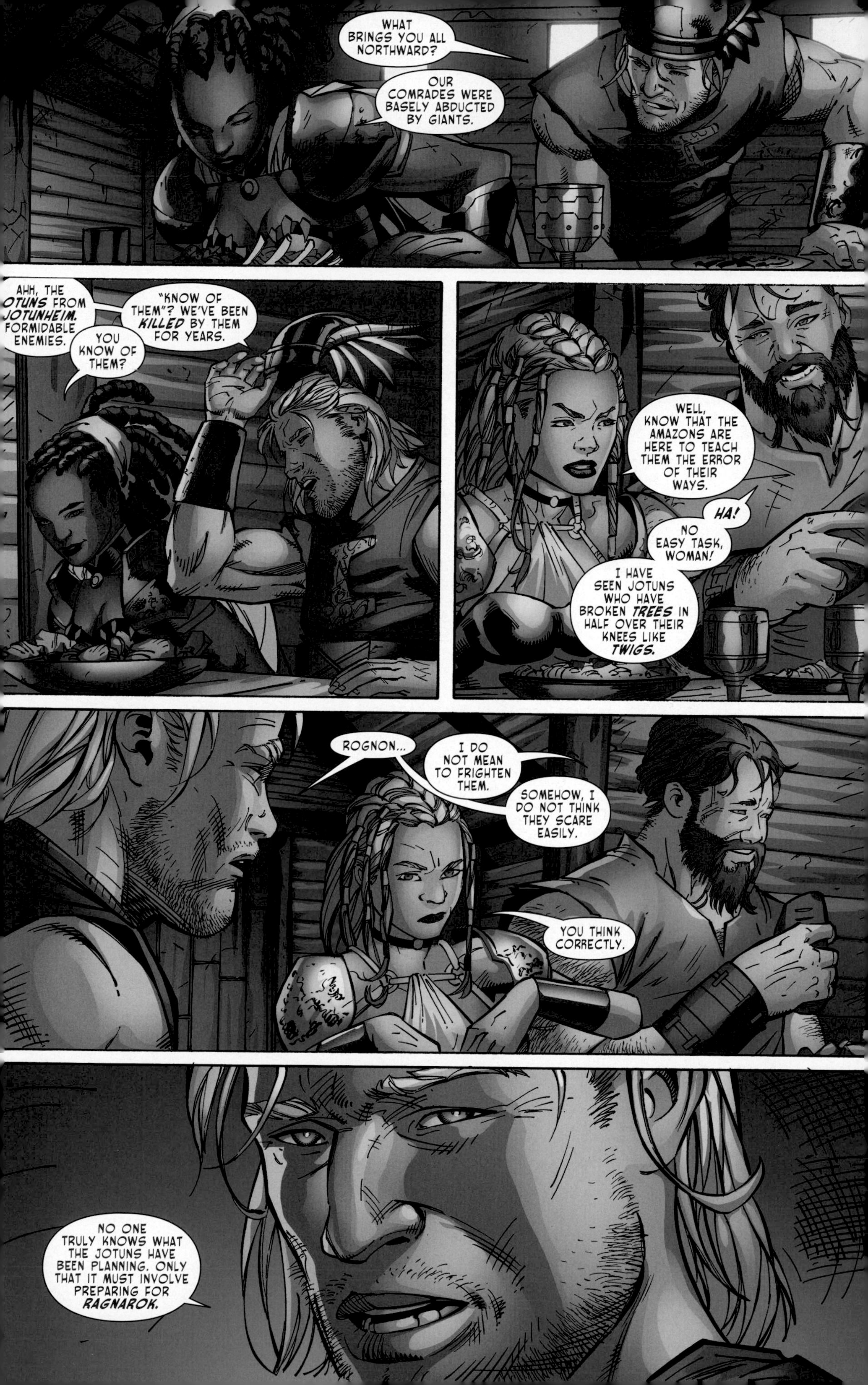
WHAT BRINGS YOU ALL NORTHWARD?
OUR COMRADES WERE BASELY ABDUCTED BY GIANTS.
AHH, THE JOTUNS FROM JOTUNHEIM. FORMIDABLE ENEMIES.
YOU KNOW OF THEM?
"KNOW OF THEM"? WE'VE BEEN KILLED BY THEM FOR YEARS.
WELL, KNOW THAT THE AMAZONS ARE HERE TO TEACH THEM THE ERROR OF THEIR WAYS.
HA!
NO EASY TASK, WOMAN!
I HAVE SEEN JOTUNS WHO HAVE BROKEN TREES IN HALF OVER THEIR KNEES LIKE TWIGS.
ROGNON...
I DO NOT MEAN TO FRIGHTEN THEM.
SOMEHOW, I DO NOT THINK THEY SCARE EASILY.
YOU THINK CORRECTLY.
NO ONE TRULY KNOWS WHAT THE JOTUNS HAVE BEEN PLANNING. ONLY THAT IT MUST INVOLVE PREPARING FOR RAGNAROK.

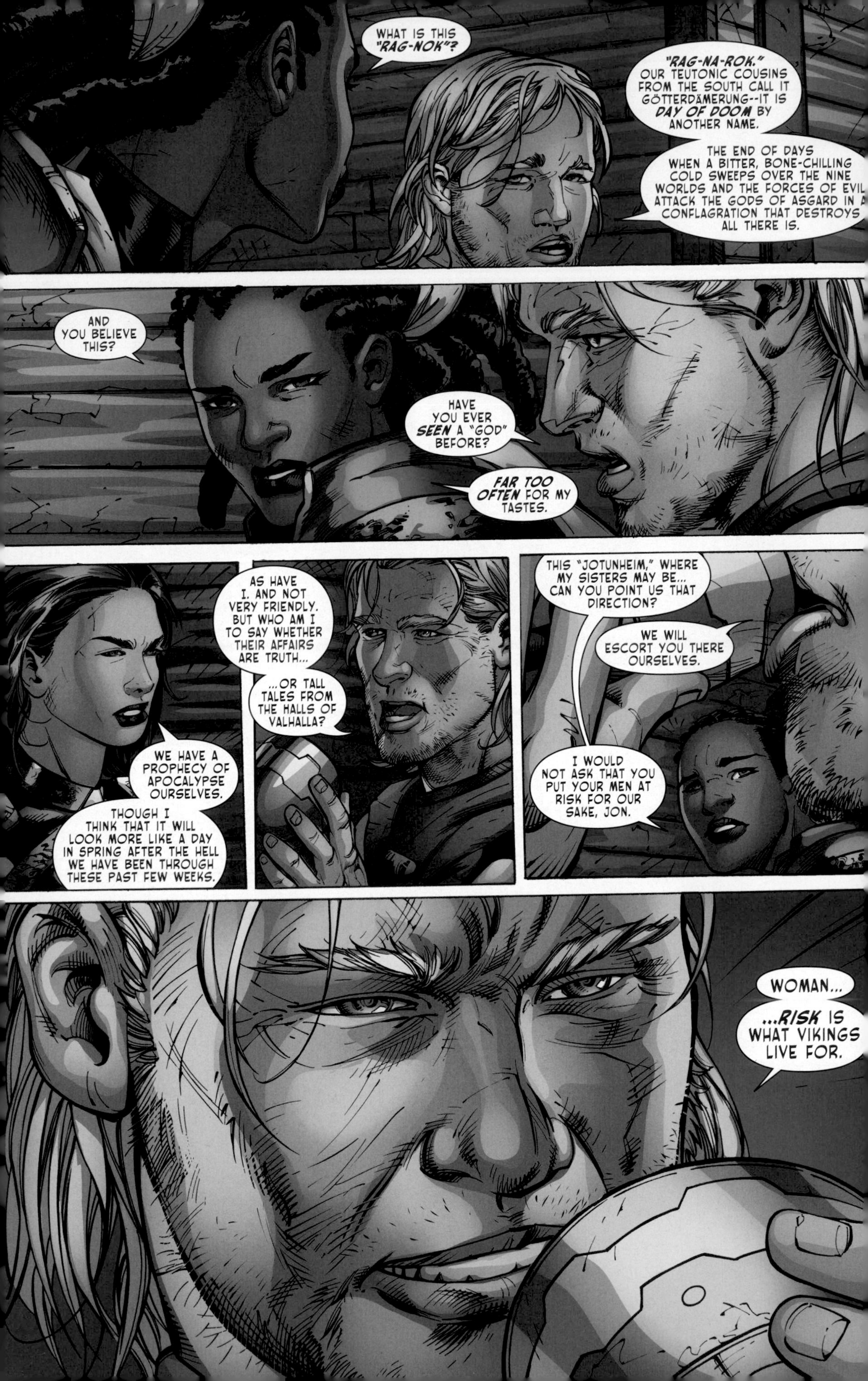
WHAT IS THIS "RAG-NOK"?
"RAG-NA-ROK." OUR TEUTONIC COUSINS FROM THE SOUTH CALL IT GÖTTERDÄMERUNG--IT IS DAY OF DOOM BY ANOTHER NAME.
THE END OF DAYS WHEN A BITTER, BONE-CHILLING COLD SWEEPS OVER THE NINE WORLDS AND THE FORCES OF EVIL ATTACK THE GODS OF ASGARD IN A CONFLAGRATION THAT DESTROYS ALL THERE IS.
AND YOU BELIEVE THIS?
HAVE YOU EVER SEEN A "GOD" BEFORE?
FAR TOO OFTEN FOR MY TASTES.
AS HAVE I. AND NOT VERY FRIENDLY. BUT WHO AM I TO SAY WHETHER THEIR AFFAIRS ARE TRUTH...
...OR TALL TALES FROM THE HALLS OF VALHALLA?
WE HAVE A PROPHECY OF APOCALYPSE OURSELVES.
THOUGH I THINK THAT IT WILL LOOK MORE LIKE A DAY IN SPRING AFTER THE HELL WE HAVE BEEN THROUGH THESE PAST FEW WEEKS.
THIS "JOTUNHEIM," WHERE MY SISTERS MAY BE... CAN YOU POINT US THAT DIRECTION?
WE WILL ESCORT YOU THERE OURSELVES.
I WOULD NOT ASK THAT YOU PUT YOUR MEN AT RISK FOR OUR SAKE, JON.
WOMAN...
...RISK IS WHAT VIKINGS LIVE FOR.

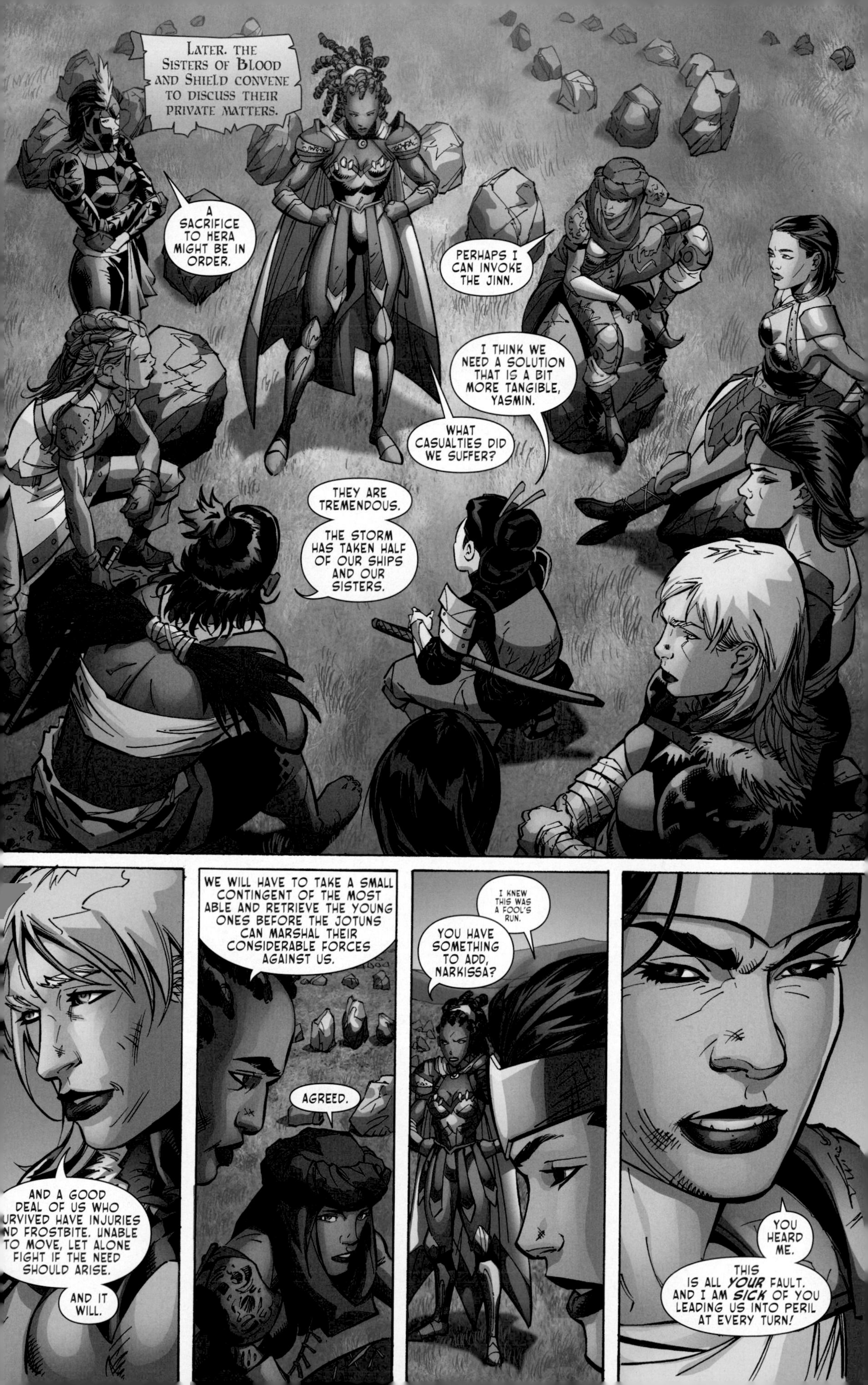
LATER. THE SISTERS OF BLOOD AND SHIELD CONVENE TO DISCUSS THEIR PRIVATE MATTERS.
A SACRIFICE TO HERA MIGHT BE IN ORDER.
PERHAPS I CAN INVOKE THE JINN.
I THINK WE NEED A SOLUTION THAT IS A BIT MORE TANGIBLE, YASMIN.
WHAT CASUALTIES DID WE SUFFER?
THEY ARE TREMENDOUS.
THE STORM HAS TAKEN HALF OF OUR SHIPS AND OUR SISTERS.
AND A GOOD DEAL OF US WHO URVIVED HAVE INJURIES ND FROSTBITE. UNABLE TO MOVE, LET ALONE FIGHT IF THE NEED SHOULD ARISE.
AND IT WILL.
WE WILL HAVE TO TAKE A SMALL CONTINGENT OF THE MOST ABLE AND RETRIEVE THE YOUNG ONES BEFORE THE JOTUNS CAN MARSHAL THEIR CONSIDERABLE FORCES AGAINST US.
AGREED.
I KNEW THIS WAS A FOOL'S RUN.
YOU HAVE SOMETHING TO ADD, NARKISSA?
YOU HEARD ME.
THIS IS ALL YOUR FAULT. AND I AM SICK OF YOU LEADING US INTO PERIL AT EVERY TURN!

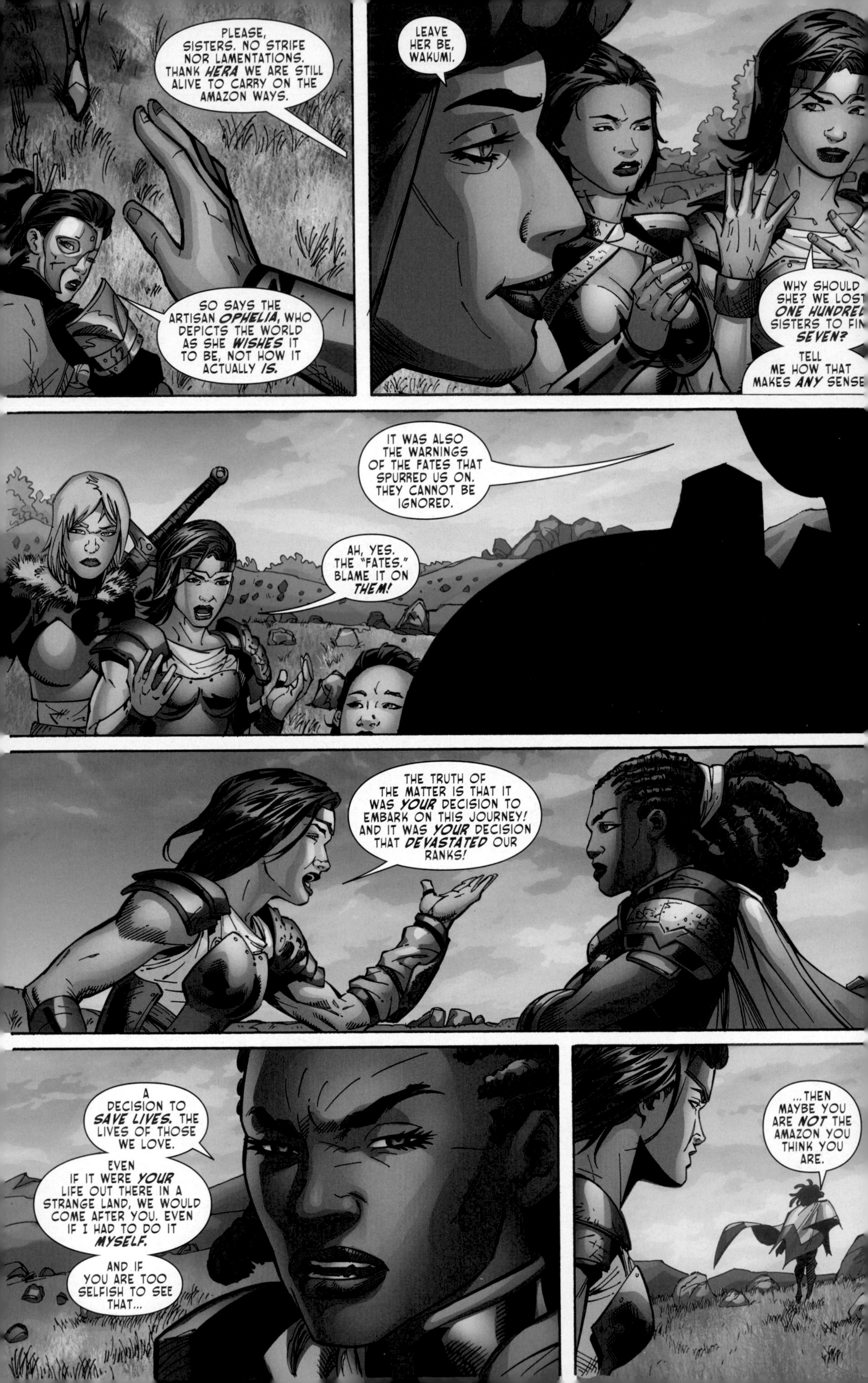
PLEASE, SISTERS. NO STRIFE NOR LAMENTATIONS. THANK HERA WE ARE STILL ALIVE TO CARRY ON THE AMAZON WAYS.
SO SAYS THE ARTISAN OPHELIA, WHO DEPICTS THE WORLD AS SHE WISHES IT TO BE, NOT HOW IT ACTUALLY IS.
LEAVE HER BE, WAKUMI.
WHY SHOULD SHE? WE LOST ONE HUNDRED SISTERS TO FIN SEVEN?
TELL ME HOW THAT MAKES ANY SENSE
IT WAS ALSO THE WARNINGS OF THE FATES THAT SPURRED US ON. THEY CANNOT BE IGNORED.
AH, YES. THE "FATES." BLAME IT ON THEM!
THE TRUTH OF THE MATTER IS THAT IT WAS YOUR DECISION TO EMBARK ON THIS JOURNEY! AND IT WAS YOUR DECISION THAT DEVASTATED OUR RANKS!
A DECISION TO SAVE LIVES. THE LIVES OF THOSE WE LOVE.
EVEN IF IT WERE YOUR LIFE OUT THERE IN A STRANGE LAND, WE WOULD COME AFTER YOU. EVEN IF I HAD TO DO IT MYSELF.
AND IF YOU ARE TOO SELFISH TO SEE THAT...
...THEN MAYBE YOU ARE NOT THE AMAZON YOU THINK YOU ARE.

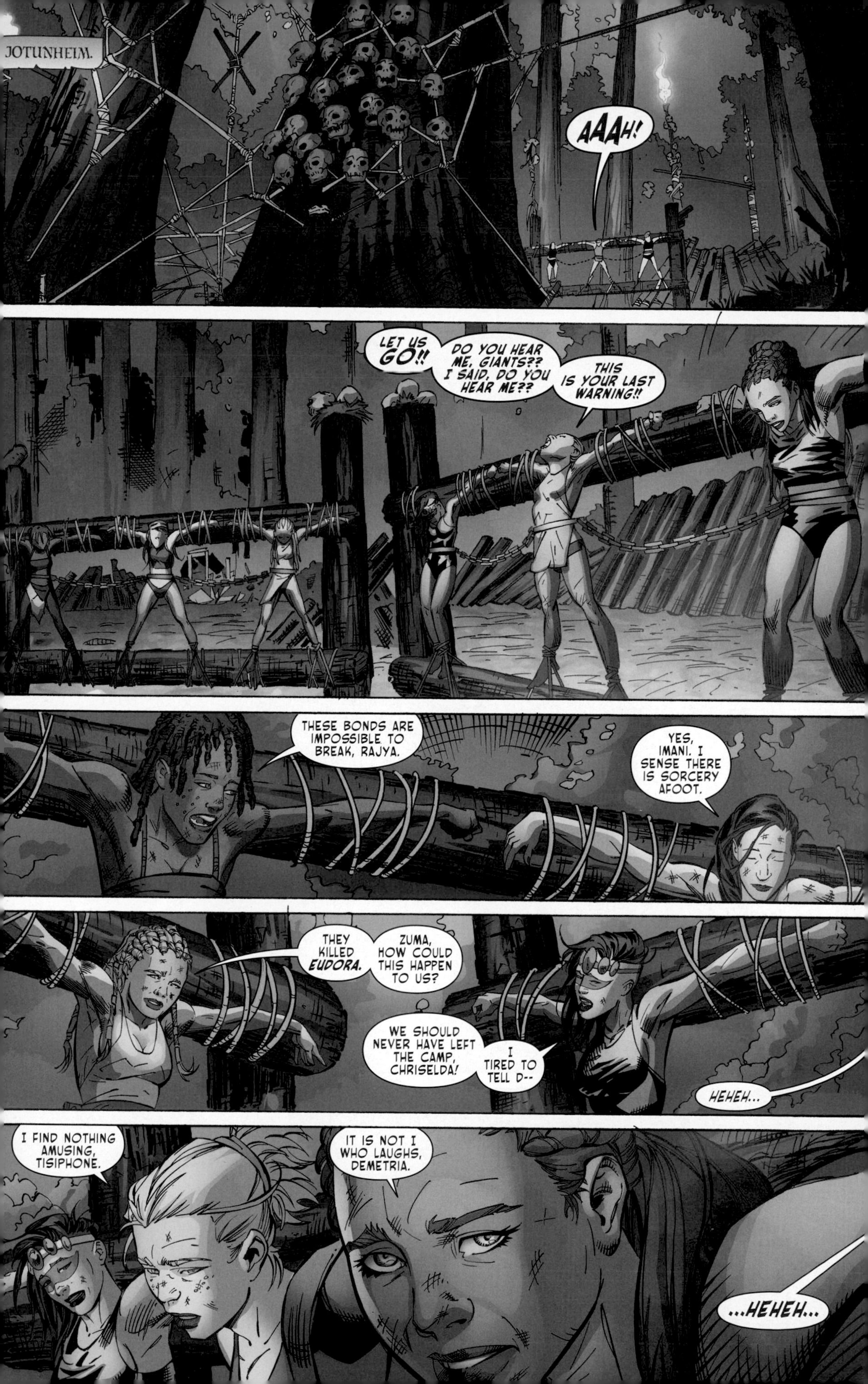
JOTUNHEIM.
AAAH!
LET US GO!!
DO YOU HEAR ME, GIANTS?? I SAID, DO YOU HEAR ME??
THIS IS YOUR LAST WARNING!!
THESE BONDS ARE IMPOSSIBLE TO BREAK, RAJYA.
YES, IMANI. I SENSE THERE IS SORCERY AFOOT.
THEY KILLED EUDORA.
ZUMA, HOW COULD THIS HAPPEN TO US?
WE SHOULD NEVER HAVE LEFT THE CAMP, CHRISELDA!
I TIRED TO TELL D--
HEHEH...
I FIND NOTHING AMUSING, TISIPHONE.
IT IS NOT I WHO LAUGHS, DEMETRIA.
...HEHEH...

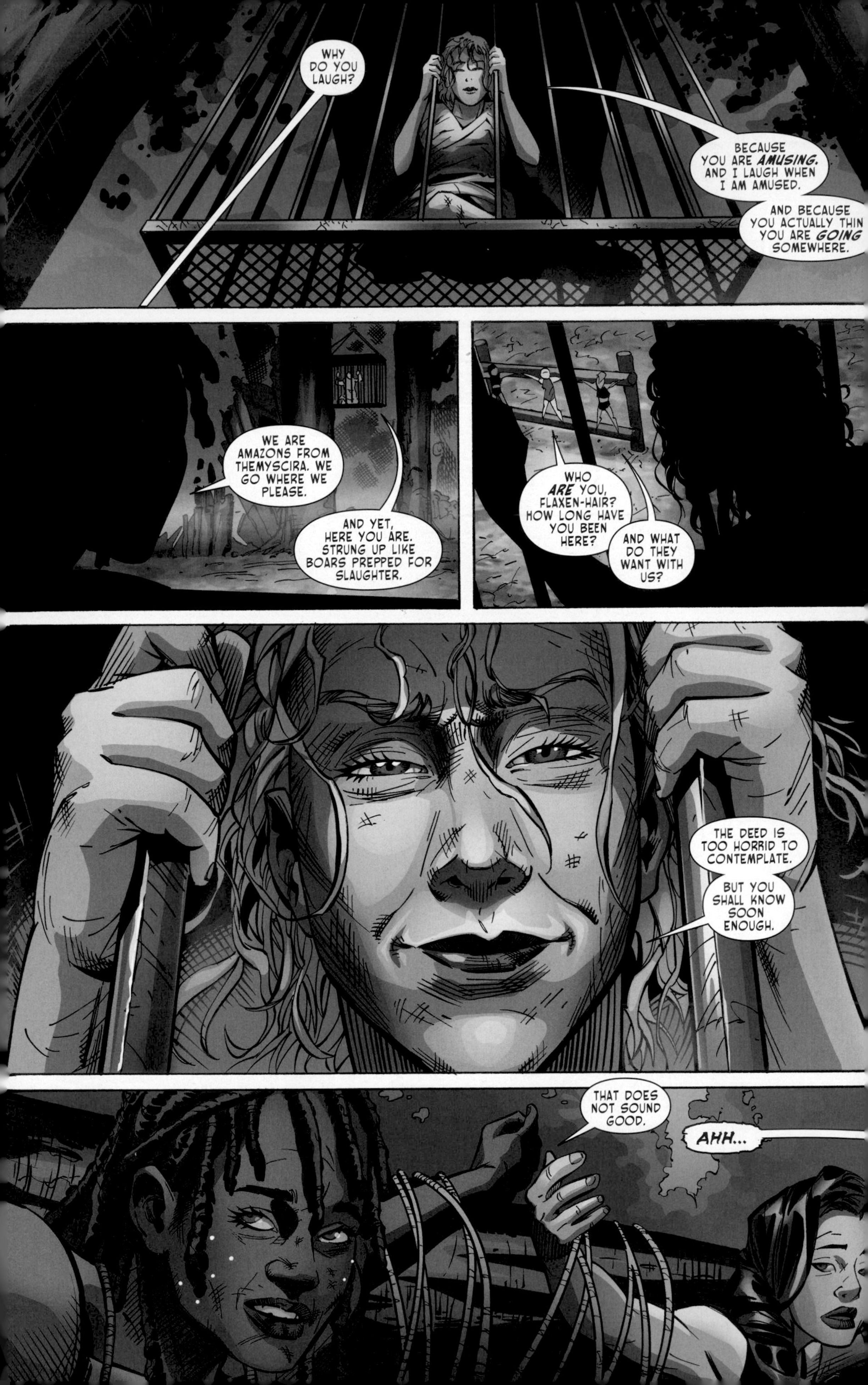
WHY DO YOU LAUGH?
BECAUSE YOU ARE *AMUSING.* AND I LAUGH WHEN I AM AMUSED.
AND BECAUSE YOU ACTUALLY THIN YOU ARE *GOING* SOMEWHERE.
WE ARE AMAZONS FROM THEMYSCIRA. WE GO WHERE WE PLEASE.
AND YET, HERE YOU ARE. STRUNG UP LIKE BOARS PREPPED FOR SLAUGHTER.
WHO *ARE* YOU, FLAXEN-HAIR? HOW LONG HAVE YOU BEEN HERE?
AND WHAT DO THEY WANT WITH US?
THE DEED IS TOO HORRID TO CONTEMPLATE.
BUT YOU SHALL KNOW SOON ENOUGH.
THAT DOES NOT SOUND GOOD.
AHH...

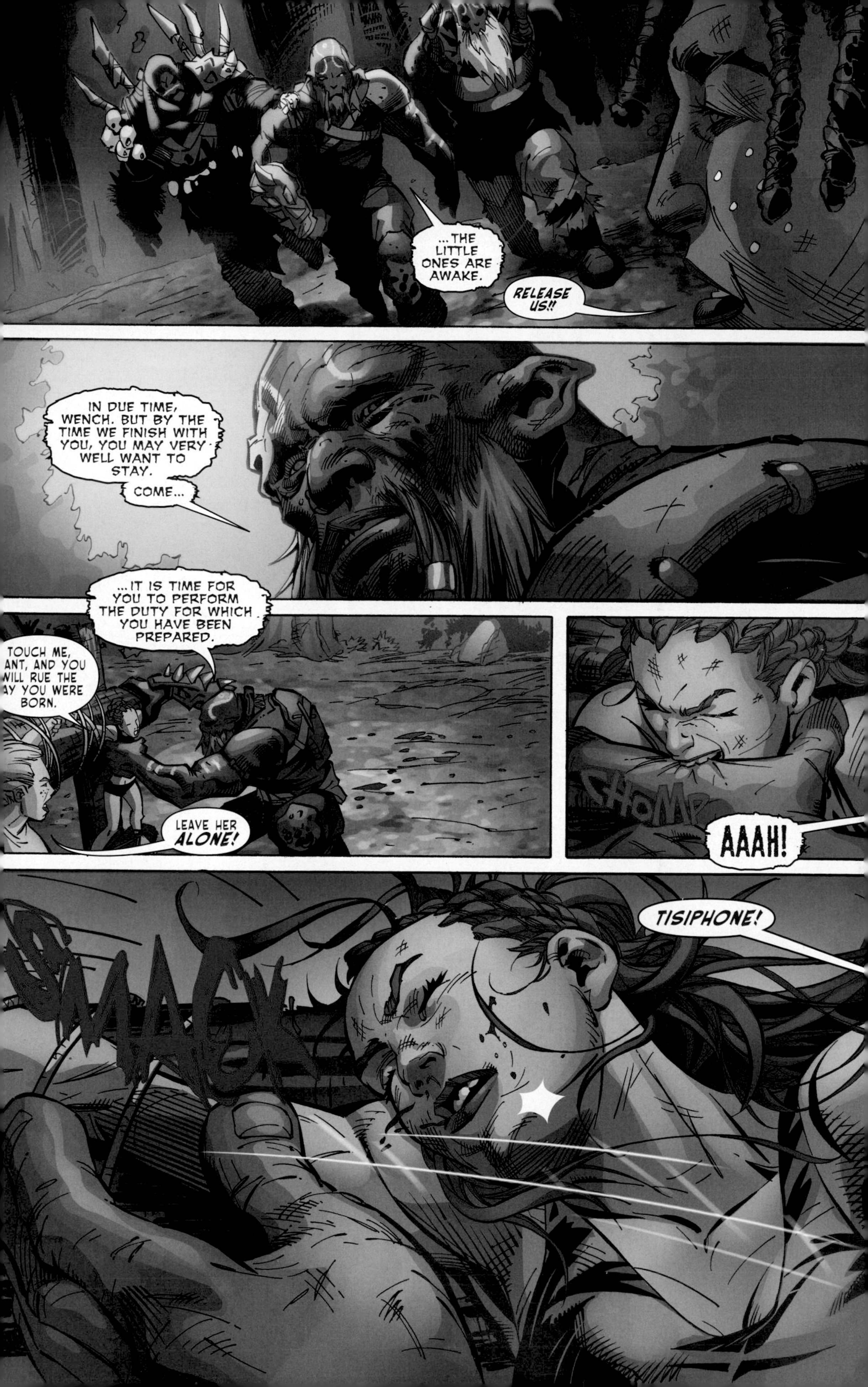
...THE LITTLE ONES ARE AWAKE.
RELEASE US!!
IN DUE TIME, WENCH. BUT BY THE TIME WE FINISH WITH YOU, YOU MAY VERY WELL WANT TO STAY.
COME...
...IT IS TIME FOR YOU TO PERFORM THE DUTY FOR WHICH YOU HAVE BEEN PREPARED.
TOUCH ME, ANT, AND YOU WILL RUE THE AY YOU WERE BORN.
LEAVE HER ALONE!
CHOMP
AAAH!
TISIPHONE!
SMACK

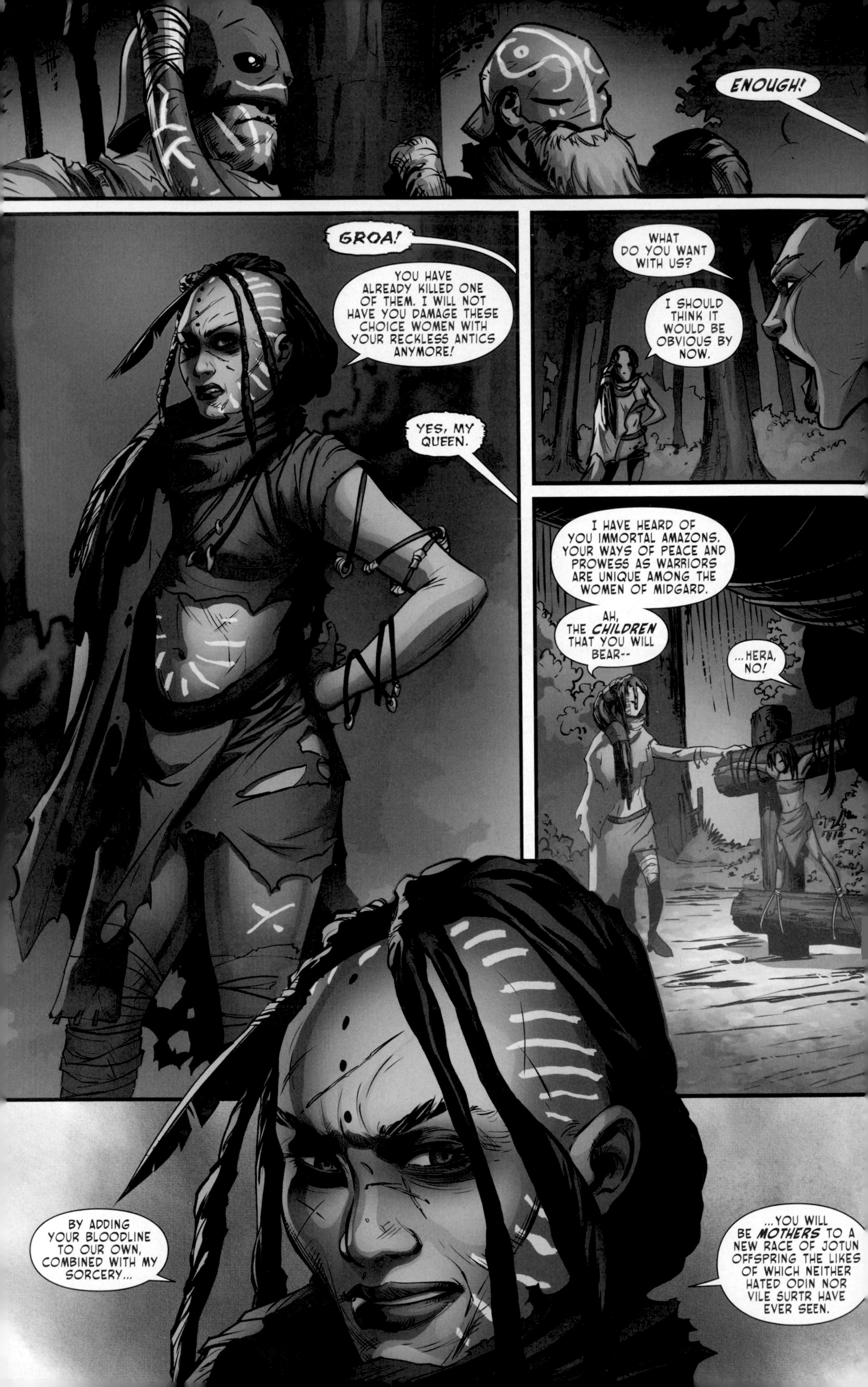
ENOUGH!
GROA!
YOU HAVE ALREADY KILLED ONE OF THEM. I WILL NOT HAVE YOU DAMAGE THESE CHOICE WOMEN WITH YOUR RECKLESS ANTICS ANYMORE!
YES, MY QUEEN.
WHAT DO YOU WANT WITH US?
I SHOULD THINK IT WOULD BE OBVIOUS BY NOW.
I HAVE HEARD OF YOU IMMORTAL AMAZONS. YOUR WAYS OF PEACE AND PROWESS AS WARRIORS ARE UNIQUE AMONG THE WOMEN OF MIDGARD.
AH, THE CHILDREN THAT YOU WILL BEAR--
...HERA, NO!
BY ADDING YOUR BLOODLINE TO OUR OWN, COMBINED WITH MY SORCERY...
...YOU WILL BE MOTHERS TO A NEW RACE OF JOTUN OFFSPRING THE LIKES OF WHICH NEITHER HATED ODIN NOR VILE SURTR HAVE EVER SEEN.

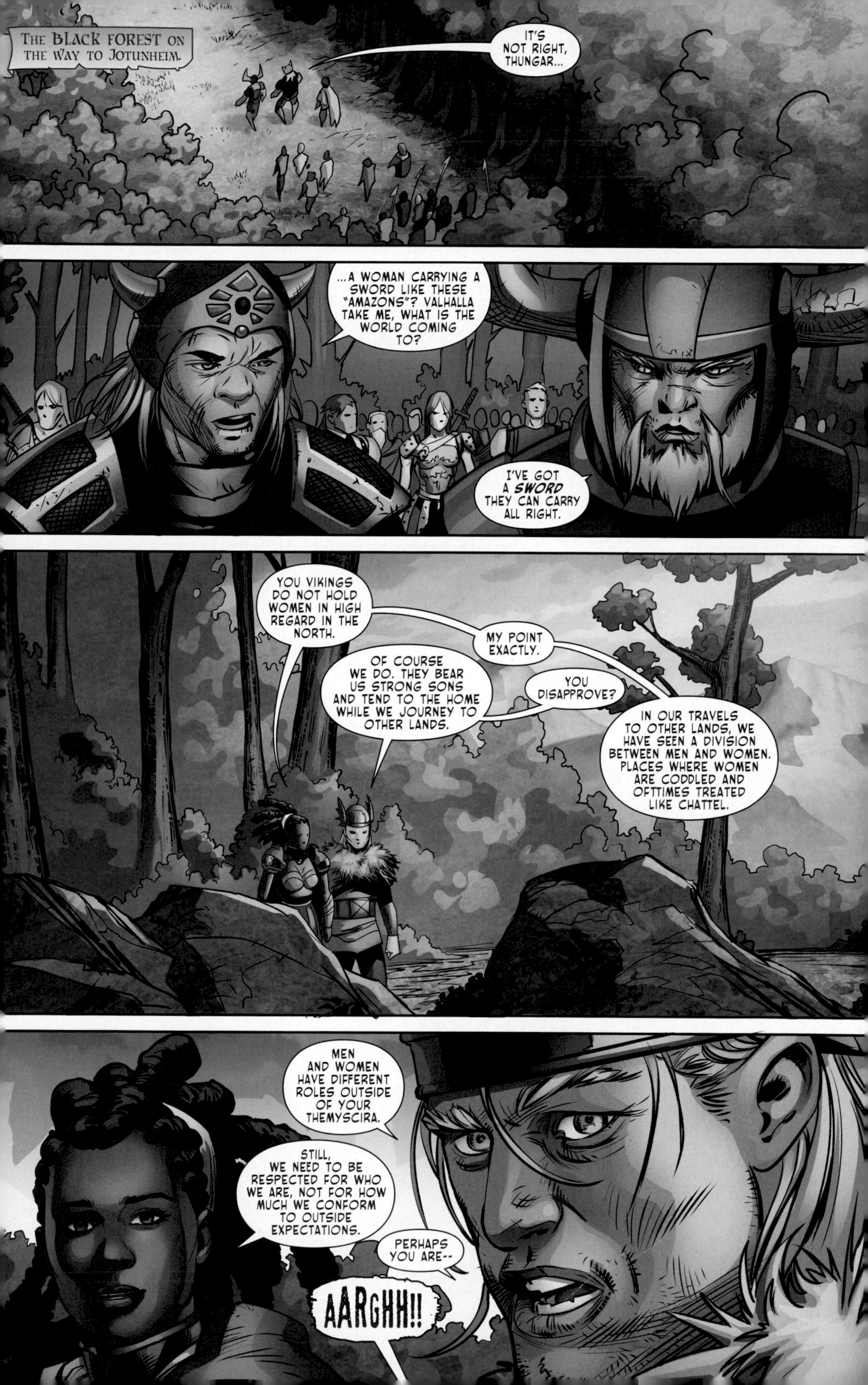
THE BLACK FOREST ON THE WAY TO JOTUNHEIM.
IT'S NOT RIGHT, THUNGAR...
...A WOMAN CARRYING A SWORD LIKE THESE "AMAZONS"? VALHALLA TAKE ME, WHAT IS THE WORLD COMING TO?
I'VE GOT A *SWORD* THEY CAN CARRY ALL RIGHT.
YOU VIKINGS DO NOT HOLD WOMEN IN HIGH REGARD IN THE NORTH.
MY POINT EXACTLY.
OF COURSE WE DO. THEY BEAR US STRONG SONS AND TEND TO THE HOME WHILE WE JOURNEY TO OTHER LANDS.
YOU DISAPPROVE?
IN OUR TRAVELS TO OTHER LANDS, WE HAVE SEEN A DIVISION BETWEEN MEN AND WOMEN. PLACES WHERE WOMEN ARE CODDLED AND OFTTIMES TREATED LIKE CHATTEL.
MEN AND WOMEN HAVE DIFFERENT ROLES OUTSIDE OF YOUR THEMYSCIRA.
STILL, WE NEED TO BE RESPECTED FOR WHO WE ARE, NOT FOR HOW MUCH WE CONFORM TO OUTSIDE EXPECTATIONS.
PERHAPS YOU ARE--
AARGHH!!

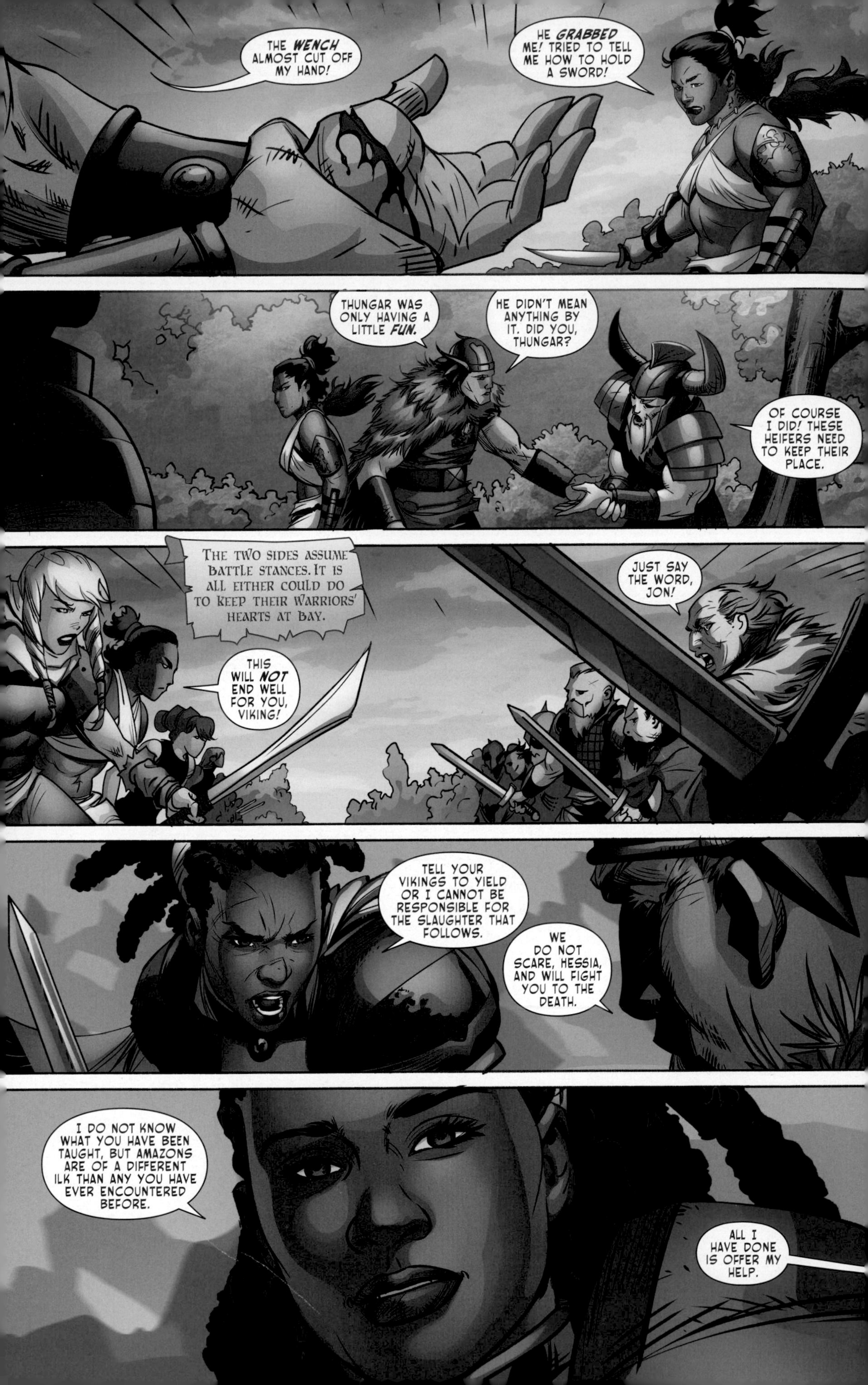
THE WENCH ALMOST CUT OFF MY HAND!
HE GRABBED ME! TRIED TO TELL ME HOW TO HOLD A SWORD!
THUNGAR WAS ONLY HAVING A LITTLE FUN.
HE DIDN'T MEAN ANYTHING BY IT. DID YOU, THUNGAR?
OF COURSE I DID! THESE HEIFERS NEED TO KEEP THEIR PLACE.
THE TWO SIDES ASSUME BATTLE STANCES. IT IS ALL EITHER COULD DO TO KEEP THEIR WARRIORS' HEARTS AT BAY.
THIS WILL NOT END WELL FOR YOU, VIKING!
JUST SAY THE WORD, JON!
TELL YOUR VIKINGS TO YIELD OR I CANNOT BE RESPONSIBLE FOR THE SLAUGHTER THAT FOLLOWS.
WE DO NOT SCARE, HESSIA, AND WILL FIGHT YOU TO THE DEATH.
I DO NOT KNOW WHAT YOU HAVE BEEN TAUGHT, BUT AMAZONS ARE OF A DIFFERENT ILK THAN ANY YOU HAVE EVER ENCOUNTERED BEFORE.
ALL I HAVE DONE IS OFFER MY HELP.

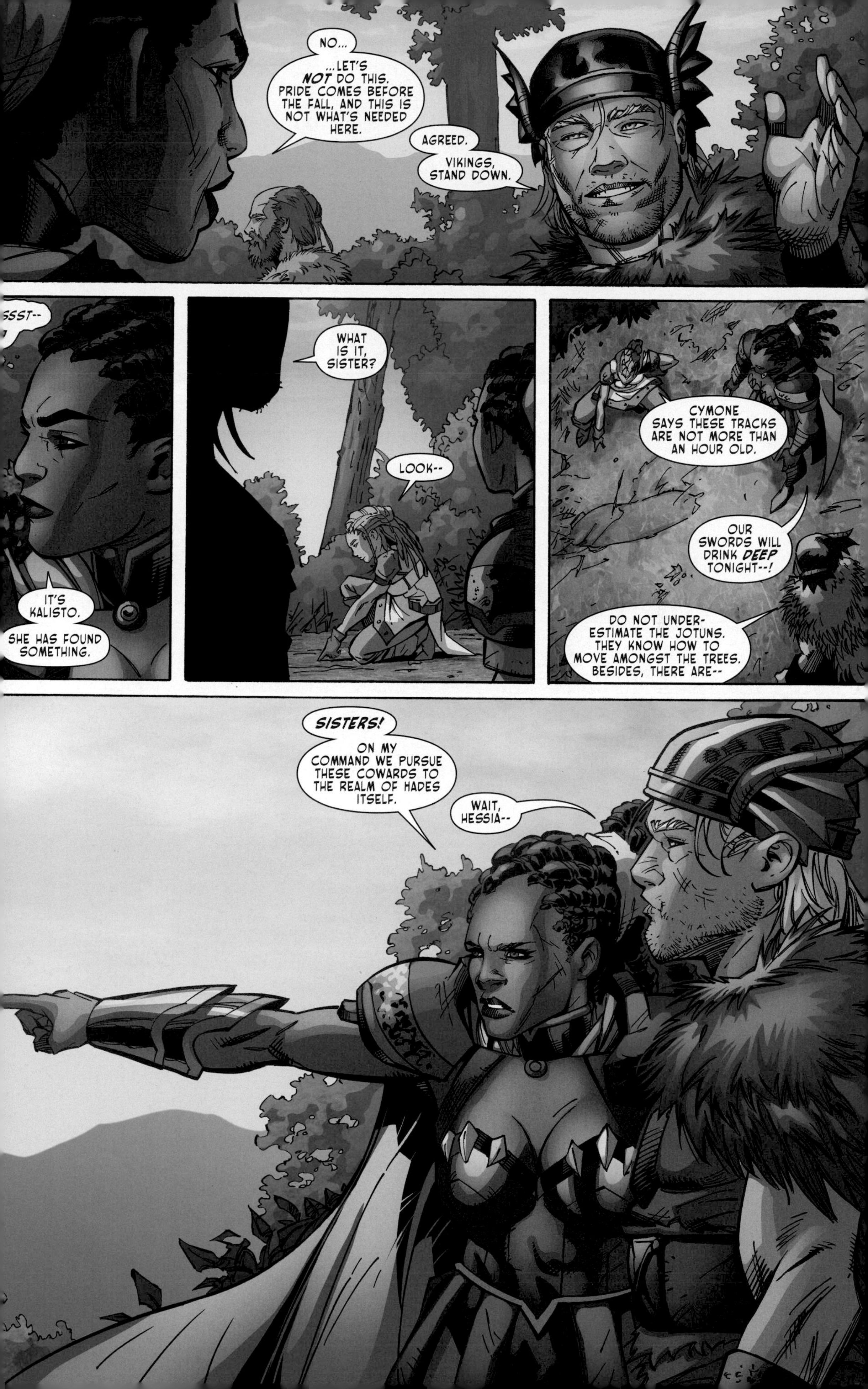
NO...
...LET'S *NOT* DO THIS. PRIDE COMES BEFORE THE FALL, AND THIS IS NOT WHAT'S NEEDED HERE.
AGREED.
VIKINGS, STAND DOWN.
SSST--
IT'S KALISTO.
SHE HAS FOUND SOMETHING.
WHAT IS IT, SISTER?
LOOK--
CYMONE SAYS THESE TRACKS ARE NOT MORE THAN AN HOUR OLD.
OUR SWORDS WILL DRINK *DEEP* TONIGHT--!
DO NOT UNDER-ESTIMATE THE JOTUNS. THEY KNOW HOW TO MOVE AMONGST THE TREES. BESIDES, THERE ARE--
SISTERS!
ON MY COMMAND WE PURSUE THESE COWARDS TO THE REALM OF HADES ITSELF.
WAIT, HESSIA--

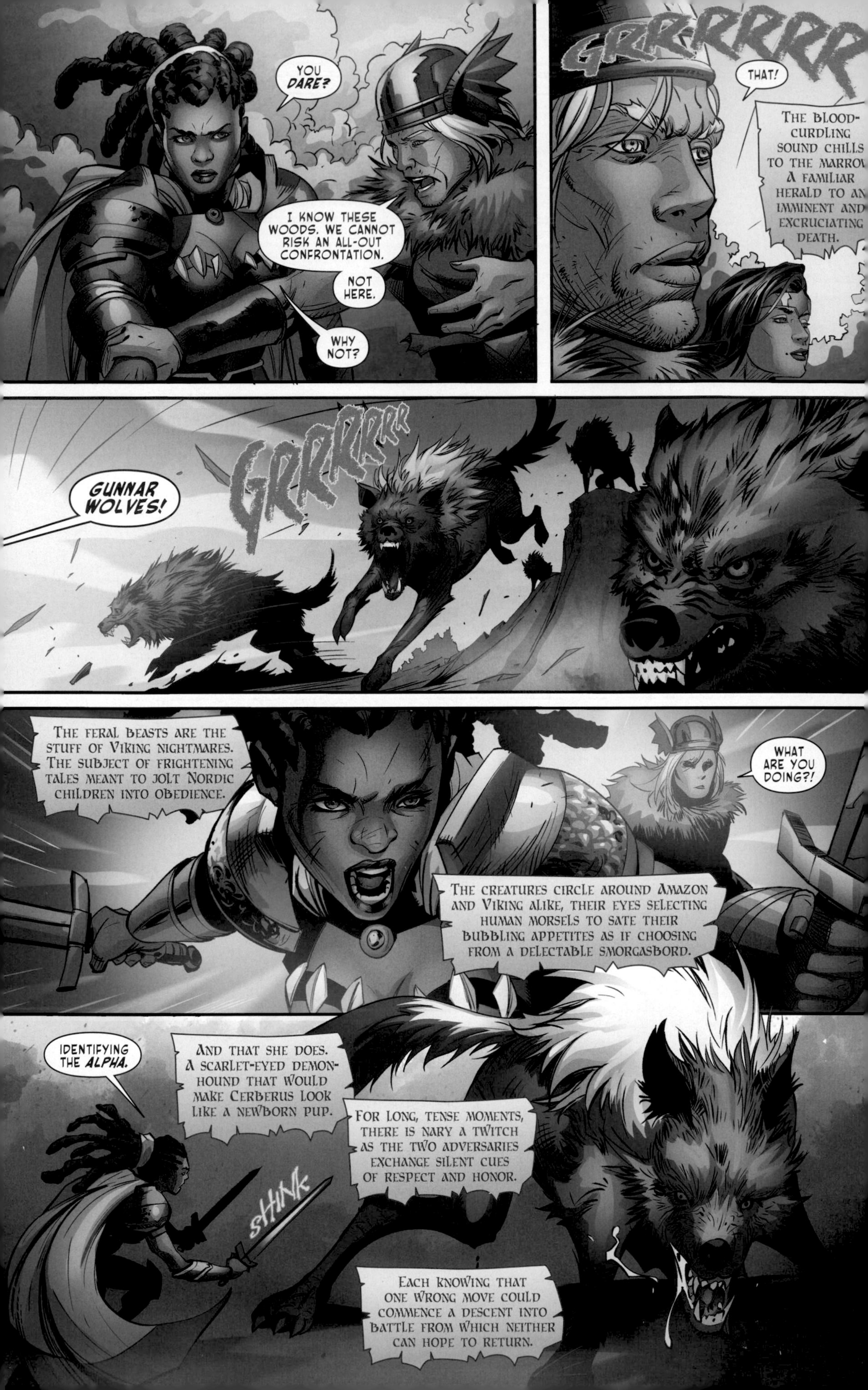
YOU DARE?
I KNOW THESE WOODS. WE CANNOT RISK AN ALL-OUT CONFRONTATION.
NOT HERE.
WHY NOT?
GRRRRRRR
THAT!
THE BLOOD-CURDLING SOUND CHILLS TO THE MARROW. A FAMILIAR HERALD TO AN IMMINENT AND EXCRUCIATING DEATH.
GUNNAR WOLVES!
GRRRRRR
THE FERAL BEASTS ARE THE STUFF OF VIKING NIGHTMARES. THE SUBJECT OF FRIGHTENING TALES MEANT TO JOLT NORDIC CHILDREN INTO OBEDIENCE.
WHAT ARE YOU DOING?!
THE CREATURES CIRCLE AROUND AMAZON AND VIKING ALIKE, THEIR EYES SELECTING HUMAN MORSELS TO SATE THEIR BUBBLING APPETITES AS IF CHOOSING FROM A DELECTABLE SMORGASBORD.
IDENTIFYING THE ALPHA.
AND THAT SHE DOES. A SCARLET-EYED DEMON-HOUND THAT WOULD MAKE CERBERUS LOOK LIKE A NEWBORN PUP.
FOR LONG, TENSE MOMENTS, THERE IS NARY A TWITCH AS THE TWO ADVERSARIES EXCHANGE SILENT CUES OF RESPECT AND HONOR.
SHINK
EACH KNOWING THAT ONE WRONG MOVE COULD COMMENCE A DESCENT INTO BATTLE FROM WHICH NEITHER CAN HOPE TO RETURN.

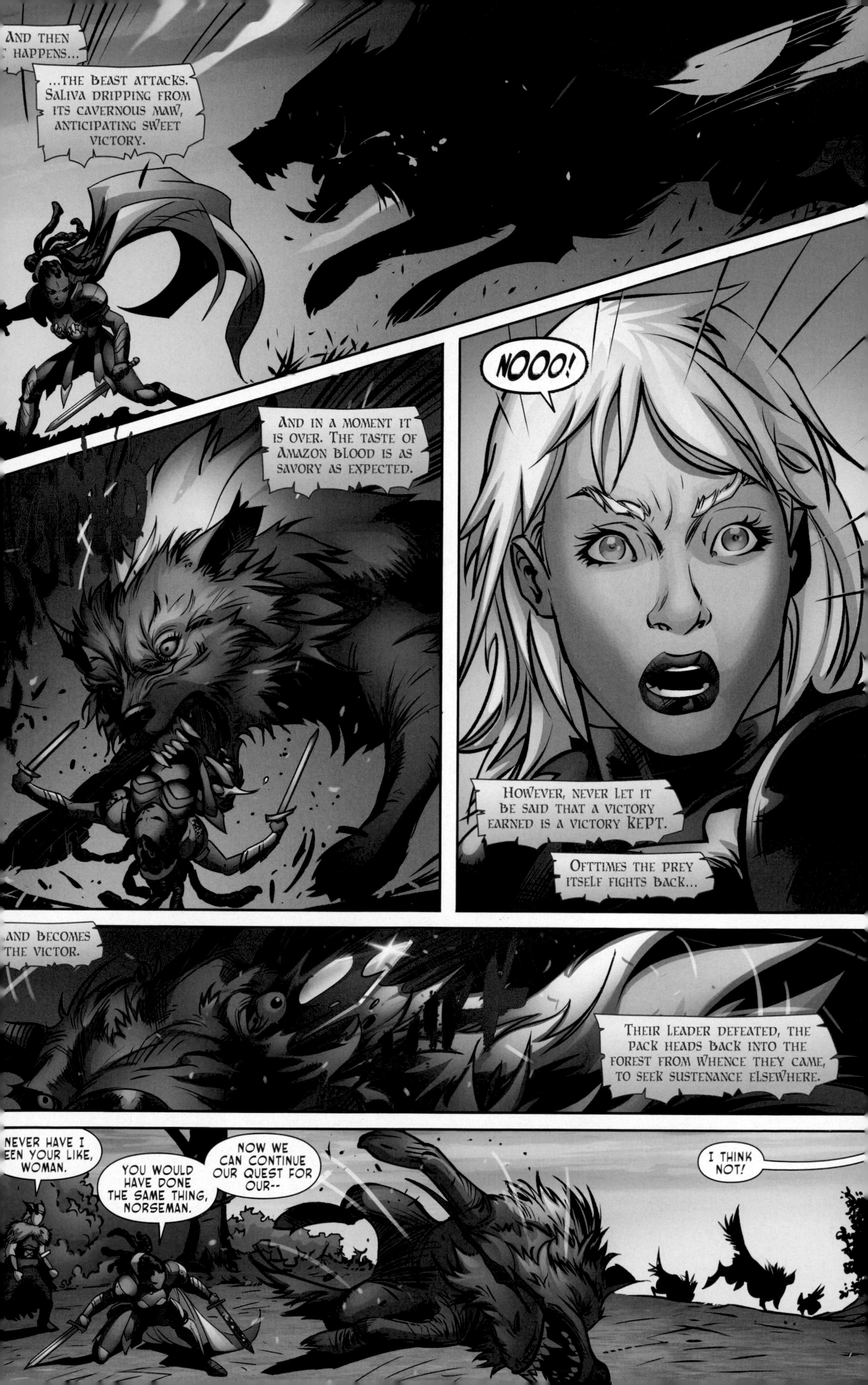

AND THEN
HAPPENS...
...THE BEAST ATTACKS. SALIVA DRIPPING FROM ITS CAVERNOUS MAW, ANTICIPATING SWEET VICTORY.
AND IN A MOMENT IT IS OVER. THE TASTE OF AMAZON BLOOD IS AS SAVORY AS EXPECTED.
NOOO!
HOWEVER, NEVER LET IT BE SAID THAT A VICTORY EARNED IS A VICTORY KEPT.
OFTTIMES THE PREY ITSELF FIGHTS BACK...
AND BECOMES THE VICTOR.
THEIR LEADER DEFEATED, THE PACK HEADS BACK INTO THE FOREST FROM WHENCE THEY CAME, TO SEEK SUSTENANCE ELSEWHERE.
NEVER HAVE I
EEN YOUR LIKE, WOMAN.
YOU WOULD HAVE DONE THE SAME THING, NORSEMAN.
NOW WE CAN CONTINUE OUR QUEST FOR OUR--
I THINK NOT!

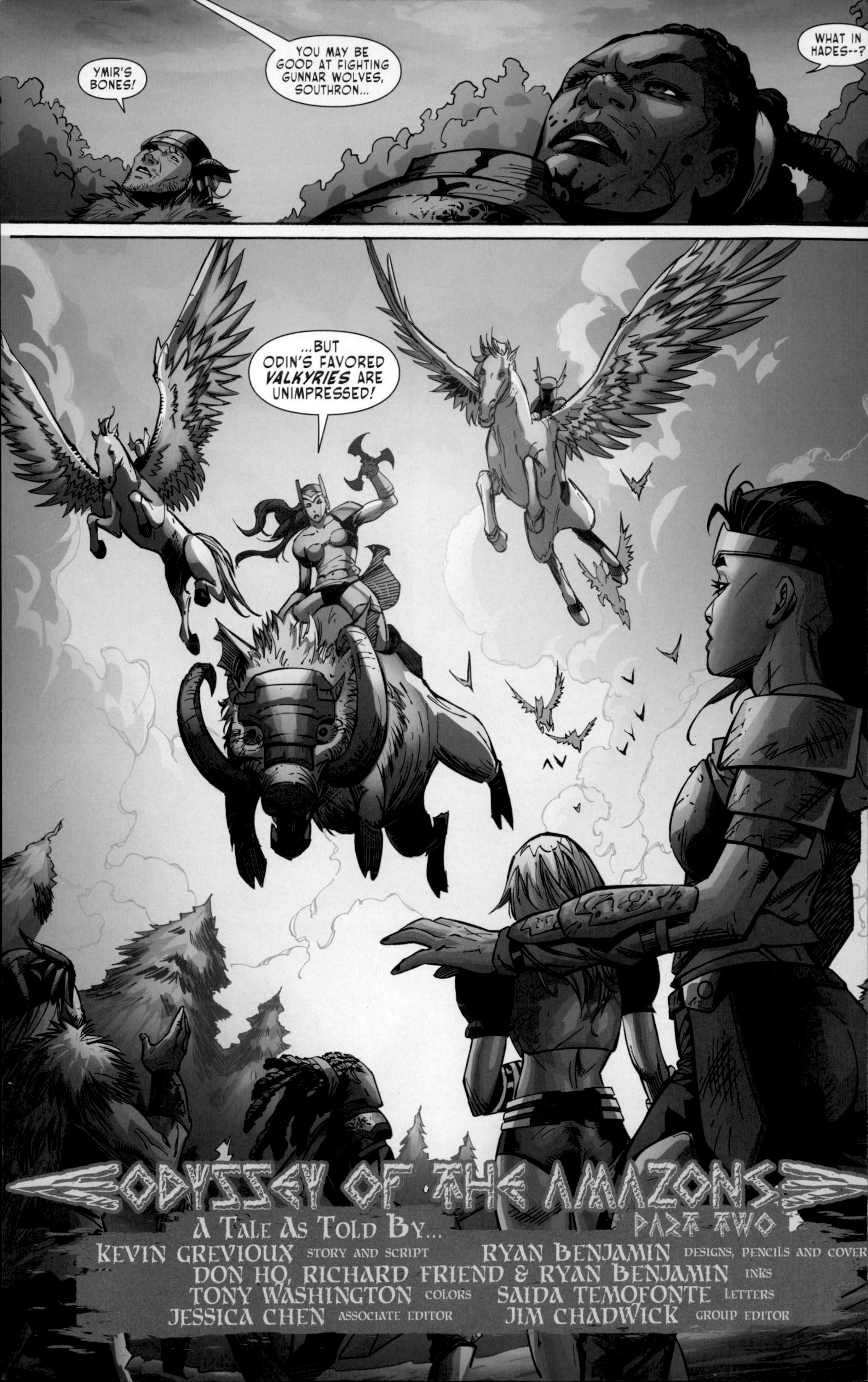
YMIR'S BONES!
YOU MAY BE GOOD AT FIGHTING GUNNAR WOLVES, SOUTHRON...
WHAT IN HADES--?
...BUT ODIN'S FAVORED VALKYRIES ARE UNIMPRESSED!
ODYSSEY OF THE AMAZONS
PART TWO
A TALE AS TOLD BY...
KEVIN GREVIOUX STORY AND SCRIPT
RYAN BENJAMIN DESIGNS, PENCILS AND COVER
DON HO, RICHARD FRIEND & RYAN BENJAMIN INKS
TONY WASHINGTON COLORS
SAIDA TEMOFONTE LETTERS
JESSICA CHEN ASSOCIATE EDITOR
JIM CHADWICK GROUP EDITOR

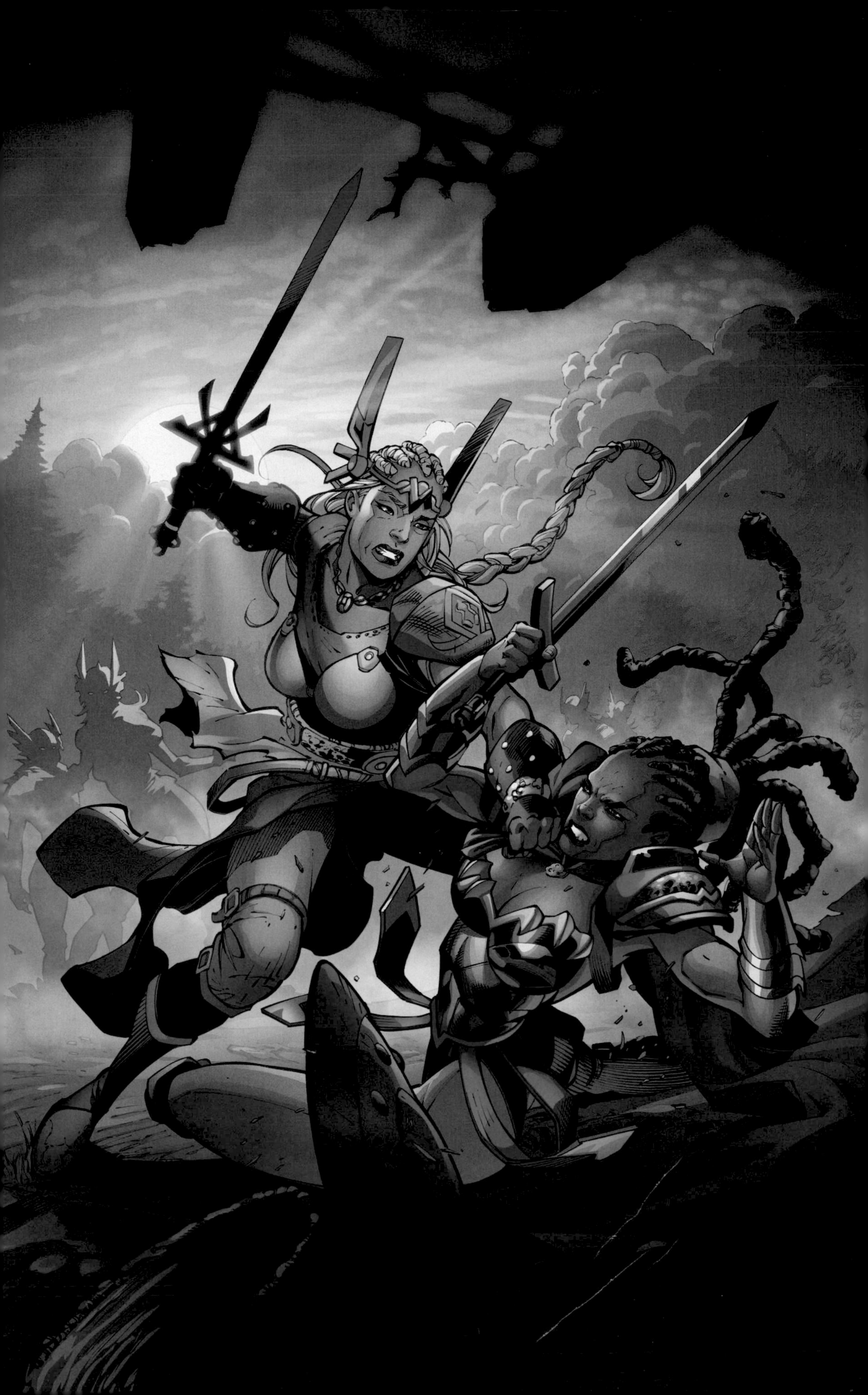

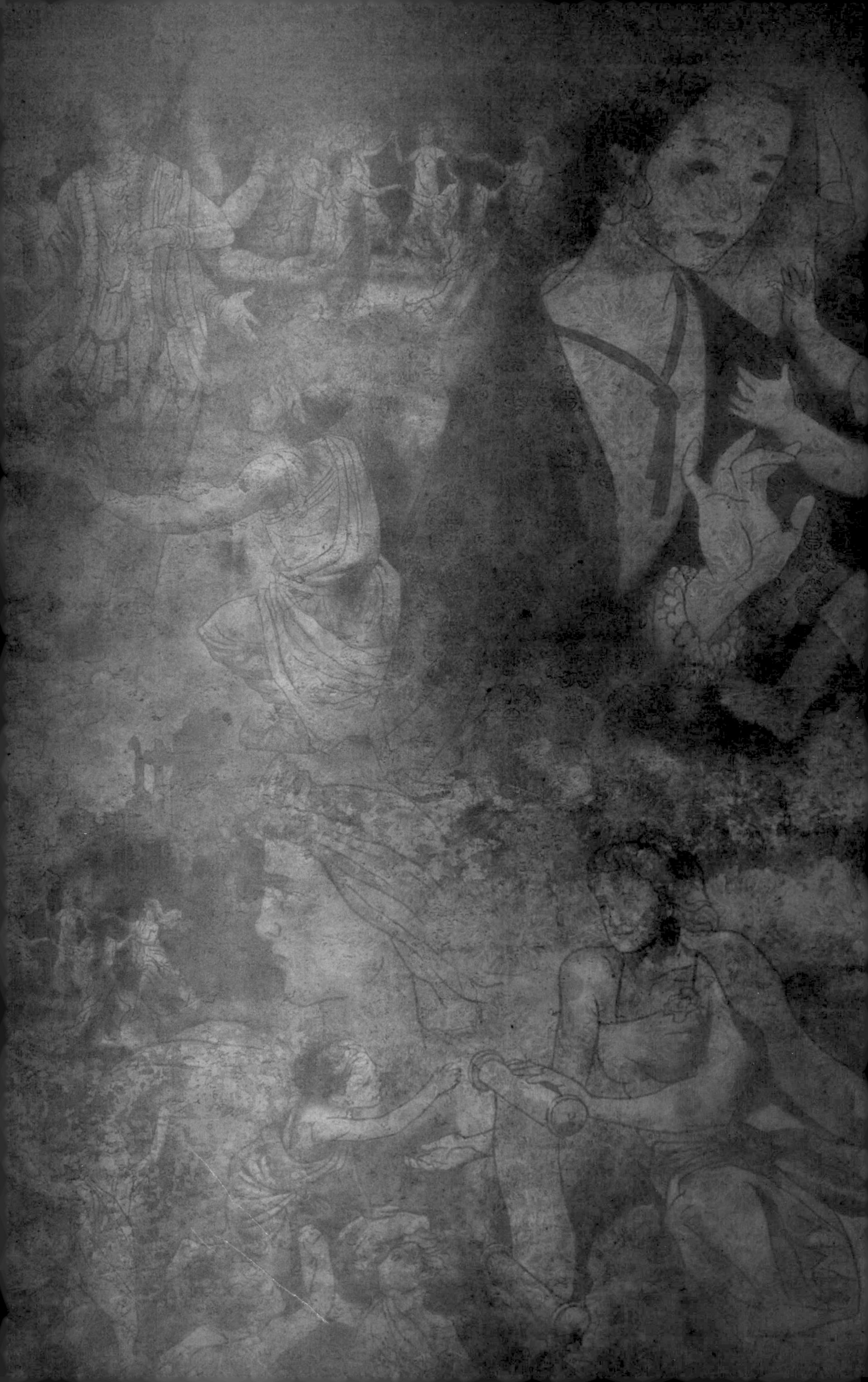

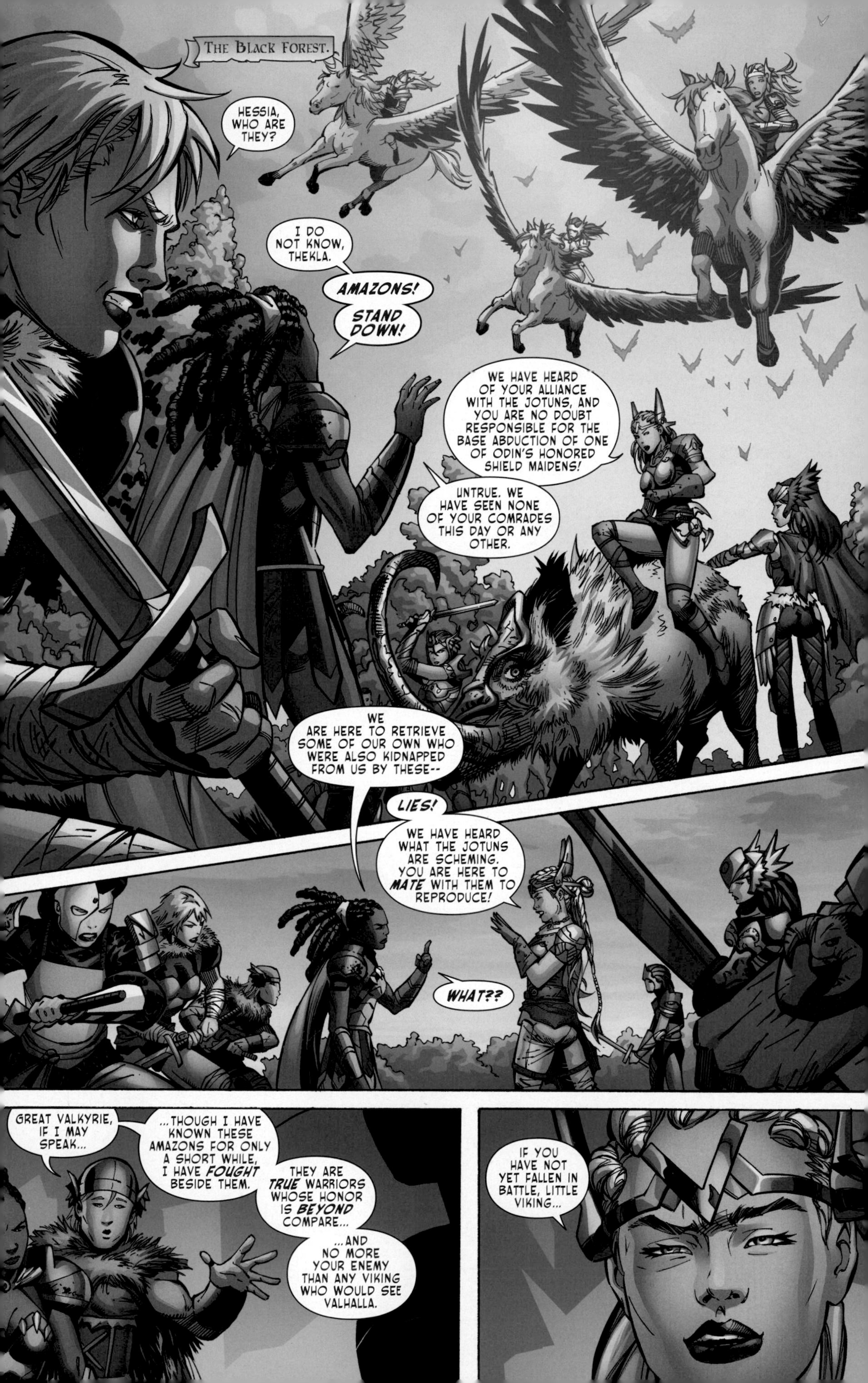
THE BLACK FOREST.
HESSIA, WHO ARE THEY?
I DO NOT KNOW, THEKLA.
AMAZONS! STAND DOWN!
WE HAVE HEARD OF YOUR ALLIANCE WITH THE JOTUNS, AND YOU ARE NO DOUBT RESPONSIBLE FOR THE BASE ABDUCTION OF ONE OF ODIN'S HONORED SHIELD MAIDENS!
UNTRUE. WE HAVE SEEN NONE OF YOUR COMRADES THIS DAY OR ANY OTHER.
WE ARE HERE TO RETRIEVE SOME OF OUR OWN WHO WERE ALSO KIDNAPPED FROM US BY THESE--
LIES!
WE HAVE HEARD WHAT THE JOTUNS ARE SCHEMING. YOU ARE HERE TO MATE WITH THEM TO REPRODUCE!
WHAT??
GREAT VALKYRIE, IF I MAY SPEAK...
...THOUGH I HAVE KNOWN THESE AMAZONS FOR ONLY A SHORT WHILE, I HAVE FOUGHT BESIDE THEM.
THEY ARE TRUE WARRIORS WHOSE HONOR IS BEYOND COMPARE...
...AND NO MORE YOUR ENEMY THAN ANY VIKING WHO WOULD SEE VALHALLA.
IF YOU HAVE NOT YET FALLEN IN BATTLE, LITTLE VIKING...

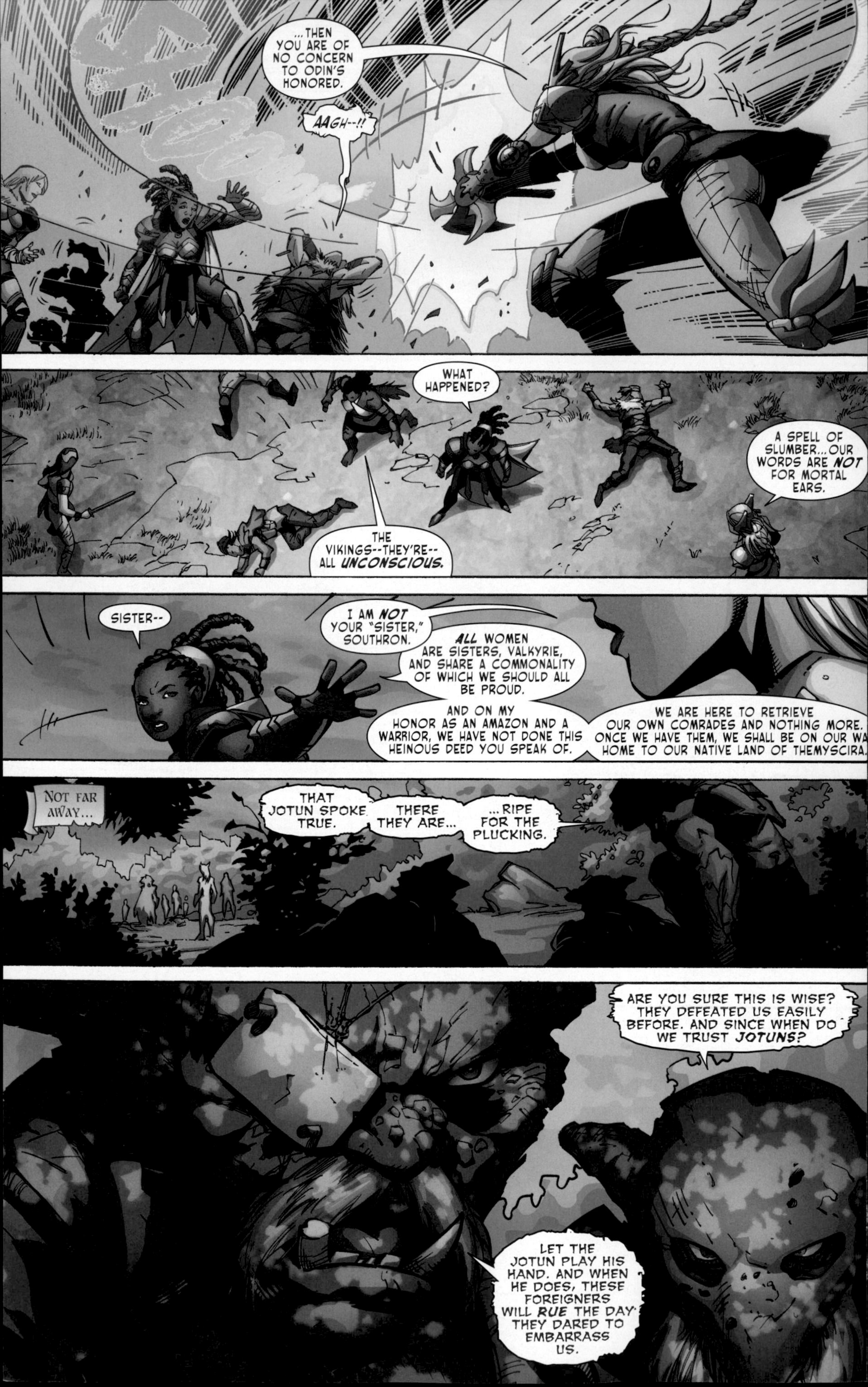

...THEN YOU ARE OF NO CONCERN TO ODIN'S HONORED.
AAGH--!!
WHAT HAPPENED?
A SPELL OF SLUMBER...OUR WORDS ARE NOT FOR MORTAL EARS.
THE VIKINGS--THEY'RE--ALL UNCONSCIOUS.
SISTER--
I AM NOT YOUR "SISTER," SOUTHRON.
ALL WOMEN ARE SISTERS, VALKYRIE, AND SHARE A COMMONALITY OF WHICH WE SHOULD ALL BE PROUD.
AND ON MY HONOR AS AN AMAZON AND A WARRIOR, WE HAVE NOT DONE THIS HEINOUS DEED YOU SPEAK OF.
WE ARE HERE TO RETRIEVE OUR OWN COMRADES AND NOTHING MORE. ONCE WE HAVE THEM, WE SHALL BE ON OUR WA HOME TO OUR NATIVE LAND OF THEMYSCIRA.
NOT FAR AWAY...
THAT JOTUN SPOKE TRUE.
THERE THEY ARE...
...RIPE FOR THE PLUCKING.
ARE YOU SURE THIS IS WISE? THEY DEFEATED US EASILY BEFORE. AND SINCE WHEN DO WE TRUST JOTUNS?
LET THE JOTUN PLAY HIS HAND. AND WHEN HE DOES, THESE FOREIGNERS WILL RUE THE DAY THEY DARED TO EMBARRASS US.

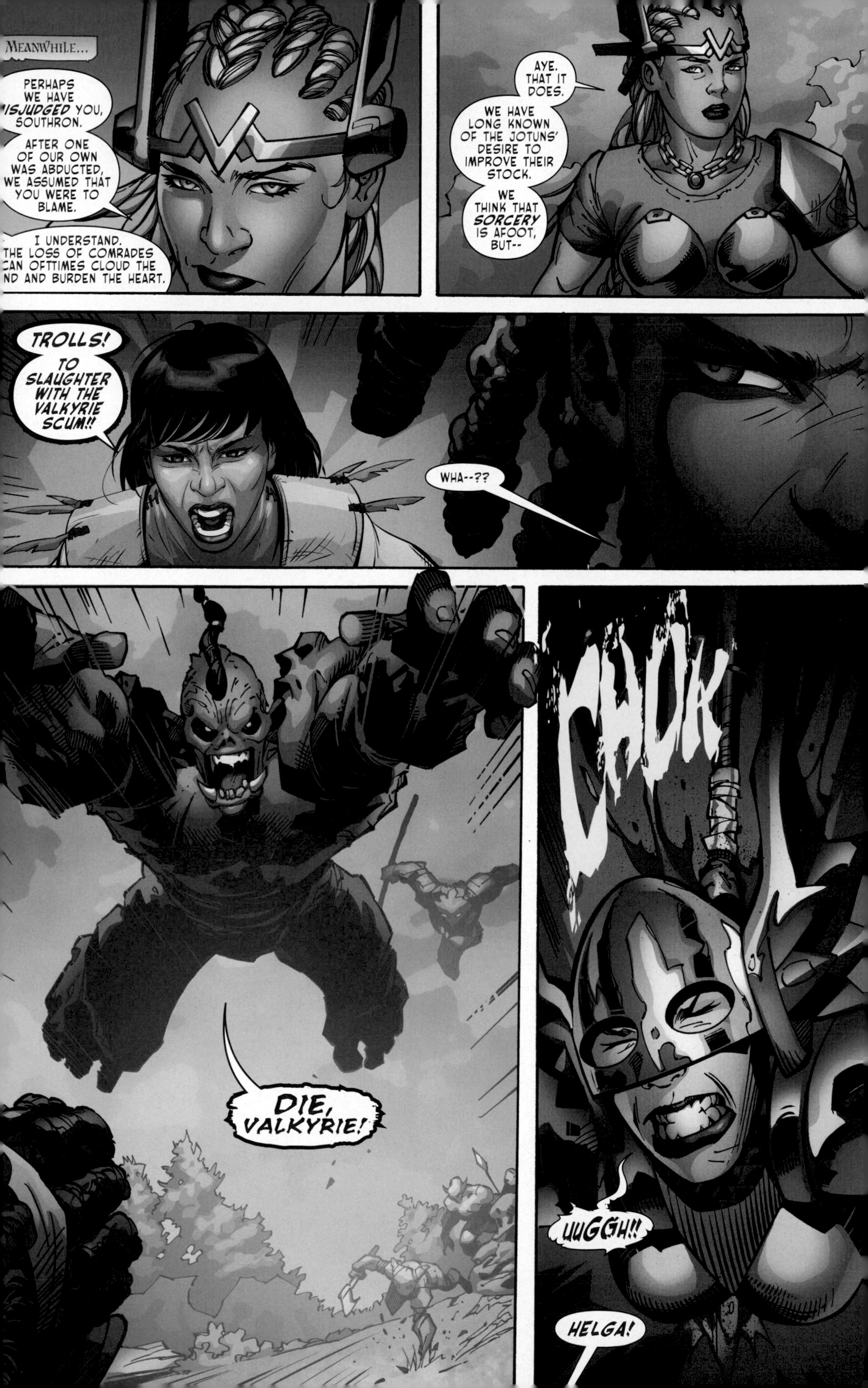
MEANWHILE...
PERHAPS WE HAVE ISJUDGED YOU, SOUTHRON.
AFTER ONE OF OUR OWN WAS ABDUCTED, WE ASSUMED THAT YOU WERE TO BLAME.
I UNDERSTAND. THE LOSS OF COMRADES CAN OFTTIMES CLOUD THE ND AND BURDEN THE HEART.
AYE. THAT IT DOES.
WE HAVE LONG KNOWN OF THE JOTUNS' DESIRE TO IMPROVE THEIR STOCK.
WE THINK THAT SORCERY IS AFOOT, BUT--
TROLLS!
TO SLAUGHTER WITH THE VALKYRIE SCUM!!
WHA--??
DIE, VALKYRIE!
CHUK
UUGGH!!
HELGA!

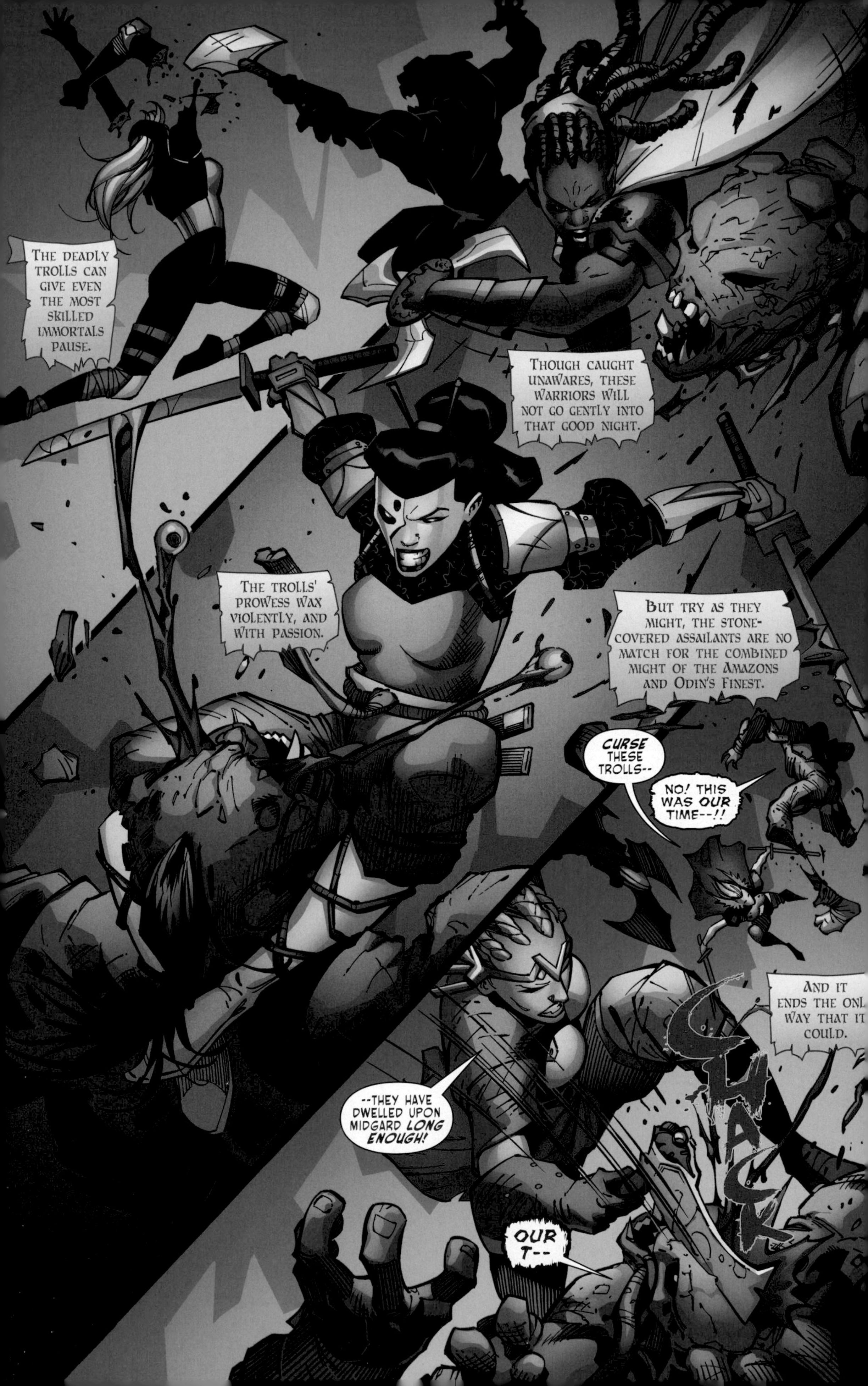
The deadly trolls can give even the most skilled immortals pause.
Though caught unawares, these warriors will not go gently into that good night.
The trolls' prowess wax violently, and with passion.
But try as they might, the stone-covered assailants are no match for the combined might of the Amazons and Odin's Finest.
Curse these trolls--
No! This was our time--!!
--They have dwelled upon Midgard long enough!
And it ends the onl way that it could.
CHACK
Our t--

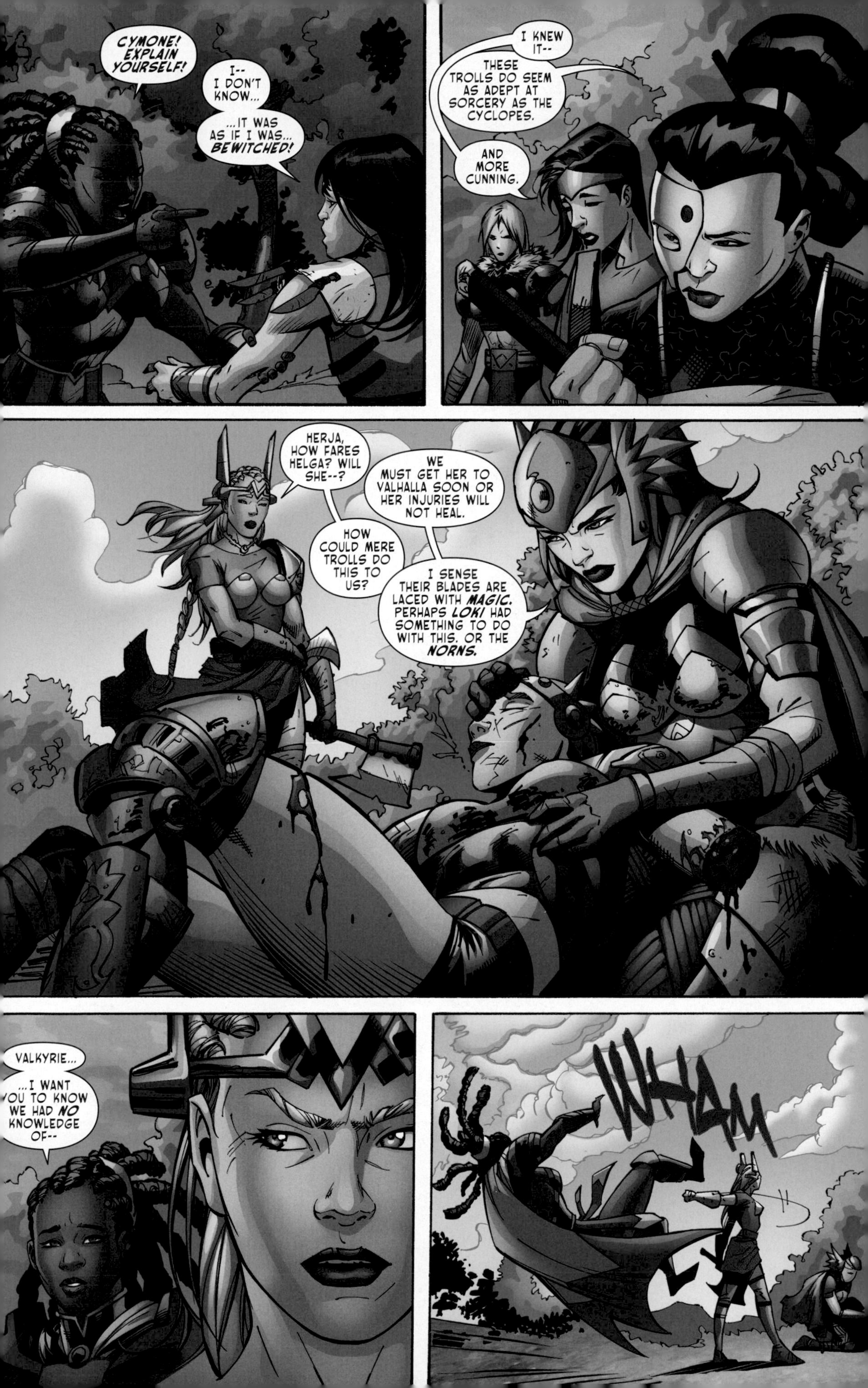

CYMONE! EXPLAIN YOURSELF!
I-- I DON'T KNOW...
...IT WAS AS IF I WAS... BEWITCHED!
I KNEW IT--
THESE TROLLS DO SEEM AS ADEPT AT SORCERY AS THE CYCLOPES.
AND MORE CUNNING.
HERJA, HOW FARES HELGA? WILL SHE--?
WE MUST GET HER TO VALHALLA SOON OR HER INJURIES WILL NOT HEAL.
HOW COULD MERE TROLLS DO THIS TO US?
I SENSE THEIR BLADES ARE LACED WITH MAGIC. PERHAPS LOKI HAD SOMETHING TO DO WITH THIS. OR THE NORNS.
VALKYRIE...
...I WANT YOU TO KNOW WE HAD NO KNOWLEDGE OF--
WHAM

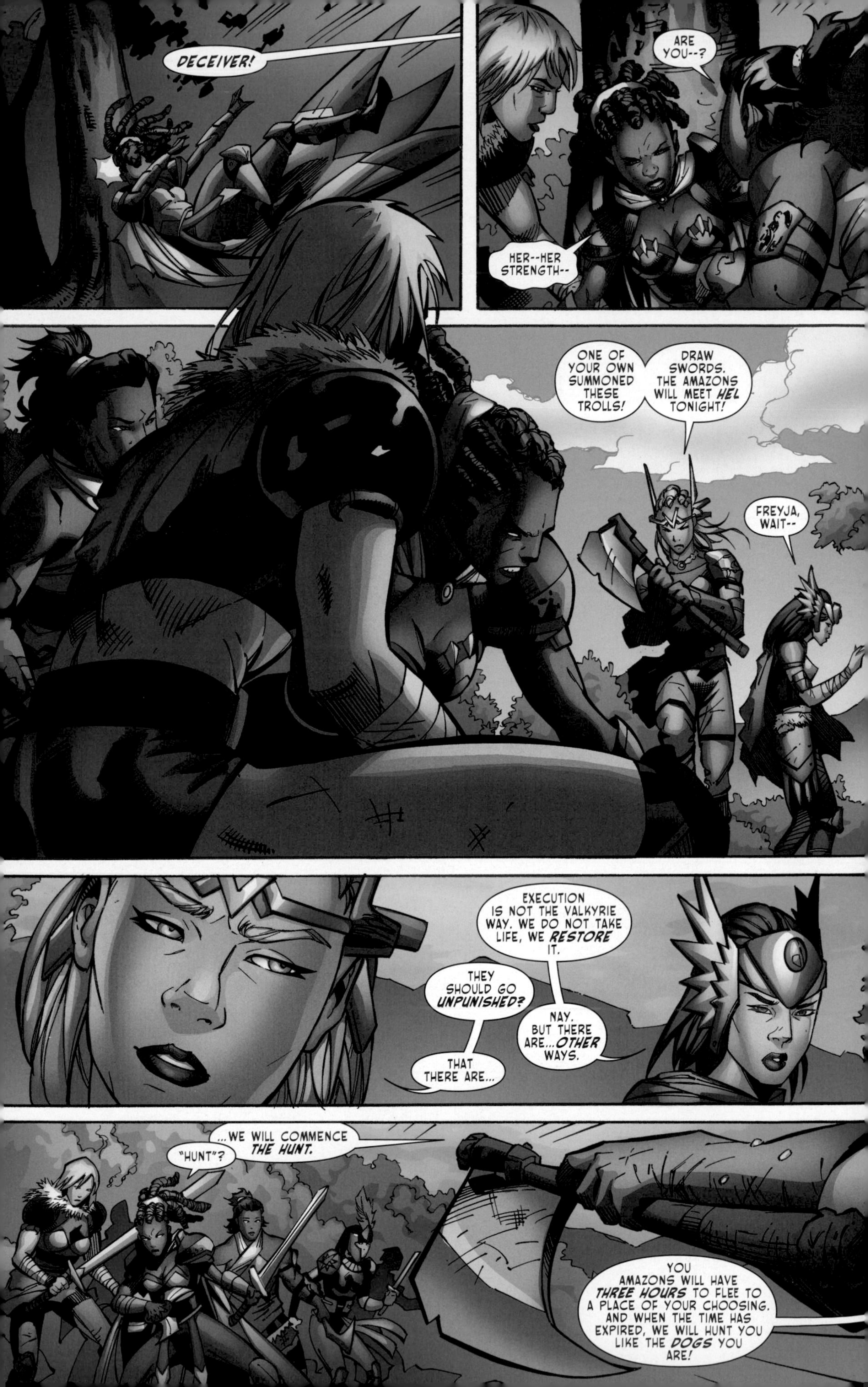
DECEIVER!
ARE YOU--?
HER--HER STRENGTH--
ONE OF YOUR OWN SUMMONED THESE TROLLS!
DRAW SWORDS. THE AMAZONS WILL MEET HEL TONIGHT!
FREYJA, WAIT--
EXECUTION IS NOT THE VALKYRIE WAY. WE DO NOT TAKE LIFE, WE RESTORE IT.
THEY SHOULD GO UNPUNISHED?
NAY. BUT THERE ARE...OTHER WAYS.
THAT THERE ARE...
...WE WILL COMMENCE THE HUNT.
"HUNT"?
YOU AMAZONS WILL HAVE THREE HOURS TO FLEE TO A PLACE OF YOUR CHOOSING. AND WHEN THE TIME HAS EXPIRED, WE WILL HUNT YOU LIKE THE DOGS YOU ARE!

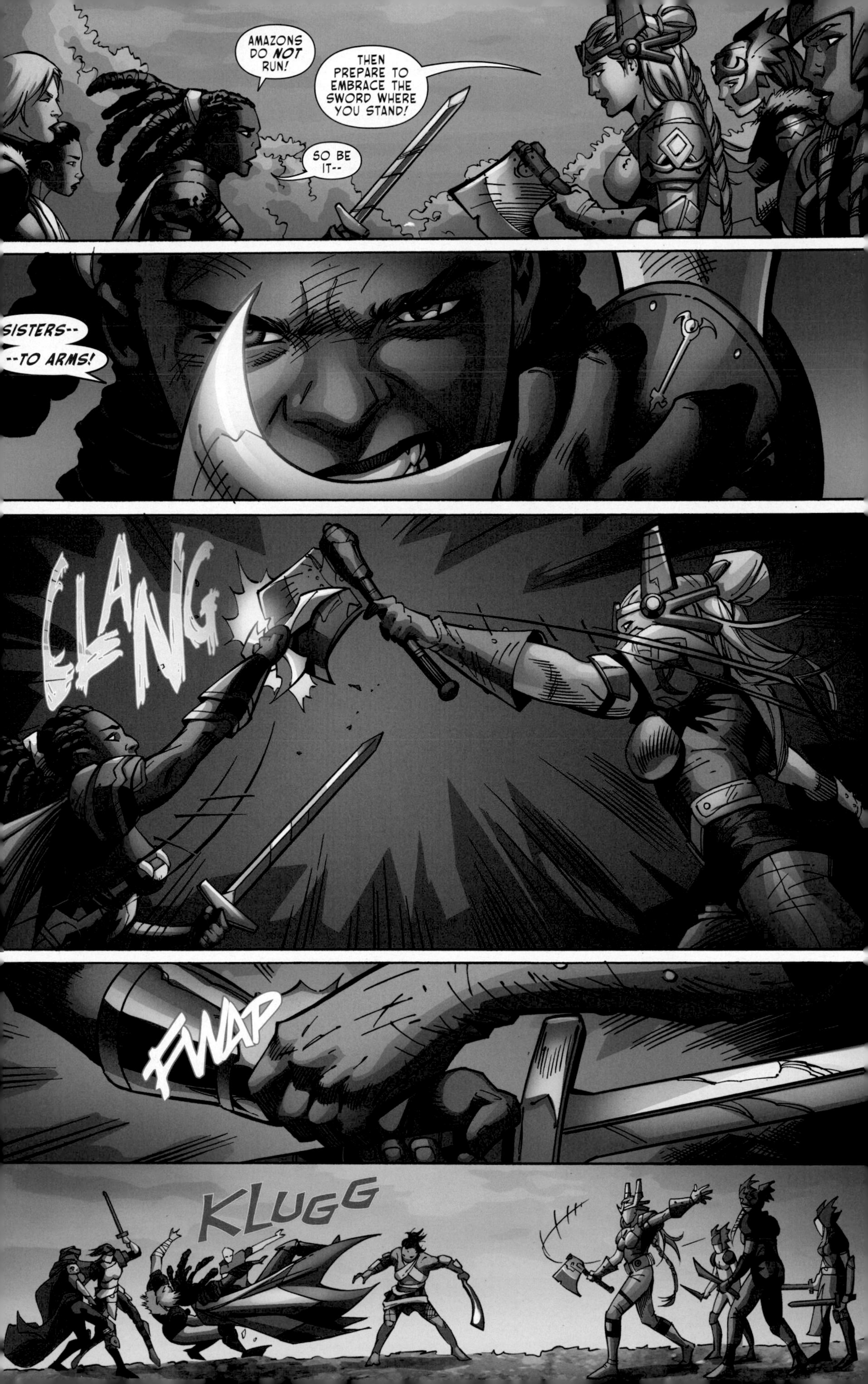
AMAZONS DO NOT RUN!
THEN PREPARE TO EMBRACE THE SWORD WHERE YOU STAND!
SO BE IT--
SISTERS--
--TO ARMS!
CLANG
FWAP
KLUGG

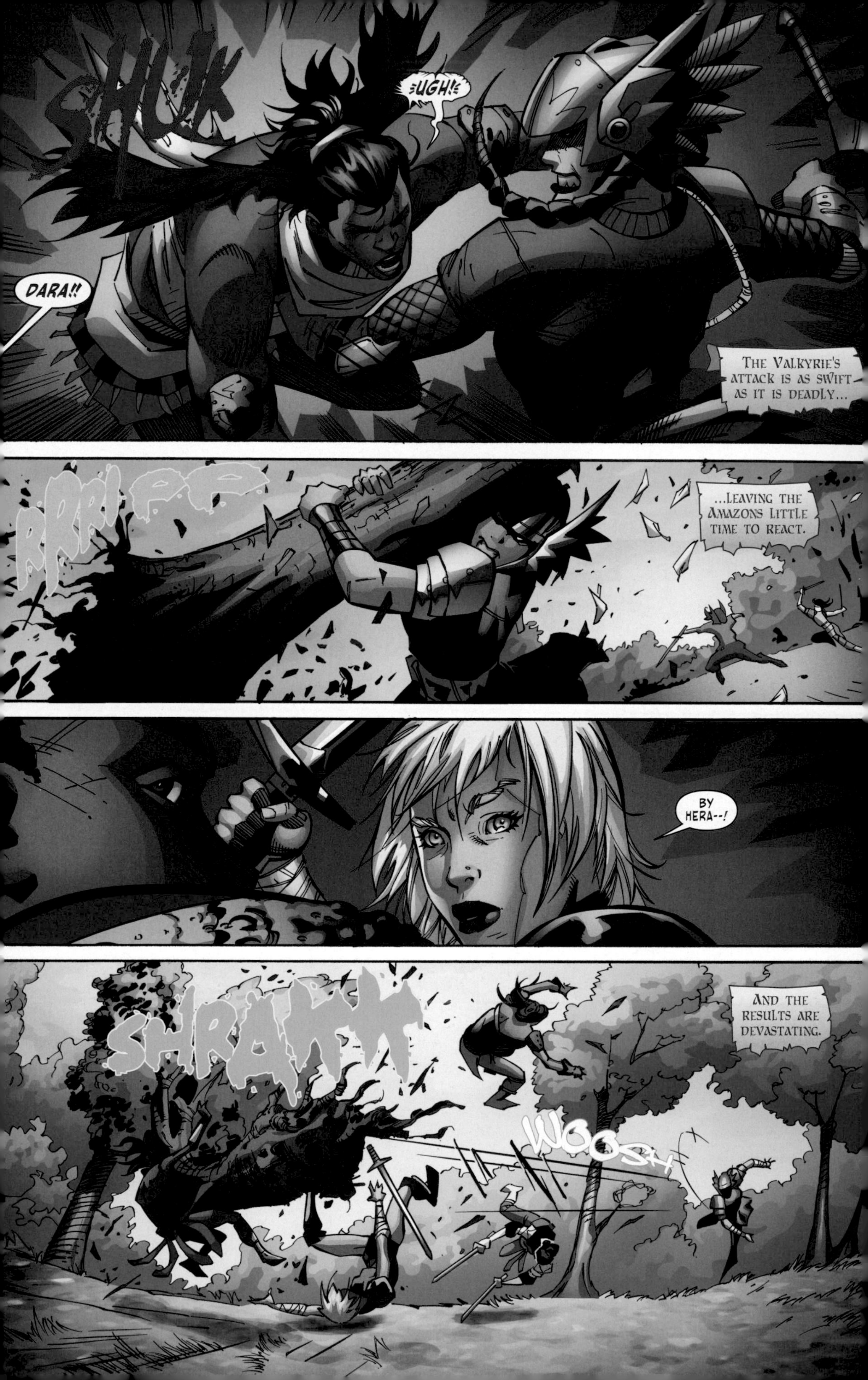
SHUK
UGH!
DARA!!
THE VALKYRIE'S ATTACK IS AS SWIFT AS IT IS DEADLY...
RRRIPP
...LEAVING THE AMAZONS LITTLE TIME TO REACT.
BY HERA--!
SHRAKK
AND THE RESULTS ARE DEVASTATING.
WOOSH

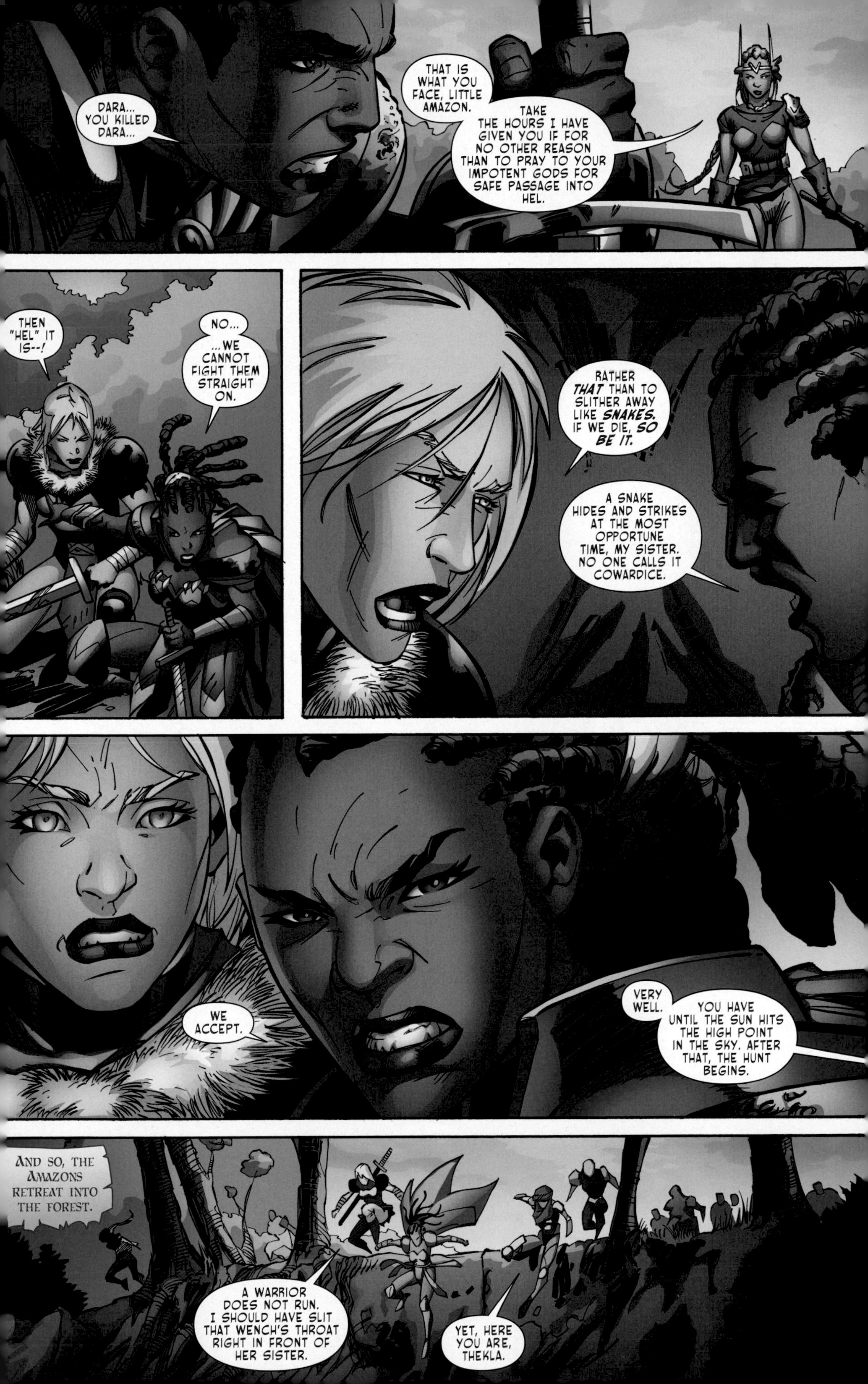
DARA... YOU KILLED DARA...
THAT IS WHAT YOU FACE, LITTLE AMAZON.
TAKE THE HOURS I HAVE GIVEN YOU IF FOR NO OTHER REASON THAN TO PRAY TO YOUR IMPOTENT GODS FOR SAFE PASSAGE INTO HEL.
THEN "HEL" IT IS--!
NO...
...WE CANNOT FIGHT THEM STRAIGHT ON.
RATHER *THAT* THAN TO SLITHER AWAY LIKE *SNAKES.* IF WE DIE, *SO BE IT.*
A SNAKE HIDES AND STRIKES AT THE MOST OPPORTUNE TIME, MY SISTER. NO ONE CALLS IT COWARDICE.
WE ACCEPT.
VERY WELL.
YOU HAVE UNTIL THE SUN HITS THE HIGH POINT IN THE SKY. AFTER THAT, THE HUNT BEGINS.
AND SO, THE AMAZONS RETREAT INTO THE FOREST.
A WARRIOR DOES NOT RUN. I SHOULD HAVE SLIT THAT WENCH'S THROAT RIGHT IN FRONT OF HER SISTER.
YET, HERE YOU ARE, THEKLA.

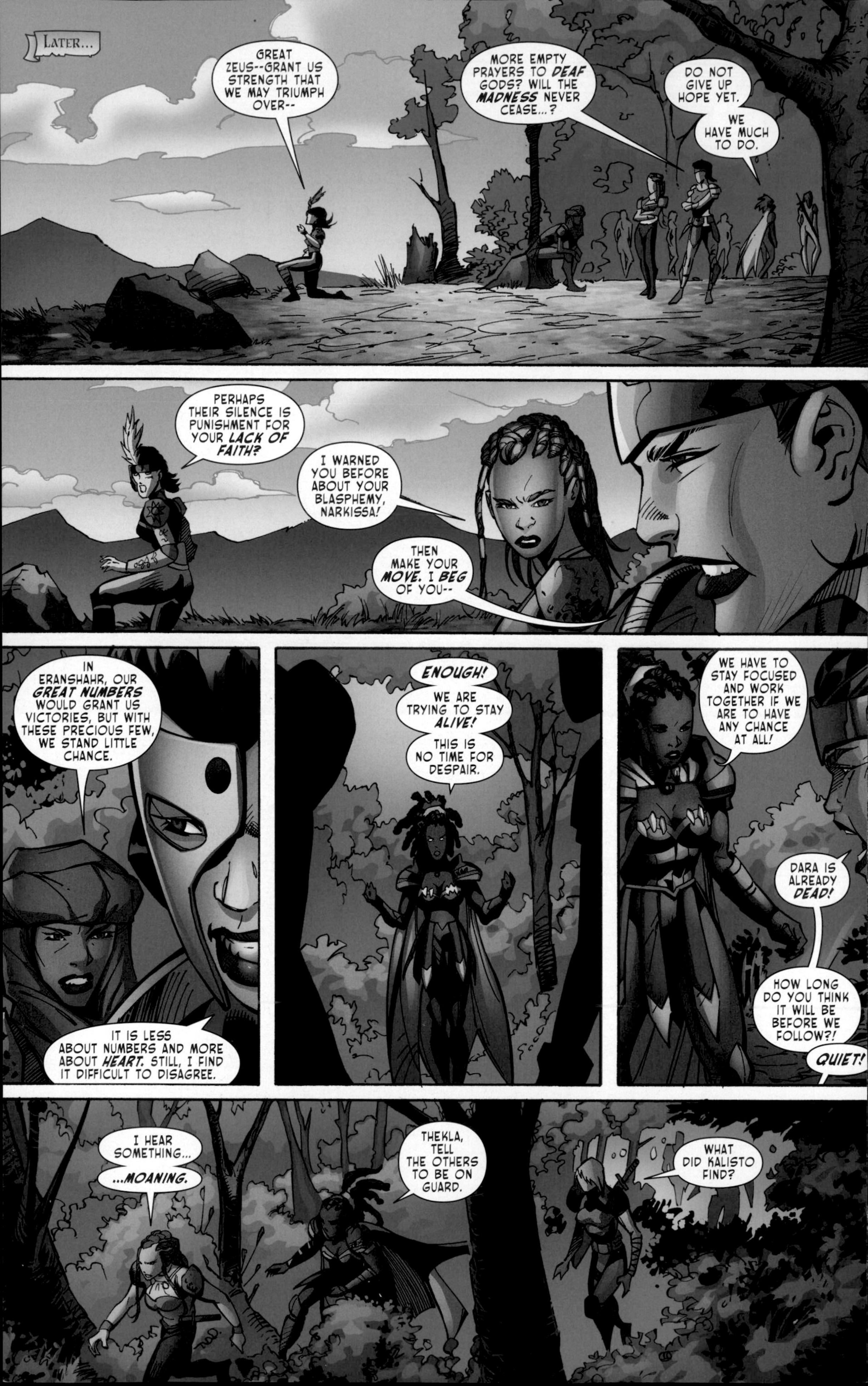
LATER...
GREAT ZEUS--GRANT US STRENGTH THAT WE MAY TRIUMPH OVER--
MORE EMPTY PRAYERS TO DEAF GODS? WILL THE MADNESS NEVER CEASE...?
DO NOT GIVE UP HOPE YET.
WE HAVE MUCH TO DO.
PERHAPS THEIR SILENCE IS PUNISHMENT FOR YOUR LACK OF FAITH?
I WARNED YOU BEFORE ABOUT YOUR BLASPHEMY, NARKISSA!
THEN MAKE YOUR MOVE. I BEG OF YOU--
IN ERANSHAHR, OUR GREAT NUMBERS WOULD GRANT US VICTORIES, BUT WITH THESE PRECIOUS FEW, WE STAND LITTLE CHANCE.
IT IS LESS ABOUT NUMBERS AND MORE ABOUT HEART. STILL, I FIND IT DIFFICULT TO DISAGREE.
ENOUGH!
WE ARE TRYING TO STAY ALIVE!
THIS IS NO TIME FOR DESPAIR.
WE HAVE TO STAY FOCUSED AND WORK TOGETHER IF WE ARE TO HAVE ANY CHANCE AT ALL!
DARA IS ALREADY DEAD!
HOW LONG DO YOU THINK IT WILL BE BEFORE WE FOLLOW?!
QUIET!
I HEAR SOMETHING...
...MOANING.
THEKLA, TELL THE OTHERS TO BE ON GUARD.
WHAT DID KALISTO FIND?

MY SISTERS... HELP...

CYMONE--!

HOW--?

FOOLISH AMAZON...

...THE DEED IS DONE!

THEN WHO--?

THE OTHER CYMONE! SHE WAS A JOTUN!

DIE, BASE DECEIVER!

I WAS SCOUTING--LOOKING FOR CLUES TO THE OTHERS' WHEREABOUTS WHEN I WAS ATTACKED.

THEY WERE AFRAID WE WERE GETTING CLOSER TO FINDING THE OTHERS.

YOU DID WELL, SISTER.

THIS ALL SEEMS SO FUTILE.

I JUST NEVER EXPECTED IT TO END THIS WAY.

PERHAPS IT IS THE GODS' WILL THAT WE DIE THIS DAY.

I DO NOT ACCEPT THAT, XANDRA. AND NEITHER SHOULD ANY OF YOU.

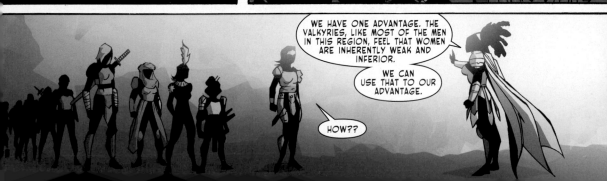

WE HAVE ONE ADVANTAGE. THE VALKYRIES, LIKE MOST OF THE MEN IN THIS REGION, FEEL THAT WOMEN ARE INHERENTLY WEAK AND INFERIOR.

WE CAN USE THAT TO OUR ADVANTAGE.

HOW??

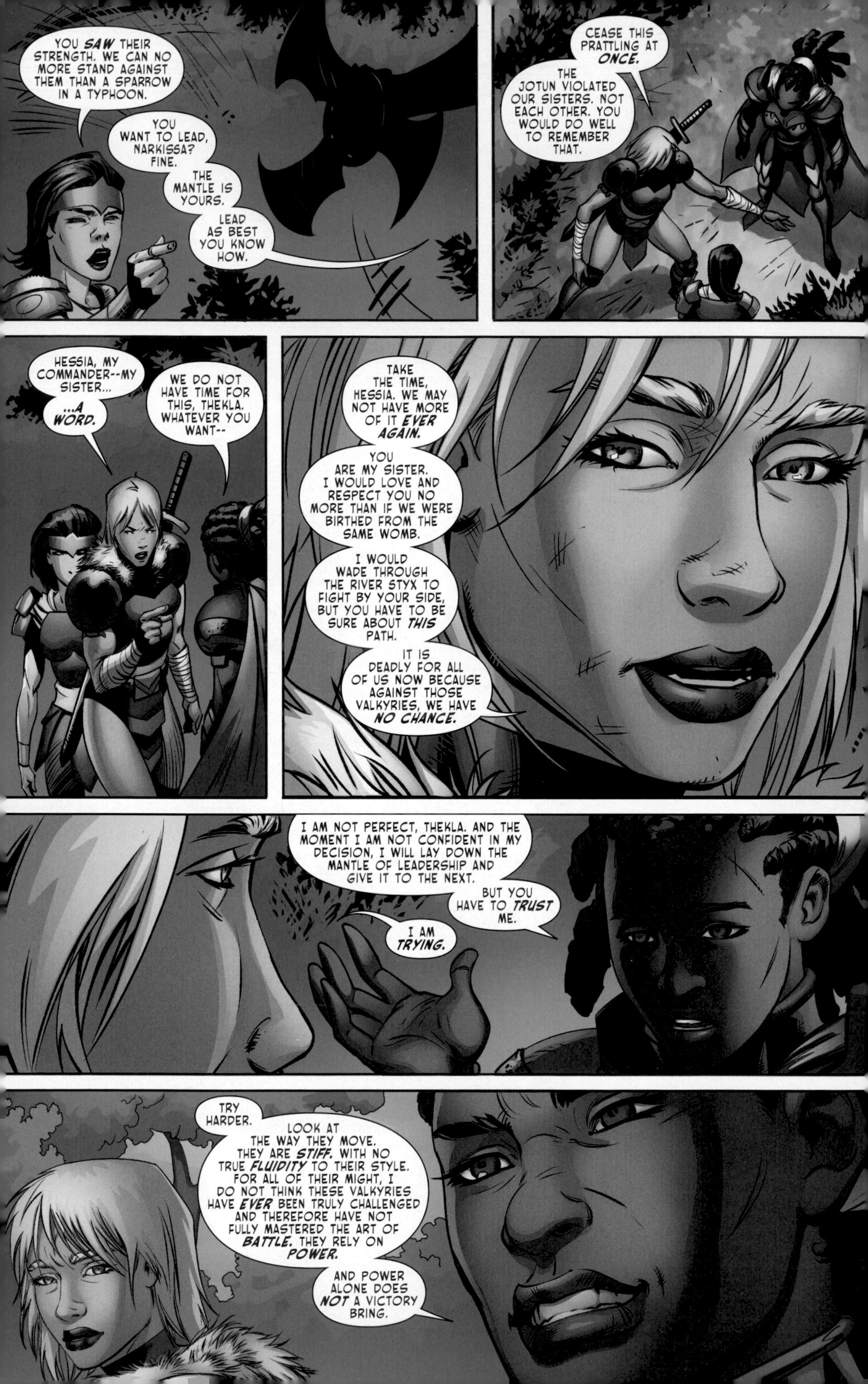
YOU SAW THEIR STRENGTH. WE CAN NO MORE STAND AGAINST THEM THAN A SPARROW IN A TYPHOON.
YOU WANT TO LEAD, NARKISSA? FINE.
THE MANTLE IS YOURS.
LEAD AS BEST YOU KNOW HOW.
CEASE THIS PRATTLING AT ONCE.
THE JOTUN VIOLATED OUR SISTERS. NOT EACH OTHER. YOU WOULD DO WELL TO REMEMBER THAT.
HESSIA, MY COMMANDER--MY SISTER...
...A WORD.
WE DO NOT HAVE TIME FOR THIS, THEKLA. WHATEVER YOU WANT--
TAKE THE TIME, HESSIA. WE MAY NOT HAVE MORE OF IT EVER AGAIN.
YOU ARE MY SISTER. I WOULD LOVE AND RESPECT YOU NO MORE THAN IF WE WERE BIRTHED FROM THE SAME WOMB.
I WOULD WADE THROUGH THE RIVER STYX TO FIGHT BY YOUR SIDE, BUT YOU HAVE TO BE SURE ABOUT THIS PATH.
IT IS DEADLY FOR ALL OF US NOW BECAUSE AGAINST THOSE VALKYRIES, WE HAVE NO CHANCE.
I AM NOT PERFECT, THEKLA. AND THE MOMENT I AM NOT CONFIDENT IN MY DECISION, I WILL LAY DOWN THE MANTLE OF LEADERSHIP AND GIVE IT TO THE NEXT.
BUT YOU HAVE TO TRUST ME.
I AM TRYING.
TRY HARDER.
LOOK AT THE WAY THEY MOVE. THEY ARE STIFF. WITH NO TRUE FLUIDITY TO THEIR STYLE. FOR ALL OF THEIR MIGHT, I DO NOT THINK THESE VALKYRIES HAVE EVER BEEN TRULY CHALLENGED AND THEREFORE HAVE NOT FULLY MASTERED THE ART OF BATTLE. THEY RELY ON POWER.
AND POWER ALONE DOES NOT A VICTORY BRING.

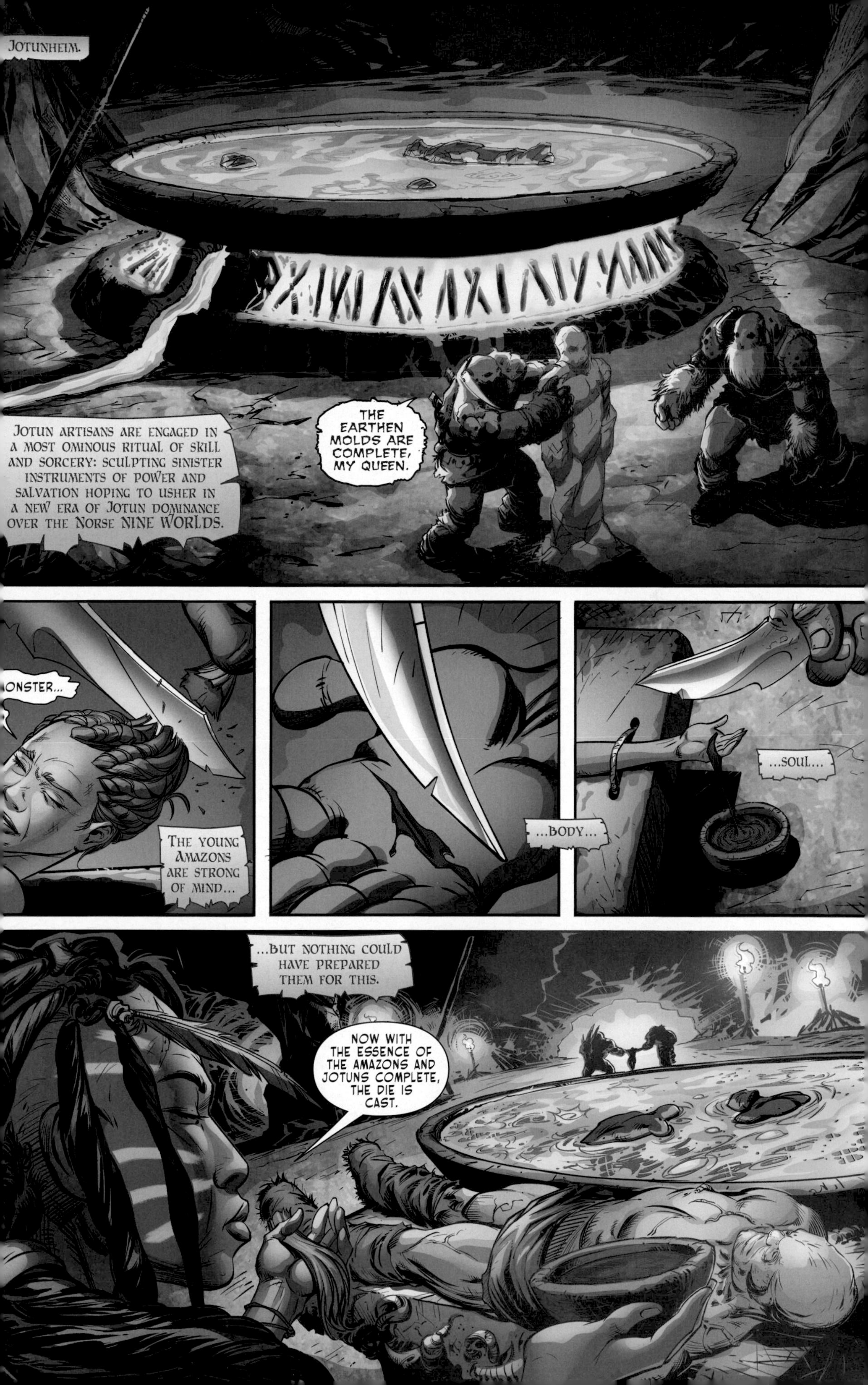
Jotunheim.
Jotun artisans are engaged in a most ominous ritual of skill and sorcery: sculpting sinister instruments of power and salvation hoping to usher in a new era of Jotun dominance over the Norse NINE WORLDS.
THE EARTHEN MOLDS ARE COMPLETE, MY QUEEN.
ONSTER...
The young Amazons are strong of mind...
...BODY...
...SOUL...
...But nothing could have prepared them for this.
NOW WITH THE ESSENCE OF THE AMAZONS AND JOTUNS COMPLETE, THE DIE IS CAST.

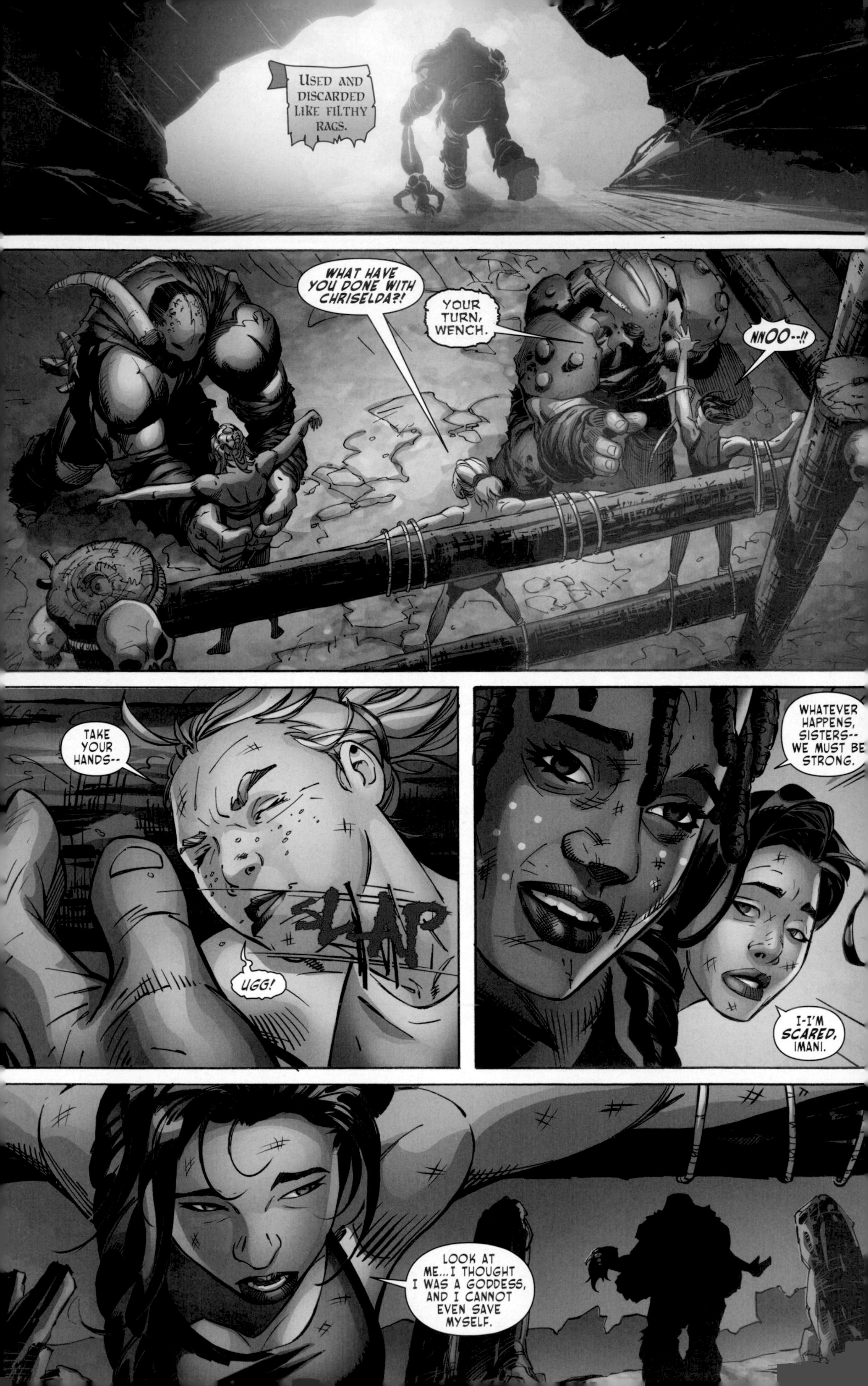
USED AND DISCARDED LIKE FILTHY RAGS.
WHAT HAVE YOU DONE WITH CHRISELDA?!
YOUR TURN, WENCH.
NNOO--!!
TAKE YOUR HANDS--
SLAP
UGG!
WHATEVER HAPPENS, SISTERS-- WE MUST BE STRONG.
I-I'M SCARED, IMANI.
LOOK AT ME...I THOUGHT I WAS A GODDESS, AND I CANNOT EVEN SAVE MYSELF.

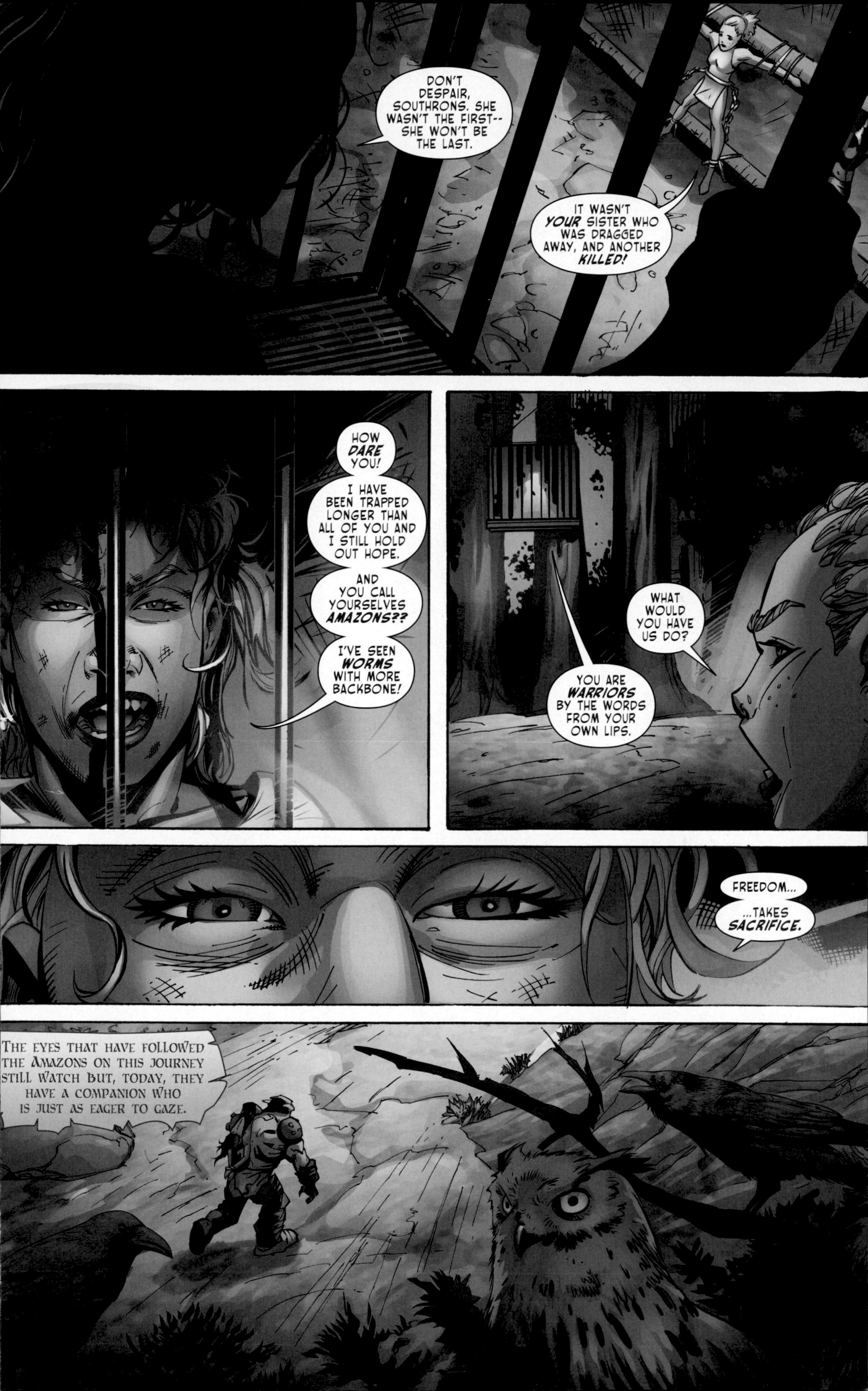
DON'T DESPAIR, SOUTHRONS. SHE WASN'T THE FIRST-- SHE WON'T BE THE LAST.
IT WASN'T YOUR SISTER WHO WAS DRAGGED AWAY, AND ANOTHER KILLED!
HOW DARE YOU!
I HAVE BEEN TRAPPED LONGER THAN ALL OF YOU AND I STILL HOLD OUT HOPE.
AND YOU CALL YOURSELVES AMAZONS??
I'VE SEEN WORMS WITH MORE BACKBONE!
WHAT WOULD YOU HAVE US DO?
YOU ARE WARRIORS BY THE WORDS FROM YOUR OWN LIPS.
FREEDOM...
...TAKES SACRIFICE.
THE EYES THAT HAVE FOLLOWED THE AMAZONS ON THIS JOURNEY STILL WATCH BUT, TODAY, THEY HAVE A COMPANION WHO IS JUST AS EAGER TO GAZE.

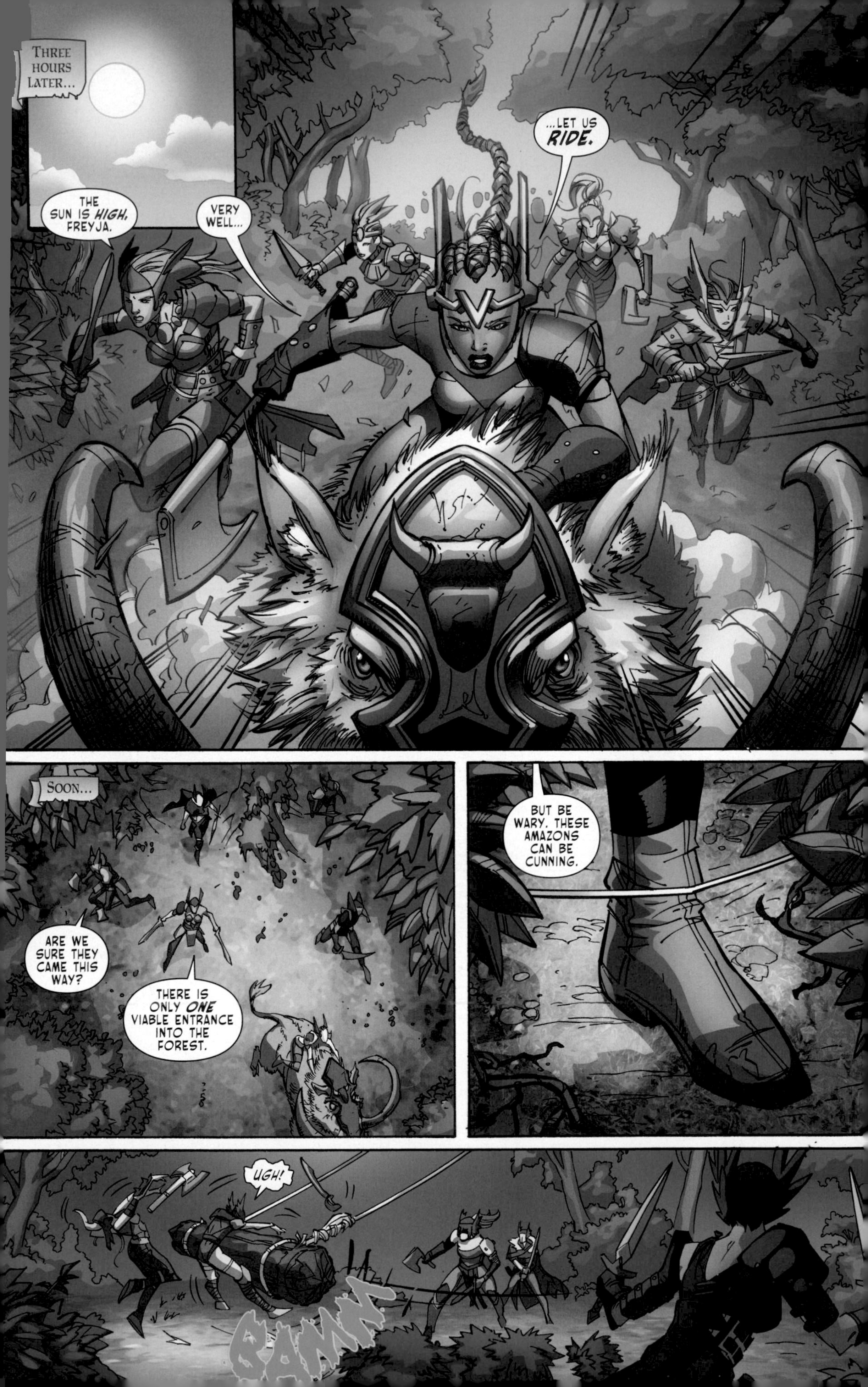
THREE HOURS LATER...
THE SUN IS HIGH, FREYJA.
VERY WELL...
...LET US RIDE.
SOON...
ARE WE SURE THEY CAME THIS WAY?
THERE IS ONLY ONE VIABLE ENTRANCE INTO THE FOREST.
BUT BE WARY. THESE AMAZONS CAN BE CUNNING.
UGH!

ZOUNDS! THIS ENTIRE AREA COULD BE A TRAP.

I SAY WE SPREAD OUT TO COVER MORE GROUND.

THAT IS WHAT THEY WANT. WE NEED TO REMAIN CAUTIOUS.

BUT WE WILL *NOT* BE DIVIDED.

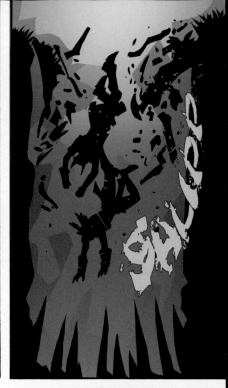

SPLURP

ROTA! THOSE AMAZONS WILL PAY DEARLY FOR THIS.

SNAP

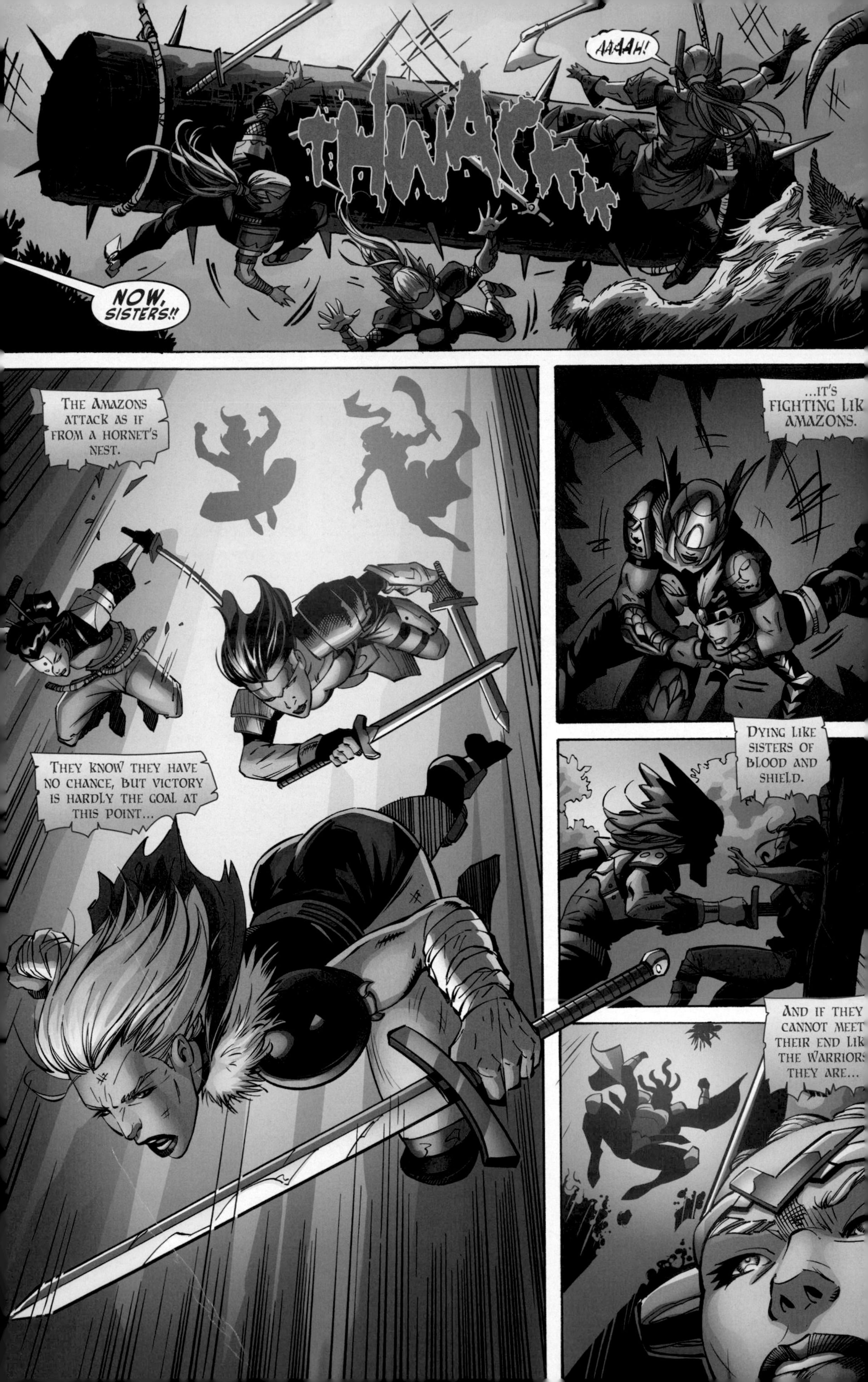
AAAAH!
THWACK
NOW, SISTERS!!
THE AMAZONS ATTACK AS IF FROM A HORNET'S NEST.
THEY KNOW THEY HAVE NO CHANCE, BUT VICTORY IS HARDLY THE GOAL AT THIS POINT...
...IT'S FIGHTING LIK AMAZONS.
DYING LIKE SISTERS OF BLOOD AND SHIELD.
AND IF THEY CANNOT MEET THEIR END LIK THE WARRIORS THEY ARE...

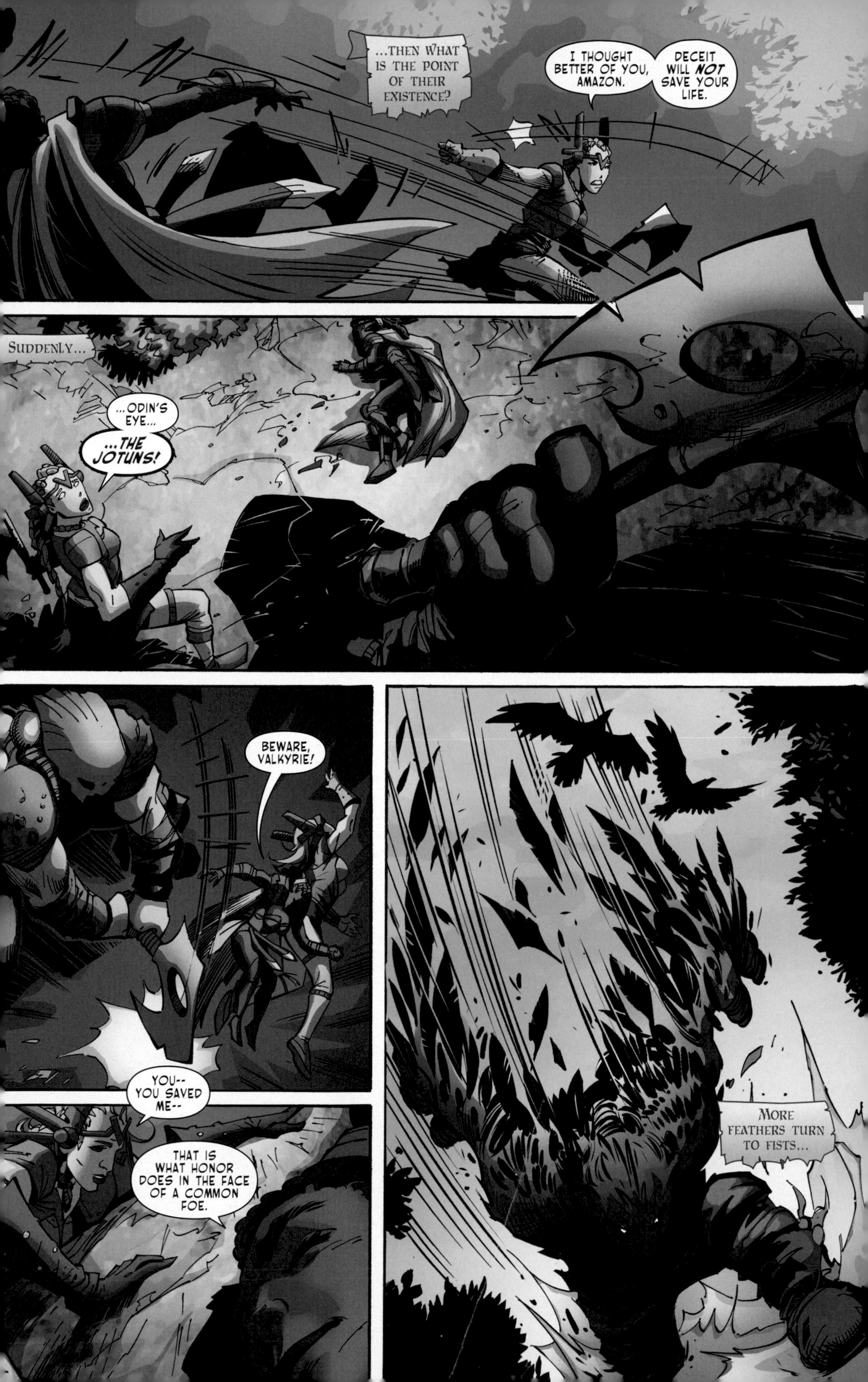
...THEN WHAT IS THE POINT OF THEIR EXISTENCE?
I THOUGHT BETTER OF YOU, AMAZON.
DECEIT WILL *NOT* SAVE YOUR LIFE.
SUDDENLY...
...ODIN'S EYE...
...THE JOTUNS!
BEWARE, VALKYRIE!
YOU-- YOU SAVED ME--
THAT IS WHAT HONOR DOES IN THE FACE OF A COMMON FOE.
MORE FEATHERS TURN TO FISTS...

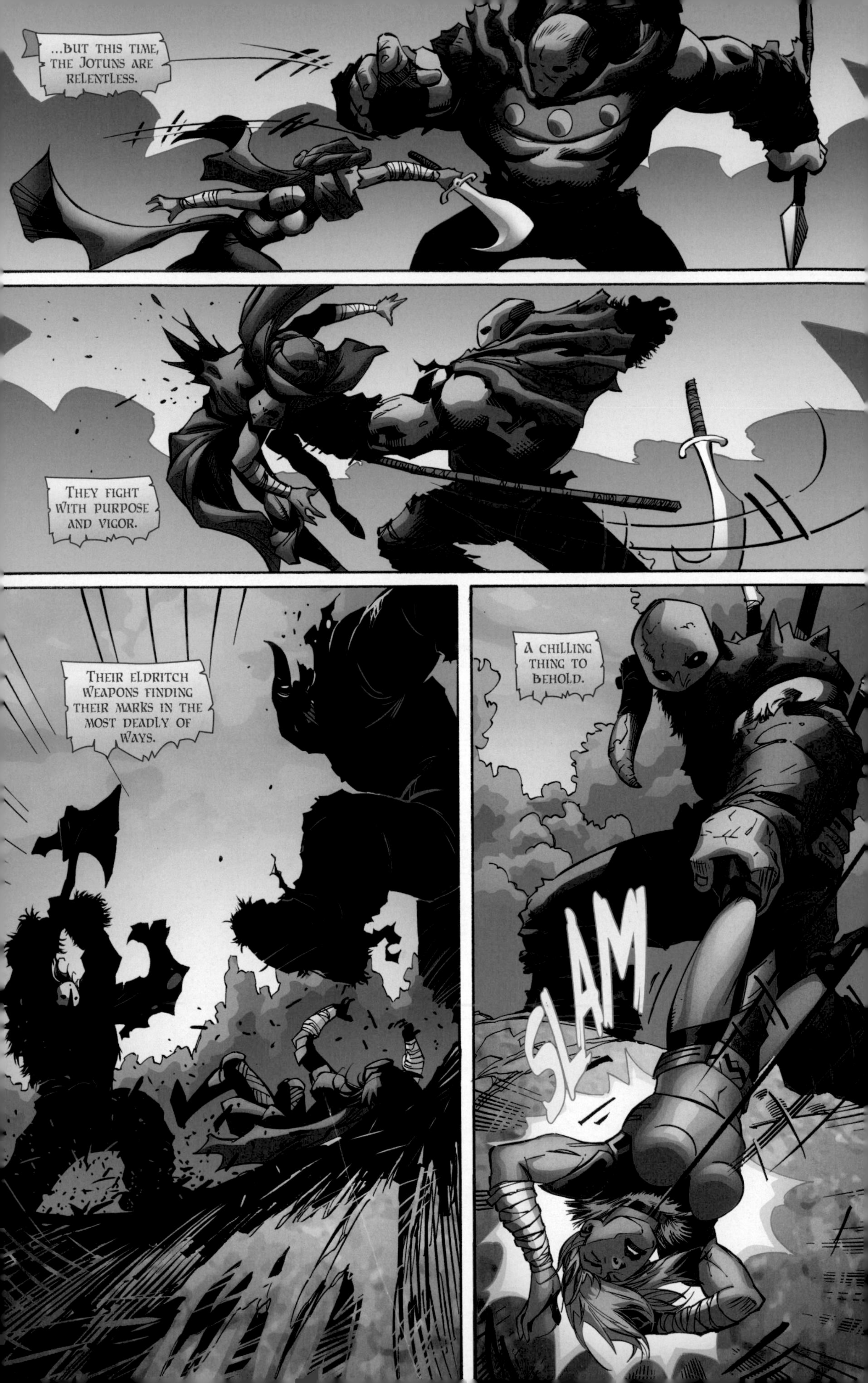
...But this time, the Jotuns are relentless.
They fight with purpose and vigor.
Their eldritch weapons finding their marks in the most deadly of ways.
A chilling thing to behold.
SLAM

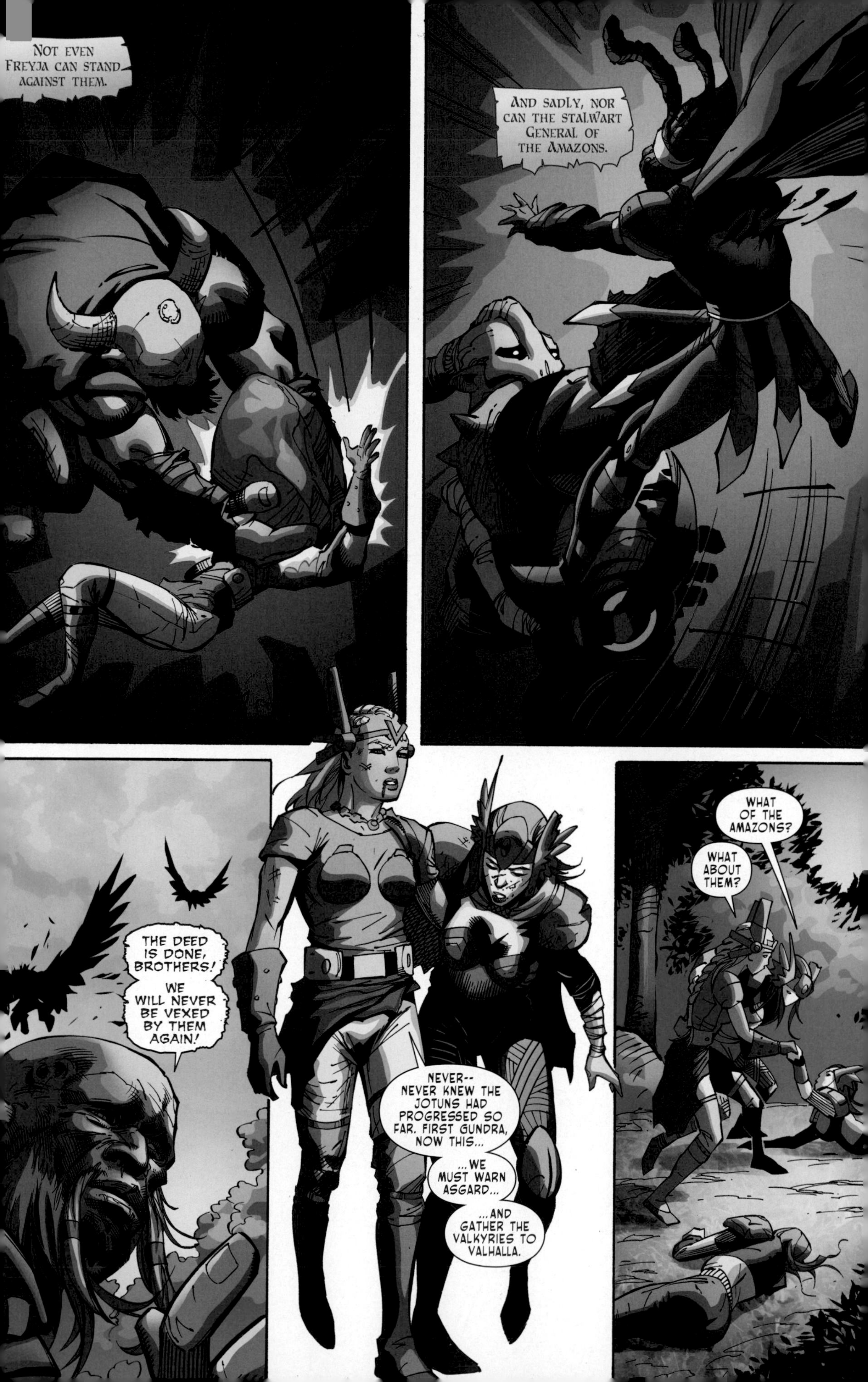
NOT EVEN FREYJA CAN STAND AGAINST THEM.
AND SADLY, NOR CAN THE STALWART GENERAL OF THE AMAZONS.
THE DEED IS DONE, BROTHERS!
WE WILL NEVER BE VEXED BY THEM AGAIN!
NEVER-- NEVER KNEW THE JOTUNS HAD PROGRESSED SO FAR. FIRST GUNDRA, NOW THIS...
...WE MUST WARN ASGARD...
...AND GATHER THE VALKYRIES TO VALHALLA.
WHAT OF THE AMAZONS?
WHAT ABOUT THEM?

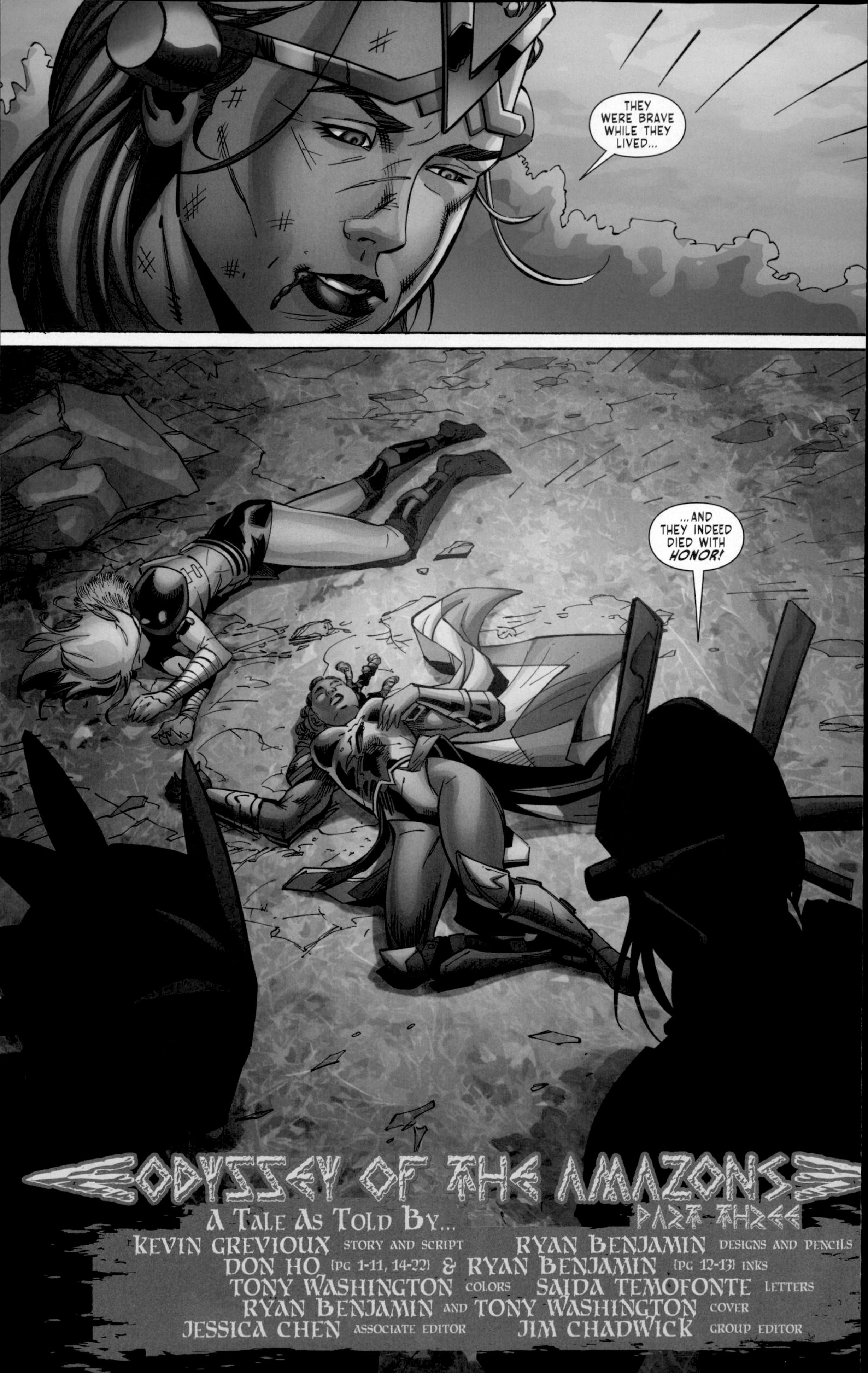
THEY WERE BRAVE WHILE THEY LIVED...
...AND THEY INDEED DIED WITH *HONOR!*
ODYSSEY OF THE AMAZONS
A TALE AS TOLD BY...
PART THREE
KEVIN GREVIOUX STORY AND SCRIPT
RYAN BENJAMIN DESIGNS AND PENCILS
DON HO [PG 1-11, 14-22] & RYAN BENJAMIN [PG 12-13] INKS
TONY WASHINGTON COLORS
SAIDA TEMOFONTE LETTERS
RYAN BENJAMIN AND TONY WASHINGTON COVER
JESSICA CHEN ASSOCIATE EDITOR
JIM CHADWICK GROUP EDITOR

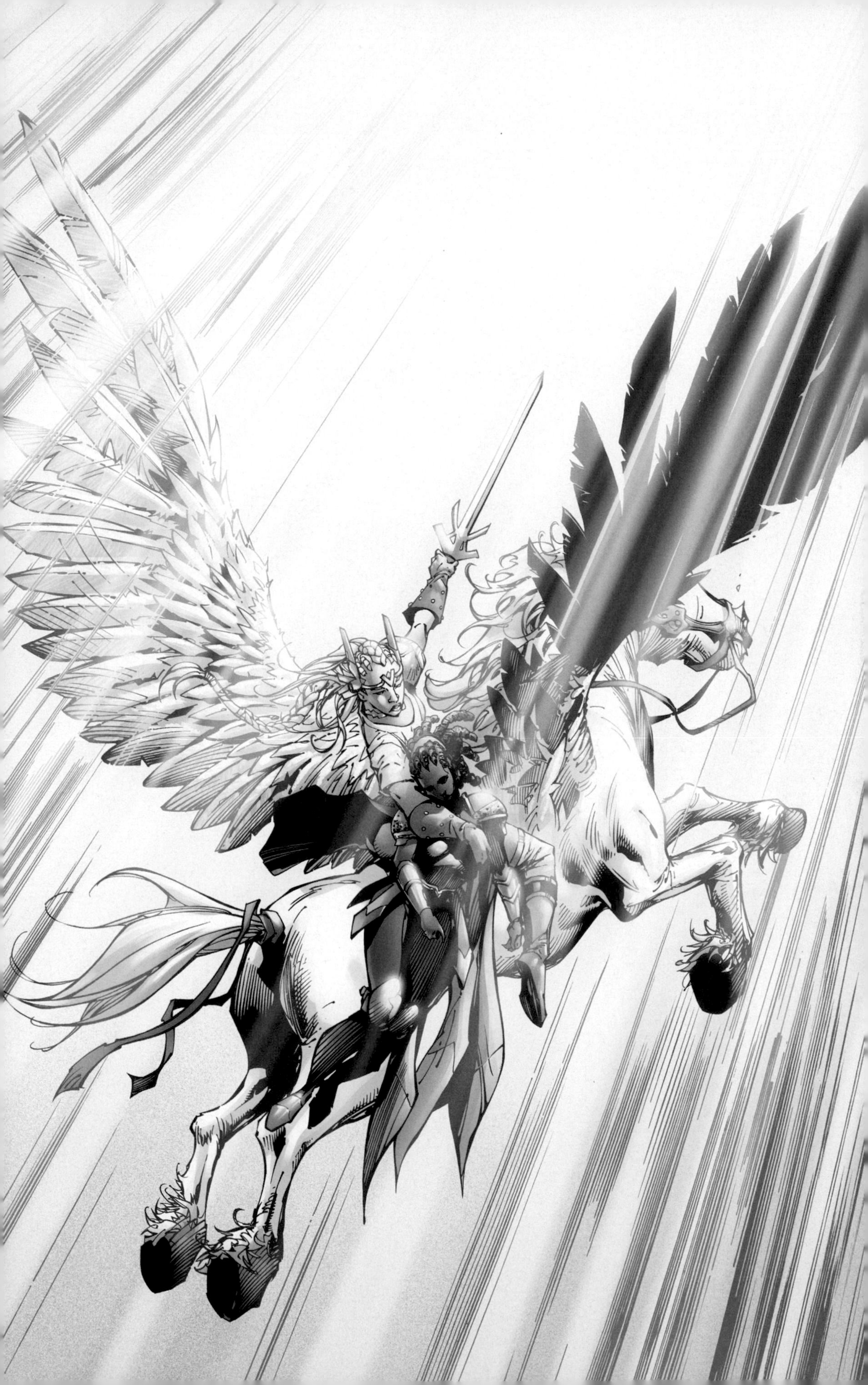

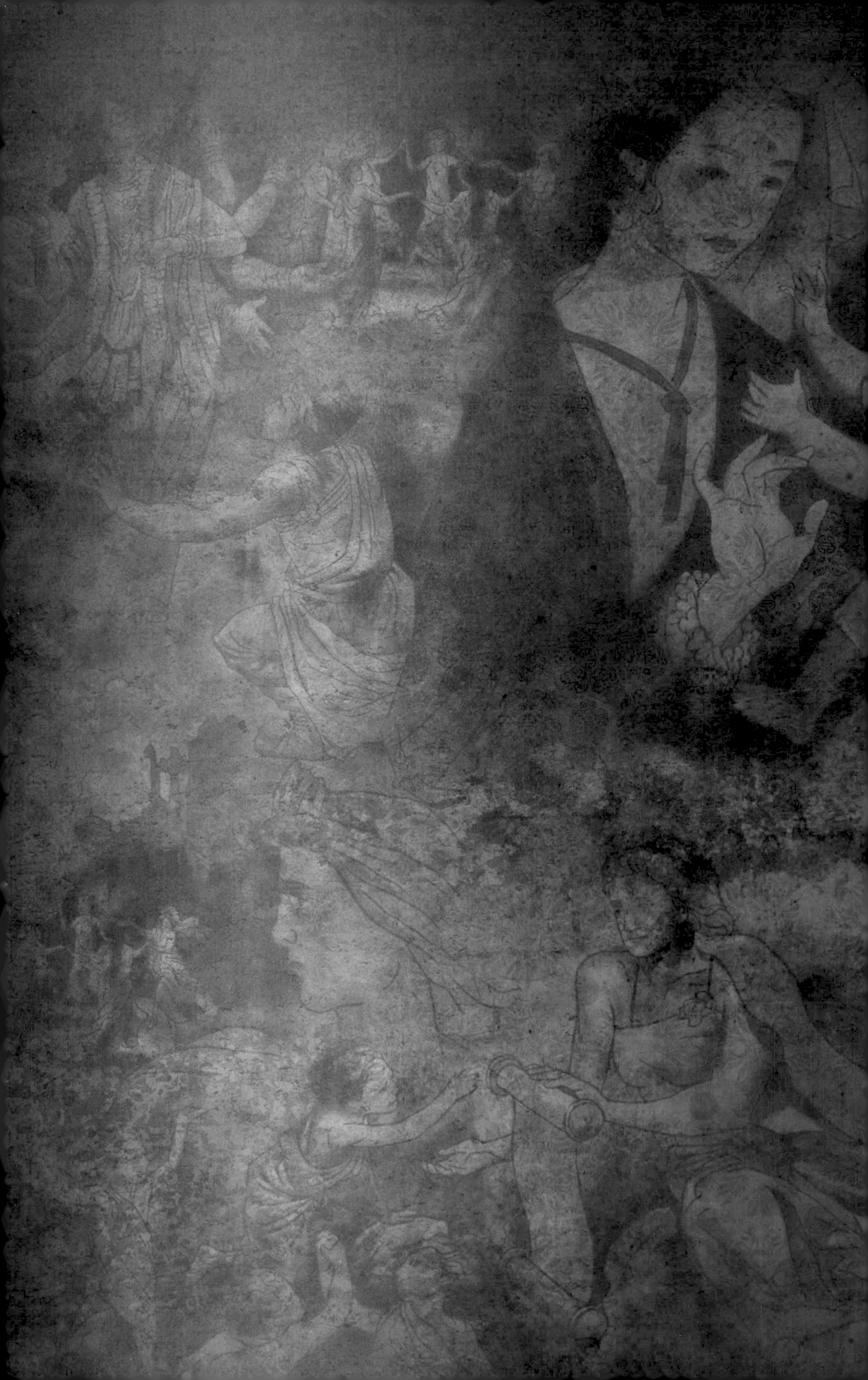

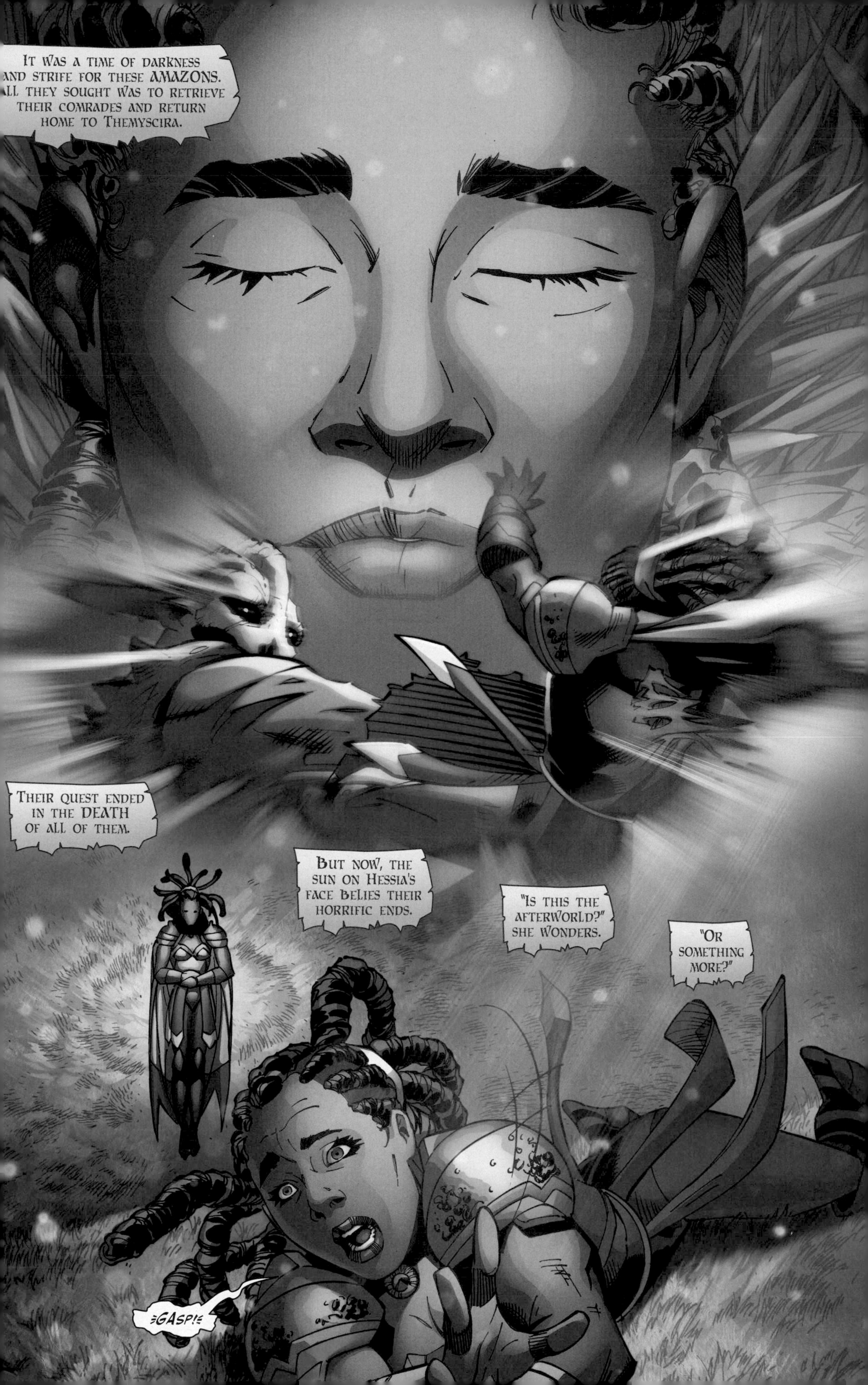
It was a time of darkness and strife for these AMAZONS. All they sought was to retrieve their comrades and return home to Themyscira.
Their quest ended in the DEATH of all of them.
But now, the sun on Hessia's face belies their horrific ends.
"Is this the afterworld?" she wonders.
"Or something more?"
GASP!

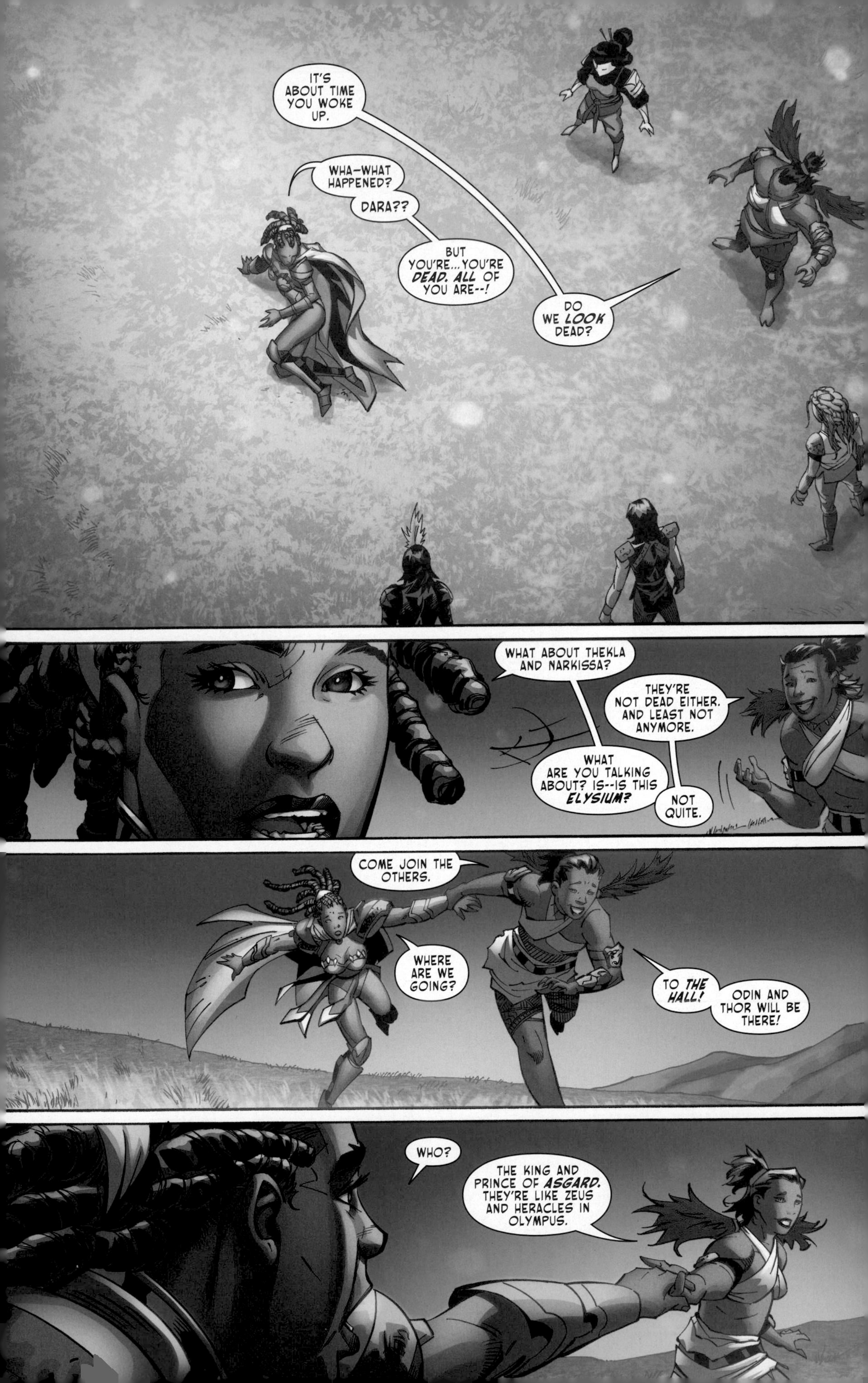
IT'S ABOUT TIME YOU WOKE UP.
WHA-WHAT HAPPENED?
DARA??
BUT YOU'RE...YOU'RE DEAD. ALL OF YOU ARE--!
DO WE LOOK DEAD?
WHAT ABOUT THEKLA AND NARKISSA?
THEY'RE NOT DEAD EITHER. AND LEAST NOT ANYMORE.
WHAT ARE YOU TALKING ABOUT? IS--IS THIS ELYSIUM?
NOT QUITE.
COME JOIN THE OTHERS.
WHERE ARE WE GOING?
TO THE HALL!
ODIN AND THOR WILL BE THERE!
WHO?
THE KING AND PRINCE OF ASGARD. THEY'RE LIKE ZEUS AND HERACLES IN OLYMPUS.

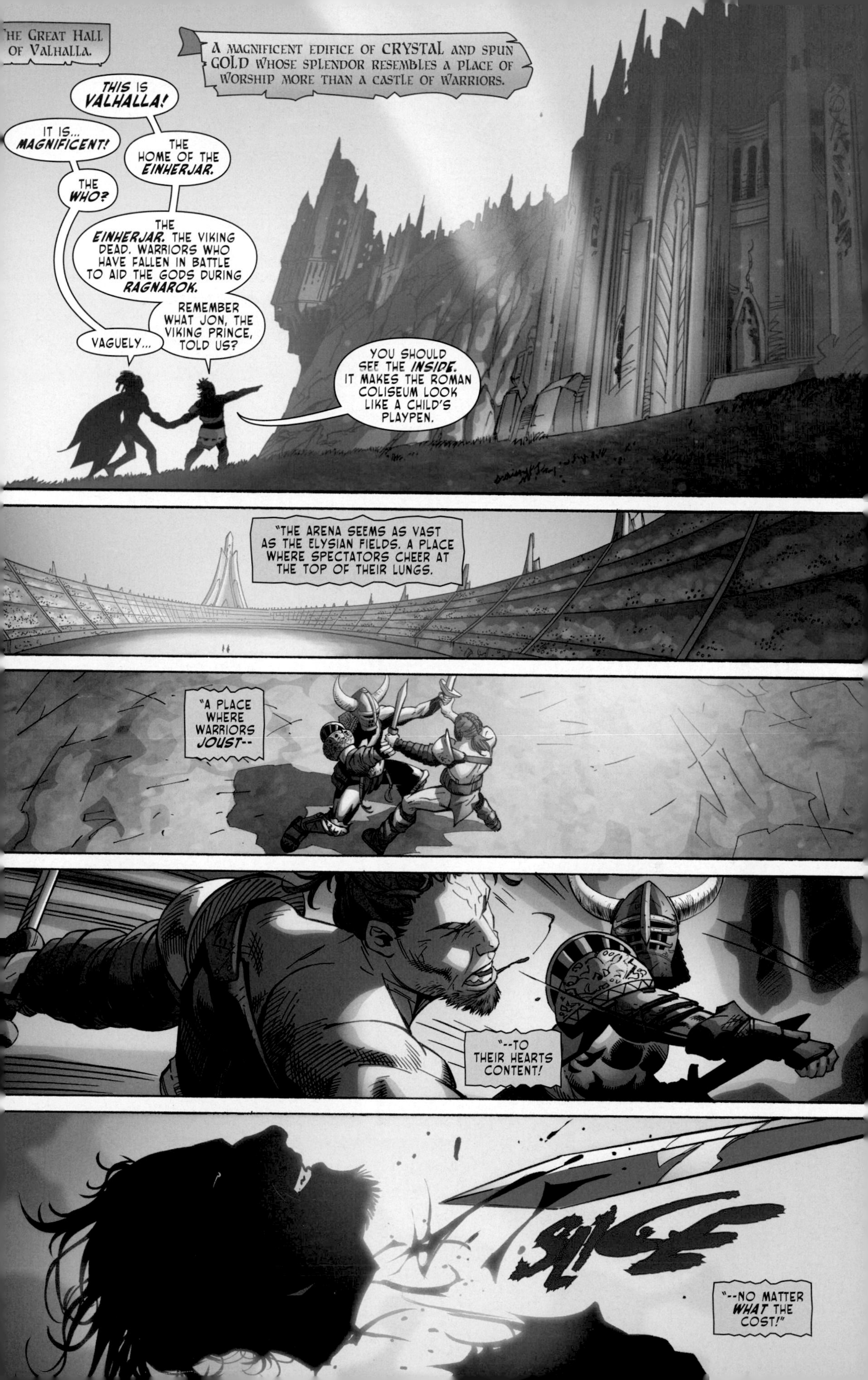
THE GREAT HALL OF VALHALLA.
A MAGNIFICENT EDIFICE OF CRYSTAL AND SPUN GOLD WHOSE SPLENDOR RESEMBLES A PLACE OF WORSHIP MORE THAN A CASTLE OF WARRIORS.
THIS IS VALHALLA!
IT IS... MAGNIFICENT!
THE HOME OF THE EINHERJAR.
THE WHO?
THE EINHERJAR. THE VIKING DEAD. WARRIORS WHO HAVE FALLEN IN BATTLE TO AID THE GODS DURING RAGNAROK.
REMEMBER WHAT JON, THE VIKING PRINCE, TOLD US?
VAGUELY...
YOU SHOULD SEE THE INSIDE. IT MAKES THE ROMAN COLISEUM LOOK LIKE A CHILD'S PLAYPEN.
"THE ARENA SEEMS AS VAST AS THE ELYSIAN FIELDS. A PLACE WHERE SPECTATORS CHEER AT THE TOP OF THEIR LUNGS.
"A PLACE WHERE WARRIORS JOUST--
"--TO THEIR HEARTS CONTENT!
SLICE
"--NO MATTER WHAT THE COST!"

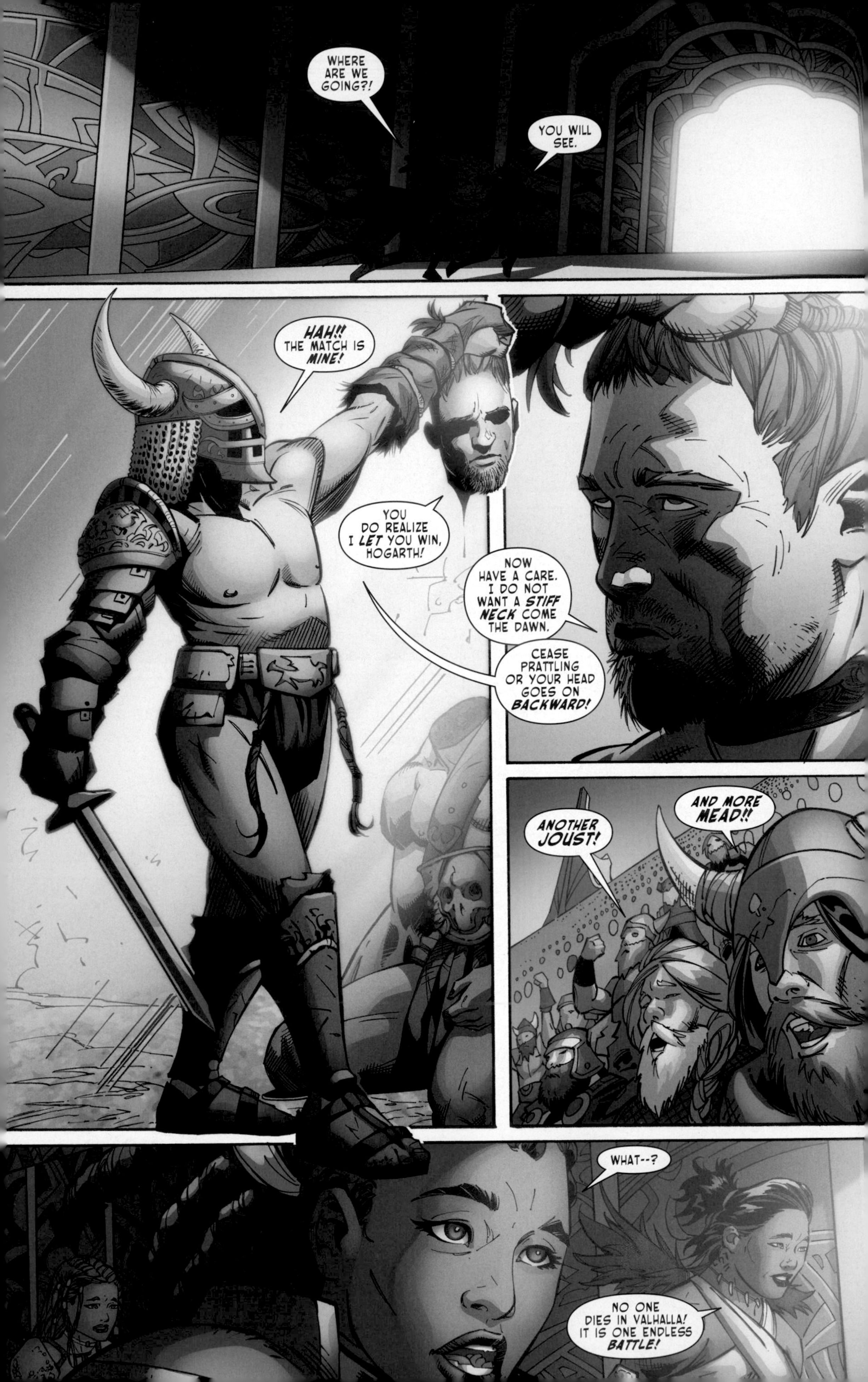
WHERE ARE WE GOING?!
YOU WILL SEE.
HAH!! THE MATCH IS MINE!
YOU DO REALIZE I LET YOU WIN, HOGARTH!
NOW HAVE A CARE. I DO NOT WANT A STIFF NECK COME THE DAWN.
CEASE PRATTLING OR YOUR HEAD GOES ON BACKWARD!
ANOTHER JOUST!
AND MORE MEAD!!
WHAT--?
NO ONE DIES IN VALHALLA! IT IS ONE ENDLESS BATTLE!

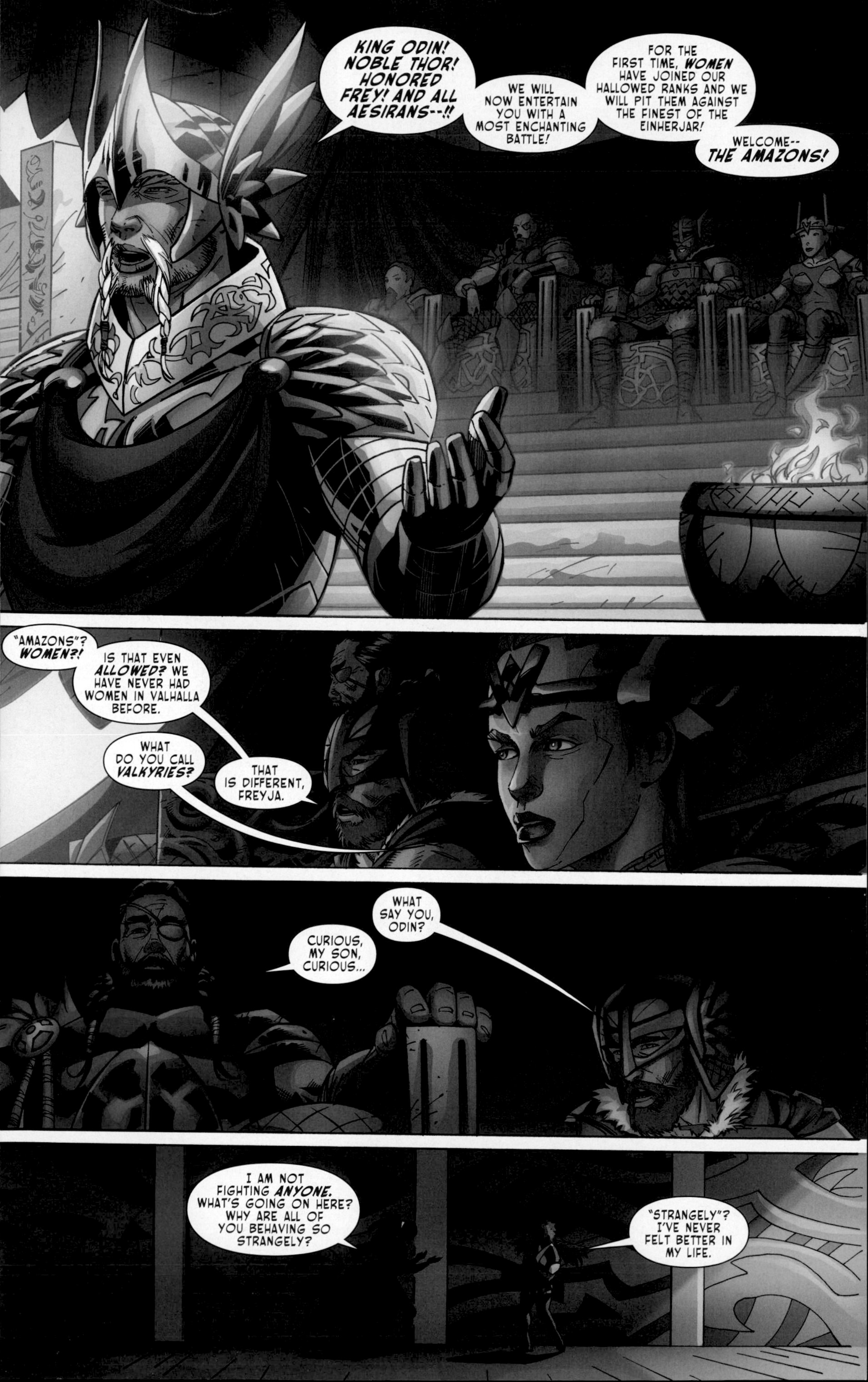
KING ODIN! NOBLE THOR! HONORED FREY! AND ALL AESIRANS--!!
WE WILL NOW ENTERTAIN YOU WITH A MOST ENCHANTING BATTLE!
FOR THE FIRST TIME, WOMEN HAVE JOINED OUR HALLOWED RANKS AND WE WILL PIT THEM AGAINST THE FINEST OF THE EINHERJAR!
WELCOME-- THE AMAZONS!
"AMAZONS"? WOMEN?!
IS THAT EVEN ALLOWED? WE HAVE NEVER HAD WOMEN IN VALHALLA BEFORE.
WHAT DO YOU CALL VALKYRIES?
THAT IS DIFFERENT, FREYJA.
WHAT SAY YOU, ODIN?
CURIOUS, MY SON, CURIOUS...
I AM NOT FIGHTING ANYONE. WHAT'S GOING ON HERE? WHY ARE ALL OF YOU BEHAVING SO STRANGELY?
"STRANGELY"? I'VE NEVER FELT BETTER IN MY LIFE.

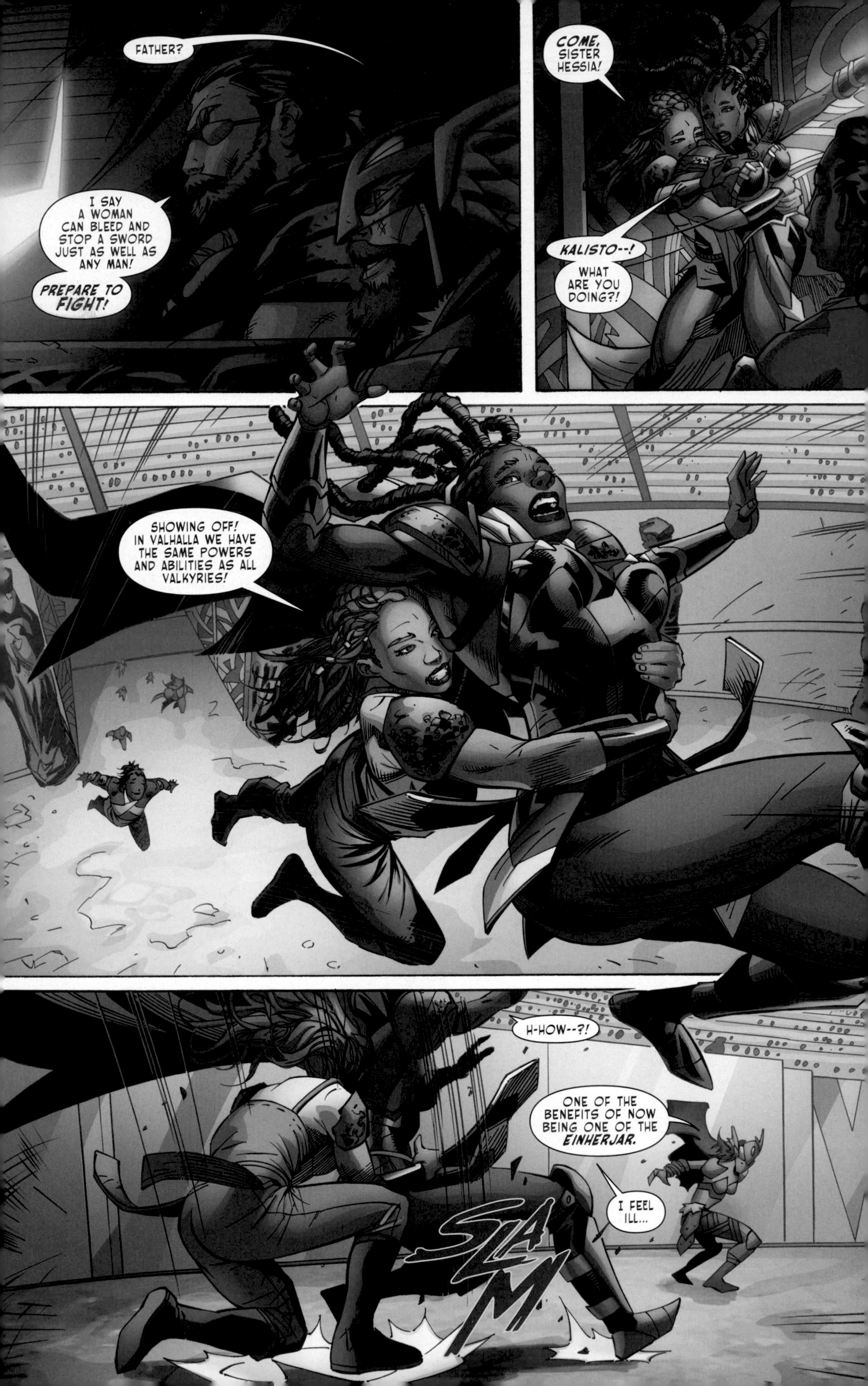
FATHER?
I SAY A WOMAN CAN BLEED AND STOP A SWORD JUST AS WELL AS ANY MAN!
PREPARE TO FIGHT!
COME, SISTER HESSIA!
KALISTO--!
WHAT ARE YOU DOING?!
SHOWING OFF! IN VALHALLA WE HAVE THE SAME POWERS AND ABILITIES AS ALL VALKYRIES!
H-HOW--?!
ONE OF THE BENEFITS OF NOW BEING ONE OF THE EINHERJAR.
I FEEL ILL...
SLAM

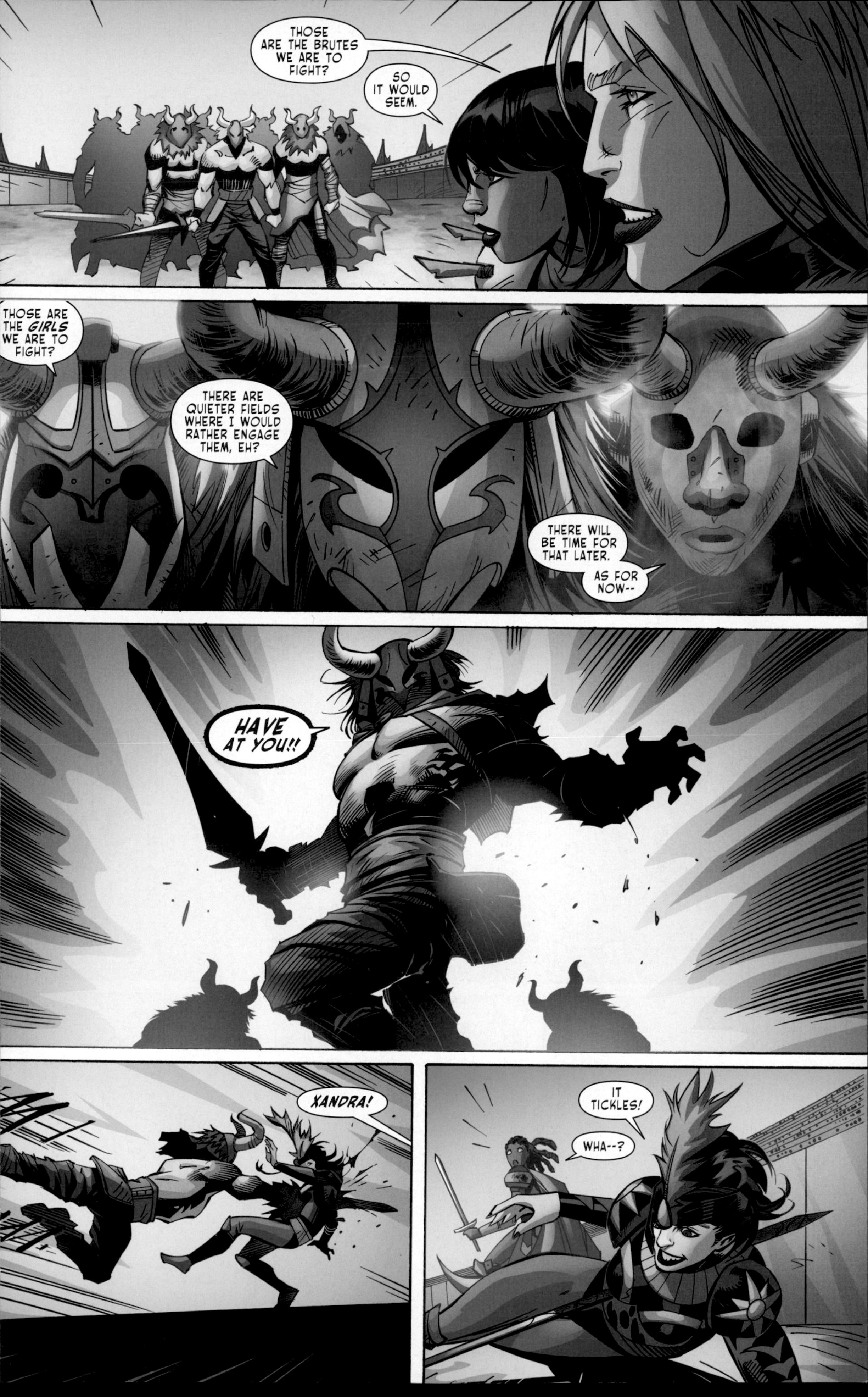
THOSE ARE THE BRUTES WE ARE TO FIGHT?
SO IT WOULD SEEM.
THOSE ARE THE *GIRLS* WE ARE TO FIGHT?
THERE ARE QUIETER FIELDS WHERE I WOULD RATHER ENGAGE THEM, EH?
THERE WILL BE TIME FOR THAT LATER.
AS FOR NOW--
HAVE AT YOU!!
XANDRA!
IT TICKLES!
WHA--?

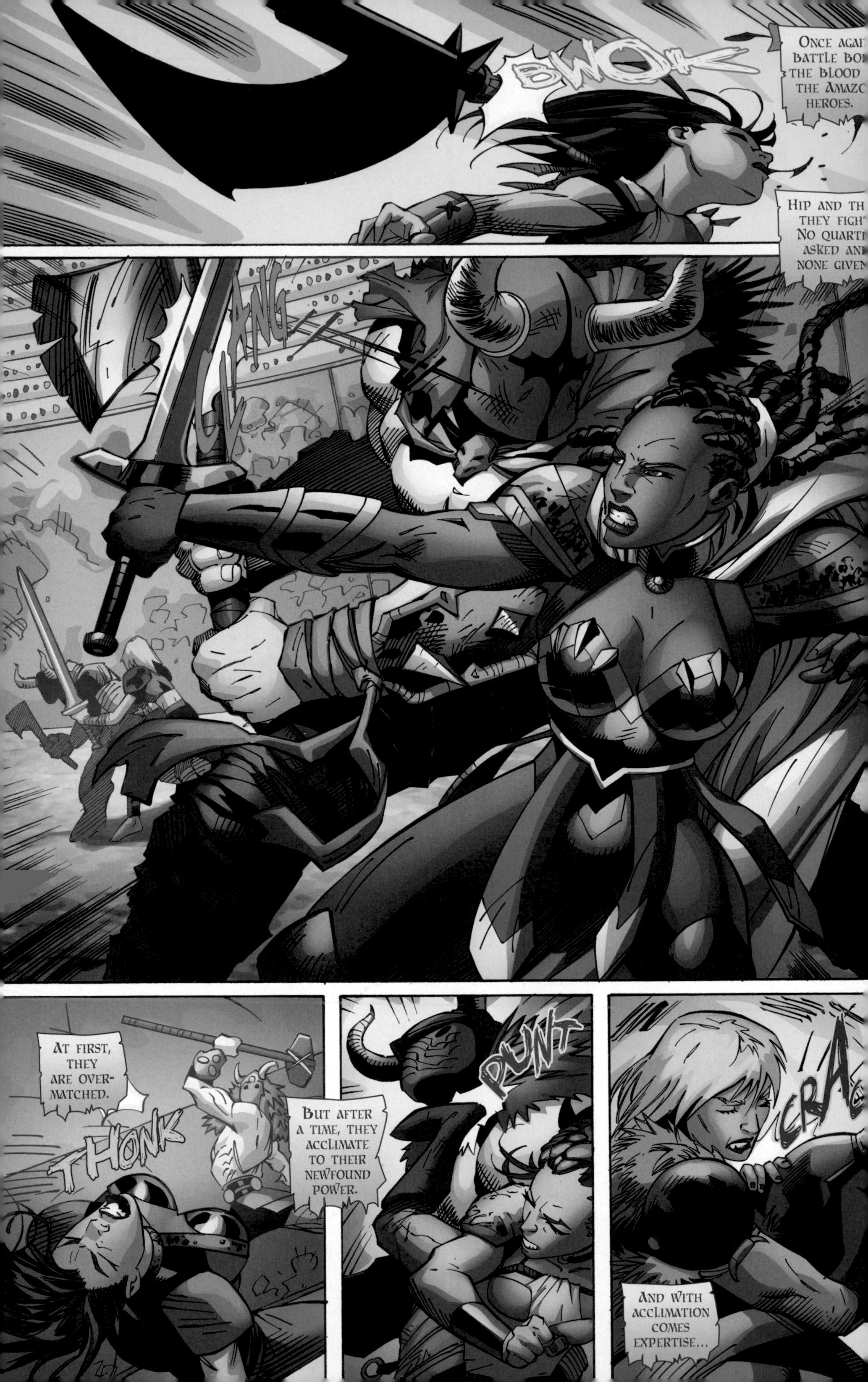
BWOK
ONCE AGAI
BATTLE BO
THE BLOOD
THE AMAZO
HEROES.
HIP AND TH
THEY FIGH
NO QUART
ASKED AN
NONE GIVEN
CLANG
AT FIRST, THEY ARE OVER-MATCHED.
THONK
BUT AFTER A TIME, THEY ACCLIMATE TO THEIR NEWFOUND POWER.
CRA
AND WITH ACCLIMATION COMES EXPERTISE...

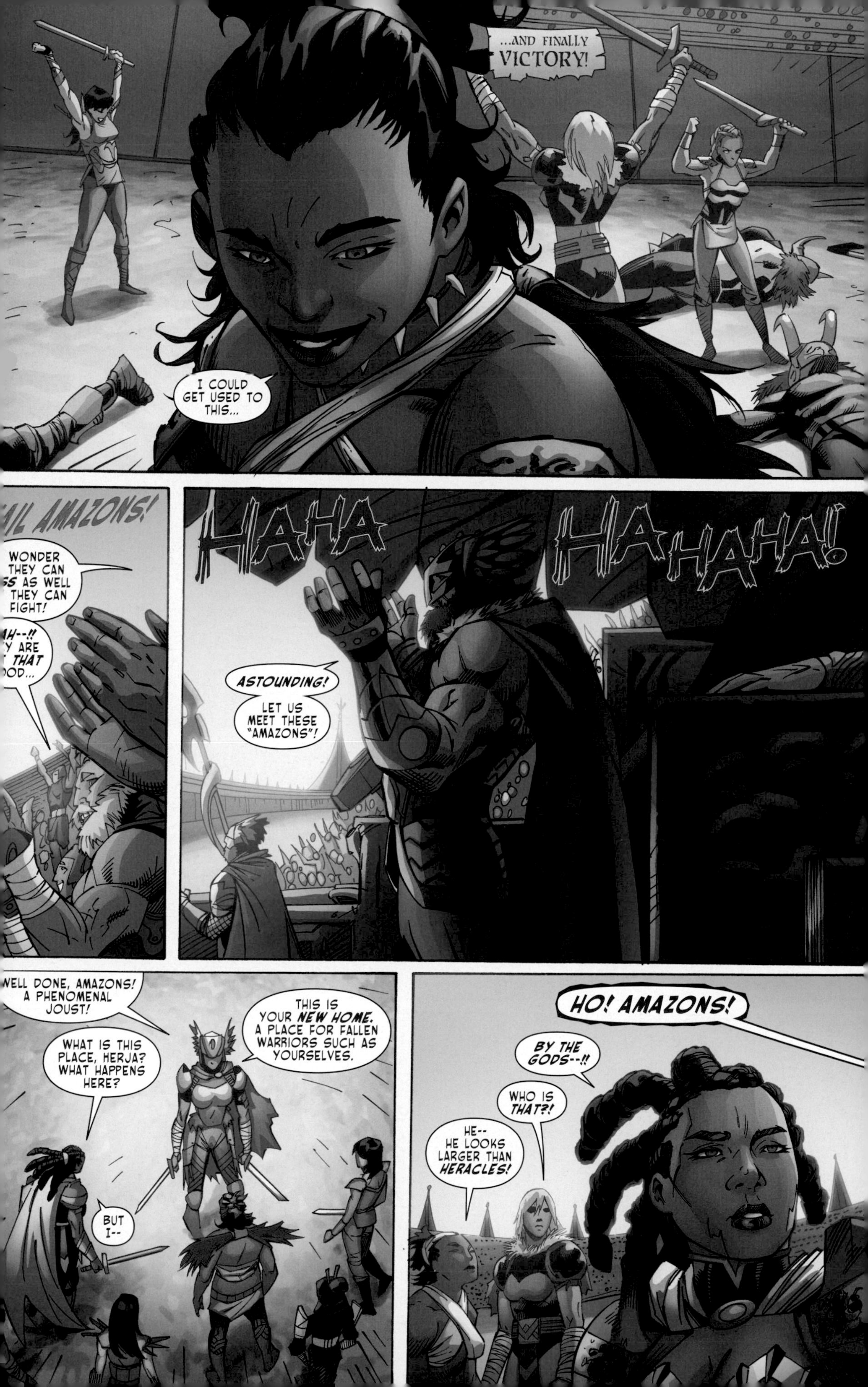

...AND FINALLY VICTORY!
I COULD GET USED TO THIS...
AIL AMAZONS!
WONDER THEY CAN SS AS WELL THEY CAN FIGHT!
AH--!! Y ARE THAT OOD...
HAHA HAHAHA!
ASTOUNDING!
LET US MEET THESE "AMAZONS"!
WELL DONE, AMAZONS! A PHENOMENAL JOUST!
WHAT IS THIS PLACE, HERJA? WHAT HAPPENS HERE?
THIS IS YOUR NEW HOME. A PLACE FOR FALLEN WARRIORS SUCH AS YOURSELVES.
BUT I--
HO! AMAZONS!
BY THE GODS--!!
WHO IS THAT?!
HE-- HE LOOKS LARGER THAN HERACLES!

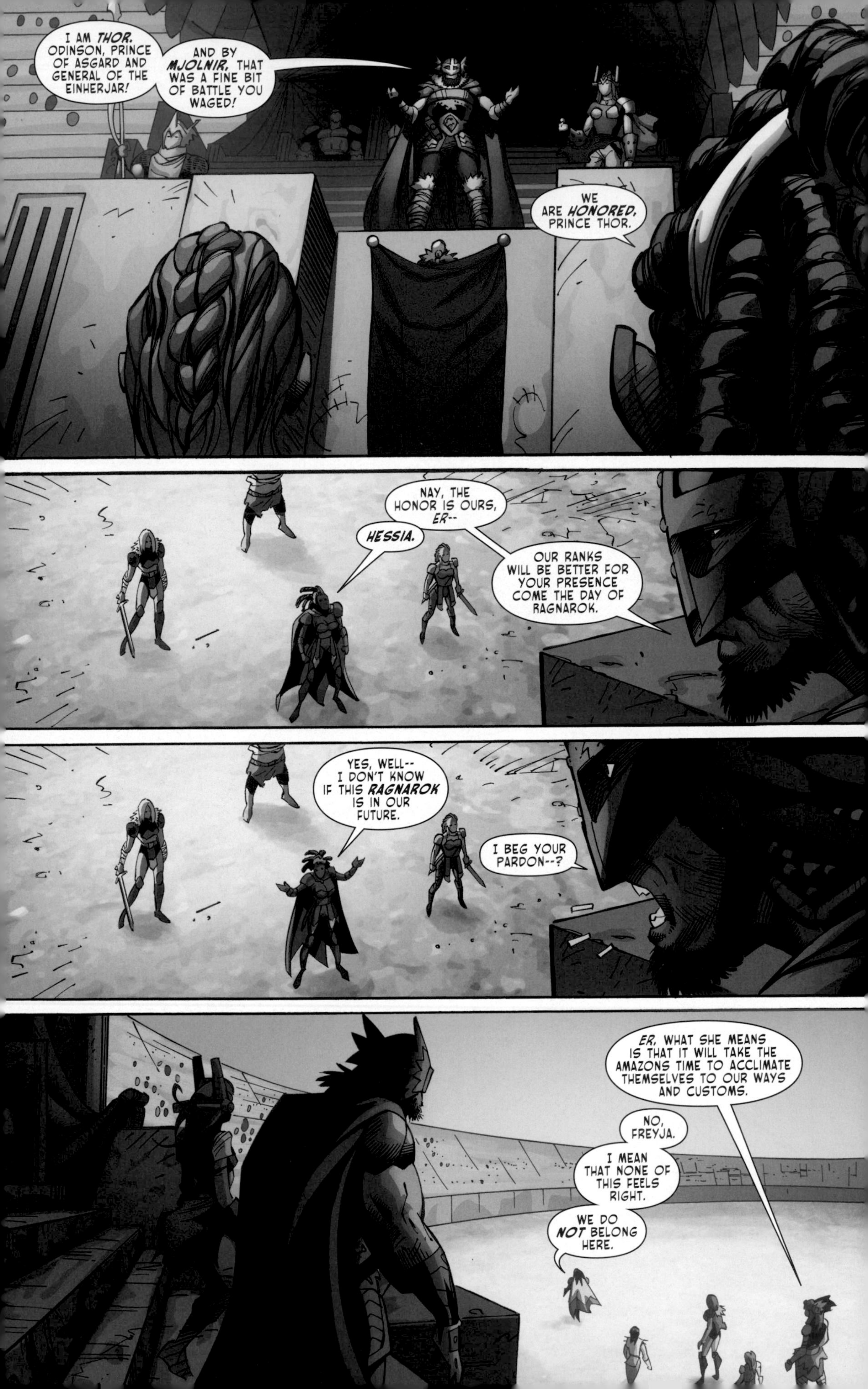
I AM THOR. ODINSON, PRINCE OF ASGARD AND GENERAL OF THE EINHERJAR!
AND BY MJOLNIR, THAT WAS A FINE BIT OF BATTLE YOU WAGED!
WE ARE HONORED, PRINCE THOR.
NAY, THE HONOR IS OURS, ER--
HESSIA.
OUR RANKS WILL BE BETTER FOR YOUR PRESENCE COME THE DAY OF RAGNAROK.
YES, WELL-- I DON'T KNOW IF THIS RAGNAROK IS IN OUR FUTURE.
I BEG YOUR PARDON--?
ER, WHAT SHE MEANS IS THAT IT WILL TAKE THE AMAZONS TIME TO ACCLIMATE THEMSELVES TO OUR WAYS AND CUSTOMS.
NO, FREYJA.
I MEAN THAT NONE OF THIS FEELS RIGHT.
WE DO NOT BELONG HERE.

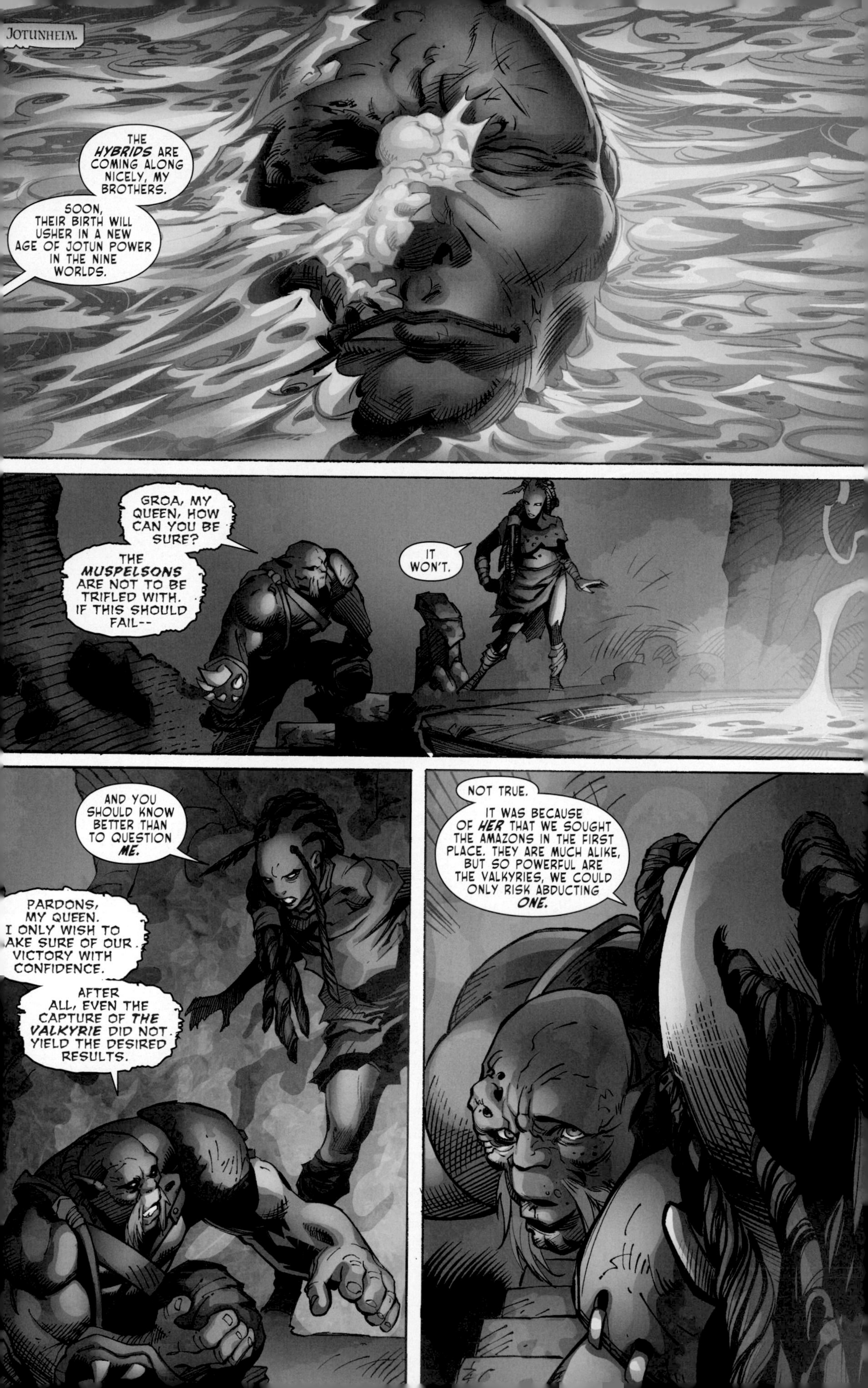
JOTUNHEIM.
THE HYBRIDS ARE COMING ALONG NICELY, MY BROTHERS.
SOON, THEIR BIRTH WILL USHER IN A NEW AGE OF JOTUN POWER IN THE NINE WORLDS.
GROA, MY QUEEN, HOW CAN YOU BE SURE?
THE MUSPELSONS ARE NOT TO BE TRIFLED WITH. IF THIS SHOULD FAIL--
IT WON'T.
AND YOU SHOULD KNOW BETTER THAN TO QUESTION ME.
PARDONS, MY QUEEN. I ONLY WISH TO AKE SURE OF OUR VICTORY WITH CONFIDENCE.
AFTER ALL, EVEN THE CAPTURE OF THE VALKYRIE DID NOT YIELD THE DESIRED RESULTS.
NOT TRUE.
IT WAS BECAUSE OF HER THAT WE SOUGHT THE AMAZONS IN THE FIRST PLACE. THEY ARE MUCH ALIKE, BUT SO POWERFUL ARE THE VALKYRIES, WE COULD ONLY RISK ABDUCTING ONE.

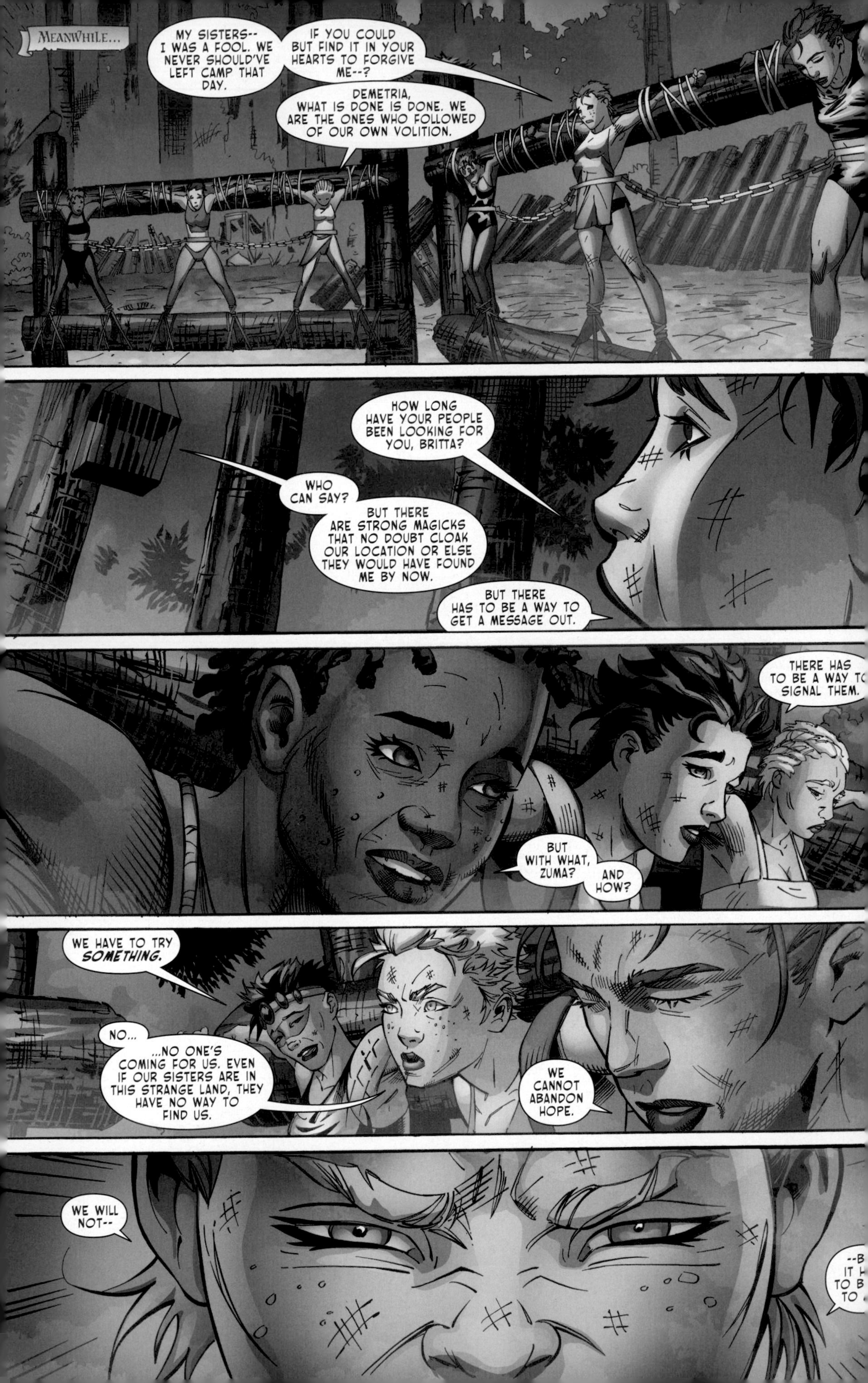
MEANWHILE...
MY SISTERS-- I WAS A FOOL. WE NEVER SHOULD'VE LEFT CAMP THAT DAY.
IF YOU COULD BUT FIND IT IN YOUR HEARTS TO FORGIVE ME--?
DEMETRIA, WHAT IS DONE IS DONE. WE ARE THE ONES WHO FOLLOWED OF OUR OWN VOLITION.
HOW LONG HAVE YOUR PEOPLE BEEN LOOKING FOR YOU, BRITTA?
WHO CAN SAY?
BUT THERE ARE STRONG MAGICKS THAT NO DOUBT CLOAK OUR LOCATION OR ELSE THEY WOULD HAVE FOUND ME BY NOW.
BUT THERE HAS TO BE A WAY TO GET A MESSAGE OUT.
THERE HAS TO BE A WAY TO SIGNAL THEM.
BUT WITH WHAT, ZUMA?
AND HOW?
WE HAVE TO TRY *SOMETHING.*
NO...
...NO ONE'S COMING FOR US. EVEN IF OUR SISTERS ARE IN THIS STRANGE LAND, THEY HAVE NO WAY TO FIND US.
WE CANNOT ABANDON HOPE.
WE WILL NOT--

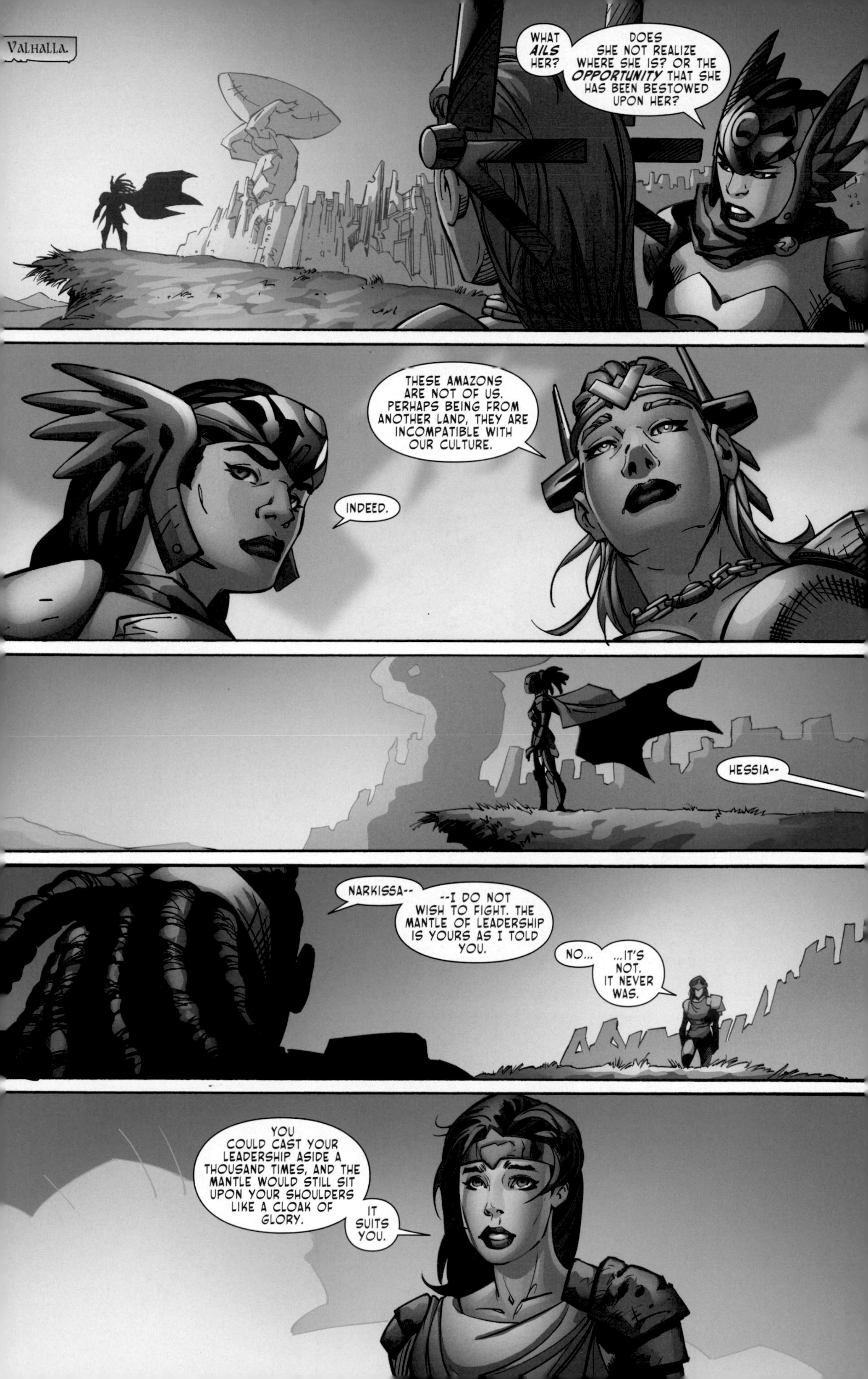
VALHALLA.
WHAT AILS HER?
DOES SHE NOT REALIZE WHERE SHE IS? OR THE OPPORTUNITY THAT SHE HAS BEEN BESTOWED UPON HER?
THESE AMAZONS ARE NOT OF US. PERHAPS BEING FROM ANOTHER LAND, THEY ARE INCOMPATIBLE WITH OUR CULTURE.
INDEED.
HESSIA--
NARKISSA--
--I DO NOT WISH TO FIGHT. THE MANTLE OF LEADERSHIP IS YOURS AS I TOLD YOU.
NO...
...IT'S NOT. IT NEVER WAS.
YOU COULD CAST YOUR LEADERSHIP ASIDE A THOUSAND TIMES, AND THE MANTLE WOULD STILL SIT UPON YOUR SHOULDERS LIKE A CLOAK OF GLORY.
IT SUITS YOU.

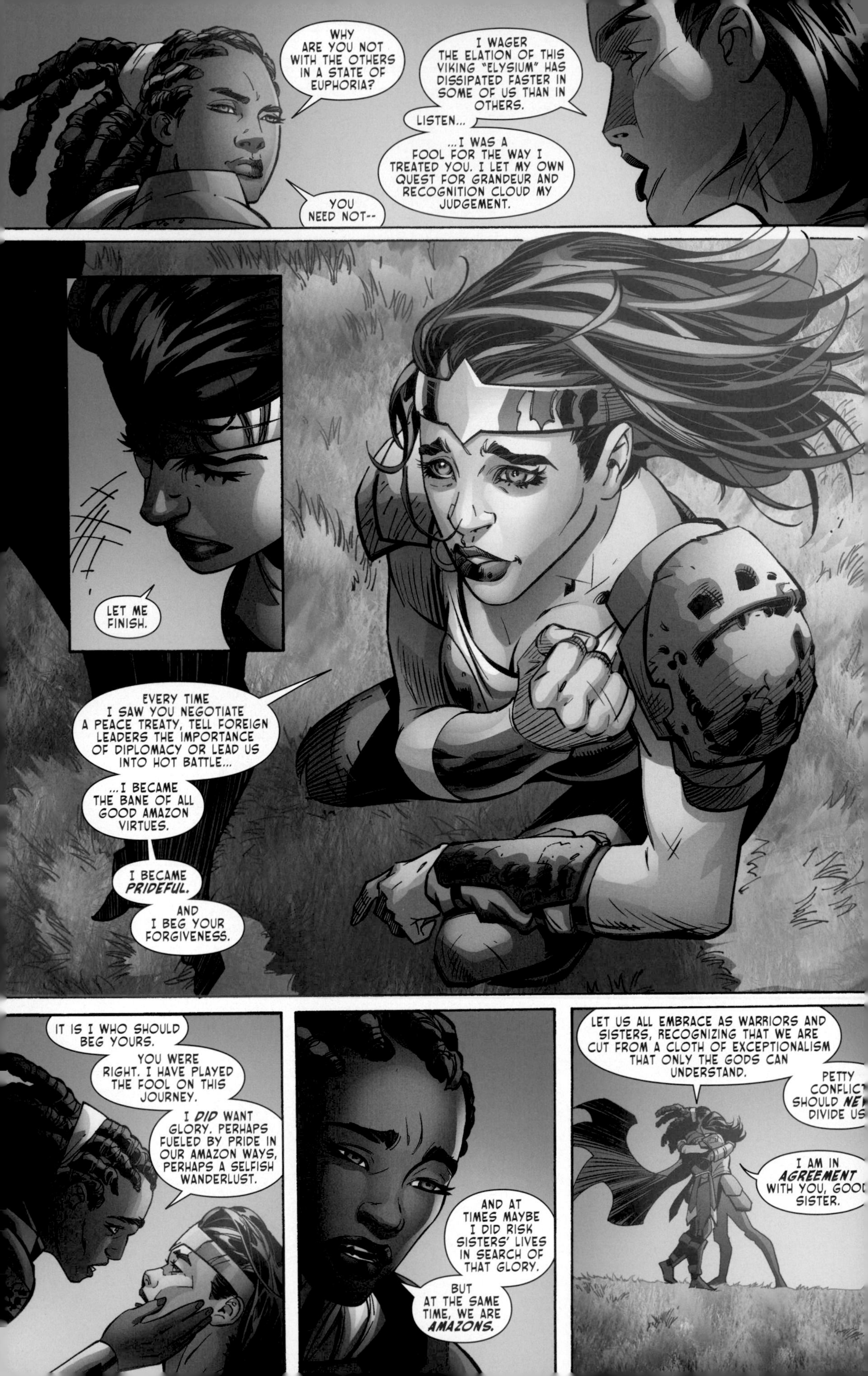
WHY ARE YOU NOT WITH THE OTHERS IN A STATE OF EUPHORIA?
I WAGER THE ELATION OF THIS VIKING "ELYSIUM" HAS DISSIPATED FASTER IN SOME OF US THAN IN OTHERS.
LISTEN...
...I WAS A FOOL FOR THE WAY I TREATED YOU. I LET MY OWN QUEST FOR GRANDEUR AND RECOGNITION CLOUD MY JUDGEMENT.
YOU NEED NOT--
LET ME FINISH.
EVERY TIME I SAW YOU NEGOTIATE A PEACE TREATY, TELL FOREIGN LEADERS THE IMPORTANCE OF DIPLOMACY OR LEAD US INTO HOT BATTLE...
...I BECAME THE BANE OF ALL GOOD AMAZON VIRTUES.
I BECAME *PRIDEFUL.*
AND I BEG YOUR FORGIVENESS.
IT IS I WHO SHOULD BEG YOURS.
YOU WERE RIGHT. I HAVE PLAYED THE FOOL ON THIS JOURNEY.
I *DID* WANT GLORY. PERHAPS FUELED BY PRIDE IN OUR AMAZON WAYS, PERHAPS A SELFISH WANDERLUST.
AND AT TIMES MAYBE I DID RISK SISTERS' LIVES IN SEARCH OF THAT GLORY.
BUT AT THE SAME TIME, WE ARE *AMAZONS.*
LET US ALL EMBRACE AS WARRIORS AND SISTERS, RECOGNIZING THAT WE ARE CUT FROM A CLOTH OF EXCEPTIONALISM THAT ONLY THE GODS CAN UNDERSTAND.
PETTY CONFLICT SHOULD NE DIVIDE US
I AM IN *AGREEMENT* WITH YOU, GOOD SISTER.

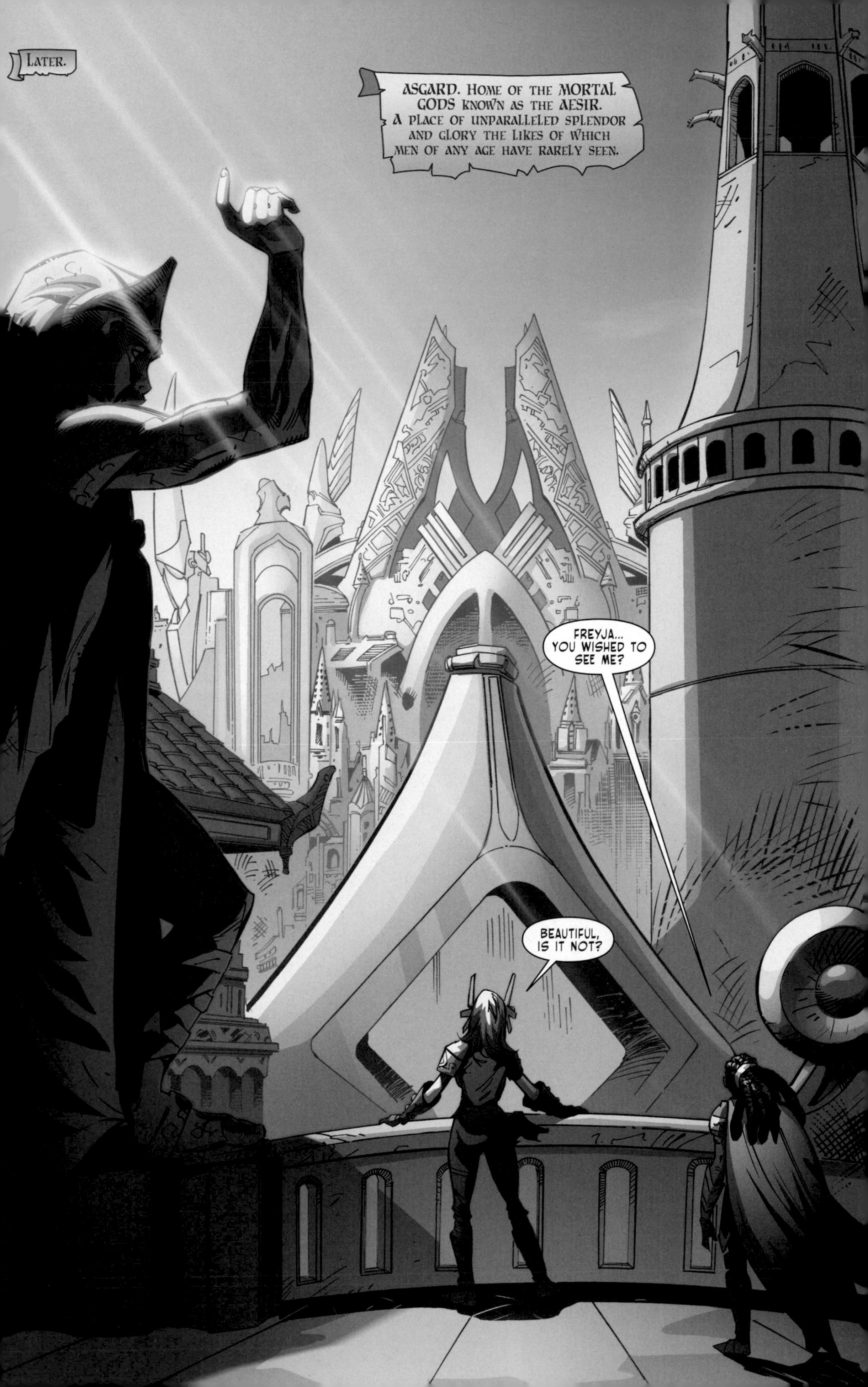
LATER.
ASGARD. HOME OF THE MORTAL GODS KNOWN AS THE AESIR. A PLACE OF UNPARALLELED SPLENDOR AND GLORY THE LIKES OF WHICH MEN OF ANY AGE HAVE RARELY SEEN.
FREYJA... YOU WISHED TO SEE ME?
BEAUTIFUL, IS IT NOT?

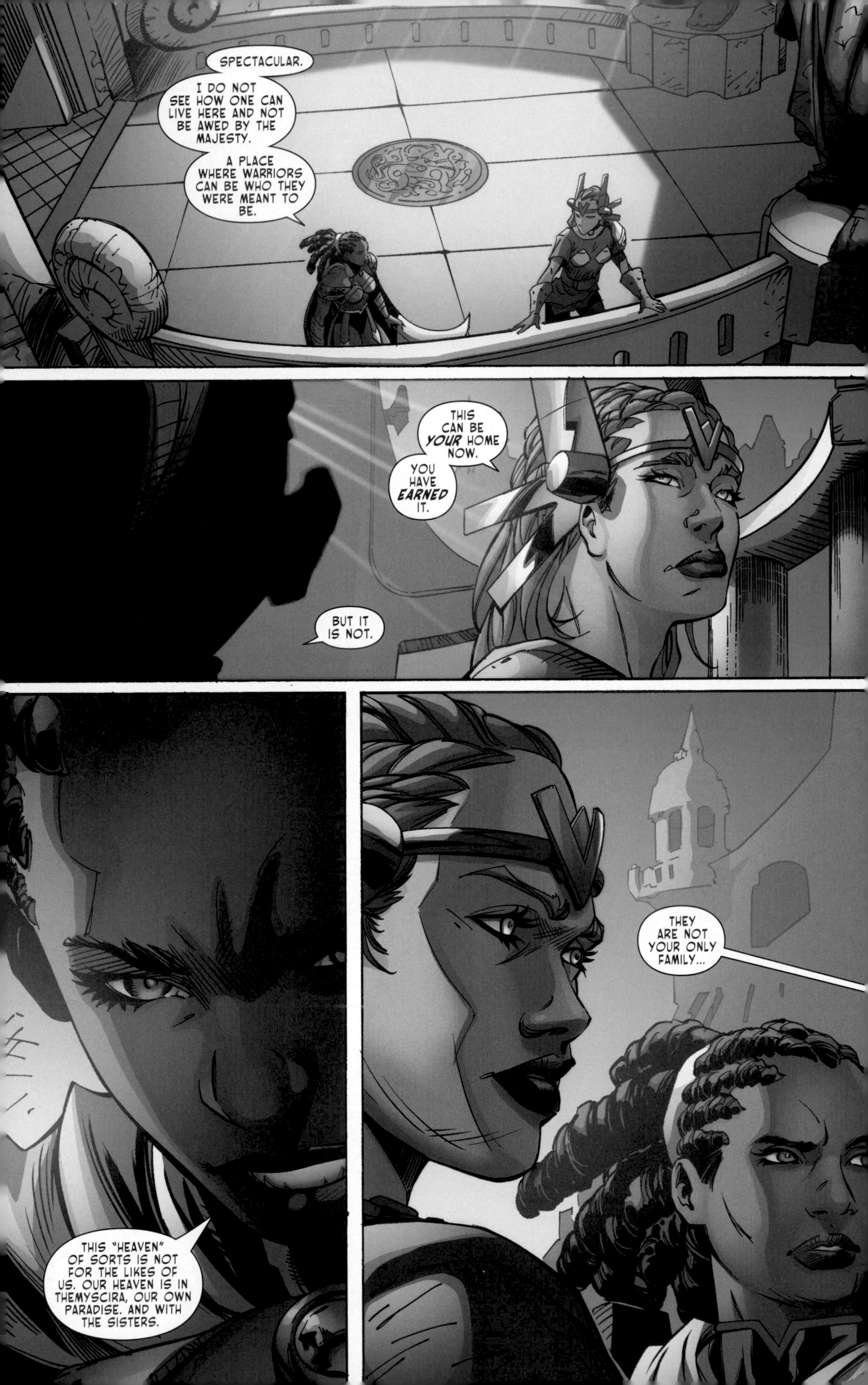
SPECTACULAR.
I DO NOT SEE HOW ONE CAN LIVE HERE AND NOT BE AWED BY THE MAJESTY.
A PLACE WHERE WARRIORS CAN BE WHO THEY WERE MEANT TO BE.
THIS CAN BE *YOUR* HOME NOW.
YOU HAVE *EARNED* IT.
BUT IT IS NOT.
THIS "HEAVEN" OF SORTS IS NOT FOR THE LIKES OF US. OUR HEAVEN IS IN THEMYSCIRA, OUR OWN PARADISE. AND WITH THE SISTERS.
THEY ARE NOT YOUR ONLY FAMILY...

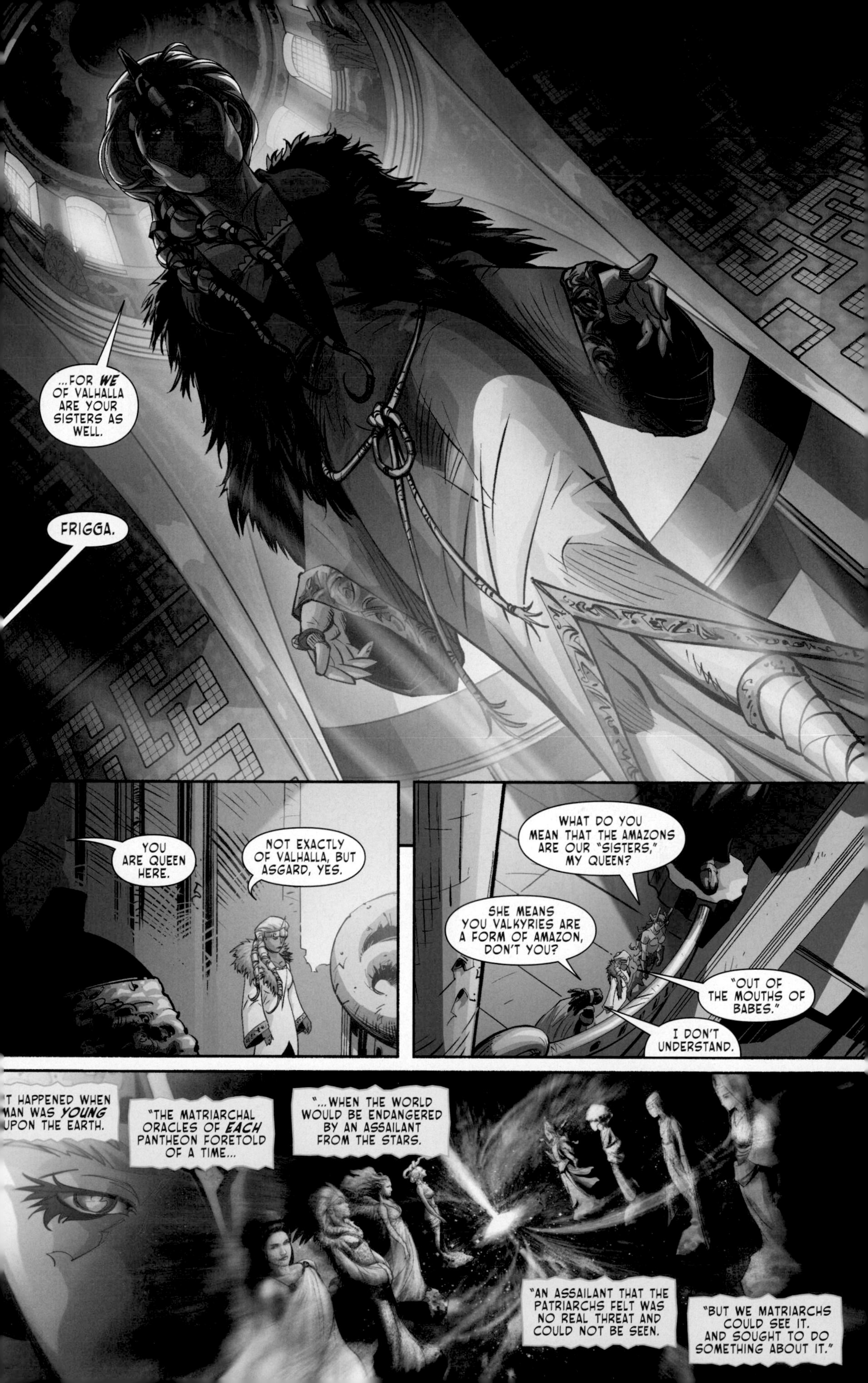
...FOR WE OF VALHALLA ARE YOUR SISTERS AS WELL.
FRIGGA.
YOU ARE QUEEN HERE.
NOT EXACTLY OF VALHALLA, BUT ASGARD, YES.
WHAT DO YOU MEAN THAT THE AMAZONS ARE OUR "SISTERS," MY QUEEN?
SHE MEANS YOU VALKYRIES ARE A FORM OF AMAZON, DON'T YOU?
"OUT OF THE MOUTHS OF BABES."
I DON'T UNDERSTAND.
T HAPPENED WHEN MAN WAS YOUNG UPON THE EARTH.
"THE MATRIARCHAL ORACLES OF EACH PANTHEON FORETOLD OF A TIME...
"...WHEN THE WORLD WOULD BE ENDANGERED BY AN ASSAILANT FROM THE STARS.
"AN ASSAILANT THAT THE PATRIARCHS FELT WAS NO REAL THREAT AND COULD NOT BE SEEN.
"BUT WE MATRIARCHS COULD SEE IT. AND SOUGHT TO DO SOMETHING ABOUT IT."

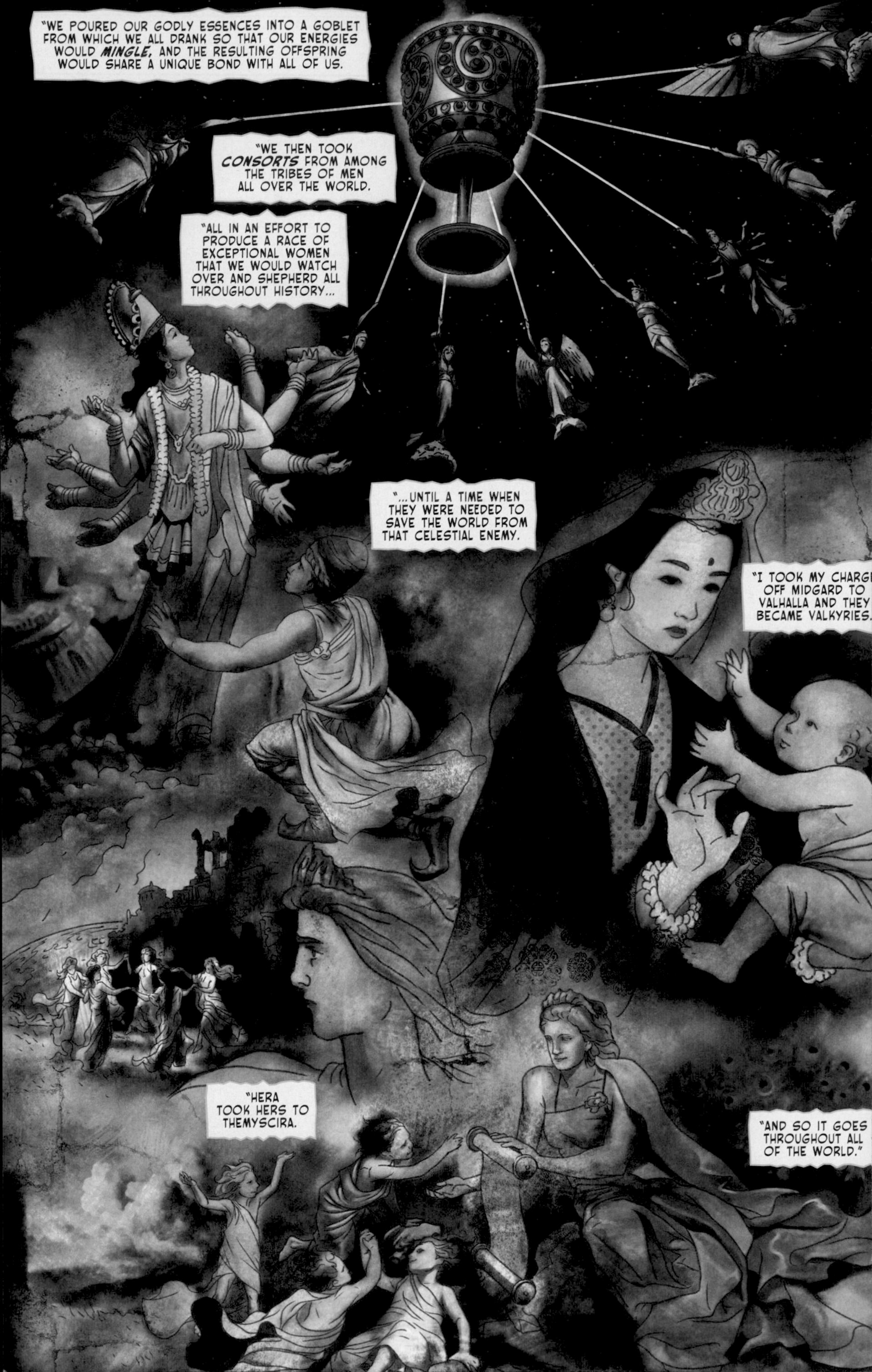
"WE POURED OUR GODLY ESSENCES INTO A GOBLET FROM WHICH WE ALL DRANK SO THAT OUR ENERGIES WOULD *MINGLE*, AND THE RESULTING OFFSPRING WOULD SHARE A UNIQUE BOND WITH ALL OF US.
"WE THEN TOOK *CONSORTS* FROM AMONG THE TRIBES OF MEN ALL OVER THE WORLD.
"ALL IN AN EFFORT TO PRODUCE A RACE OF EXCEPTIONAL WOMEN THAT WE WOULD WATCH OVER AND SHEPHERD ALL THROUGHOUT HISTORY...
"...UNTIL A TIME WHEN THEY WERE NEEDED TO SAVE THE WORLD FROM THAT CELESTIAL ENEMY.
"I TOOK MY CHARG OFF MIDGARD TO VALHALLA AND THEY BECAME VALKYRIES.
"HERA TOOK HERS TO THEMYSCIRA.
"AND SO IT GOES THROUGHOUT ALL OF THE WORLD."

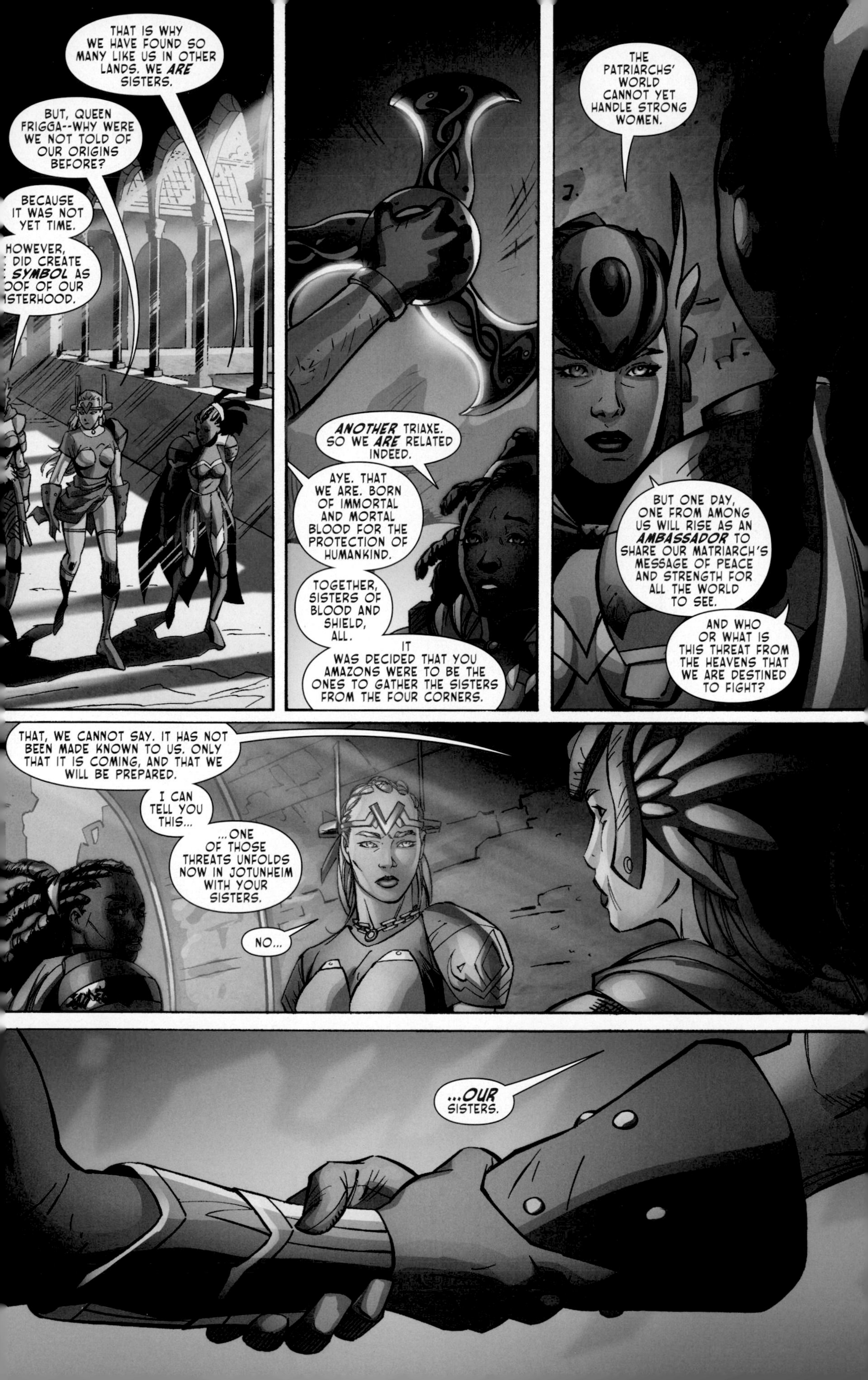
THAT IS WHY WE HAVE FOUND SO MANY LIKE US IN OTHER LANDS. WE *ARE* SISTERS.
BUT, QUEEN FRIGGA--WHY WERE WE NOT TOLD OF OUR ORIGINS BEFORE?
BECAUSE IT WAS NOT YET TIME.
HOWEVER, DID CREATE *SYMBOL* AS OOF OF OUR ISTERHOOD.
ANOTHER TRIAXE. SO WE *ARE* RELATED INDEED.
AYE. THAT WE ARE. BORN OF IMMORTAL AND MORTAL BLOOD FOR THE PROTECTION OF HUMANKIND.
TOGETHER, SISTERS OF BLOOD AND SHIELD, ALL.
IT WAS DECIDED THAT YOU AMAZONS WERE TO BE THE ONES TO GATHER THE SISTERS FROM THE FOUR CORNERS.
THE PATRIARCHS' WORLD CANNOT YET HANDLE STRONG WOMEN.
BUT ONE DAY, ONE FROM AMONG US WILL RISE AS AN *AMBASSADOR* TO SHARE OUR MATRIARCH'S MESSAGE OF PEACE AND STRENGTH FOR ALL THE WORLD TO SEE.
AND WHO OR WHAT IS THIS THREAT FROM THE HEAVENS THAT WE ARE DESTINED TO FIGHT?
THAT, WE CANNOT SAY. IT HAS NOT BEEN MADE KNOWN TO US. ONLY THAT IT IS COMING, AND THAT WE WILL BE PREPARED.
I CAN TELL YOU THIS...
...ONE OF THOSE THREATS UNFOLDS NOW IN JOTUNHEIM WITH YOUR SISTERS.
NO...
...*OUR* SISTERS.

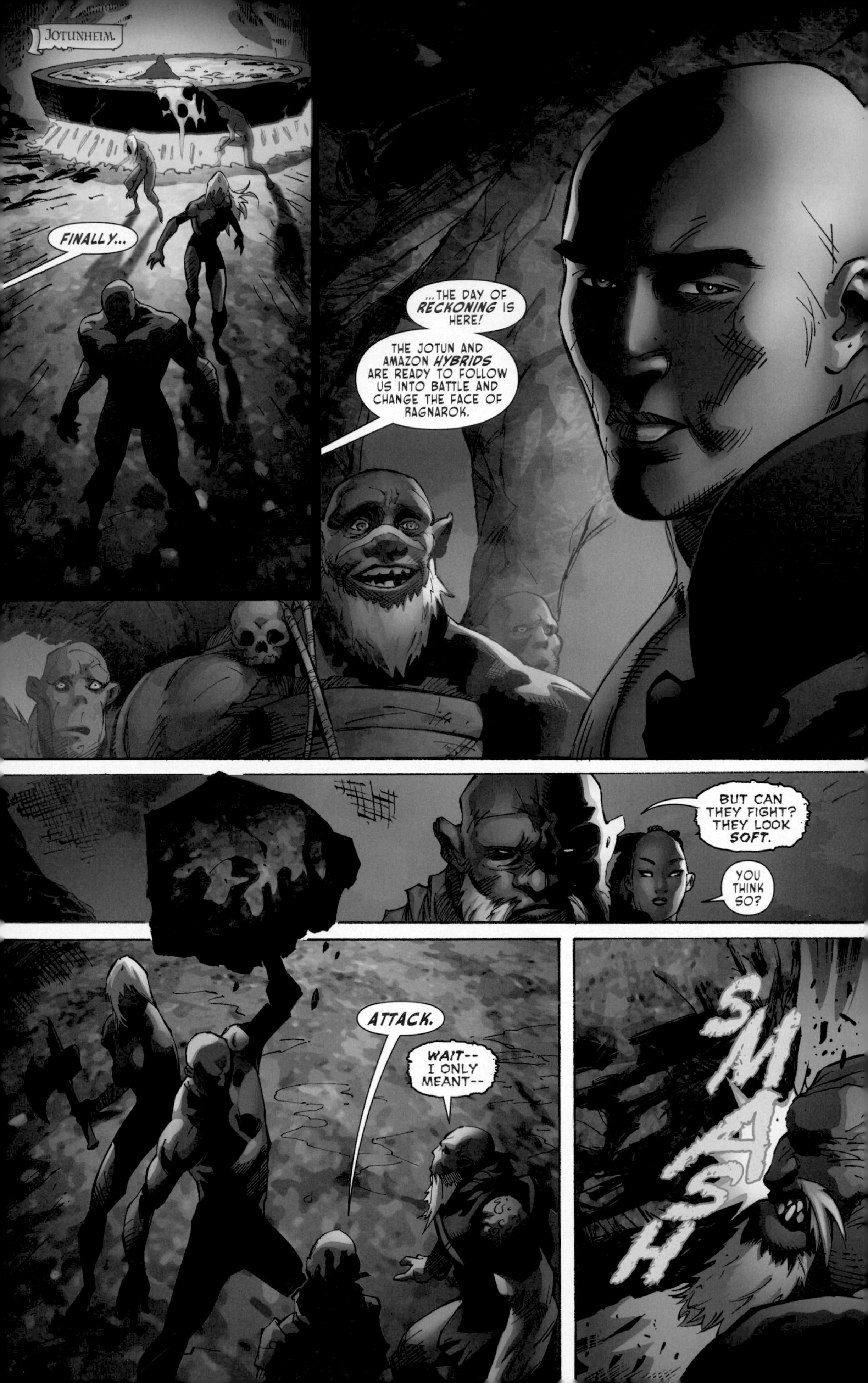
JOTUNHEIM.
FINALLY...
...THE DAY OF RECKONING IS HERE!
THE JOTUN AND AMAZON HYBRIDS ARE READY TO FOLLOW US INTO BATTLE AND CHANGE THE FACE OF RAGNAROK.
BUT CAN THEY FIGHT? THEY LOOK SOFT.
YOU THINK SO?
ATTACK.
WAIT-- I ONLY MEANT--
SMASH

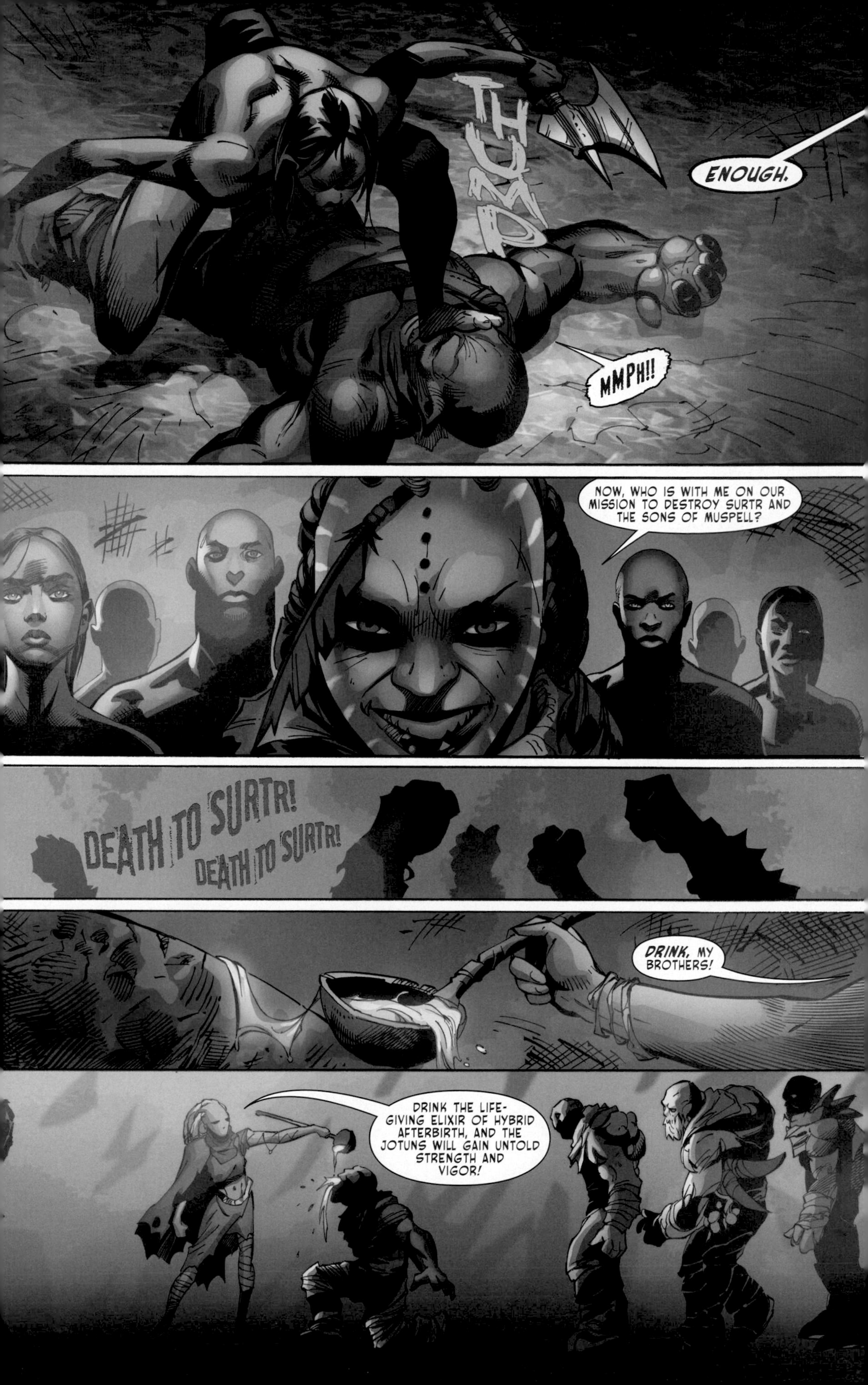
THUMP
ENOUGH.
MMPH!!
NOW, WHO IS WITH ME ON OUR MISSION TO DESTROY SURTR AND THE SONS OF MUSPELL?
DEATH TO SURTR!
DEATH TO SURTR!
DRINK, MY BROTHERS!
DRINK THE LIFE-GIVING ELIXIR OF HYBRID AFTERBIRTH, AND THE JOTUNS WILL GAIN UNTOLD STRENGTH AND VIGOR!

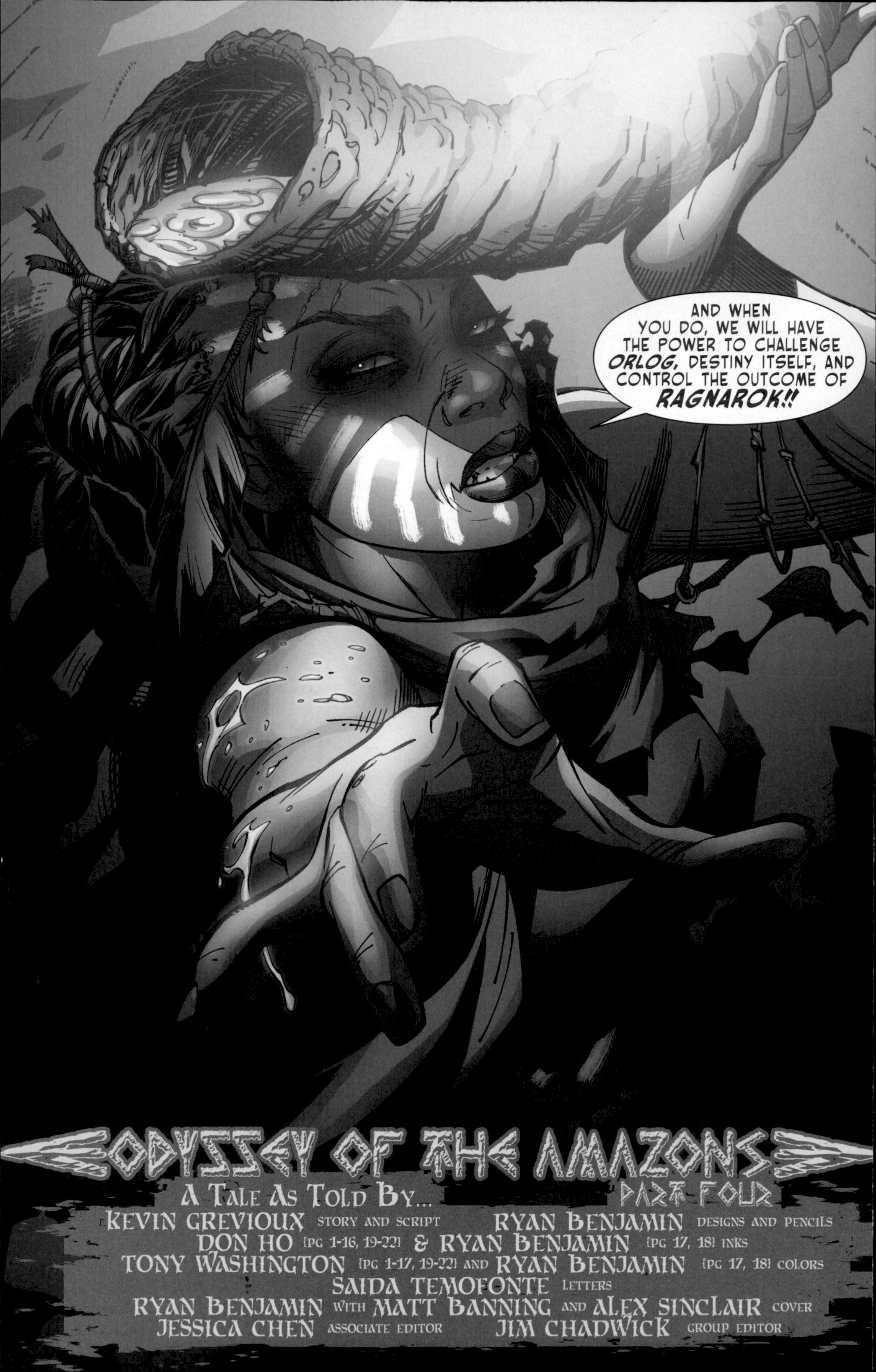
AND WHEN YOU DO, WE WILL HAVE THE POWER TO CHALLENGE ORLOG, DESTINY ITSELF, AND CONTROL THE OUTCOME OF RAGNAROK!!
ODYSSEY OF THE AMAZONS
PART FOUR
A TALE AS TOLD BY...
KEVIN GREVIOUX STORY AND SCRIPT RYAN BENJAMIN DESIGNS AND PENCILS
DON HO [PG 1-16, 19-22] & RYAN BENJAMIN [PG 17, 18] INKS
TONY WASHINGTON [PG 1-17, 19-22] AND RYAN BENJAMIN [PG 17, 18] COLORS
SAIDA TEMOFONTE LETTERS
RYAN BENJAMIN WITH MATT BANNING AND ALEX SINCLAIR COVER
JESSICA CHEN ASSOCIATE EDITOR JIM CHADWICK GROUP EDITOR

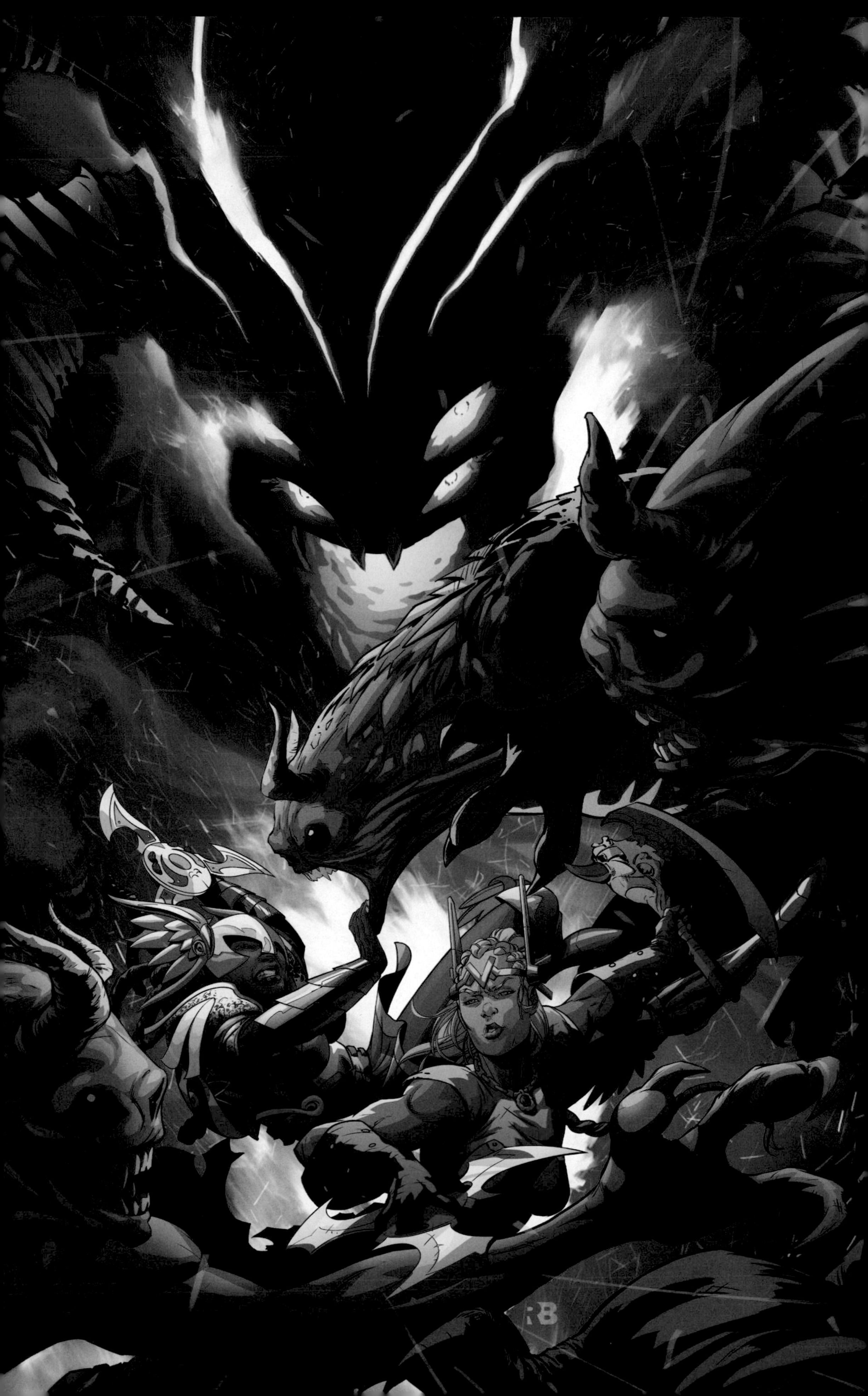

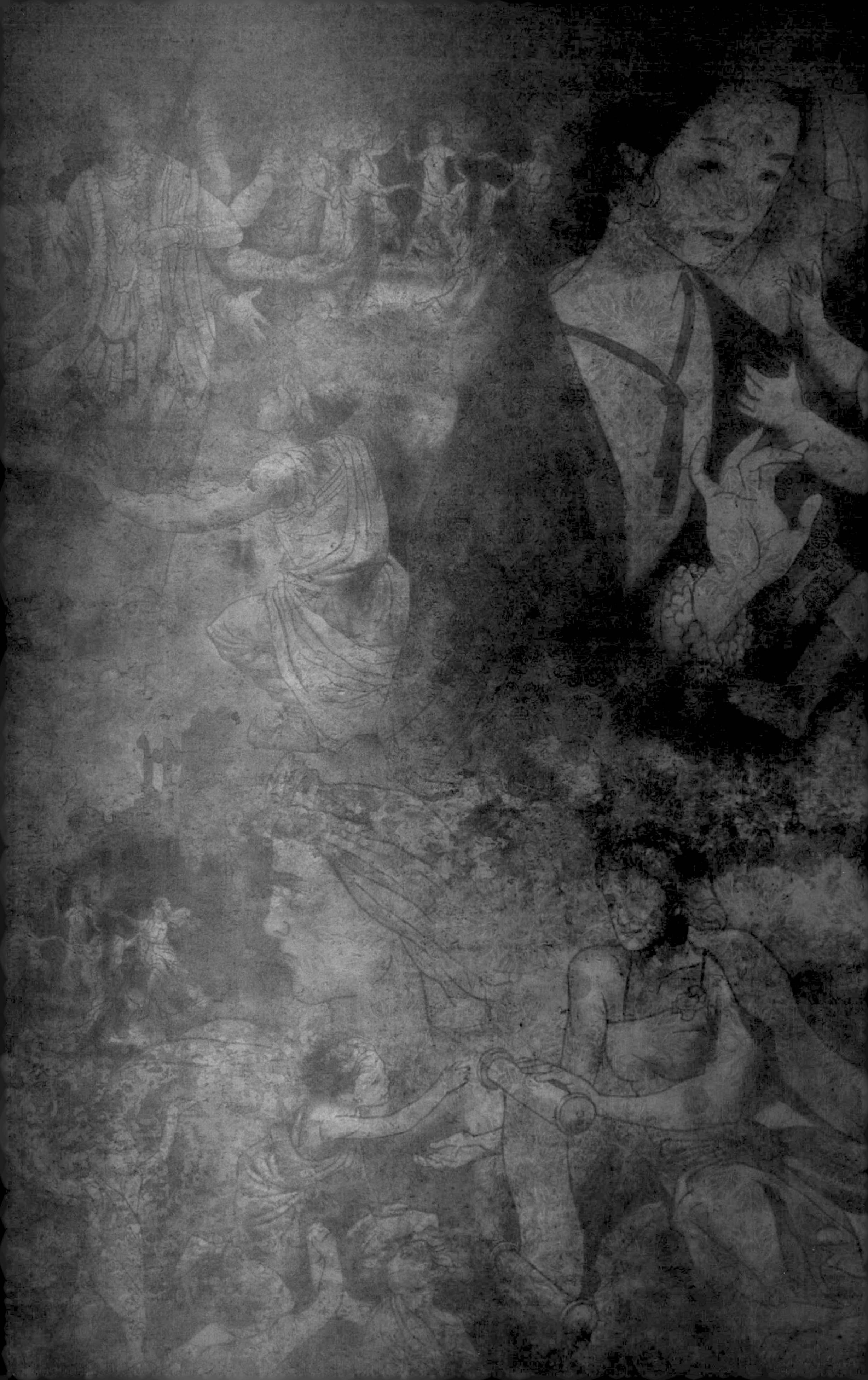

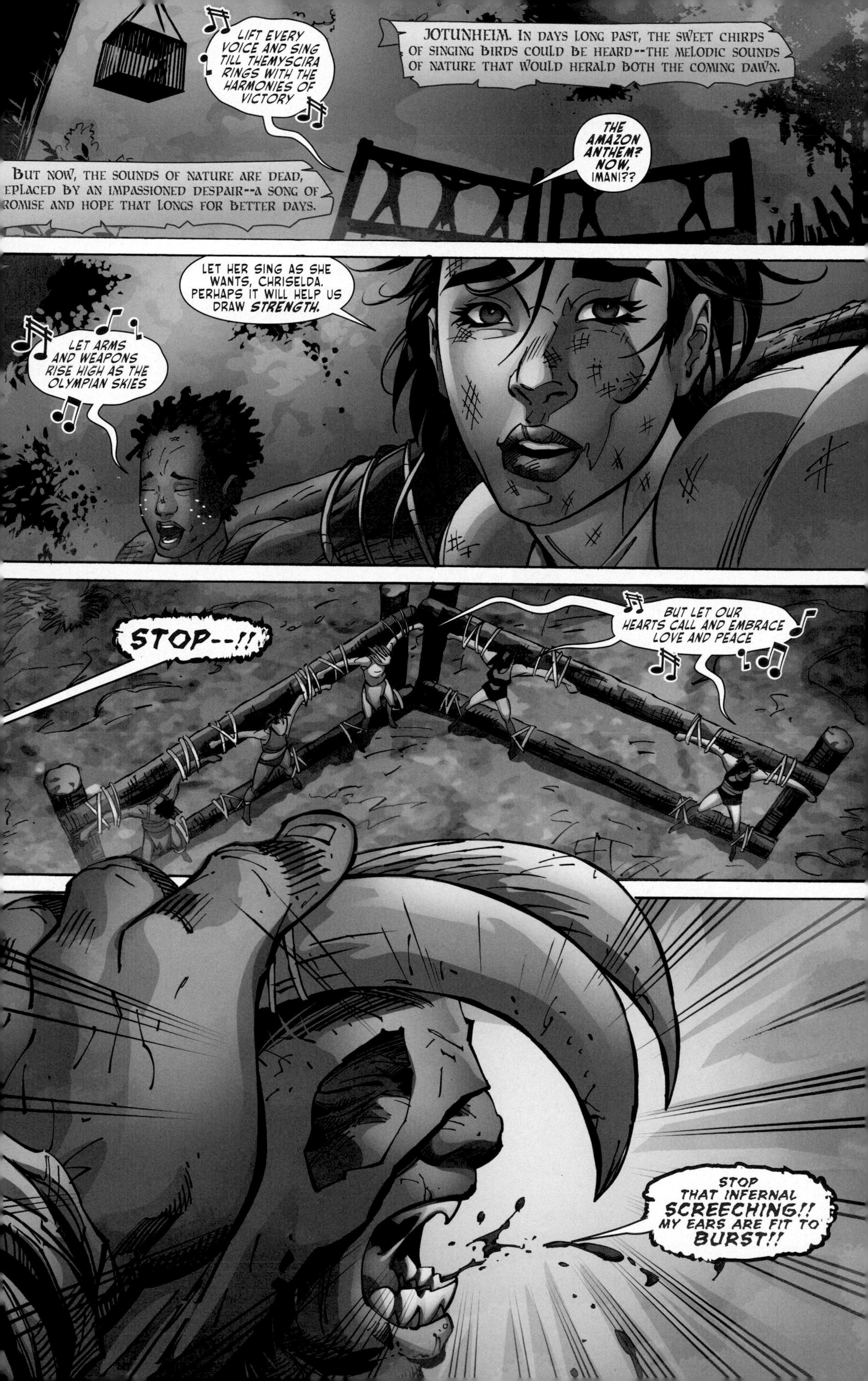
JOTUNHEIM. IN DAYS LONG PAST, THE SWEET CHIRPS OF SINGING BIRDS COULD BE HEARD--THE MELODIC SOUNDS OF NATURE THAT WOULD HERALD BOTH THE COMING DAWN.
LIFT EVERY VOICE AND SING TILL THEMYSCIRA RINGS WITH THE HARMONIES OF VICTORY
BUT NOW, THE SOUNDS OF NATURE ARE DEAD, EPLACED BY AN IMPASSIONED DESPAIR--A SONG OF ROMISE AND HOPE THAT LONGS FOR BETTER DAYS.
THE AMAZON ANTHEM? NOW, IMANI??
LET HER SING AS SHE WANTS, CHRISELDA. PERHAPS IT WILL HELP US DRAW STRENGTH.
LET ARMS AND WEAPONS RISE HIGH AS THE OLYMPIAN SKIES
STOP--!!
BUT LET OUR HEARTS CALL AND EMBRACE LOVE AND PEACE
STOP THAT INFERNAL SCREECHING!! MY EARS ARE FIT TO BURST!!

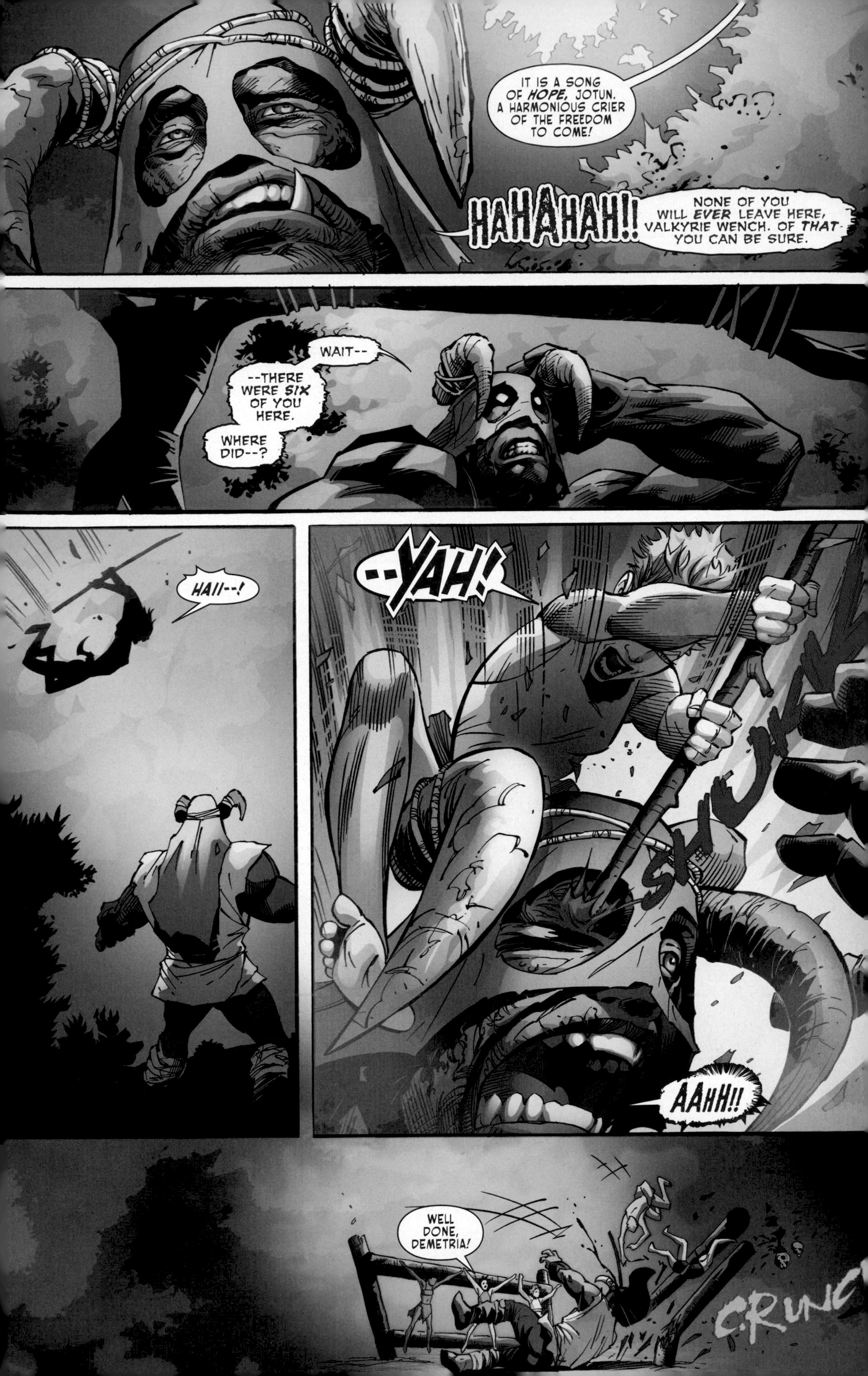

IT IS A SONG OF HOPE, JOTUN. A HARMONIOUS CRIER OF THE FREEDOM TO COME!
HAHAHAH!!
NONE OF YOU WILL EVER LEAVE HERE, VALKYRIE WENCH. OF THAT YOU CAN BE SURE.
WAIT--
--THERE WERE SIX OF YOU HERE.
WHERE DID--?
HAII--!
--YAH!
SHUNK
AAHH!!
WELL DONE, DEMETRIA!
CRUNC

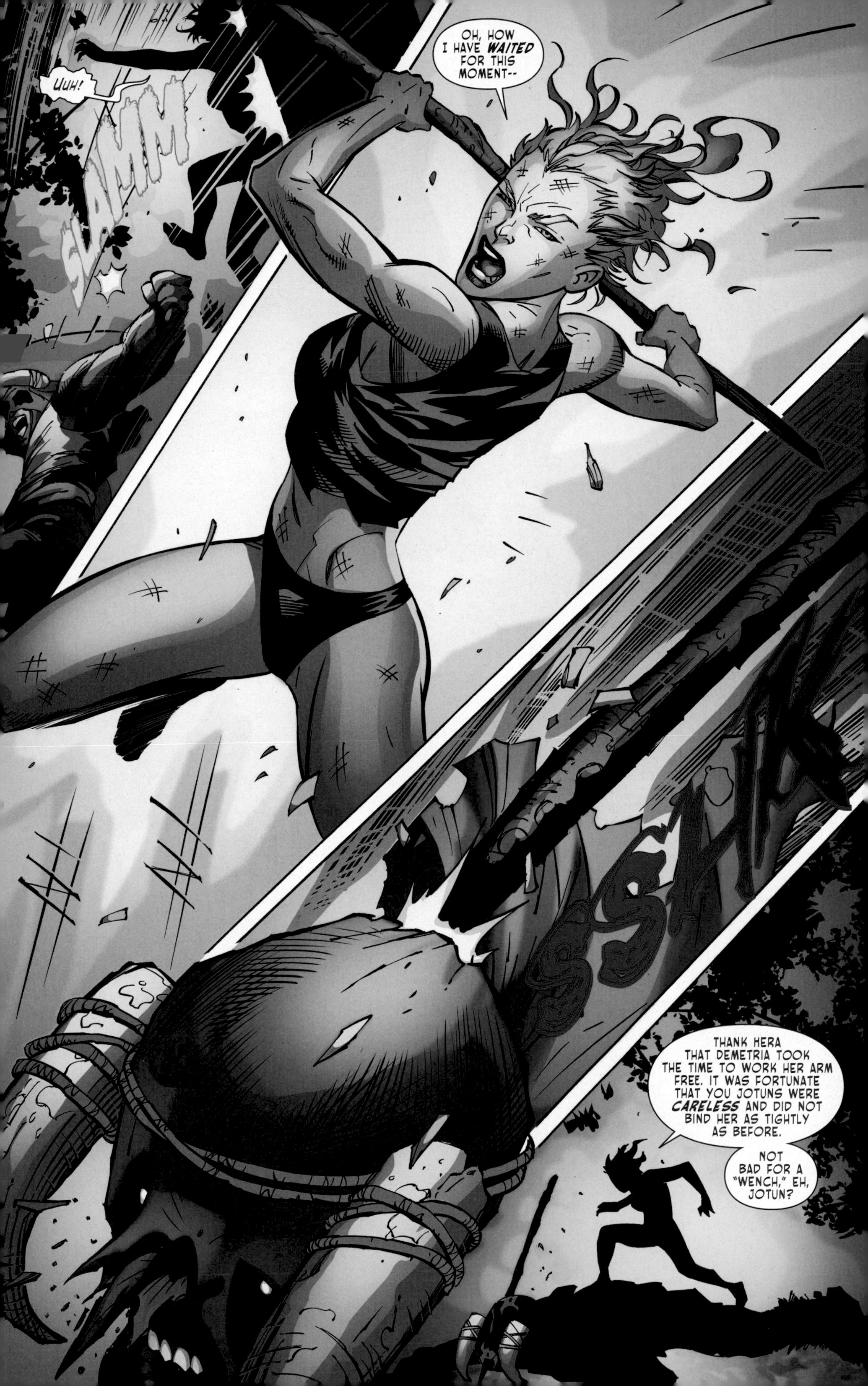
UUH!
SLAMM
OH, HOW I HAVE WAITED FOR THIS MOMENT--
THANK HERA THAT DEMETRIA TOOK THE TIME TO WORK HER ARM FREE. IT WAS FORTUNATE THAT YOU JOTUNS WERE CARELESS AND DID NOT BIND HER AS TIGHTLY AS BEFORE.
NOT BAD FOR A "WENCH," EH, JOTUN?

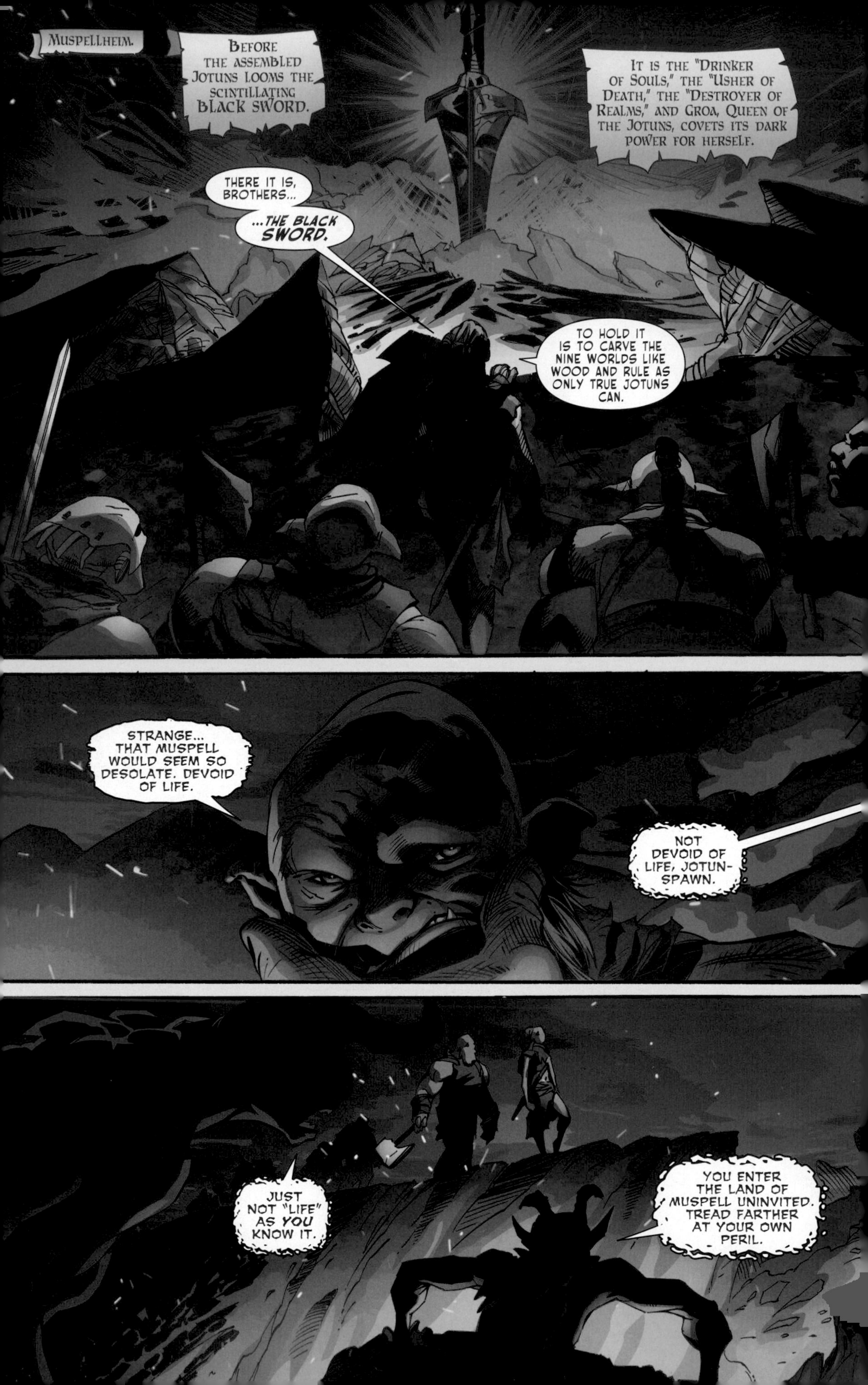
MUSPELLHEIM.
BEFORE THE ASSEMBLED JOTUNS LOOMS THE SCINTILLATING BLACK SWORD.
IT IS THE "DRINKER OF SOULS," THE "USHER OF DEATH," THE "DESTROYER OF REALMS," AND GROA, QUEEN OF THE JOTUNS, COVETS ITS DARK POWER FOR HERSELF.
THERE IT IS, BROTHERS...
...THE BLACK SWORD.
TO HOLD IT IS TO CARVE THE NINE WORLDS LIKE WOOD AND RULE AS ONLY TRUE JOTUNS CAN.
STRANGE... THAT MUSPELL WOULD SEEM SO DESOLATE. DEVOID OF LIFE.
NOT DEVOID OF LIFE, JOTUN-SPAWN.
JUST NOT "LIFE" AS YOU KNOW IT.
YOU ENTER THE LAND OF MUSPELL UNINVITED. TREAD FARTHER AT YOUR OWN PERIL.

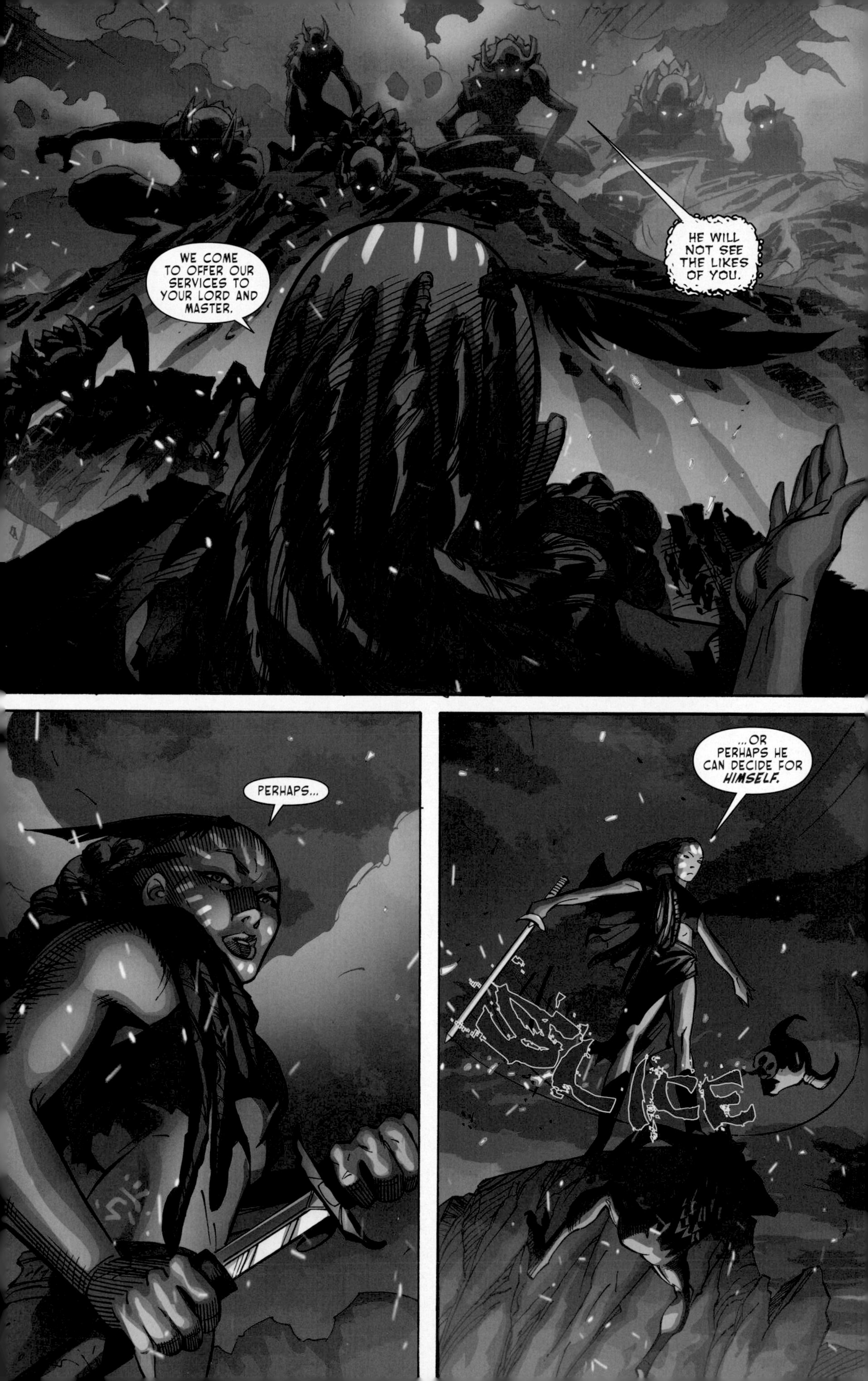
WE COME TO OFFER OUR SERVICES TO YOUR LORD AND MASTER.
HE WILL NOT SEE THE LIKES OF YOU.
PERHAPS...
...OR PERHAPS HE CAN DECIDE FOR HIMSELF.
SLICE

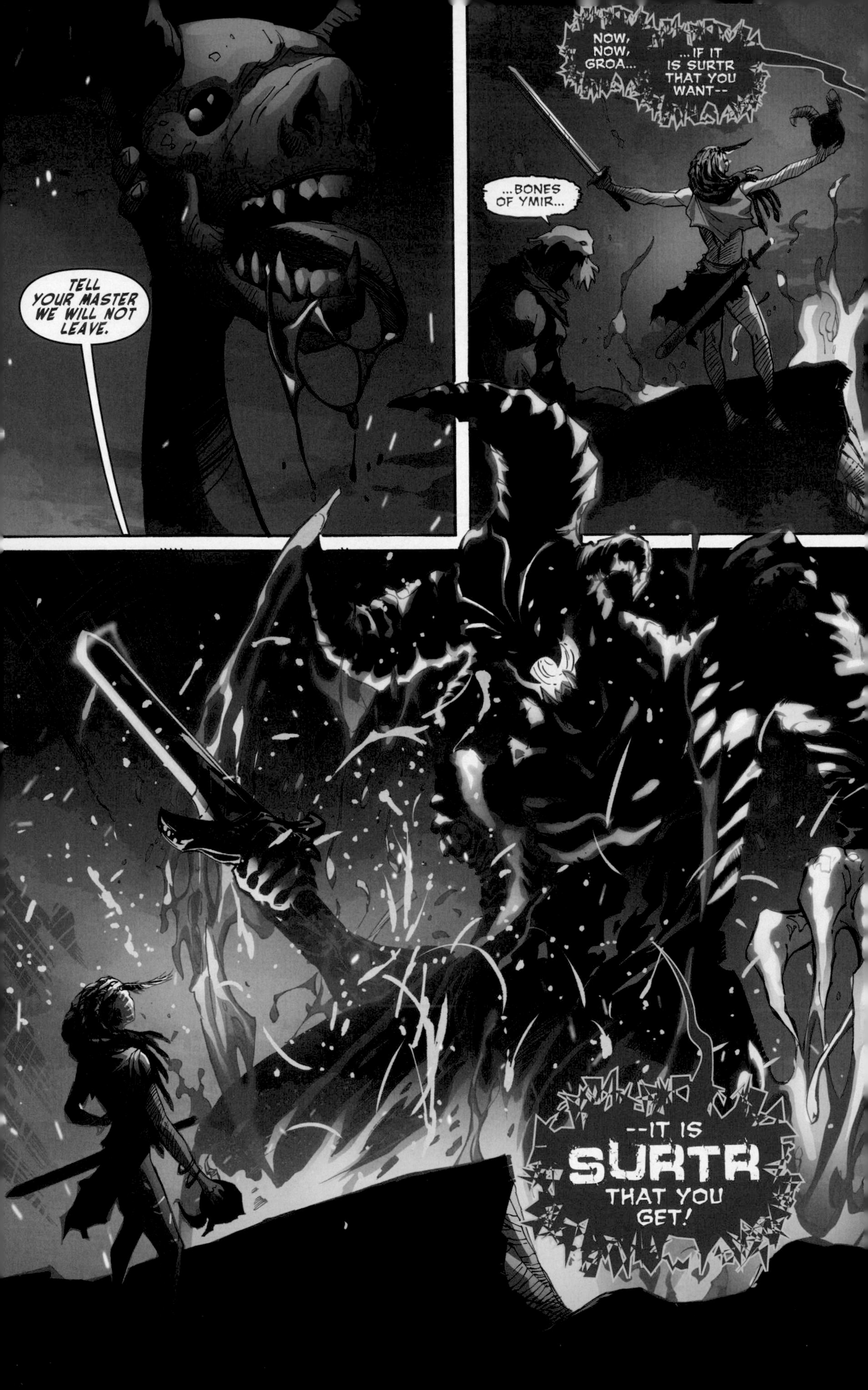
TELL YOUR MASTER WE WILL NOT LEAVE.
NOW, NOW, GROA...
...IF IT IS SURTR THAT YOU WANT--
...BONES OF YMIR...
--IT IS SURTR THAT YOU GET!

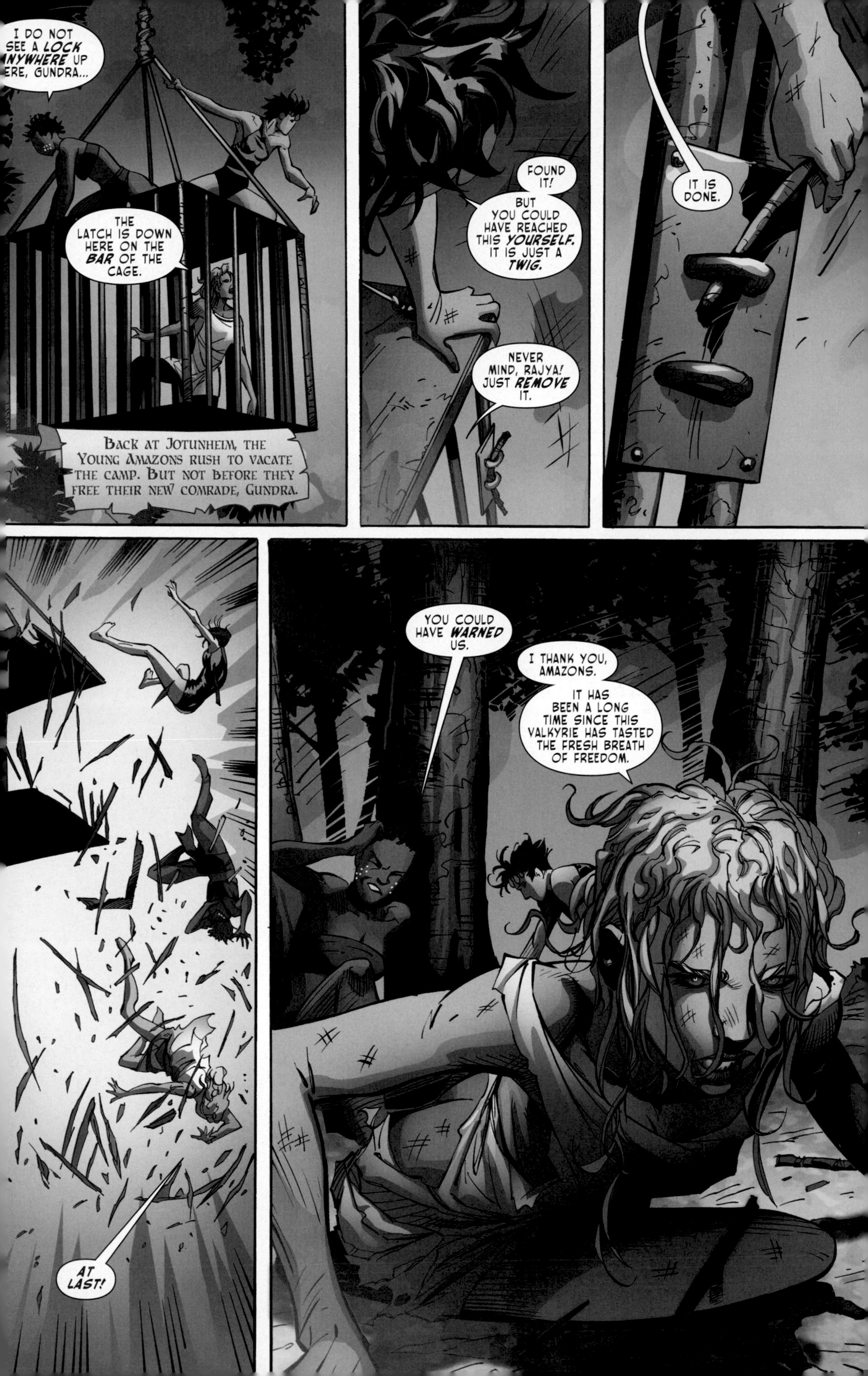
I DO NOT SEE A LOCK ANYWHERE UP HERE, GUNDRA...
THE LATCH IS DOWN HERE ON THE BAR OF THE CAGE.
BACK AT JOTUNHEIM, THE YOUNG AMAZONS RUSH TO VACATE THE CAMP. BUT NOT BEFORE THEY FREE THEIR NEW COMRADE, GUNDRA.
FOUND IT!
BUT YOU COULD HAVE REACHED THIS YOURSELF. IT IS JUST A TWIG.
NEVER MIND, RAJYA! JUST REMOVE IT.
IT IS DONE.
AT LAST!
YOU COULD HAVE WARNED US.
I THANK YOU, AMAZONS.
IT HAS BEEN A LONG TIME SINCE THIS VALKYRIE HAS TASTED THE FRESH BREATH OF FREEDOM.

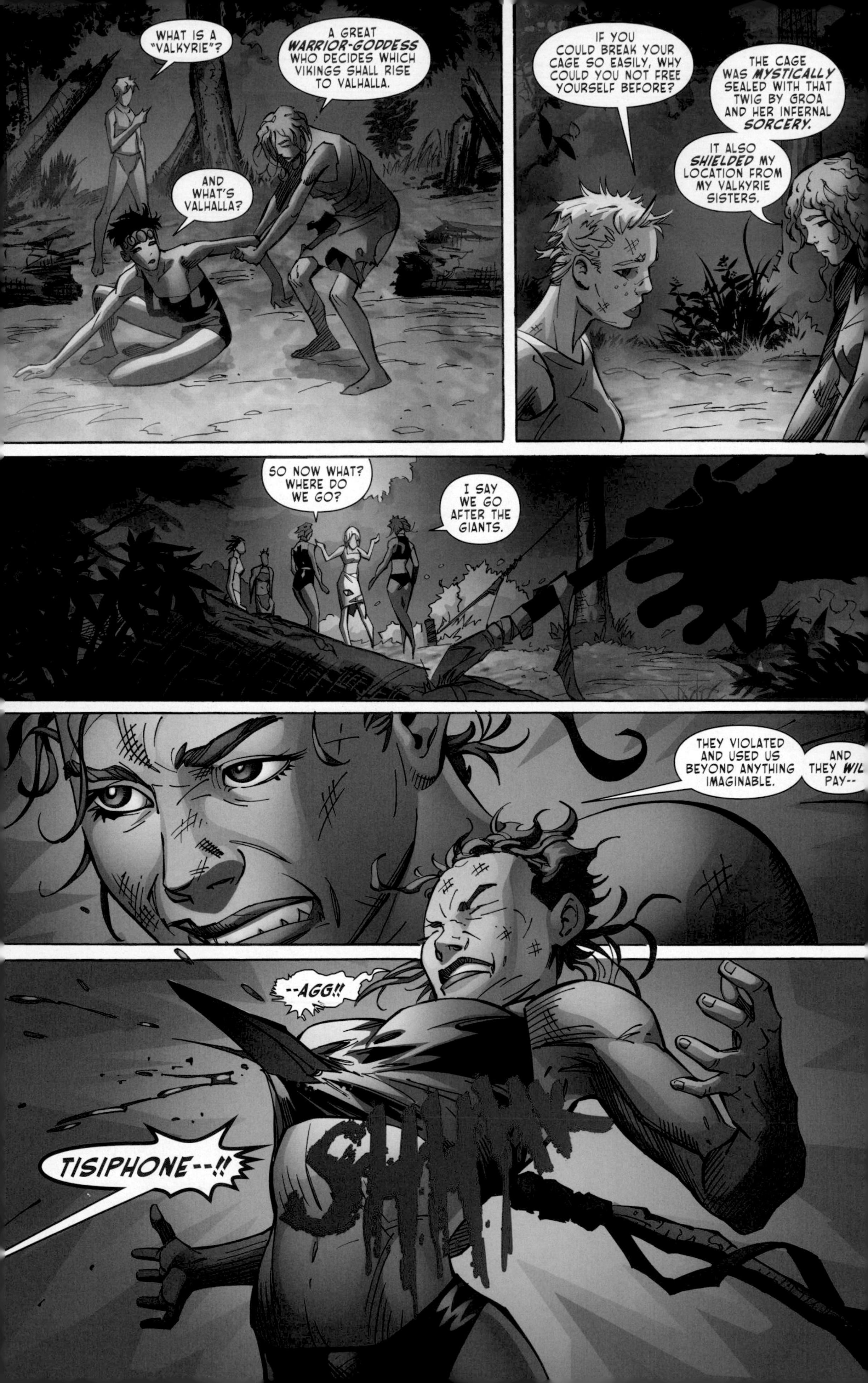
WHAT IS A "VALKYRIE"?
A GREAT WARRIOR-GODDESS WHO DECIDES WHICH VIKINGS SHALL RISE TO VALHALLA.
AND WHAT'S VALHALLA?
IF YOU COULD BREAK YOUR CAGE SO EASILY, WHY COULD YOU NOT FREE YOURSELF BEFORE?
THE CAGE WAS MYSTICALLY SEALED WITH THAT TWIG BY GROA AND HER INFERNAL SORCERY.
IT ALSO SHIELDED MY LOCATION FROM MY VALKYRIE SISTERS.
SO NOW WHAT? WHERE DO WE GO?
I SAY WE GO AFTER THE GIANTS.
THEY VIOLATED AND USED US BEYOND ANYTHING IMAGINABLE.
AND THEY WIL PAY--
--AGG!!
TISIPHONE--!!
SHHNK

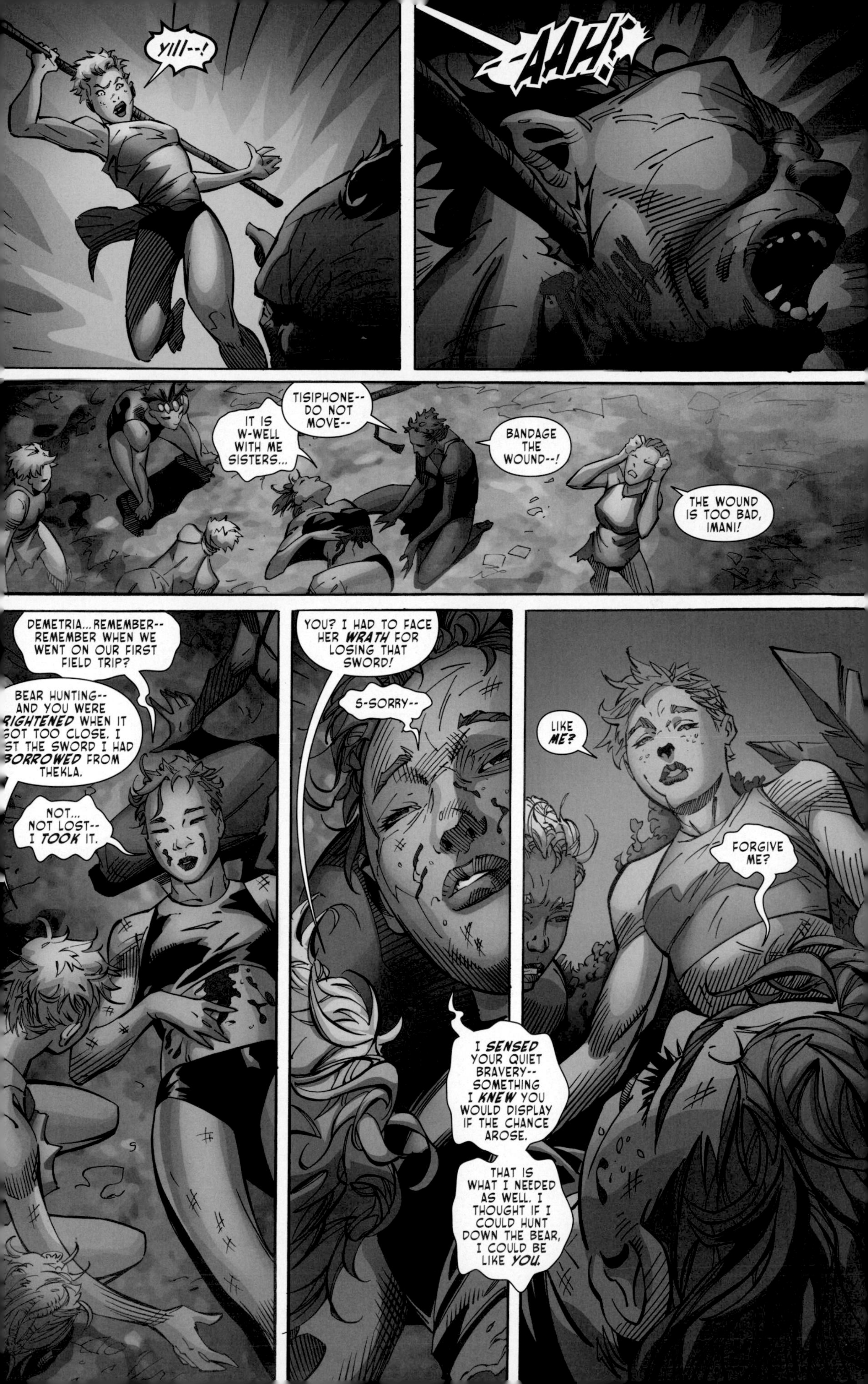
YIII--!
-AAH!
IT IS W-WELL WITH ME SISTERS...
TISIPHONE-- DO NOT MOVE--
BANDAGE THE WOUND--!
THE WOUND IS TOO BAD, IMANI!
DEMETRIA...REMEMBER-- REMEMBER WHEN WE WENT ON OUR FIRST FIELD TRIP?
BEAR HUNTING-- AND YOU WERE FRIGHTENED WHEN IT GOT TOO CLOSE. I LOST THE SWORD I HAD BORROWED FROM THEKLA.
NOT... NOT LOST-- I TOOK IT.
YOU? I HAD TO FACE HER WRATH FOR LOSING THAT SWORD!
S-SORRY--
I SENSED YOUR QUIET BRAVERY-- SOMETHING I KNEW YOU WOULD DISPLAY IF THE CHANCE AROSE.
THAT IS WHAT I NEEDED AS WELL. I THOUGHT IF I COULD HUNT DOWN THE BEAR, I COULD BE LIKE YOU.
LIKE ME?
FORGIVE ME?

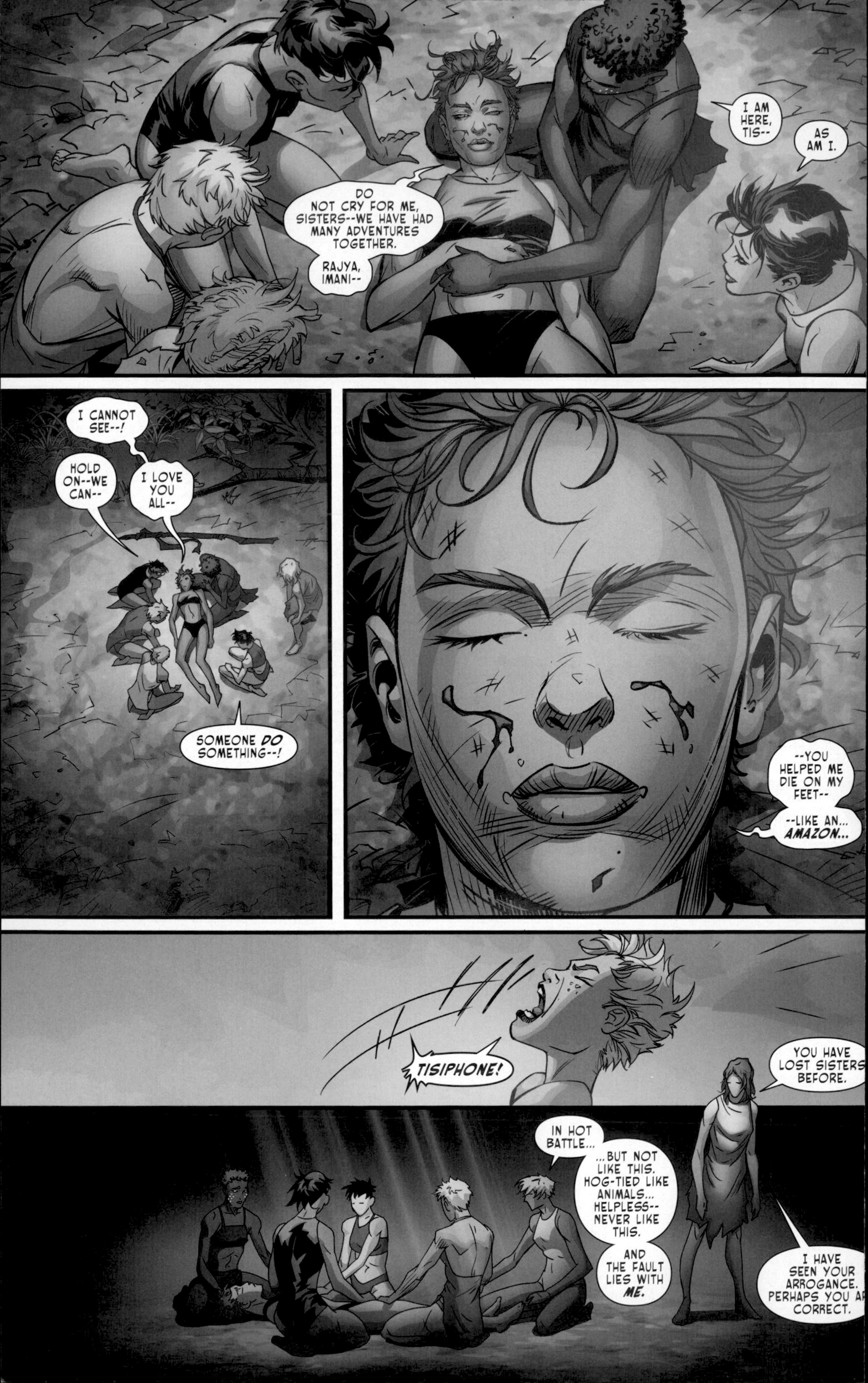
DO NOT CRY FOR ME, SISTERS--WE HAVE HAD MANY ADVENTURES TOGETHER.
RAJYA, IMANI--
I AM HERE, TIS--
AS AM I.
I CANNOT SEE--!
HOLD ON--WE CAN--
I LOVE YOU ALL--
SOMEONE DO SOMETHING--!
--YOU HELPED ME DIE ON MY FEET--
--LIKE AN... AMAZON...
TISIPHONE!
YOU HAVE LOST SISTERS BEFORE.
IN HOT BATTLE...
...BUT NOT LIKE THIS. HOG-TIED LIKE ANIMALS... HELPLESS--NEVER LIKE THIS.
AND THE FAULT LIES WITH ME.
I HAVE SEEN YOUR ARROGANCE. PERHAPS YOU AR CORRECT.

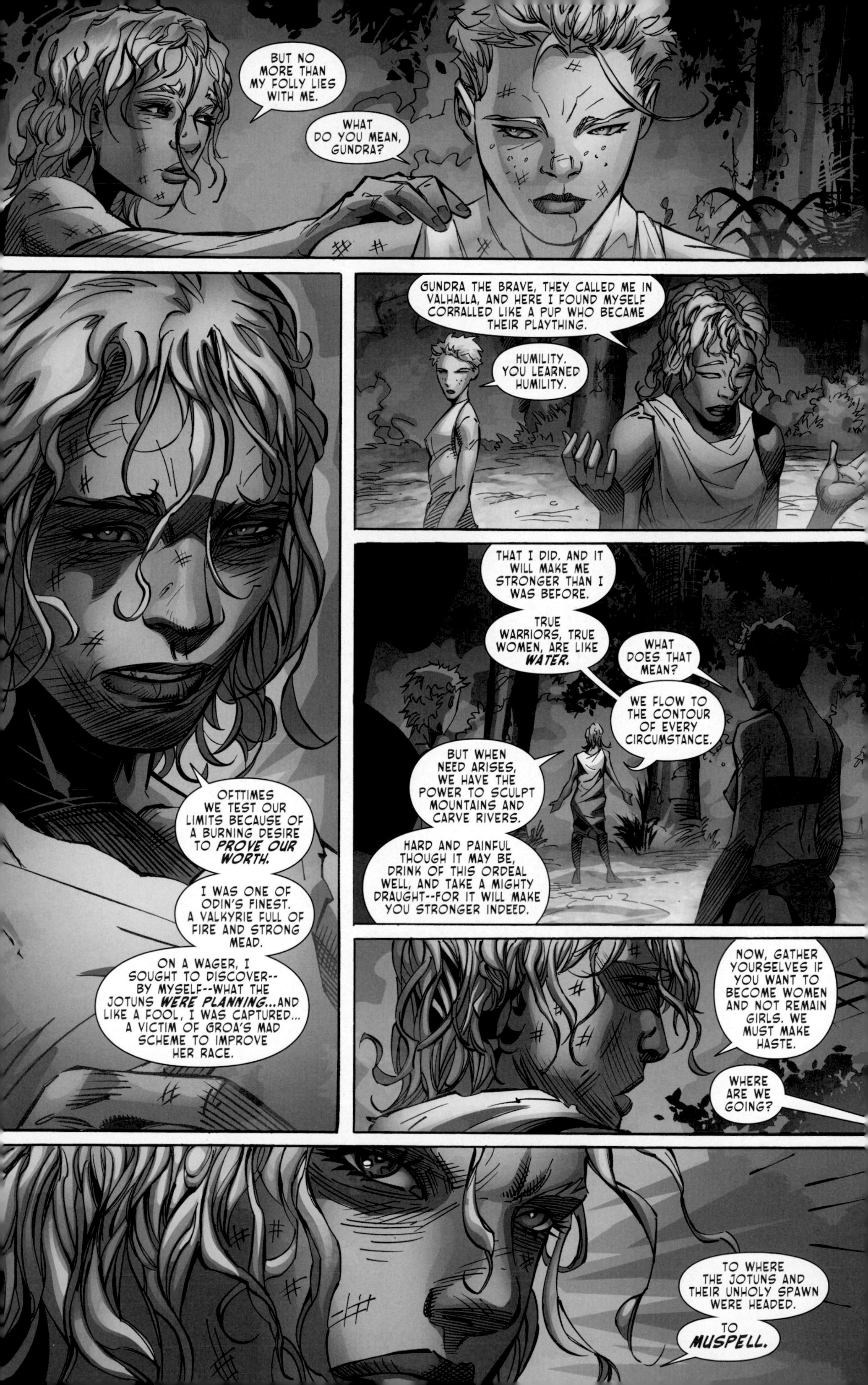
BUT NO MORE THAN MY FOLLY LIES WITH ME.
WHAT DO YOU MEAN, GUNDRA?
OFTTIMES WE TEST OUR LIMITS BECAUSE OF A BURNING DESIRE TO PROVE OUR WORTH.
I WAS ONE OF ODIN'S FINEST. A VALKYRIE FULL OF FIRE AND STRONG MEAD.
ON A WAGER, I SOUGHT TO DISCOVER-- BY MYSELF--WHAT THE JOTUNS WERE PLANNING...AND LIKE A FOOL, I WAS CAPTURED... A VICTIM OF GROA'S MAD SCHEME TO IMPROVE HER RACE.
GUNDRA THE BRAVE, THEY CALLED ME IN VALHALLA, AND HERE I FOUND MYSELF CORRALLED LIKE A PUP WHO BECAME THEIR PLAYTHING.
HUMILITY. YOU LEARNED HUMILITY.
THAT I DID. AND IT WILL MAKE ME STRONGER THAN I WAS BEFORE.
TRUE WARRIORS, TRUE WOMEN, ARE LIKE WATER.
WHAT DOES THAT MEAN?
WE FLOW TO THE CONTOUR OF EVERY CIRCUMSTANCE.
BUT WHEN NEED ARISES, WE HAVE THE POWER TO SCULPT MOUNTAINS AND CARVE RIVERS.
HARD AND PAINFUL THOUGH IT MAY BE, DRINK OF THIS ORDEAL WELL, AND TAKE A MIGHTY DRAUGHT--FOR IT WILL MAKE YOU STRONGER INDEED.
NOW, GATHER YOURSELVES IF YOU WANT TO BECOME WOMEN AND NOT REMAIN GIRLS. WE MUST MAKE HASTE.
WHERE ARE WE GOING?
TO WHERE THE JOTUNS AND THEIR UNHOLY SPAWN WERE HEADED.
TO MUSPELL.

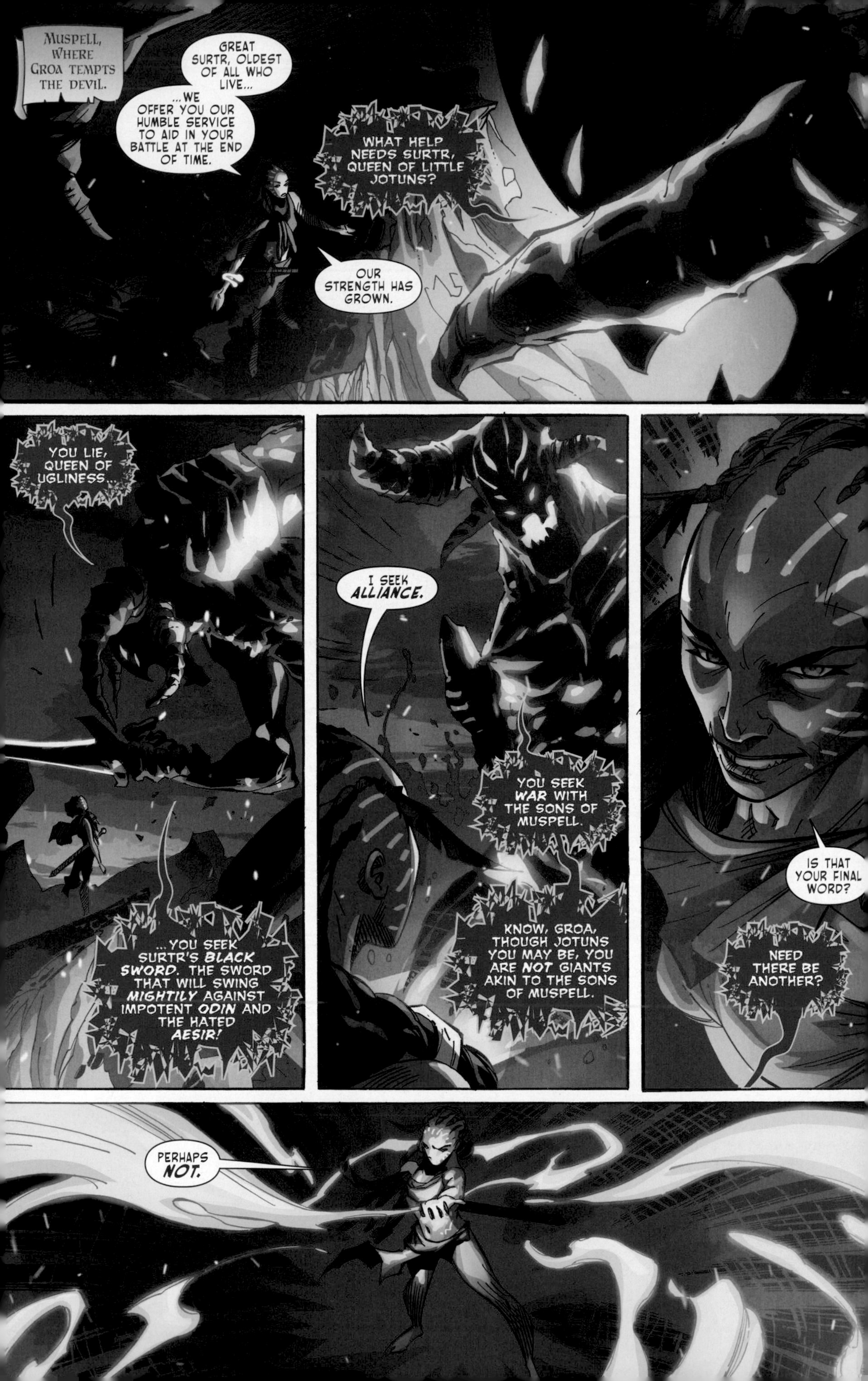
MUSPELL, WHERE GROA TEMPTS THE DEVIL.
GREAT SURTR, OLDEST OF ALL WHO LIVE...
...WE OFFER YOU OUR HUMBLE SERVICE TO AID IN YOUR BATTLE AT THE END OF TIME.
WHAT HELP NEEDS SURTR, QUEEN OF LITTLE JOTUNS?
OUR STRENGTH HAS GROWN.
YOU LIE, QUEEN OF UGLINESS...
...YOU SEEK SURTR'S BLACK SWORD. THE SWORD THAT WILL SWING MIGHTILY AGAINST IMPOTENT ODIN AND THE HATED AESIR!
I SEEK ALLIANCE.
YOU SEEK WAR WITH THE SONS OF MUSPELL.
KNOW, GROA, THOUGH JOTUNS YOU MAY BE, YOU ARE NOT GIANTS AKIN TO THE SONS OF MUSPELL.
IS THAT YOUR FINAL WORD?
NEED THERE BE ANOTHER?
PERHAPS NOT.

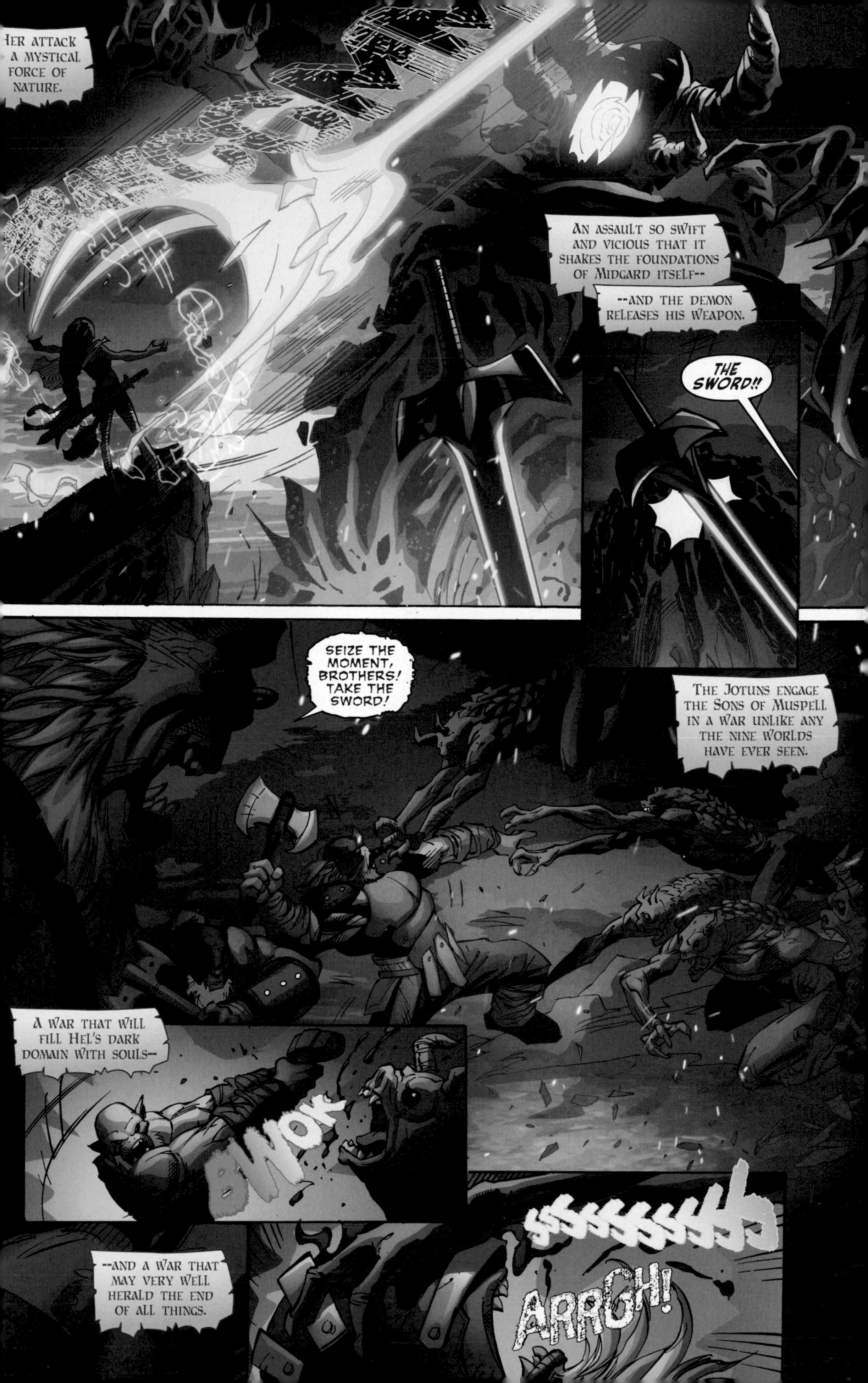
HER ATTACK A MYSTICAL FORCE OF NATURE.
AN ASSAULT SO SWIFT AND VICIOUS THAT IT SHAKES THE FOUNDATIONS OF MIDGARD ITSELF--
--AND THE DEMON RELEASES HIS WEAPON.
THE SWORD!!
SEIZE THE MOMENT, BROTHERS! TAKE THE SWORD!
THE JOTUNS ENGAGE THE SONS OF MUSPELL IN A WAR UNLIKE ANY THE NINE WORLDS HAVE EVER SEEN.
A WAR THAT WILL FILL HEL'S DARK DOMAIN WITH SOULS--
WOK
--AND A WAR THAT MAY VERY WELL HERALD THE END OF ALL THINGS.
ARRGH!

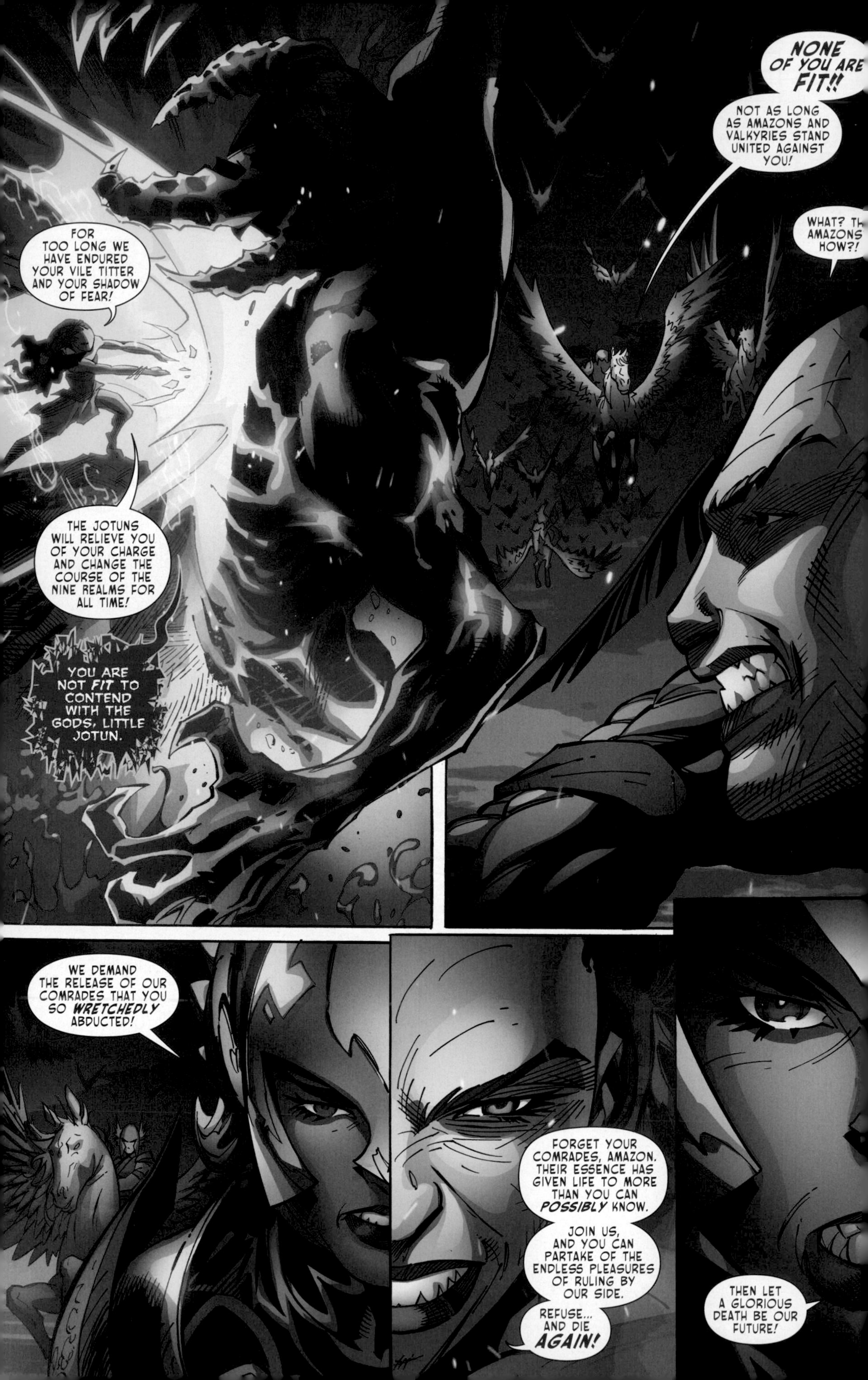
FOR TOO LONG WE HAVE ENDURED YOUR VILE TITTER AND YOUR SHADOW OF FEAR!
THE JOTUNS WILL RELIEVE YOU OF YOUR CHARGE AND CHANGE THE COURSE OF THE NINE REALMS FOR ALL TIME!
YOU ARE NOT FIT TO CONTEND WITH THE GODS, LITTLE JOTUN.
NONE OF YOU ARE FIT!!
NOT AS LONG AS AMAZONS AND VALKYRIES STAND UNITED AGAINST YOU!
WHAT? TH AMAZONS HOW?!
WE DEMAND THE RELEASE OF OUR COMRADES THAT YOU SO WRETCHEDLY ABDUCTED!
FORGET YOUR COMRADES, AMAZON. THEIR ESSENCE HAS GIVEN LIFE TO MORE THAN YOU CAN POSSIBLY KNOW.
JOIN US, AND YOU CAN PARTAKE OF THE ENDLESS PLEASURES OF RULING BY OUR SIDE.
REFUSE... AND DIE AGAIN!
THEN LET A GLORIOUS DEATH BE OUR FUTURE!

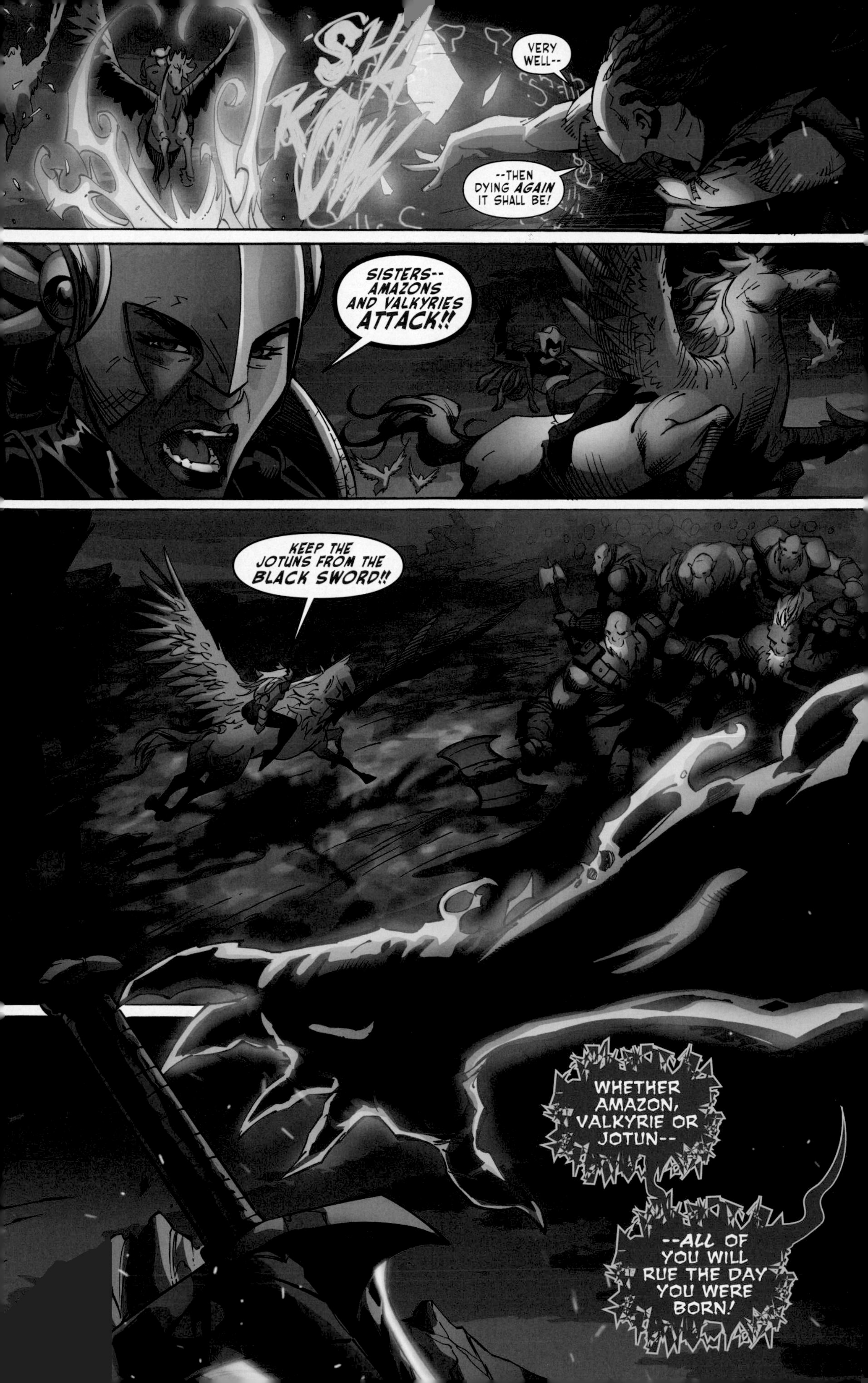
SHA KOW
VERY WELL--
--THEN DYING AGAIN IT SHALL BE!
SISTERS-- AMAZONS AND VALKYRIES ATTACK!!
KEEP THE JOTUNS FROM THE BLACK SWORD!!
WHETHER AMAZON, VALKYRIE OR JOTUN--
--ALL OF YOU WILL RUE THE DAY YOU WERE BORN!

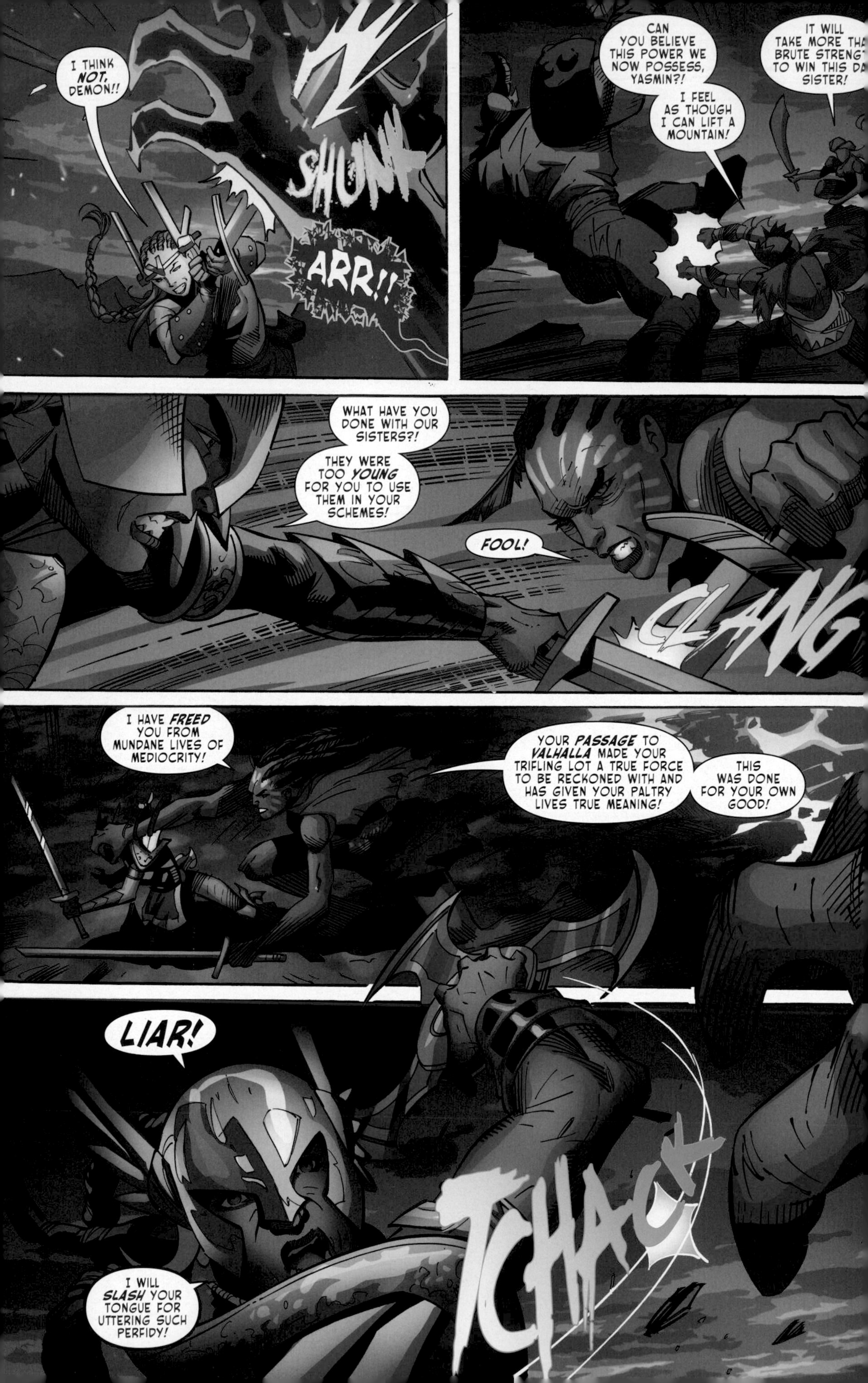
I THINK *NOT,* DEMON!!
SHUNK
ARR!!
CAN YOU BELIEVE THIS POWER WE NOW POSSESS, YASMIN?!
I FEEL AS THOUGH I CAN LIFT A MOUNTAIN!
IT WILL TAKE MORE THA BRUTE STRENGT TO WIN THIS DA SISTER!
WHAT HAVE YOU DONE WITH OUR SISTERS?!
THEY WERE TOO *YOUNG* FOR YOU TO USE THEM IN YOUR SCHEMES!
FOOL!
CLANG
I HAVE *FREED* YOU FROM MUNDANE LIVES OF MEDIOCRITY!
YOUR *PASSAGE* TO *VALHALLA* MADE YOUR TRIFLING LOT A TRUE FORCE TO BE RECKONED WITH AND HAS GIVEN YOUR PALTRY LIVES TRUE MEANING!
THIS WAS DONE FOR YOUR OWN GOOD!
LIAR!
I WILL *SLASH* YOUR TONGUE FOR UTTERING SUCH PERFIDY!
TCHACK

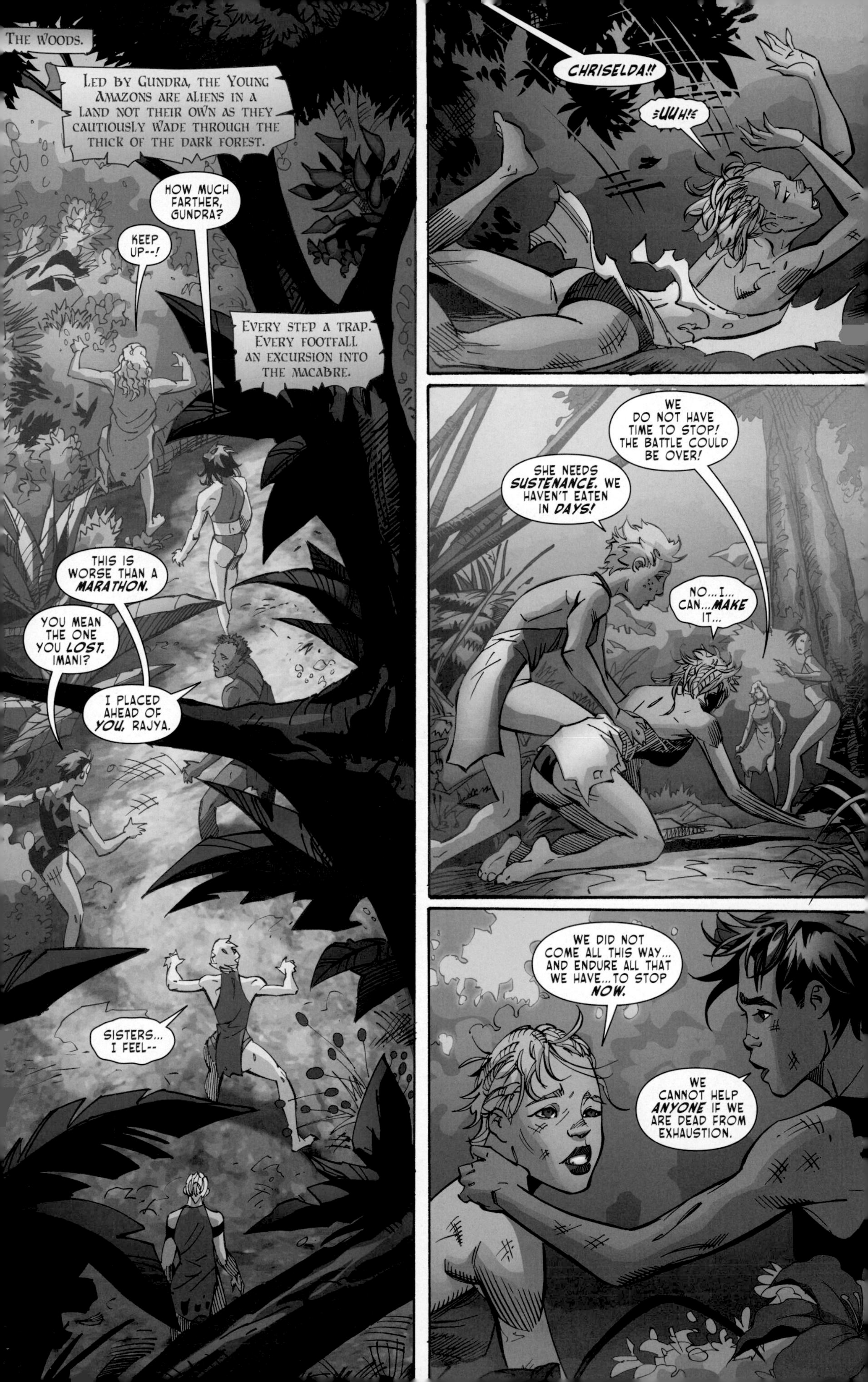
THE WOODS.
LED BY GUNDRA, THE YOUNG AMAZONS ARE ALIENS IN A LAND NOT THEIR OWN AS THEY CAUTIOUSLY WADE THROUGH THE THICK OF THE DARK FOREST.
HOW MUCH FARTHER, GUNDRA?
KEEP UP--!
EVERY STEP A TRAP. EVERY FOOTFALL AN EXCURSION INTO THE MACABRE.
THIS IS WORSE THAN A MARATHON.
YOU MEAN THE ONE YOU LOST, IMANI?
I PLACED AHEAD OF YOU, RAJYA.
SISTERS... I FEEL--
CHRISELDA!!
UUH!
SHE NEEDS SUSTENANCE. WE HAVEN'T EATEN IN DAYS!
WE DO NOT HAVE TIME TO STOP! THE BATTLE COULD BE OVER!
NO...I... CAN...MAKE IT...
WE DID NOT COME ALL THIS WAY... AND ENDURE ALL THAT WE HAVE...TO STOP NOW.
WE CANNOT HELP ANYONE IF WE ARE DEAD FROM EXHAUSTION.

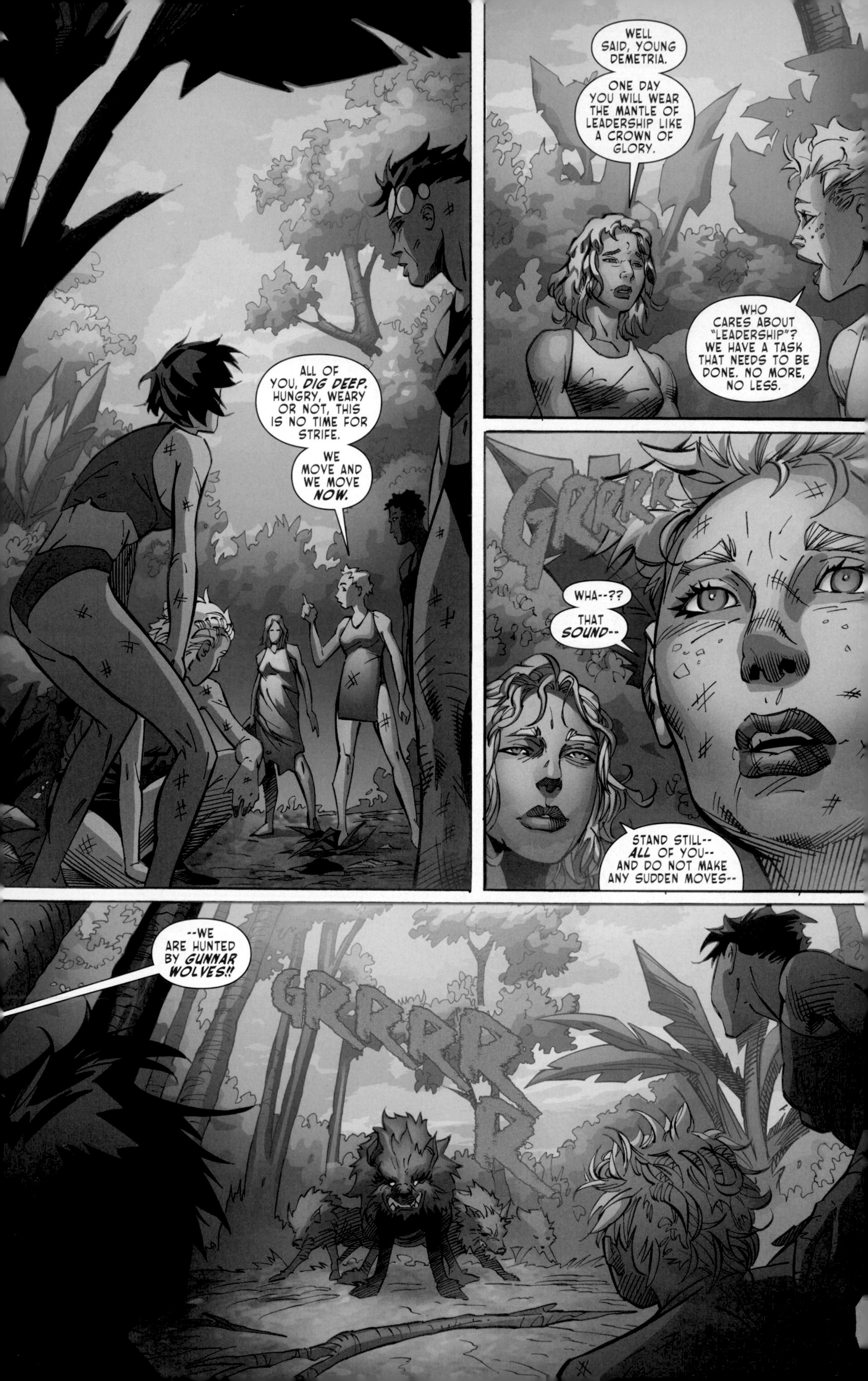
ALL OF YOU, DIG DEEP. HUNGRY, WEARY OR NOT, THIS IS NO TIME FOR STRIFE.
WE MOVE AND WE MOVE NOW.
WELL SAID, YOUNG DEMETRIA.
ONE DAY YOU WILL WEAR THE MANTLE OF LEADERSHIP LIKE A CROWN OF GLORY.
WHO CARES ABOUT "LEADERSHIP"? WE HAVE A TASK THAT NEEDS TO BE DONE. NO MORE, NO LESS.
GRRRR
WHA--??
THAT SOUND--
STAND STILL--ALL OF YOU--AND DO NOT MAKE ANY SUDDEN MOVES--
--WE ARE HUNTED BY GUNNAR WOLVES!!
GRRRRR

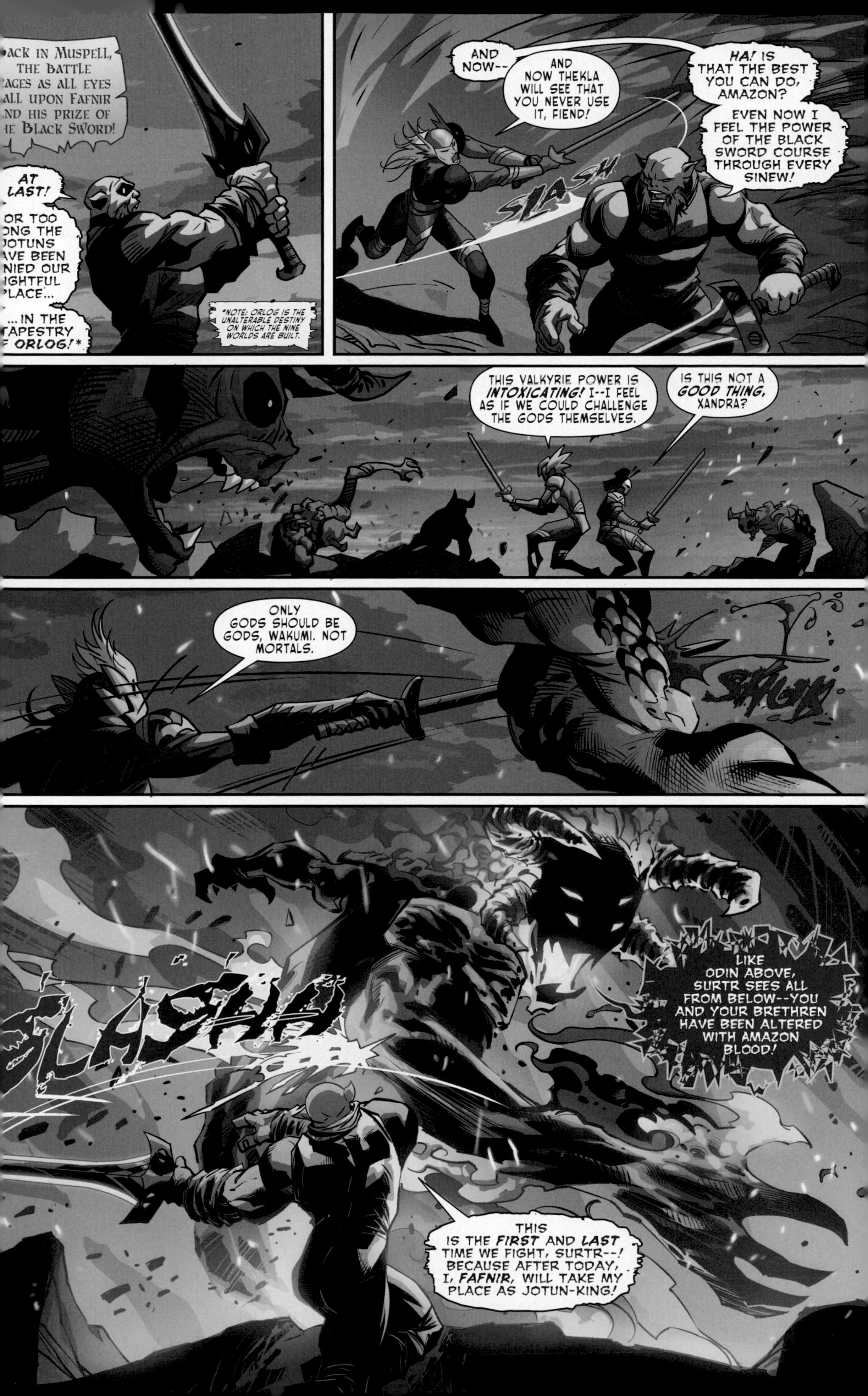

BACK IN MUSPELL, THE BATTLE RAGES AS ALL EYES FALL UPON FAFNIR AND HIS PRIZE OF THE BLACK SWORD!
AT LAST!
FOR TOO LONG THE JOTUNS HAVE BEEN DENIED OUR RIGHTFUL PLACE...
...IN THE TAPESTRY OF ORLOG!*
*NOTE: ORLOG IS THE UNALTERABLE DESTINY ON WHICH THE NINE WORLDS ARE BUILT.
AND NOW--
AND NOW THEKLA WILL SEE THAT YOU NEVER USE IT, FIEND!
SLASH
HA! IS THAT THE BEST YOU CAN DO, AMAZON?
EVEN NOW I FEEL THE POWER OF THE BLACK SWORD COURSE THROUGH EVERY SINEW!
THIS VALKYRIE POWER IS INTOXICATING! I--I FEEL AS IF WE COULD CHALLENGE THE GODS THEMSELVES.
IS THIS NOT A GOOD THING, XANDRA?
ONLY GODS SHOULD BE GODS, WAKUMI. NOT MORTALS.
SHUNK
SLASHH
LIKE ODIN ABOVE, SURTR SEES ALL FROM BELOW--YOU AND YOUR BRETHREN HAVE BEEN ALTERED WITH AMAZON BLOOD!
THIS IS THE FIRST AND LAST TIME WE FIGHT, SURTR--! BECAUSE AFTER TODAY, I, FAFNIR, WILL TAKE MY PLACE AS JOTUN-KING!

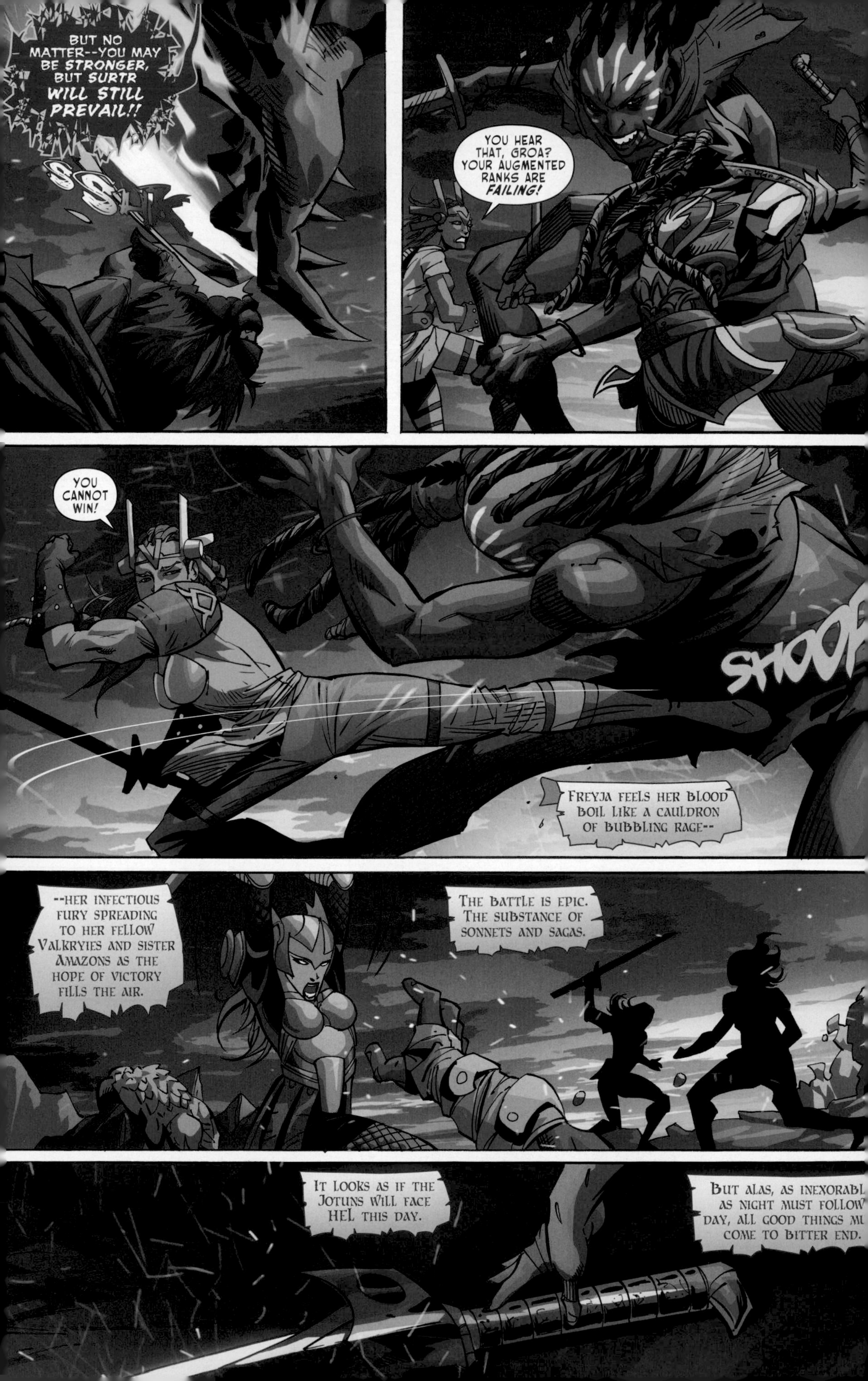
BUT NO MATTER--YOU MAY BE STRONGER, BUT SURTR WILL STILL PREVAIL!!
YOU HEAR THAT, GROA? YOUR AUGMENTED RANKS ARE FAILING!
YOU CANNOT WIN!
SHOOP
FREYJA FEELS HER BLOOD BOIL LIKE A CAULDRON OF BUBBLING RAGE--
--HER INFECTIOUS FURY SPREADING TO HER FELLOW VALKRYIES AND SISTER AMAZONS AS THE HOPE OF VICTORY FILLS THE AIR.
THE BATTLE IS EPIC. THE SUBSTANCE OF SONNETS AND SAGAS.
IT LOOKS AS IF THE JOTUNS WILL FACE HEL THIS DAY.
BUT ALAS, AS INEXORABL AS NIGHT MUST FOLLOW DAY, ALL GOOD THINGS MU COME TO BITTER END.

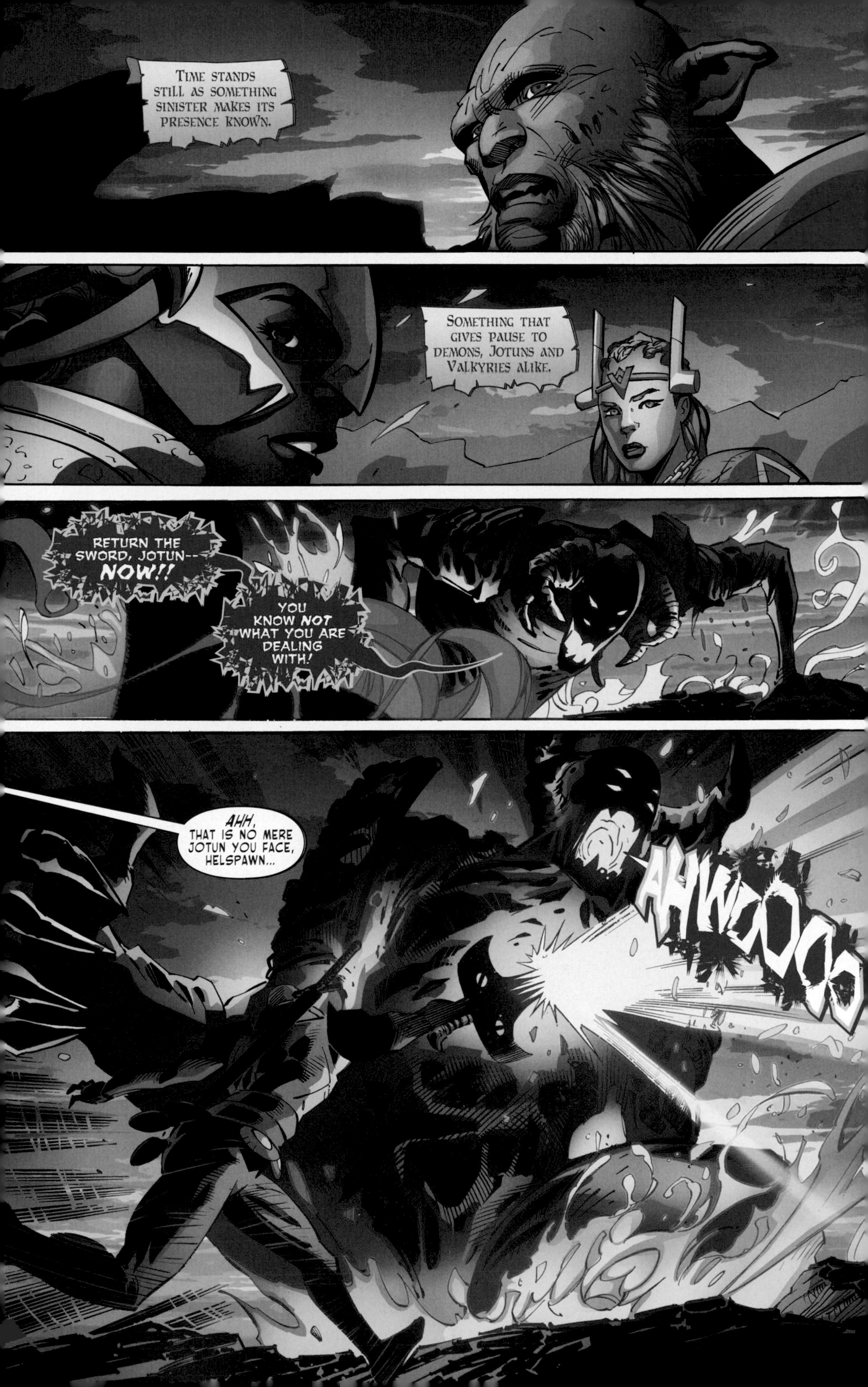
TIME STANDS STILL AS SOMETHING SINISTER MAKES ITS PRESENCE KNOWN.
SOMETHING THAT GIVES PAUSE TO DEMONS, JOTUNS AND VALKYRIES ALIKE.
RETURN THE SWORD, JOTUN-- NOW!!
YOU KNOW NOT WHAT YOU ARE DEALING WITH!
AHH, THAT IS NO MERE JOTUN YOU FACE, HELSPAWN...
AHWOOOO

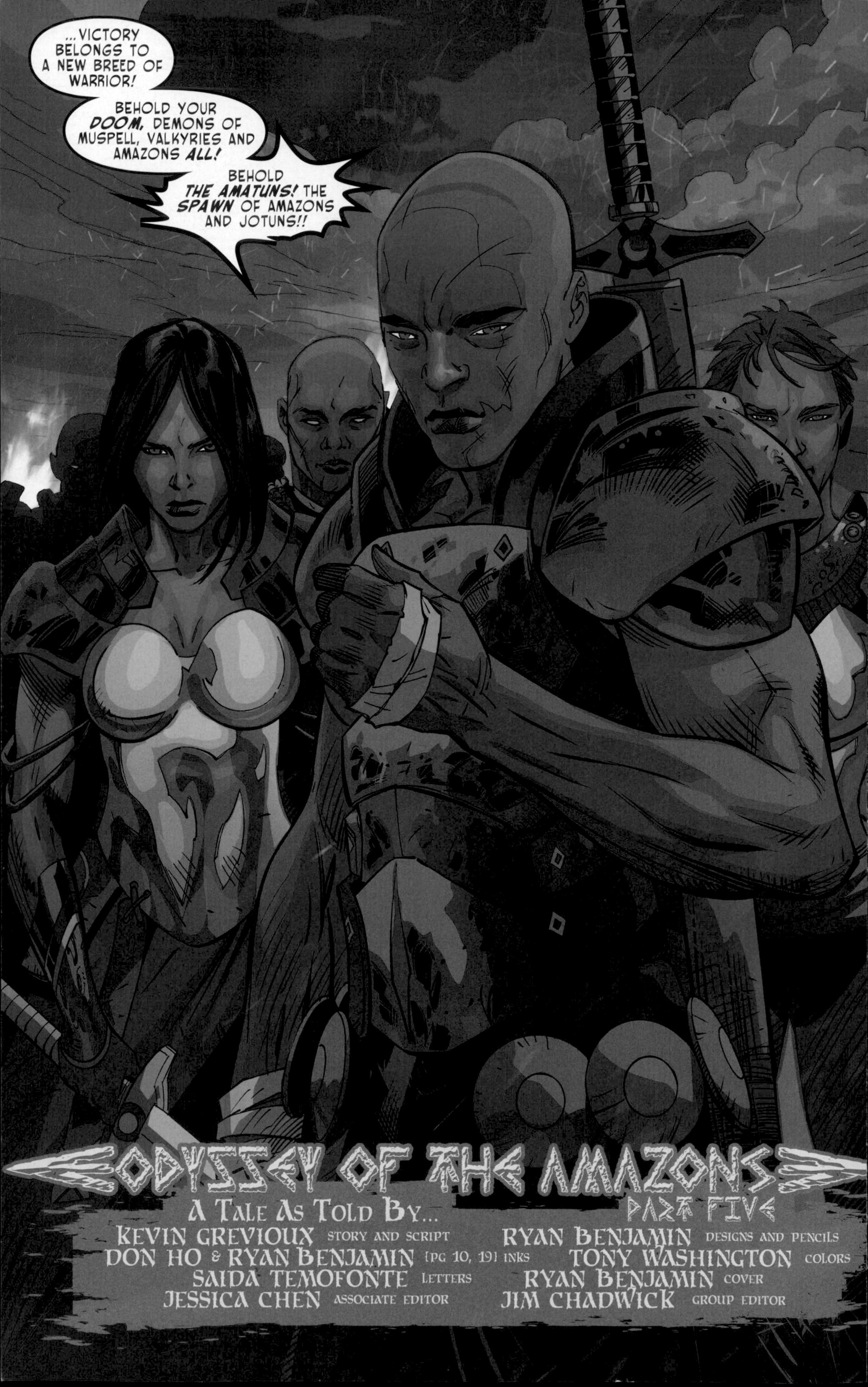
...VICTORY BELONGS TO A NEW BREED OF WARRIOR!
BEHOLD YOUR DOOM, DEMONS OF MUSPELL, VALKYRIES AND AMAZONS ALL!
BEHOLD THE AMATUNS! THE SPAWN OF AMAZONS AND JOTUNS!!
ODYSSEY OF THE AMAZONS
A TALE AS TOLD BY...
PART FIVE
KEVIN GREVIOUX STORY AND SCRIPT
RYAN BENJAMIN DESIGNS AND PENCILS
DON HO & RYAN BENJAMIN (PG 10, 19) INKS
TONY WASHINGTON COLORS
SAIDA TEMOFONTE LETTERS
RYAN BENJAMIN COVER
JESSICA CHEN ASSOCIATE EDITOR
JIM CHADWICK GROUP EDITOR

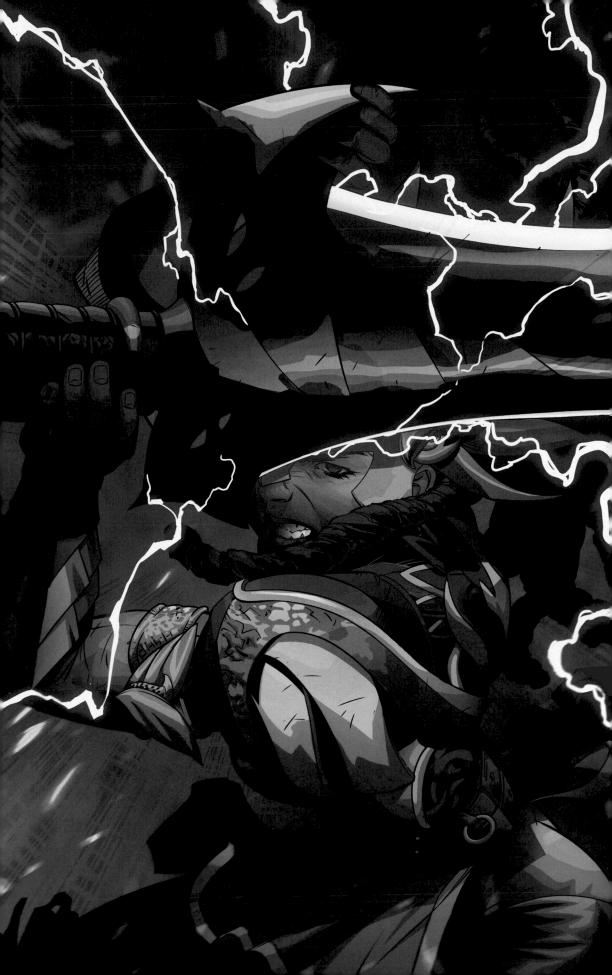

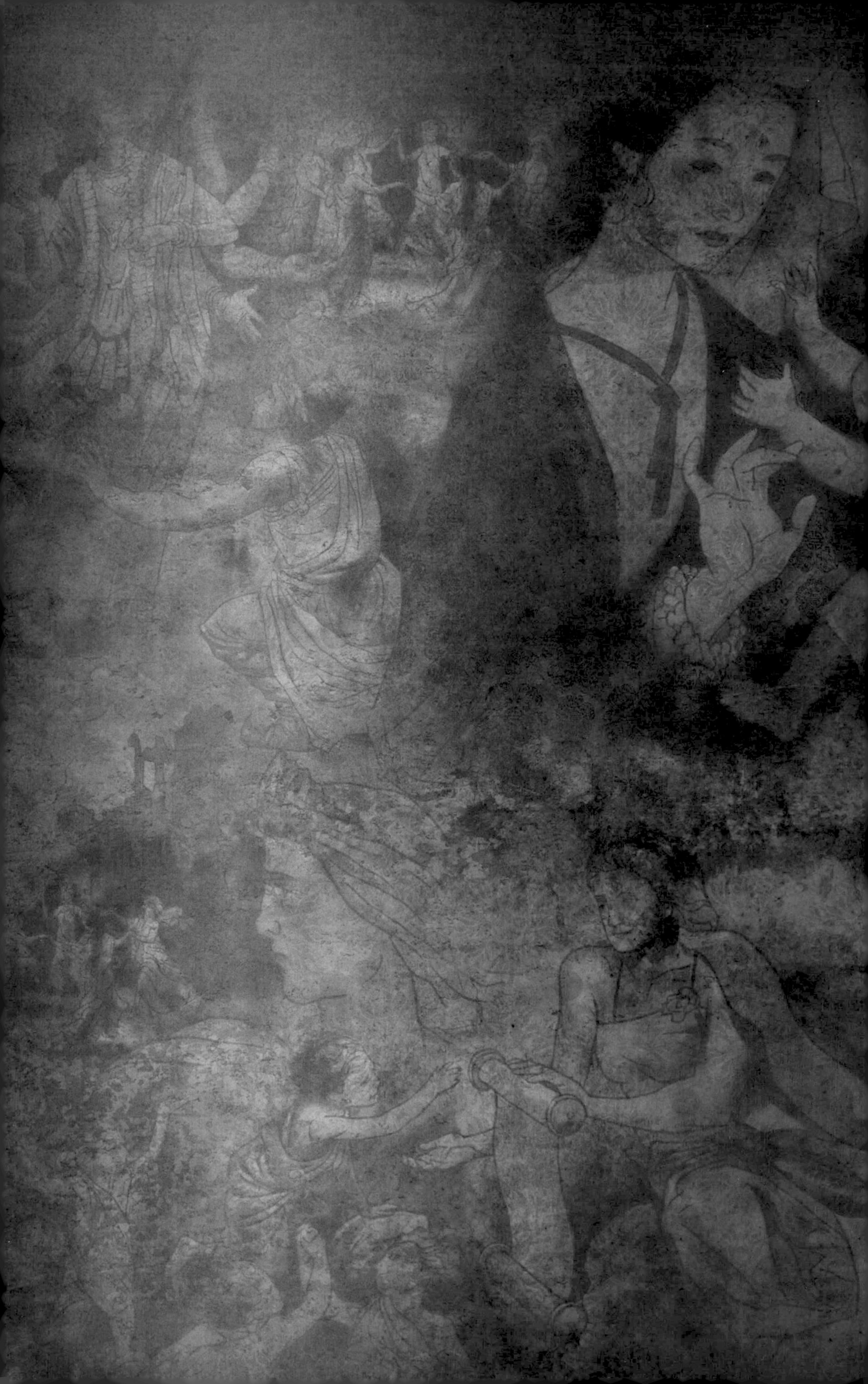

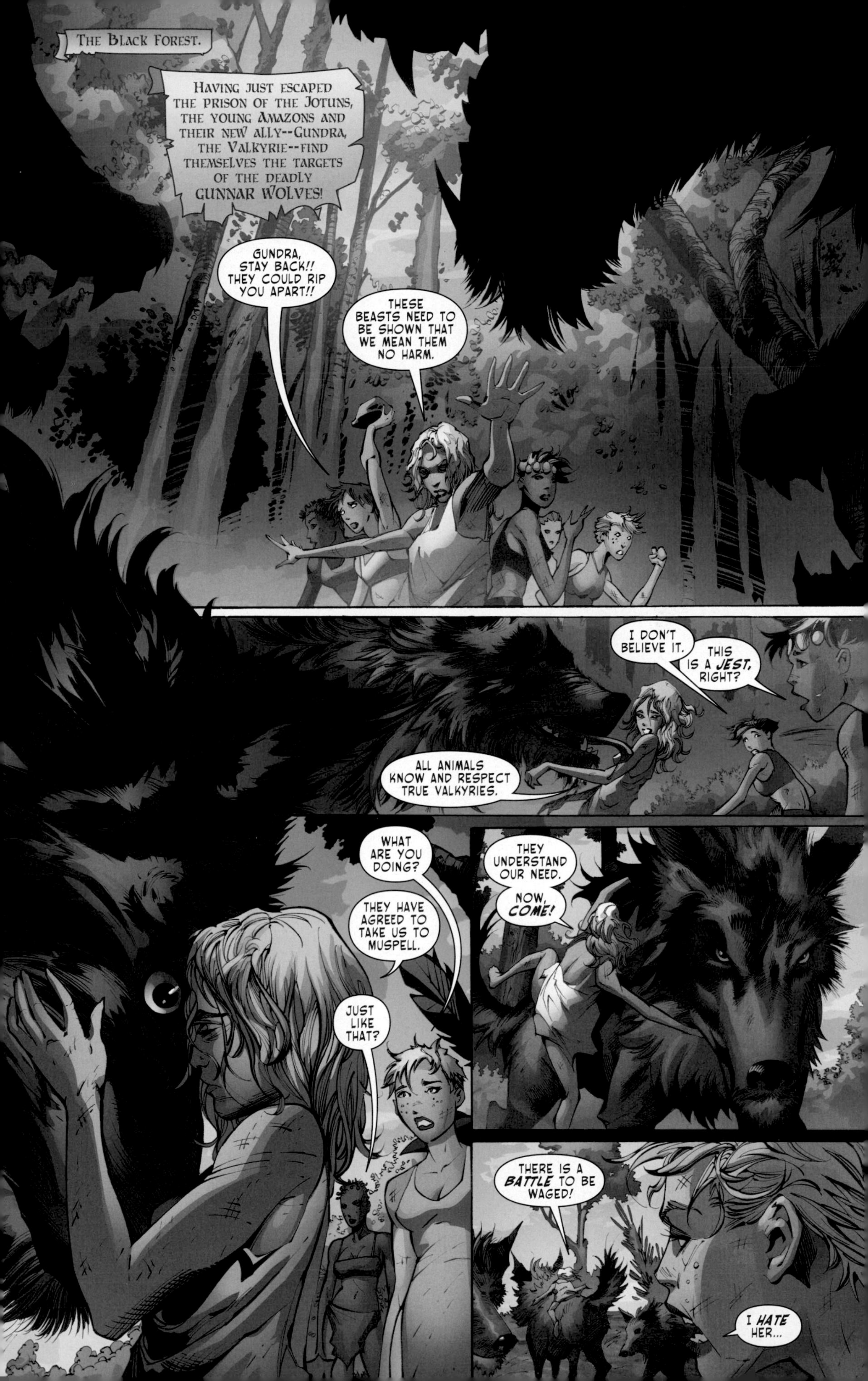
THE BLACK FOREST.
HAVING JUST ESCAPED THE PRISON OF THE JOTUNS, THE YOUNG AMAZONS AND THEIR NEW ALLY--GUNDRA, THE VALKYRIE--FIND THEMSELVES THE TARGETS OF THE DEADLY GUNNAR WOLVES!
GUNDRA, STAY BACK!! THEY COULD RIP YOU APART!!
THESE BEASTS NEED TO BE SHOWN THAT WE MEAN THEM NO HARM.
I DON'T BELIEVE IT.
THIS IS A JEST, RIGHT?
ALL ANIMALS KNOW AND RESPECT TRUE VALKYRIES.
WHAT ARE YOU DOING?
THEY HAVE AGREED TO TAKE US TO MUSPELL.
JUST LIKE THAT?
THEY UNDERSTAND OUR NEED.
NOW, COME!
THERE IS A BATTLE TO BE WAGED!
I HATE HER...

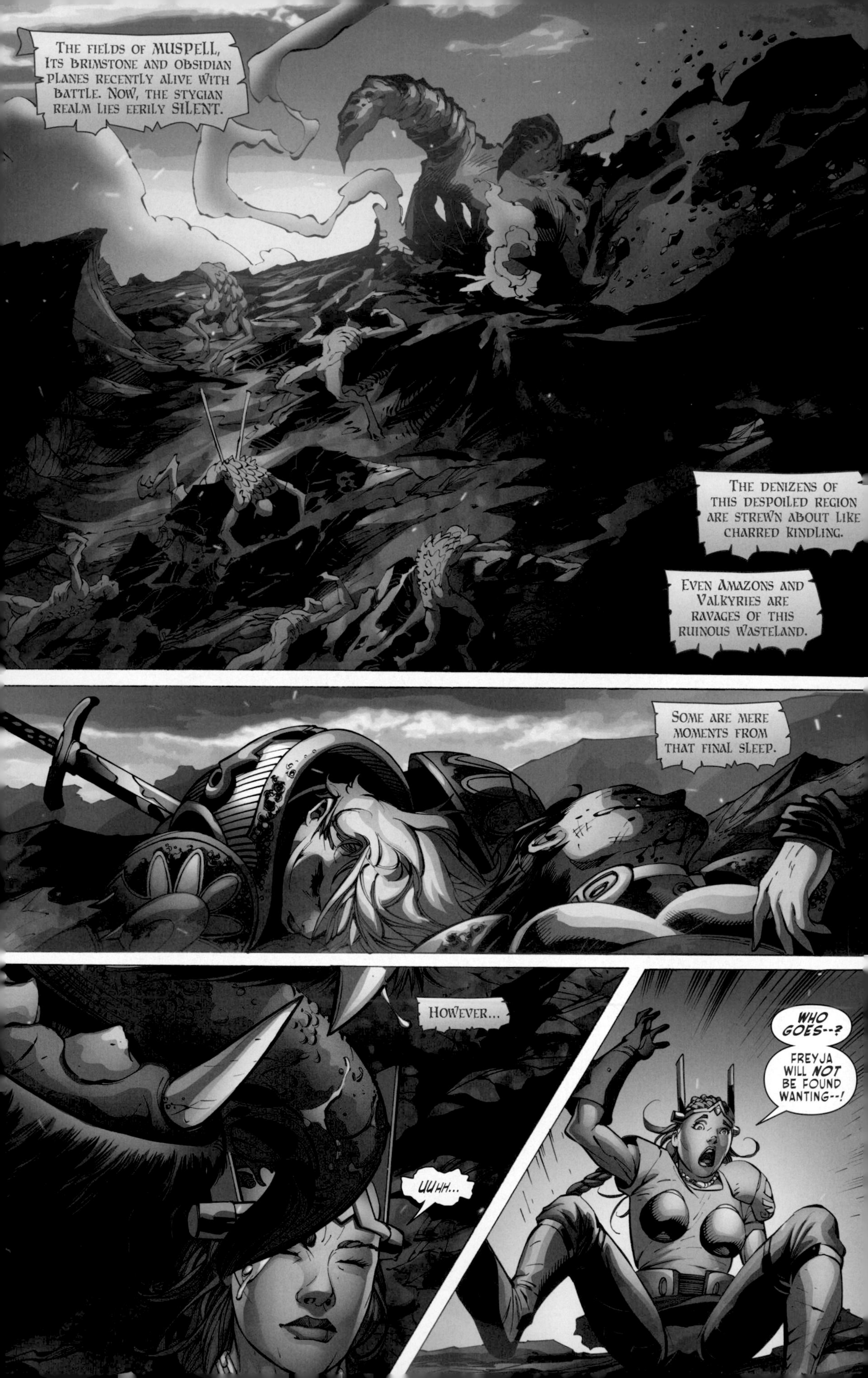
The fields of MUSPELL, its brimstone and obsidian planes recently alive with battle. Now, the stygian realm lies eerily SILENT.
The denizens of this despoiled region are strewn about like charred kindling.
Even Amazons and Valkyries are ravages of this ruinous wasteland.
Some are mere moments from that final sleep.
However...
UUHH...
WHO GOES--?
FREYJA WILL NOT BE FOUND WANTING--!

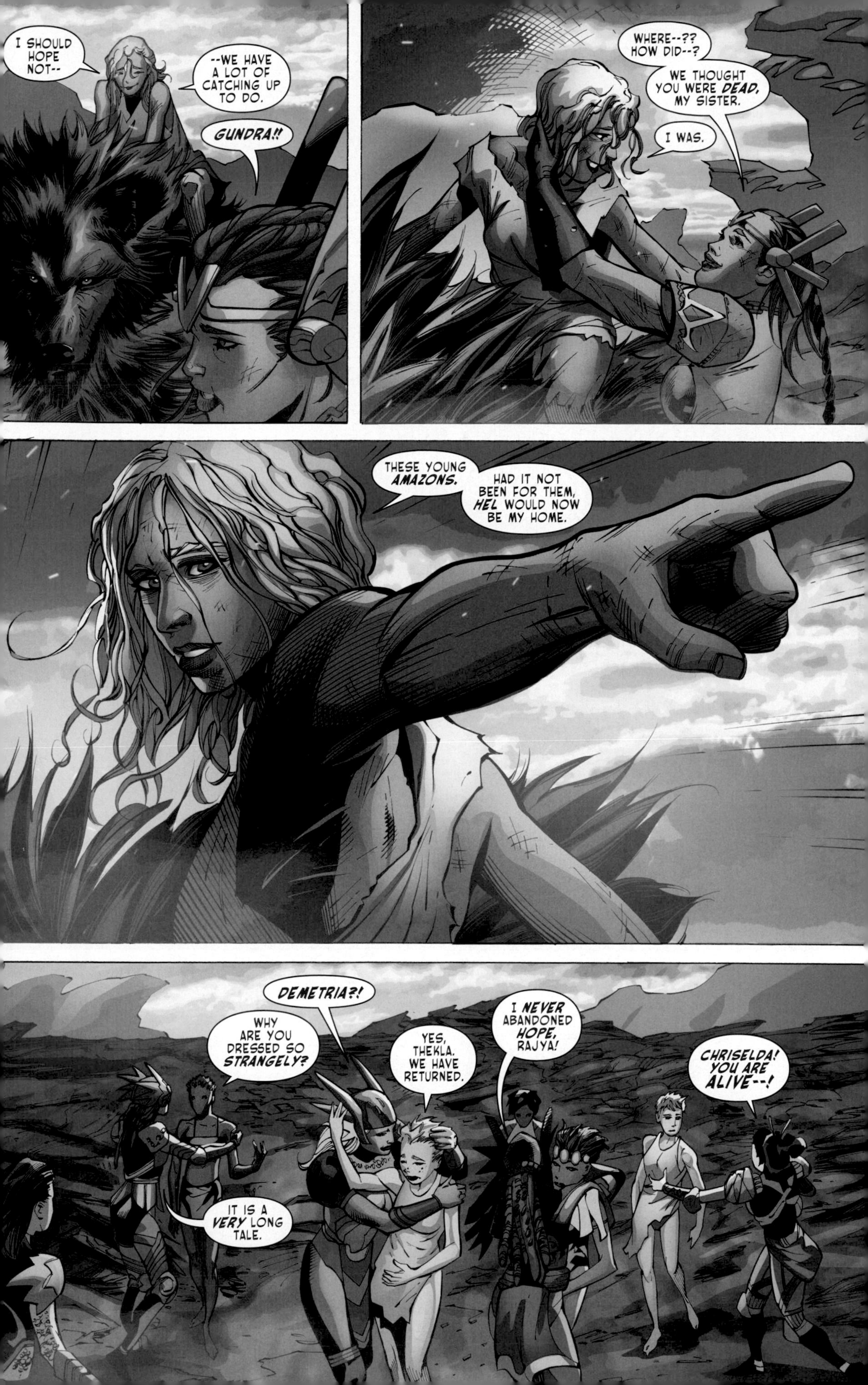
I SHOULD HOPE NOT--
--WE HAVE A LOT OF CATCHING UP TO DO.
GUNDRA!!
WHERE--?? HOW DID--?
WE THOUGHT YOU WERE DEAD, MY SISTER.
I WAS.
THESE YOUNG AMAZONS.
HAD IT NOT BEEN FOR THEM, HEL WOULD NOW BE MY HOME.
WHY ARE YOU DRESSED SO STRANGELY?
IT IS A VERY LONG TALE.
DEMETRIA?!
YES, THEKLA. WE HAVE RETURNED.
I NEVER ABANDONED HOPE, RAJYA!
CHRISELDA! YOU ARE ALIVE--!

TIME AND AGAIN I HAVE TOLD YOU ALL ABOUT RUNNING OFF--

WHATEVER WE DID IS *DONE*, THEKLA. BOTH TISIPHONE AND EUDORA ARE *DEAD*.

HOLD, WARRIORS--TIME ENOUGH FOR SCOLDING AT ANOTHER TIME.

LET IT BE ENOUGH THAT OUR SISTERS HAVE RETURNED TO US.

THERE BE WEIGHTIER MATTERS THAT REQUIRE OUR ATTENTION.

YES. RIGHT NOW I WAGER THAT GROA IS ATTACKING THE OTHER NINE REALMS.

BUT WHICH ONE?

RIGHT NOW, WE SHOULD SEE TO THE YOUNG ONES' REST. THE ORDEAL HAS SURELY WEAKENED THEM.

WE "RESTED" ENOUGH WHEN THEY STRAPPED US DOWN AND BOUND US.

NO MORE!

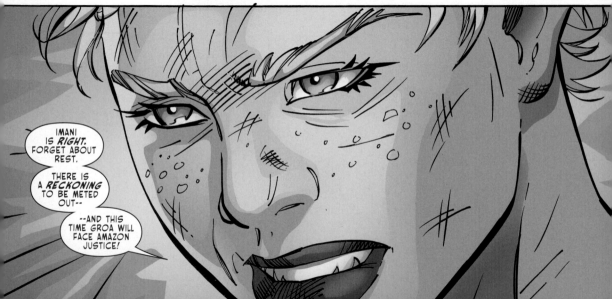

IMANI IS *RIGHT*. FORGET ABOUT REST.

THERE IS A *RECKONING* TO BE METED OUT--

--AND THIS TIME GROA WILL FACE AMAZON JUSTICE!

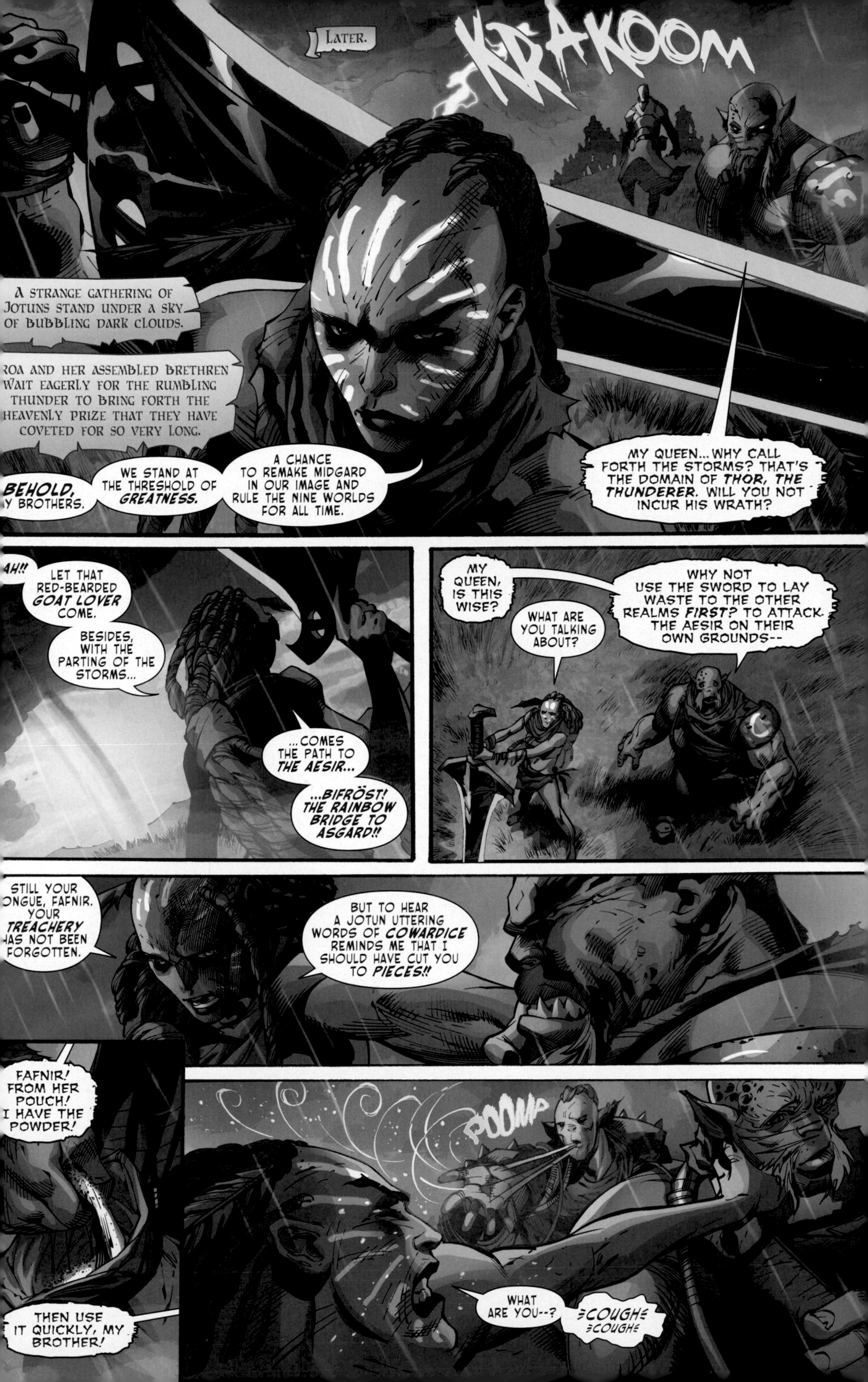
LATER.
KRAKOOM
A STRANGE GATHERING OF JOTUNS STAND UNDER A SKY OF BUBBLING DARK CLOUDS.
ROA AND HER ASSEMBLED BRETHREN WAIT EAGERLY FOR THE RUMBLING THUNDER TO BRING FORTH THE HEAVENLY PRIZE THAT THEY HAVE COVETED FOR SO VERY LONG.
BEHOLD, Y BROTHERS.
WE STAND AT THE THRESHOLD OF GREATNESS.
A CHANCE TO REMAKE MIDGARD IN OUR IMAGE AND RULE THE NINE WORLDS FOR ALL TIME.
MY QUEEN... WHY CALL FORTH THE STORMS? THAT'S THE DOMAIN OF THOR, THE THUNDERER. WILL YOU NOT INCUR HIS WRATH?
AH!!
LET THAT RED-BEARDED GOAT LOVER COME.
BESIDES, WITH THE PARTING OF THE STORMS...
...COMES THE PATH TO THE AESIR...
...BIFRÖST! THE RAINBOW BRIDGE TO ASGARD!!
MY QUEEN, IS THIS WISE?
WHY NOT USE THE SWORD TO LAY WASTE TO THE OTHER REALMS FIRST? TO ATTACK THE AESIR ON THEIR OWN GROUNDS--
WHAT ARE YOU TALKING ABOUT?
STILL YOUR ONGUE, FAFNIR. YOUR TREACHERY HAS NOT BEEN FORGOTTEN.
BUT TO HEAR A JOTUN UTTERING WORDS OF COWARDICE REMINDS ME THAT I SHOULD HAVE CUT YOU TO PIECES!!
FAFNIR! FROM HER POUCH! I HAVE THE POWDER!
THEN USE IT QUICKLY, MY BROTHER!
POOMP
WHAT ARE YOU--?
COUGH COUGH

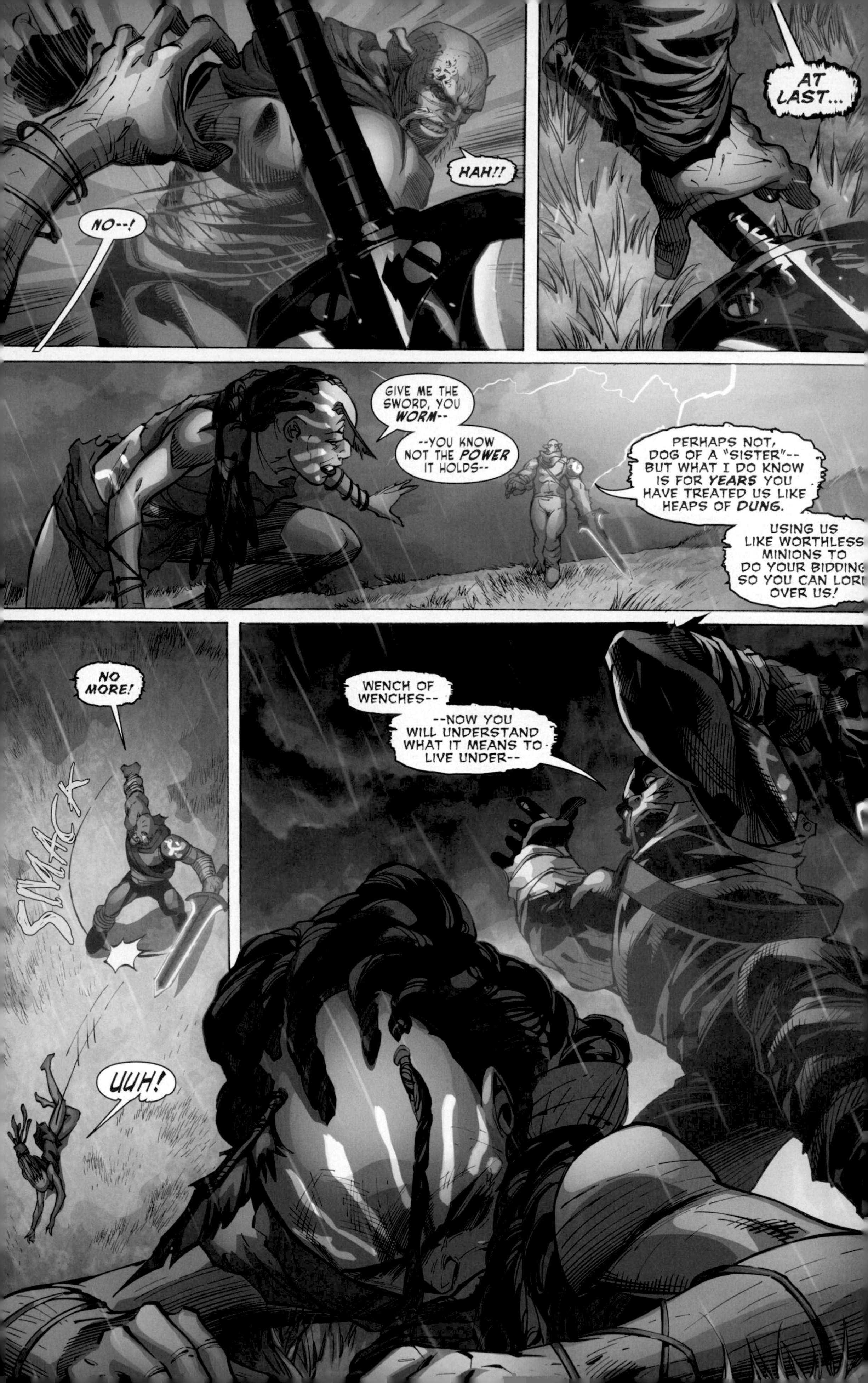

HAH!!
NO--!
AT LAST...
GIVE ME THE SWORD, YOU WORM--
--YOU KNOW NOT THE POWER IT HOLDS--
PERHAPS NOT, DOG OF A "SISTER"--BUT WHAT I DO KNOW IS FOR YEARS YOU HAVE TREATED US LIKE HEAPS OF DUNG.
USING US LIKE WORTHLESS MINIONS TO DO YOUR BIDDING SO YOU CAN LORD OVER US!
NO MORE!
SMACK
UUH!
WENCH OF WENCHES--
--NOW YOU WILL UNDERSTAND WHAT IT MEANS TO LIVE UNDER--

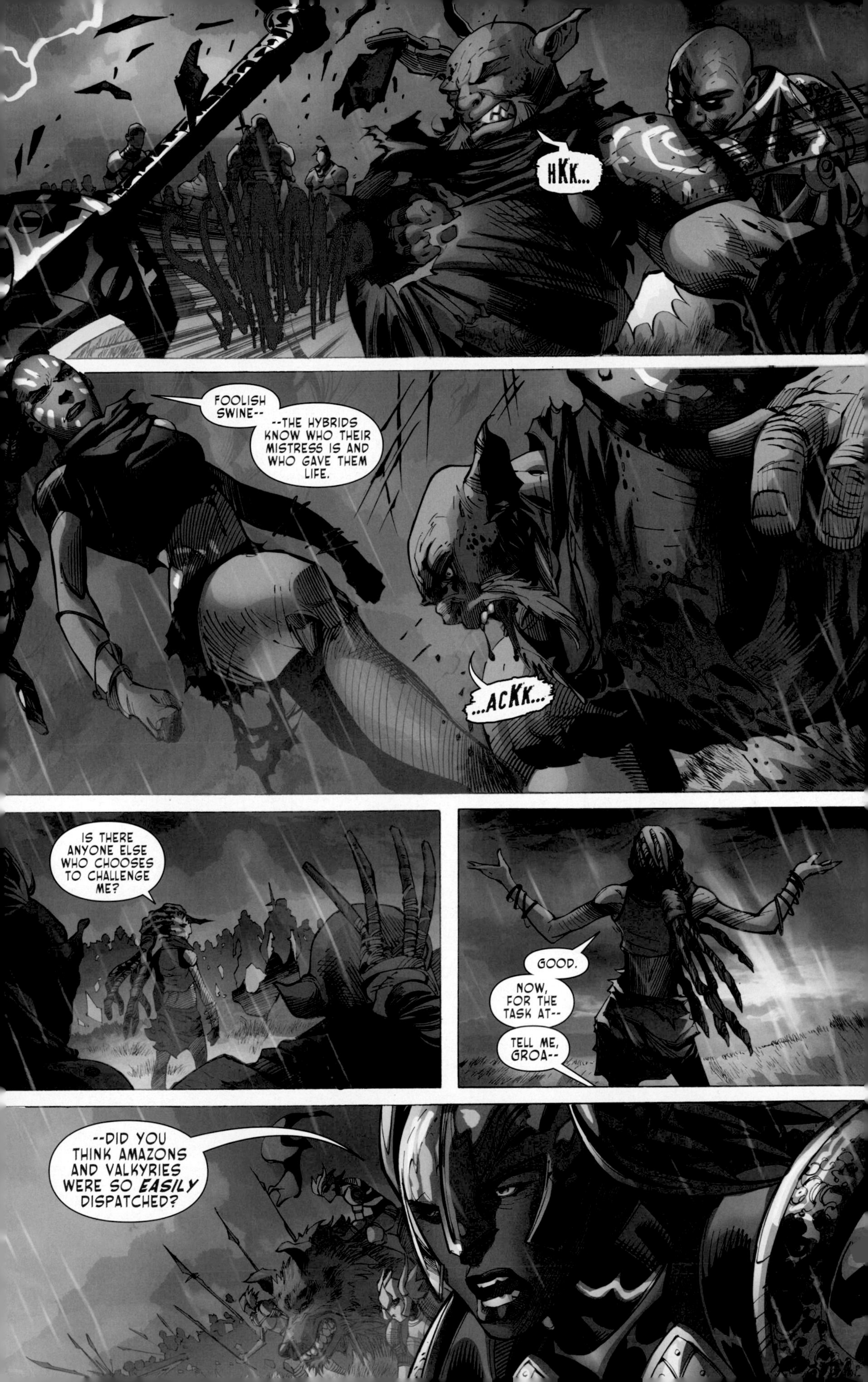
SWOMP
HKK...
FOOLISH SWINE--
--THE HYBRIDS KNOW WHO THEIR MISTRESS IS AND WHO GAVE THEM LIFE.
...ACKK...
IS THERE ANYONE ELSE WHO CHOOSES TO CHALLENGE ME?
GOOD.
NOW, FOR THE TASK AT--
TELL ME, GROA--
--DID YOU THINK AMAZONS AND VALKYRIES WERE SO *EASILY* DISPATCHED?

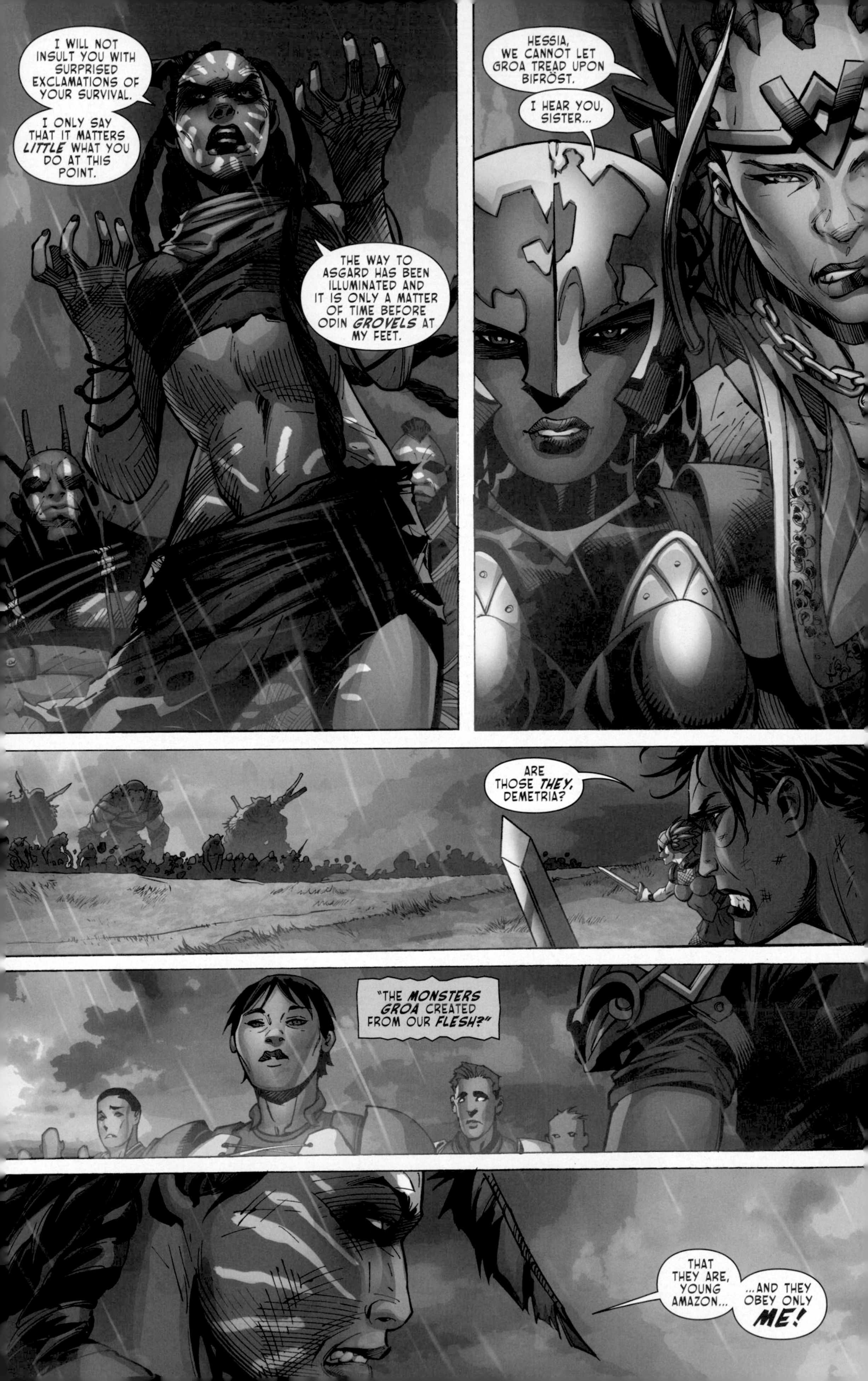
I WILL NOT INSULT YOU WITH SURPRISED EXCLAMATIONS OF YOUR SURVIVAL.
I ONLY SAY THAT IT MATTERS LITTLE WHAT YOU DO AT THIS POINT.
THE WAY TO ASGARD HAS BEEN ILLUMINATED AND IT IS ONLY A MATTER OF TIME BEFORE ODIN GROVELS AT MY FEET.
HESSIA, WE CANNOT LET GROA TREAD UPON BIFRÖST.
I HEAR YOU, SISTER...
ARE THOSE THEY, DEMETRIA?
"THE MONSTERS GROA CREATED FROM OUR FLESH?"
THAT THEY ARE, YOUNG AMAZON...
...AND THEY OBEY ONLY ME!

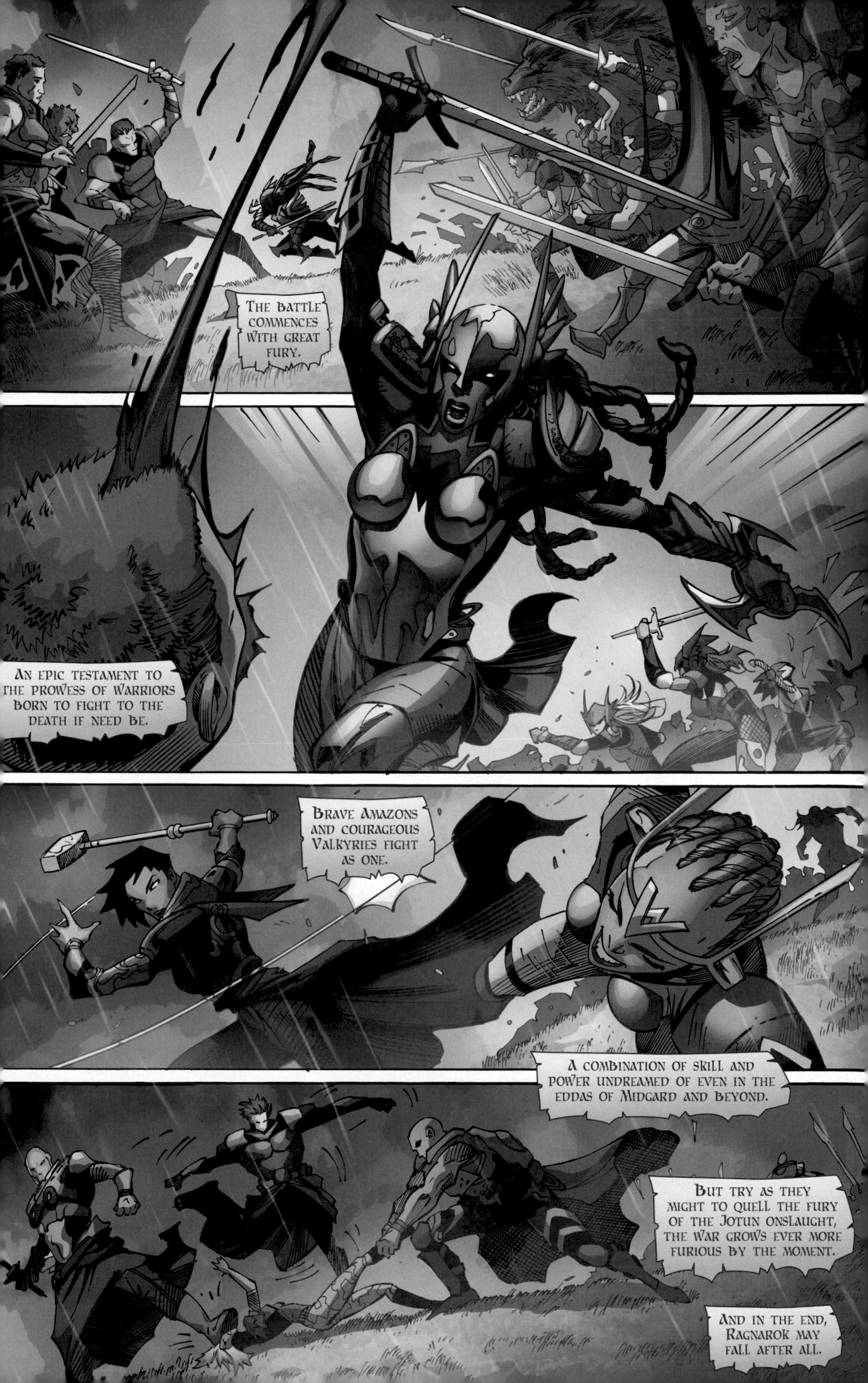
THE BATTLE COMMENCES WITH GREAT FURY.
AN EPIC TESTAMENT TO THE PROWESS OF WARRIORS BORN TO FIGHT TO THE DEATH IF NEED BE.
BRAVE AMAZONS AND COURAGEOUS VALKYRIES FIGHT AS ONE.
A COMBINATION OF SKILL AND POWER UNDREAMED OF EVEN IN THE EDDAS OF MIDGARD AND BEYOND.
BUT TRY AS THEY MIGHT TO QUELL THE FURY OF THE JOTUN ONSLAUGHT, THE WAR GROWS EVER MORE FURIOUS BY THE MOMENT.
AND IN THE END, RAGNAROK MAY FALL AFTER ALL.

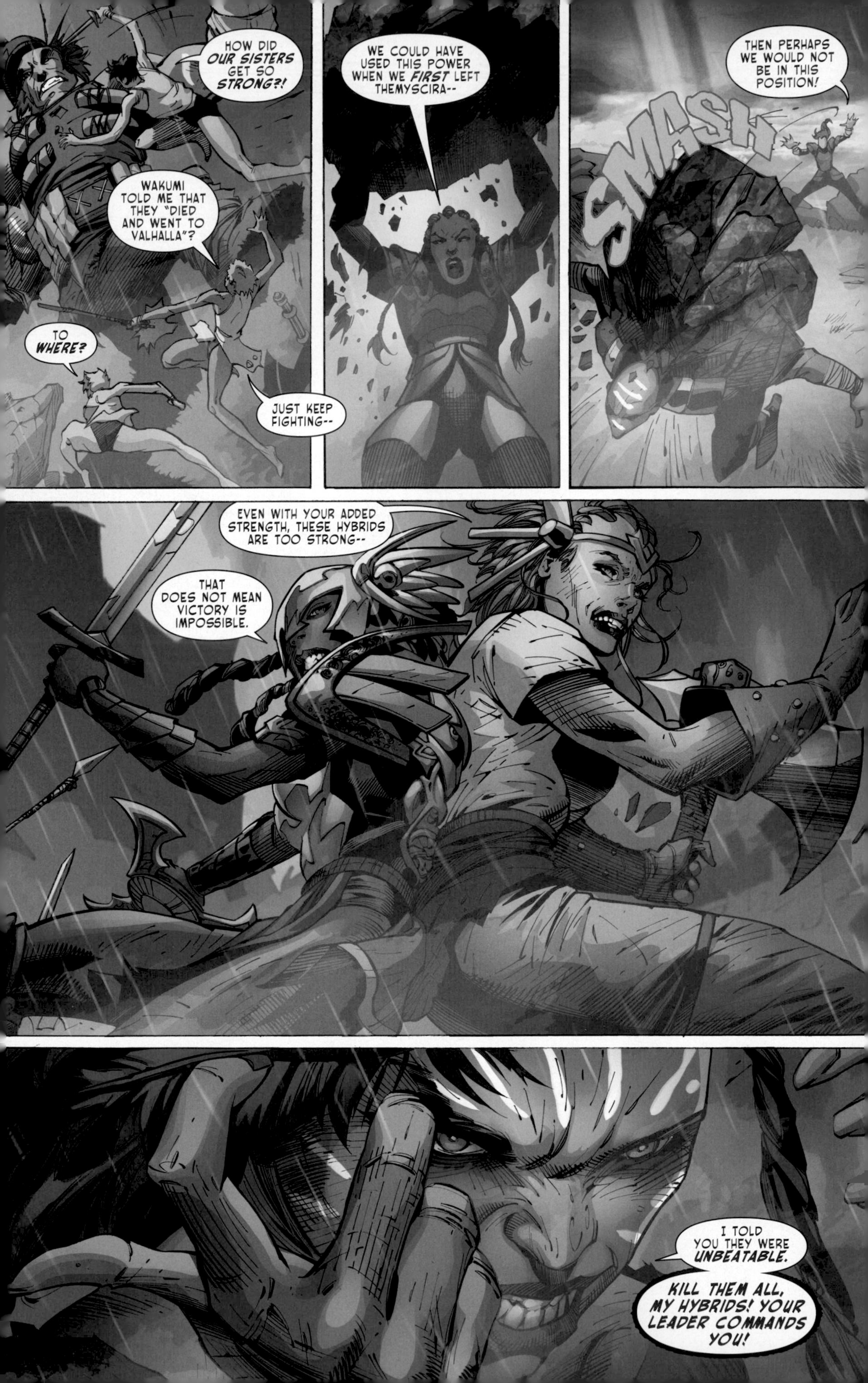
HOW DID OUR SISTERS GET SO STRONG?!
WAKUMI TOLD ME THAT THEY "DIED AND WENT TO VALHALLA"?
TO WHERE?
JUST KEEP FIGHTING--
WE COULD HAVE USED THIS POWER WHEN WE FIRST LEFT THEMYSCIRA--
THEN PERHAPS WE WOULD NOT BE IN THIS POSITION!
SMASH
EVEN WITH YOUR ADDED STRENGTH, THESE HYBRIDS ARE TOO STRONG--
THAT DOES NOT MEAN VICTORY IS IMPOSSIBLE.
I TOLD YOU THEY WERE UNBEATABLE.
KILL THEM ALL, MY HYBRIDS! YOUR LEADER COMMANDS YOU!

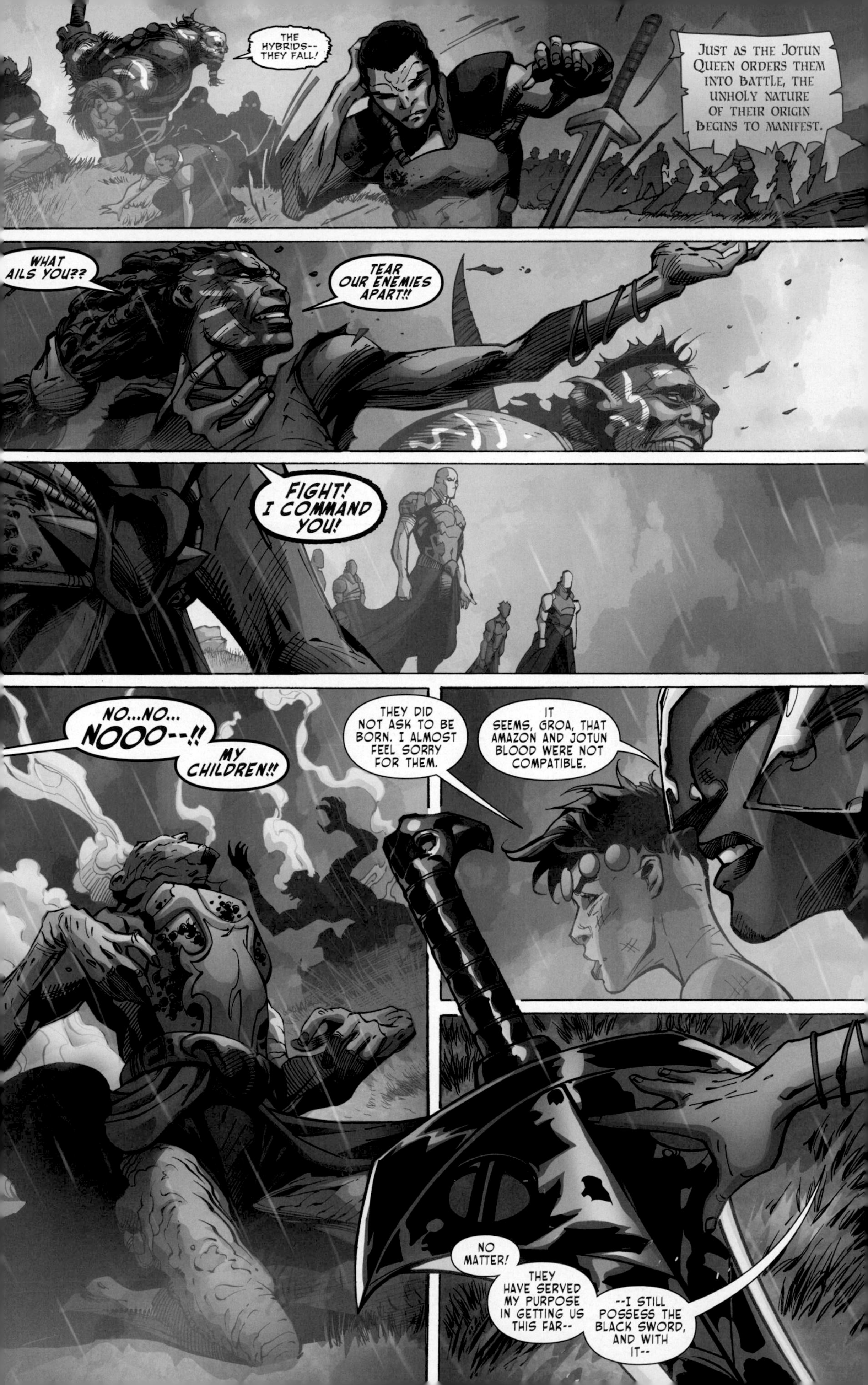
THE HYBRIDS-- THEY FALL!
JUST AS THE JOTUN QUEEN ORDERS THEM INTO BATTLE, THE UNHOLY NATURE OF THEIR ORIGIN BEGINS TO MANIFEST.
WHAT AILS YOU??
TEAR OUR ENEMIES APART!!
FIGHT! I COMMAND YOU!
NO...NO... NOOO--!!
MY CHILDREN!!
THEY DID NOT ASK TO BE BORN. I ALMOST FEEL SORRY FOR THEM.
IT SEEMS, GROA, THAT AMAZON AND JOTUN BLOOD WERE NOT COMPATIBLE.
NO MATTER!
THEY HAVE SERVED MY PURPOSE IN GETTING US THIS FAR--
--I STILL POSSESS THE BLACK SWORD, AND WITH IT--

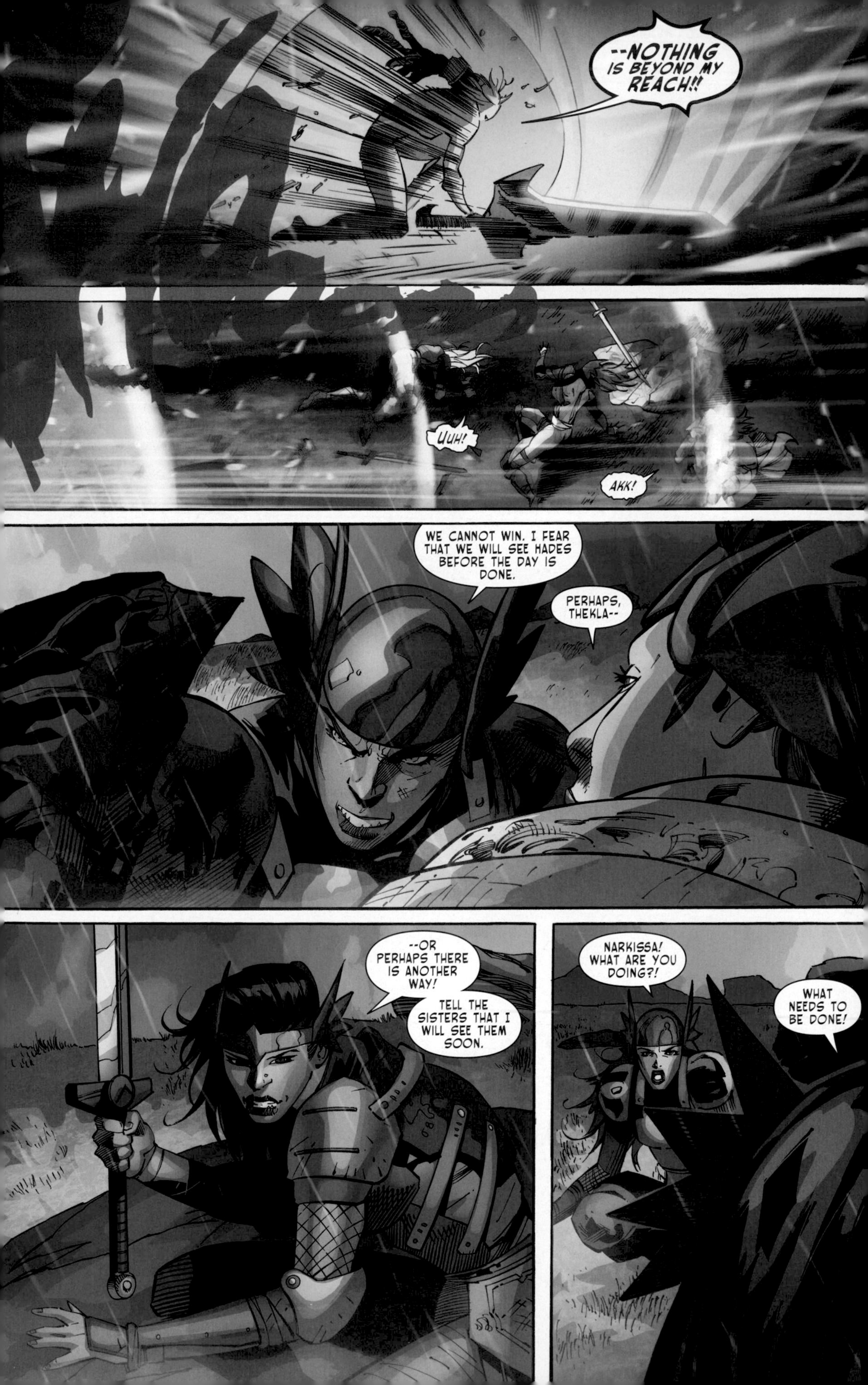
--NOTHING IS BEYOND MY REACH!!
UUH!
AKK!
WE CANNOT WIN. I FEAR THAT WE WILL SEE HADES BEFORE THE DAY IS DONE.
PERHAPS, THEKLA--
--OR PERHAPS THERE IS ANOTHER WAY!
TELL THE SISTERS THAT I WILL SEE THEM SOON.
NARKISSA! WHAT ARE YOU DOING?!
WHAT NEEDS TO BE DONE!

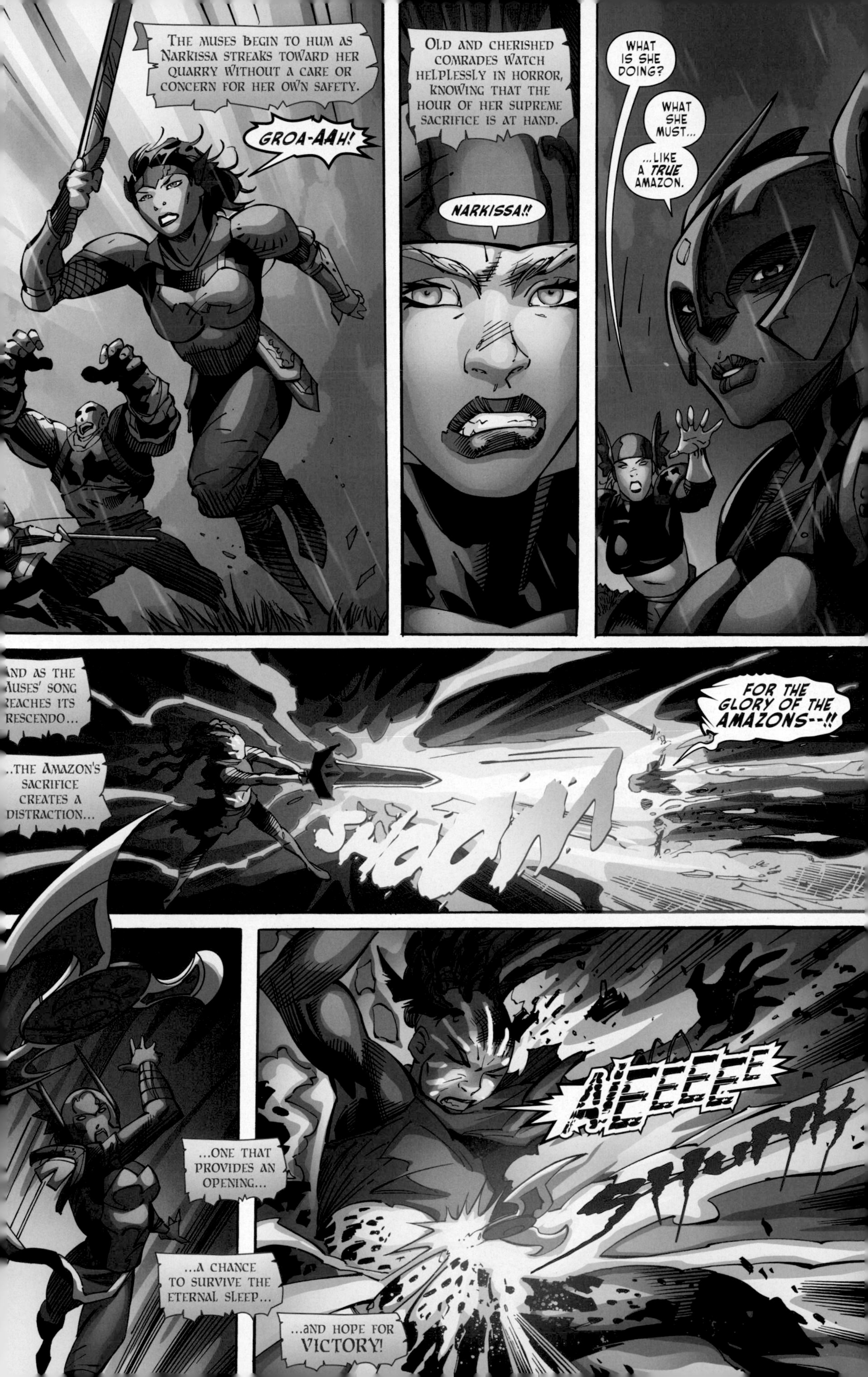

THE MUSES BEGIN TO HUM AS NARKISSA STREAKS TOWARD HER QUARRY WITHOUT A CARE OR CONCERN FOR HER OWN SAFETY.
GROA-AAH!
OLD AND CHERISHED COMRADES WATCH HELPLESSLY IN HORROR, KNOWING THAT THE HOUR OF HER SUPREME SACRIFICE IS AT HAND.
NARKISSA!!
WHAT IS SHE DOING?
WHAT SHE MUST...
...LIKE A TRUE AMAZON.
ND AS THE IUSES' SONG REACHES ITS RESCENDO...
..THE AMAZON'S SACRIFICE CREATES A DISTRACTION...
FOR THE GLORY OF THE AMAZONS--!!
...ONE THAT PROVIDES AN OPENING...
AIEEEE
...A CHANCE TO SURVIVE THE ETERNAL SLEEP...
...AND HOPE FOR VICTORY!

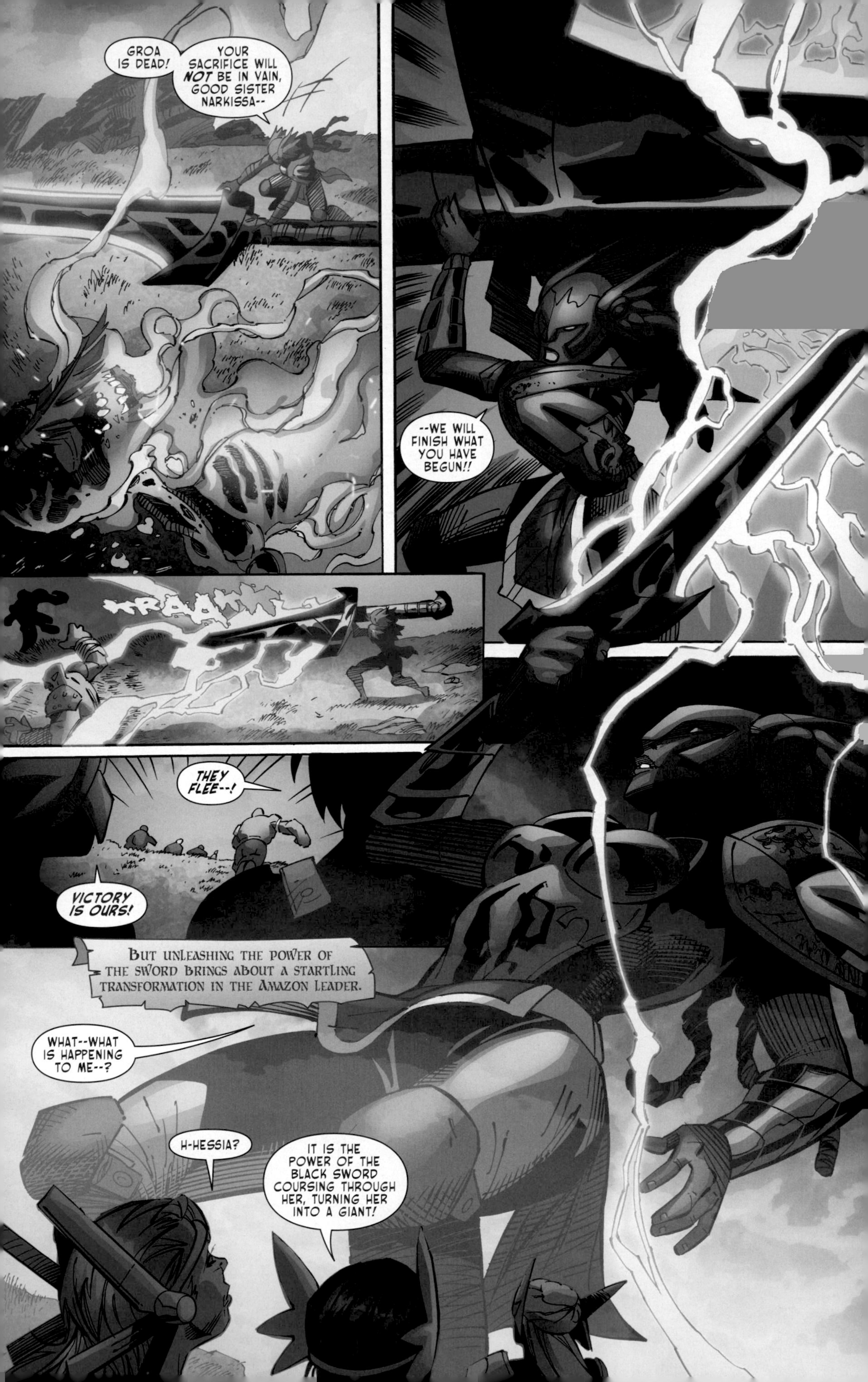

GROA IS DEAD!
YOUR SACRIFICE WILL NOT BE IN VAIN, GOOD SISTER NARKISSA--
--WE WILL FINISH WHAT YOU HAVE BEGUN!!
KRAAKK
THEY FLEE--!
VICTORY IS OURS!
BUT UNLEASHING THE POWER OF THE SWORD BRINGS ABOUT A STARTLING TRANSFORMATION IN THE AMAZON LEADER.
WHAT--WHAT IS HAPPENING TO ME--?
H-HESSIA?
IT IS THE POWER OF THE BLACK SWORD COURSING THROUGH HER, TURNING HER INTO A GIANT!

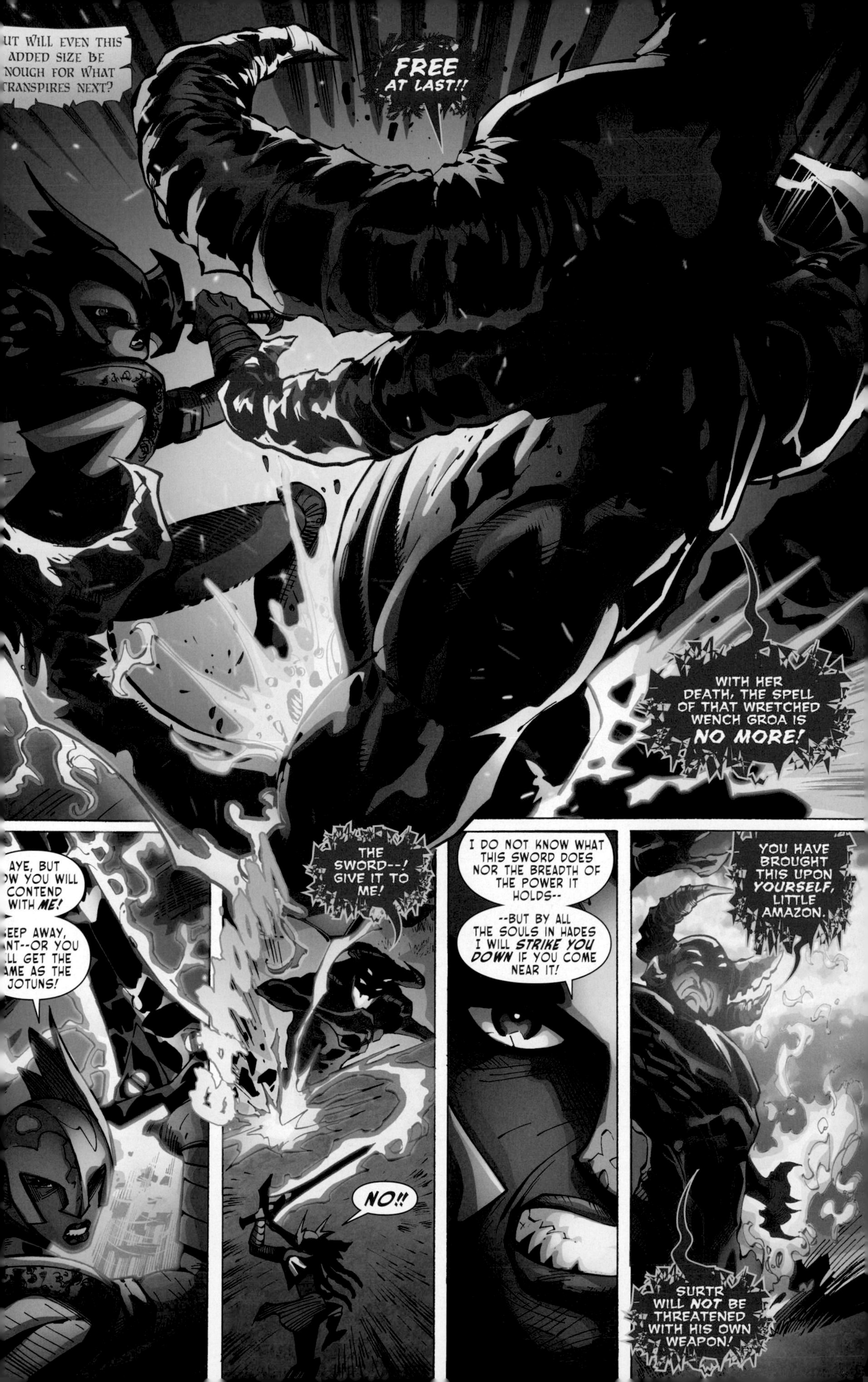
UT WILL EVEN THIS ADDED SIZE BE NOUGH FOR WHAT TRANSPIRES NEXT?
FREE AT LAST!!
WITH HER DEATH, THE SPELL OF THAT WRETCHED WENCH GROA IS NO MORE!
AYE, BUT OW YOU WILL CONTEND WITH ME!
EEP AWAY, NT--OR YOU LL GET THE AME AS THE JOTUNS!
THE SWORD--! GIVE IT TO ME!
NO!!
I DO NOT KNOW WHAT THIS SWORD DOES NOR THE BREADTH OF THE POWER IT HOLDS--
--BUT BY ALL THE SOULS IN HADES I WILL STRIKE YOU DOWN IF YOU COME NEAR IT!
YOU HAVE BROUGHT THIS UPON YOURSELF, LITTLE AMAZON.
SURTR WILL NOT BE THREATENED WITH HIS OWN WEAPON!

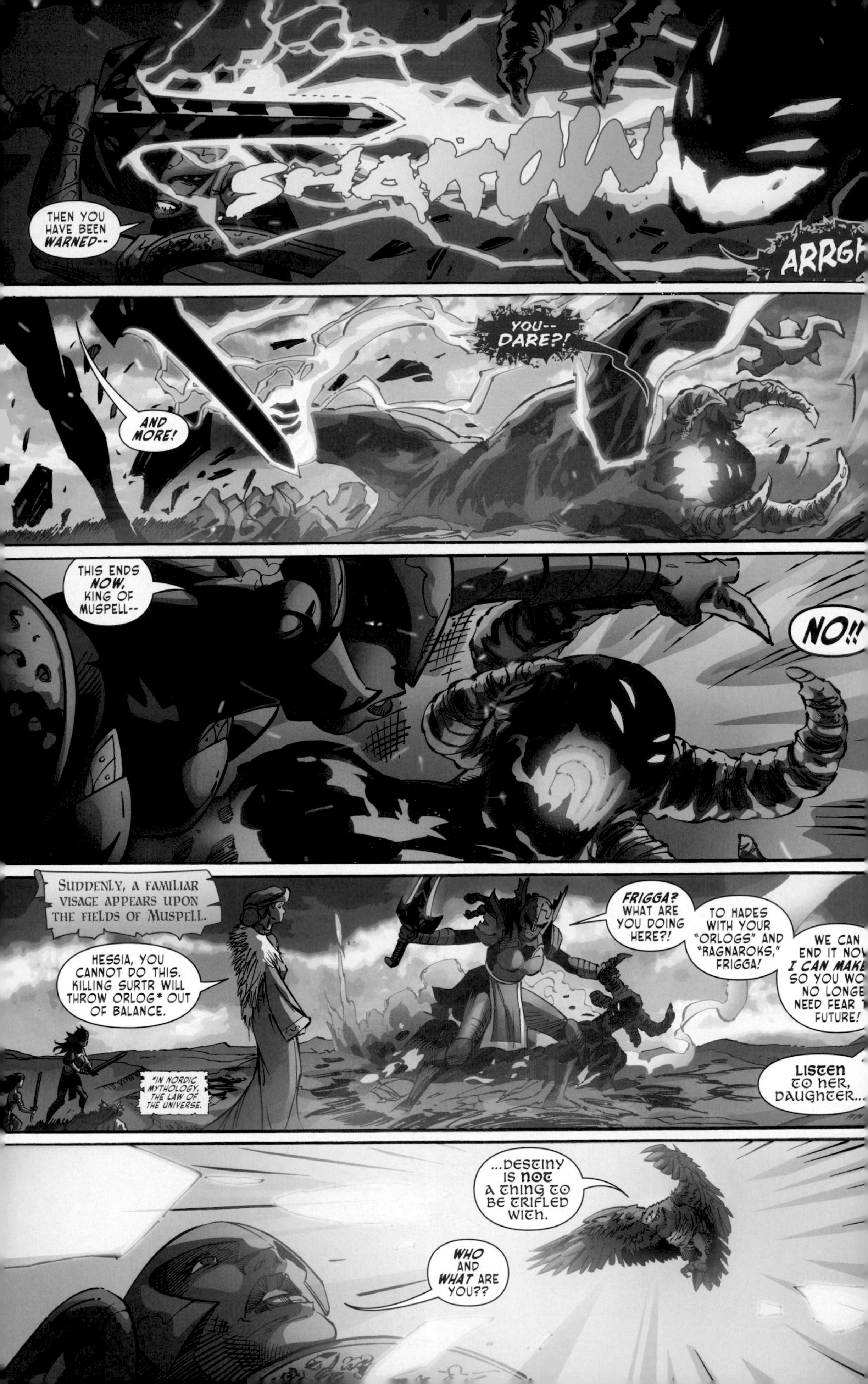
THEN YOU HAVE BEEN WARNED--
ARRGH
AND MORE!
YOU-- DARE?!
THIS ENDS NOW, KING OF MUSPELL--
NO!!
SUDDENLY, A FAMILIAR VISAGE APPEARS UPON THE FIELDS OF MUSPELL.
HESSIA, YOU CANNOT DO THIS. KILLING SURTR WILL THROW ORLOG* OUT OF BALANCE.
*IN NORDIC MYTHOLOGY, THE LAW OF THE UNIVERSE.
FRIGGA? WHAT ARE YOU DOING HERE?!
TO HADES WITH YOUR "ORLOGS" AND "RAGNAROKS," FRIGGA!
WE CAN END IT NOV I CAN MAKE SO YOU WO NO LONGE NEED FEAR T FUTURE!
LISTEN TO HER, DAUGHTER...
...DESTINY IS NOT A THING TO BE TRIFLED WITH.
WHO AND WHAT ARE YOU??

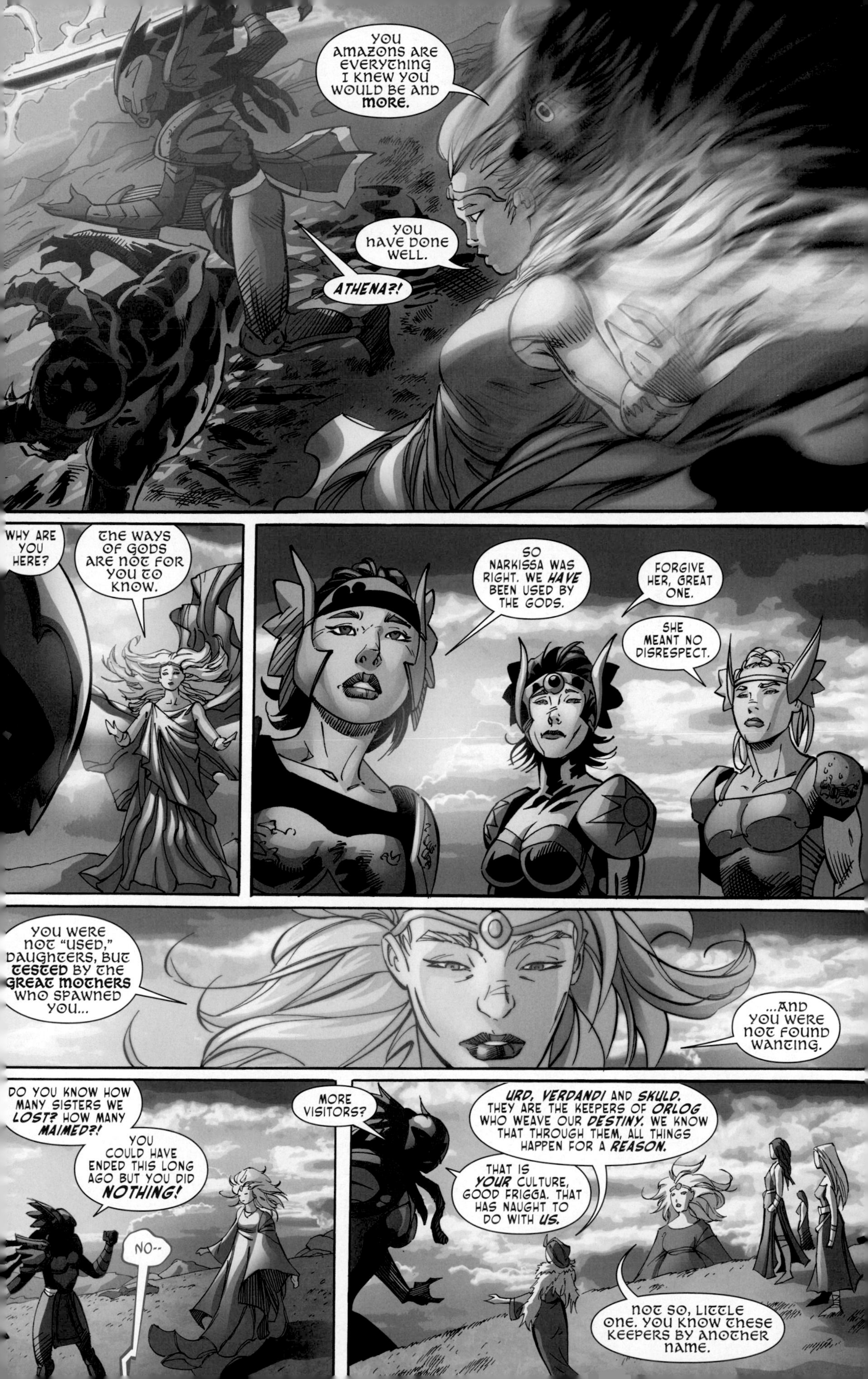
YOU AMAZONS ARE EVERYTHING I KNEW YOU WOULD BE AND MORE.
YOU HAVE DONE WELL.
ATHENA?!
WHY ARE YOU HERE?
THE WAYS OF GODS ARE NOT FOR YOU TO KNOW.
SO NARKISSA WAS RIGHT. WE HAVE BEEN USED BY THE GODS.
FORGIVE HER, GREAT ONE.
SHE MEANT NO DISRESPECT.
YOU WERE NOT "USED," DAUGHTERS, BUT TESTED BY THE GREAT MOTHERS WHO SPAWNED YOU...
...AND YOU WERE NOT FOUND WANTING.
DO YOU KNOW HOW MANY SISTERS WE LOST? HOW MANY MAIMED?!
YOU COULD HAVE ENDED THIS LONG AGO BUT YOU DID NOTHING!
NO--
MORE VISITORS?
URD, VERDANDI AND SKULD. THEY ARE THE KEEPERS OF ORLOG WHO WEAVE OUR DESTINY. WE KNOW THAT THROUGH THEM, ALL THINGS HAPPEN FOR A REASON.
THAT IS YOUR CULTURE, GOOD FRIGGA. THAT HAS NAUGHT TO DO WITH US.
NOT SO, LITTLE ONE. YOU KNOW THESE KEEPERS BY ANOTHER NAME.

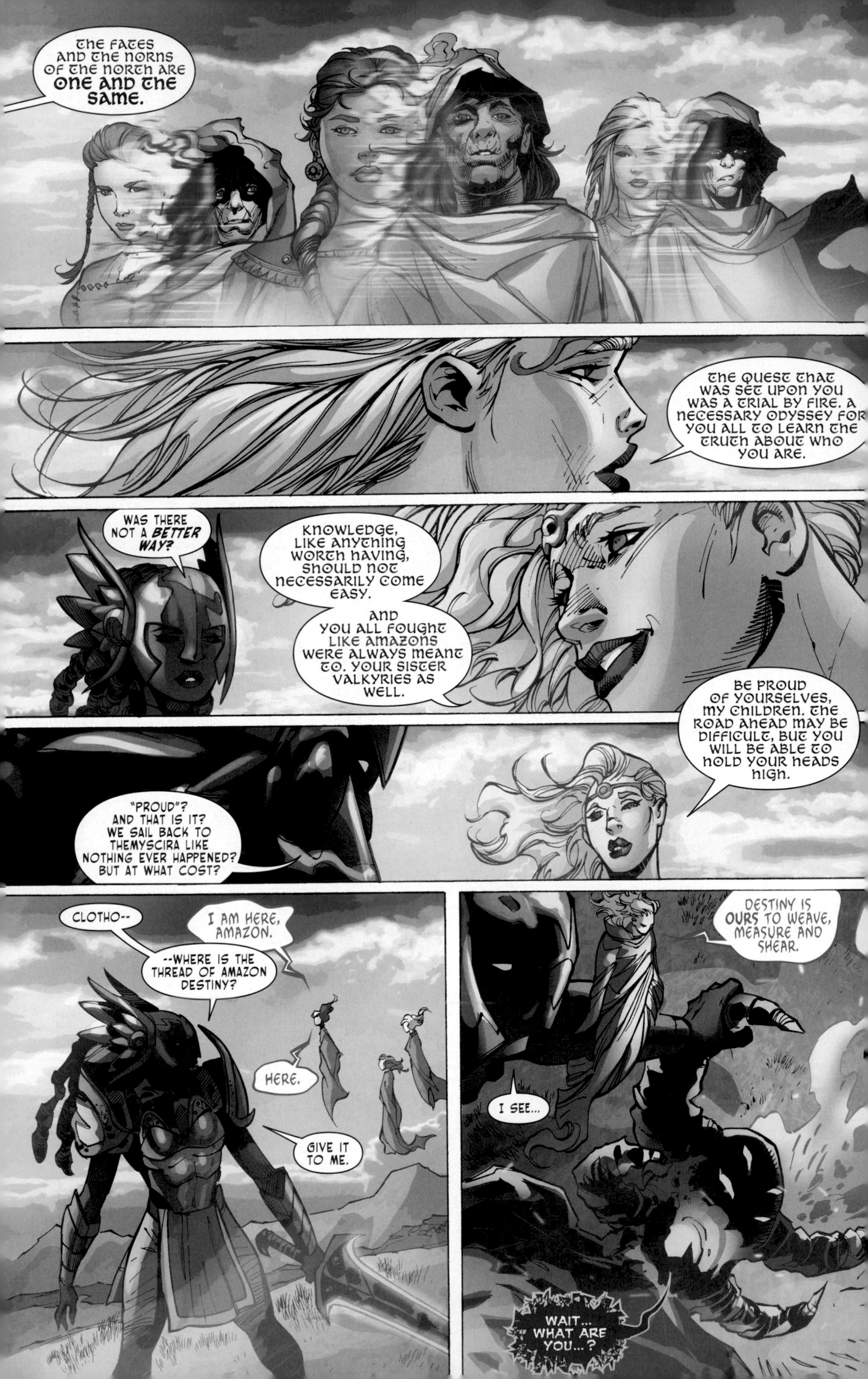
THE FATES AND THE NORNS OF THE NORTH ARE ONE AND THE SAME.
THE QUEST THAT WAS SET UPON YOU WAS A TRIAL BY FIRE. A NECESSARY ODYSSEY FOR YOU ALL TO LEARN THE TRUTH ABOUT WHO YOU ARE.
WAS THERE NOT A BETTER WAY?
KNOWLEDGE, LIKE ANYTHING WORTH HAVING, SHOULD NOT NECESSARILY COME EASY.
AND YOU ALL FOUGHT LIKE AMAZONS WERE ALWAYS MEANT TO. YOUR SISTER VALKYRIES AS WELL.
BE PROUD OF YOURSELVES, MY CHILDREN. THE ROAD AHEAD MAY BE DIFFICULT, BUT YOU WILL BE ABLE TO HOLD YOUR HEADS HIGH.
"PROUD"? AND THAT IS IT? WE SAIL BACK TO THEMYSCIRA LIKE NOTHING EVER HAPPENED? BUT AT WHAT COST?
CLOTHO--
I AM HERE, AMAZON.
--WHERE IS THE THREAD OF AMAZON DESTINY?
HERE.
GIVE IT TO ME.
DESTINY IS OURS TO WEAVE, MEASURE AND SHEAR.
I SEE...
WAIT... WHAT ARE YOU...?

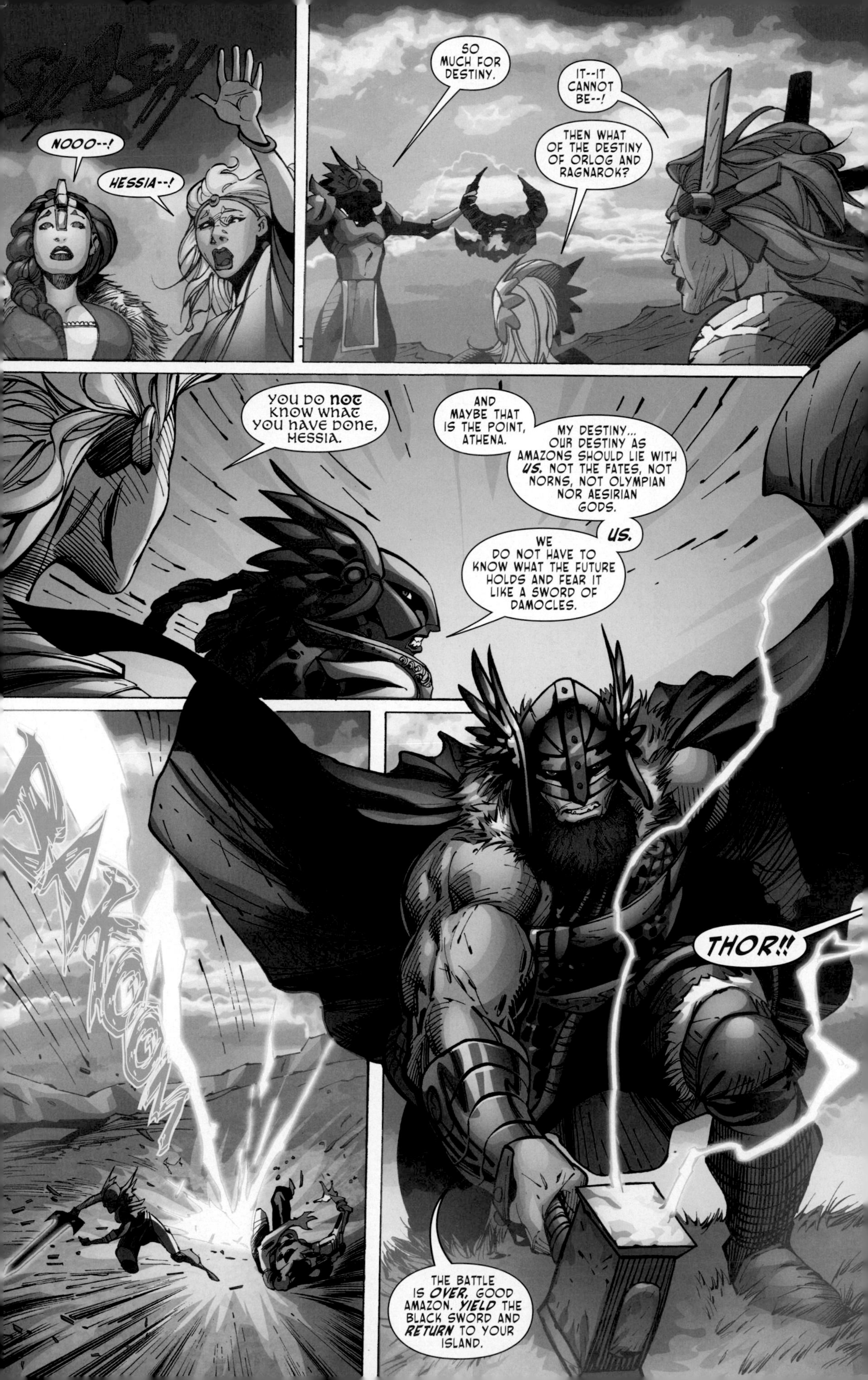
SPASH
NOOO--!
HESSIA--!
SO MUCH FOR DESTINY.
IT--IT CANNOT BE--!
THEN WHAT OF THE DESTINY OF ORLOG AND RAGNAROK?
YOU DO NOT KNOW WHAT YOU HAVE DONE, HESSIA.
AND MAYBE THAT IS THE POINT, ATHENA.
MY DESTINY... OUR DESTINY AS AMAZONS SHOULD LIE WITH US. NOT THE FATES, NOT NORNS, NOT OLYMPIAN NOR AESIRIAN GODS.
US.
WE DO NOT HAVE TO KNOW WHAT THE FUTURE HOLDS AND FEAR IT LIKE A SWORD OF DAMOCLES.
THOR!!
THE BATTLE IS OVER, GOOD AMAZON. YIELD THE BLACK SWORD AND RETURN TO YOUR ISLAND.

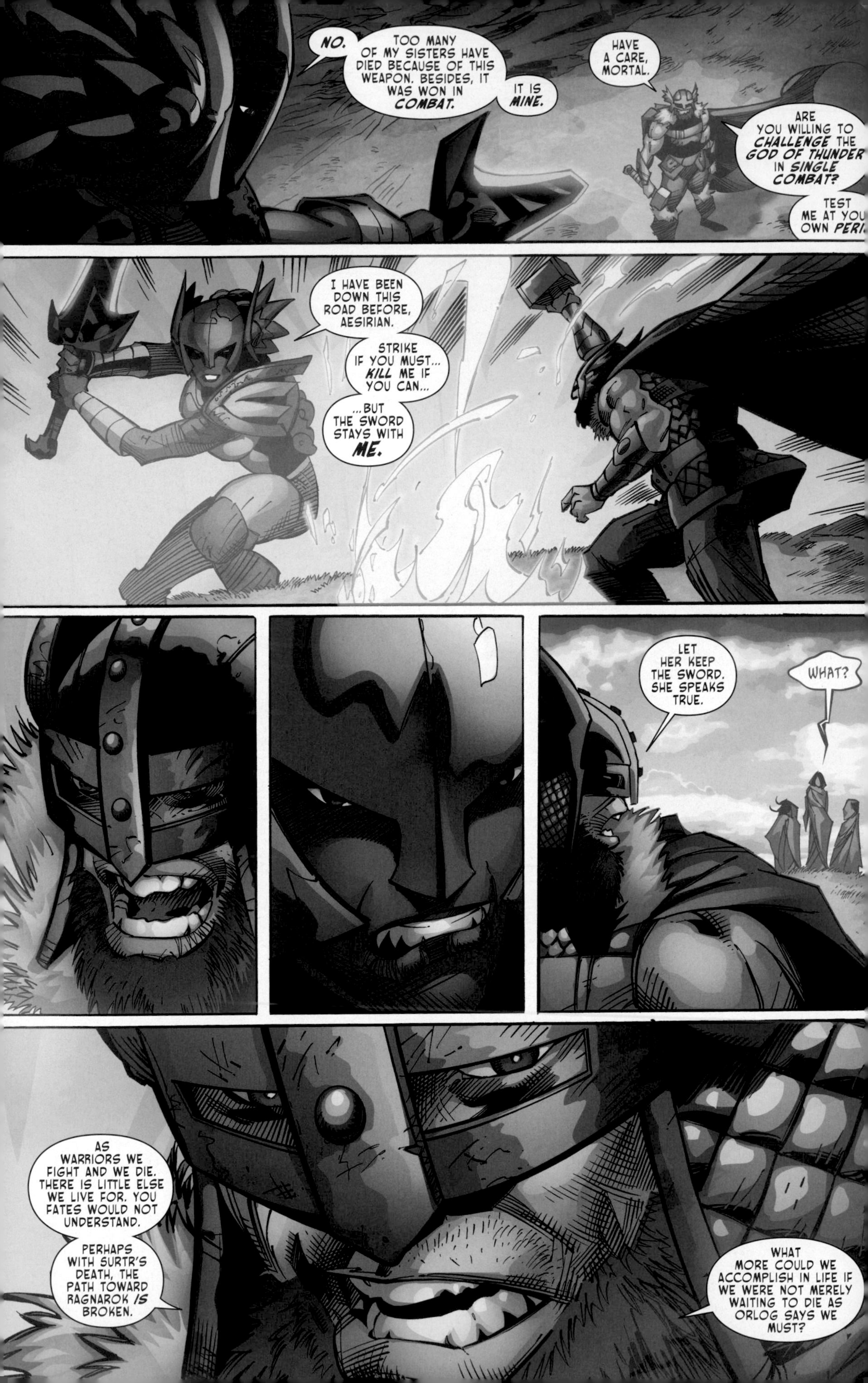
NO.
TOO MANY OF MY SISTERS HAVE DIED BECAUSE OF THIS WEAPON. BESIDES, IT WAS WON IN COMBAT.
IT IS MINE.
HAVE A CARE, MORTAL.
ARE YOU WILLING TO CHALLENGE THE GOD OF THUNDER IN SINGLE COMBAT?
TEST ME AT YOU OWN PERI
I HAVE BEEN DOWN THIS ROAD BEFORE, AESIRIAN.
STRIKE IF YOU MUST... KILL ME IF YOU CAN...
...BUT THE SWORD STAYS WITH ME.
LET HER KEEP THE SWORD. SHE SPEAKS TRUE.
WHAT?
AS WARRIORS WE FIGHT AND WE DIE. THERE IS LITTLE ELSE WE LIVE FOR. YOU FATES WOULD NOT UNDERSTAND.
PERHAPS WITH SURTR'S DEATH, THE PATH TOWARD RAGNAROK IS BROKEN.
WHAT MORE COULD WE ACCOMPLISH IN LIFE IF WE WERE NOT MERELY WAITING TO DIE AS ORLOG SAYS WE MUST?

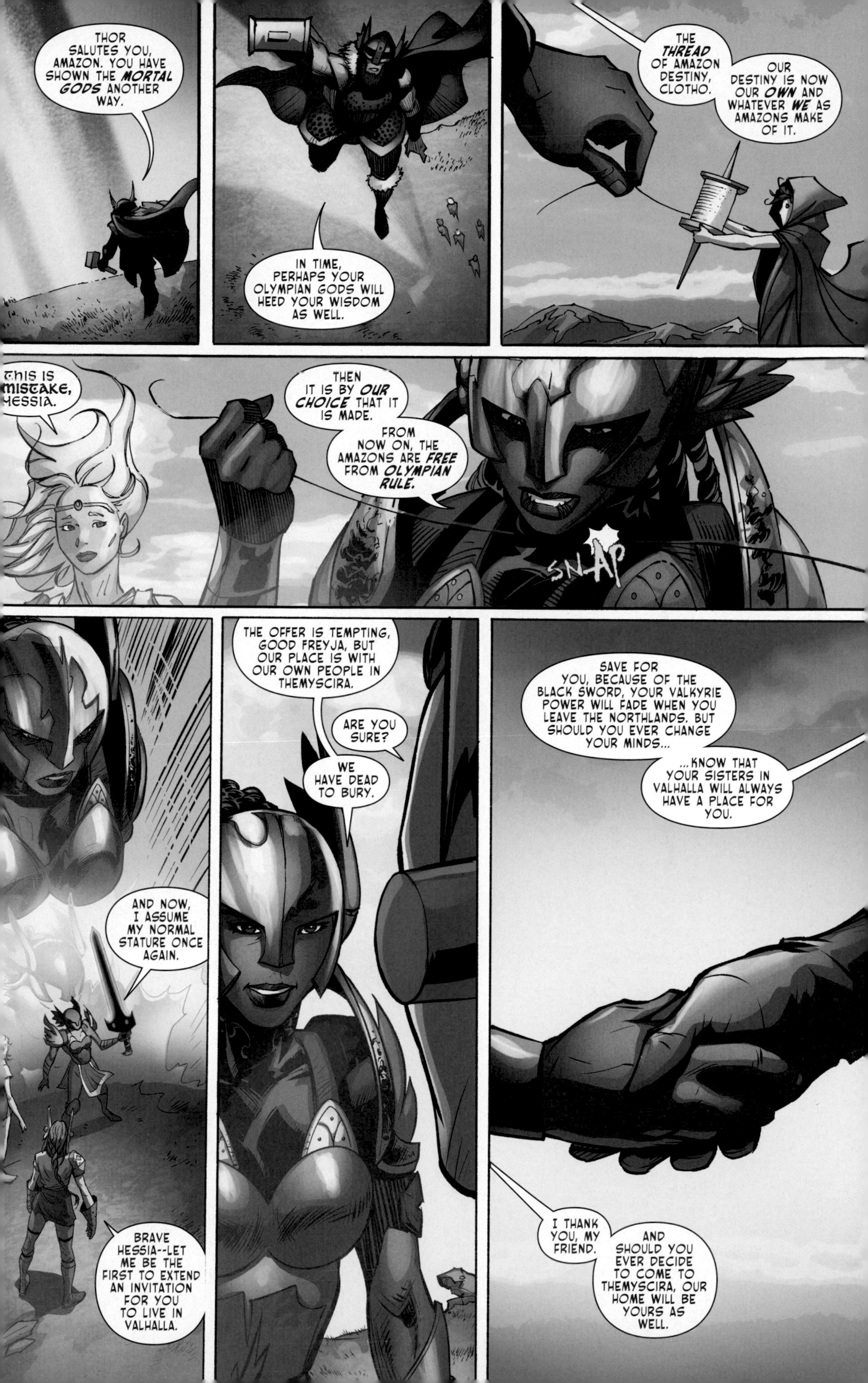
THOR SALUTES YOU, AMAZON. YOU HAVE SHOWN THE MORTAL GODS ANOTHER WAY.
IN TIME, PERHAPS YOUR OLYMPIAN GODS WILL HEED YOUR WISDOM AS WELL.
THE THREAD OF AMAZON DESTINY, CLOTHO.
OUR DESTINY IS NOW OUR OWN AND WHATEVER WE AS AMAZONS MAKE OF IT.
THIS IS MISTAKE, HESSIA.
THEN IT IS BY OUR CHOICE THAT IT IS MADE.
FROM NOW ON, THE AMAZONS ARE FREE FROM OLYMPIAN RULE.
SNAP
AND NOW, I ASSUME MY NORMAL STATURE ONCE AGAIN.
BRAVE HESSIA--LET ME BE THE FIRST TO EXTEND AN INVITATION FOR YOU TO LIVE IN VALHALLA.
THE OFFER IS TEMPTING, GOOD FREYJA, BUT OUR PLACE IS WITH OUR OWN PEOPLE IN THEMYSCIRA.
ARE YOU SURE?
WE HAVE DEAD TO BURY.
SAVE FOR YOU, BECAUSE OF THE BLACK SWORD, YOUR VALKYRIE POWER WILL FADE WHEN YOU LEAVE THE NORTHLANDS. BUT SHOULD YOU EVER CHANGE YOUR MINDS...
...KNOW THAT YOUR SISTERS IN VALHALLA WILL ALWAYS HAVE A PLACE FOR YOU.
I THANK YOU, MY FRIEND.
AND SHOULD YOU EVER DECIDE TO COME TO THEMYSCIRA, OUR HOME WILL BE YOURS AS WELL.

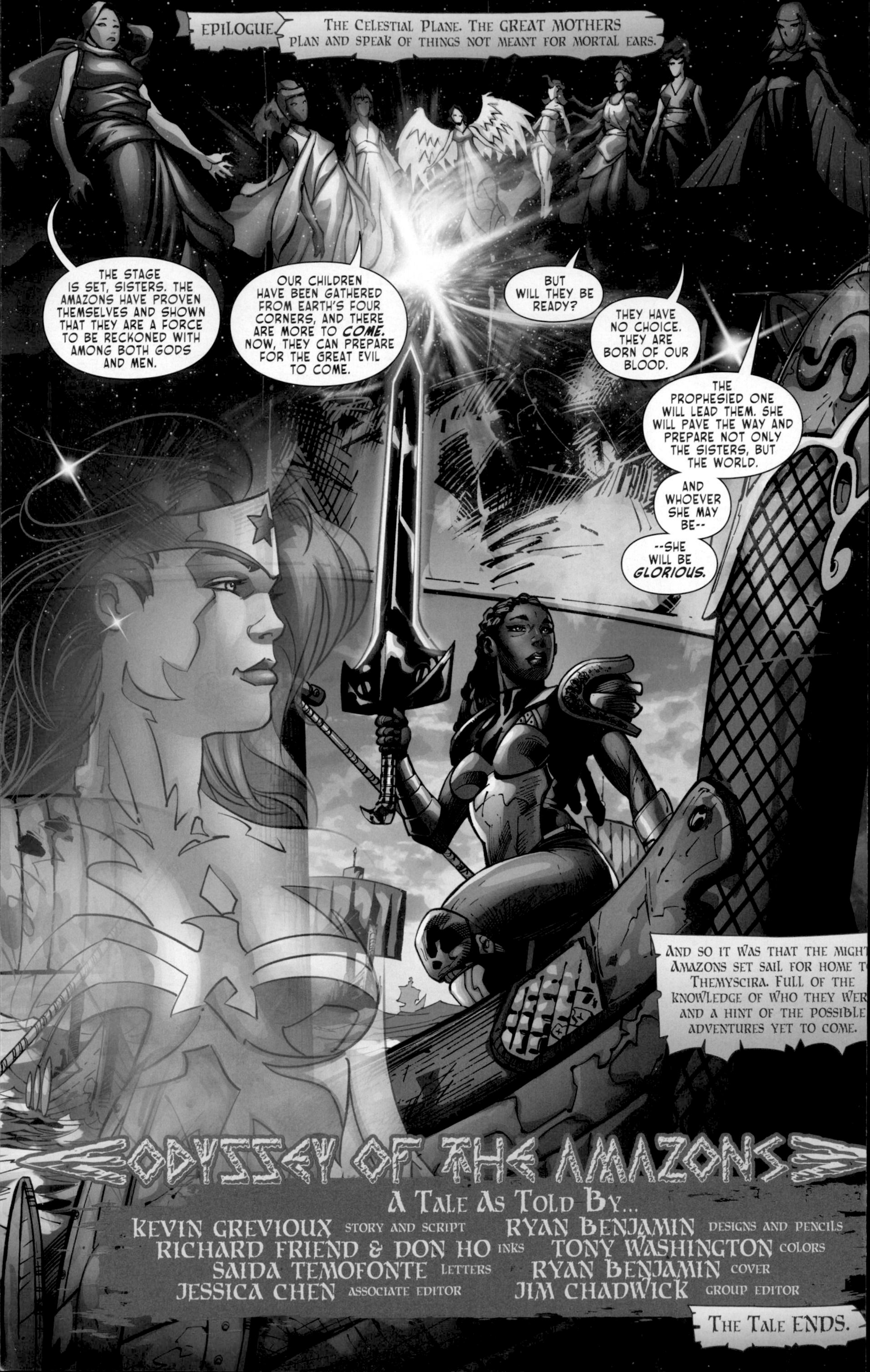
EPILOGUE
THE CELESTIAL PLANE. THE GREAT MOTHERS PLAN AND SPEAK OF THINGS NOT MEANT FOR MORTAL EARS.
THE STAGE IS SET, SISTERS. THE AMAZONS HAVE PROVEN THEMSELVES AND SHOWN THAT THEY ARE A FORCE TO BE RECKONED WITH AMONG BOTH GODS AND MEN.
OUR CHILDREN HAVE BEEN GATHERED FROM EARTH'S FOUR CORNERS, AND THERE ARE MORE TO *COME.* NOW, THEY CAN PREPARE FOR THE GREAT EVIL TO COME.
BUT WILL THEY BE READY?
THEY HAVE NO CHOICE. THEY ARE BORN OF OUR BLOOD.
THE PROPHESIED ONE WILL LEAD THEM. SHE WILL PAVE THE WAY AND PREPARE NOT ONLY THE SISTERS, BUT THE WORLD.
AND WHOEVER SHE MAY BE--
--SHE WILL BE *GLORIOUS.*
AND SO IT WAS THAT THE MIGHT AMAZONS SET SAIL FOR HOME T THEMYSCIRA. FULL OF THE KNOWLEDGE OF WHO THEY WER AND A HINT OF THE POSSIBLE ADVENTURES YET TO COME.
ODYSSEY OF THE AMAZONS
A TALE AS TOLD BY...
KEVIN GREVIOUX STORY AND SCRIPT RYAN BENJAMIN DESIGNS AND PENCILS
RICHARD FRIEND & DON HO INKS TONY WASHINGTON COLORS
SAIDA TEMOFONTE LETTERS RYAN BENJAMIN COVER
JESSICA CHEN ASSOCIATE EDITOR JIM CHADWICK GROUP EDITOR
THE TALE ENDS.

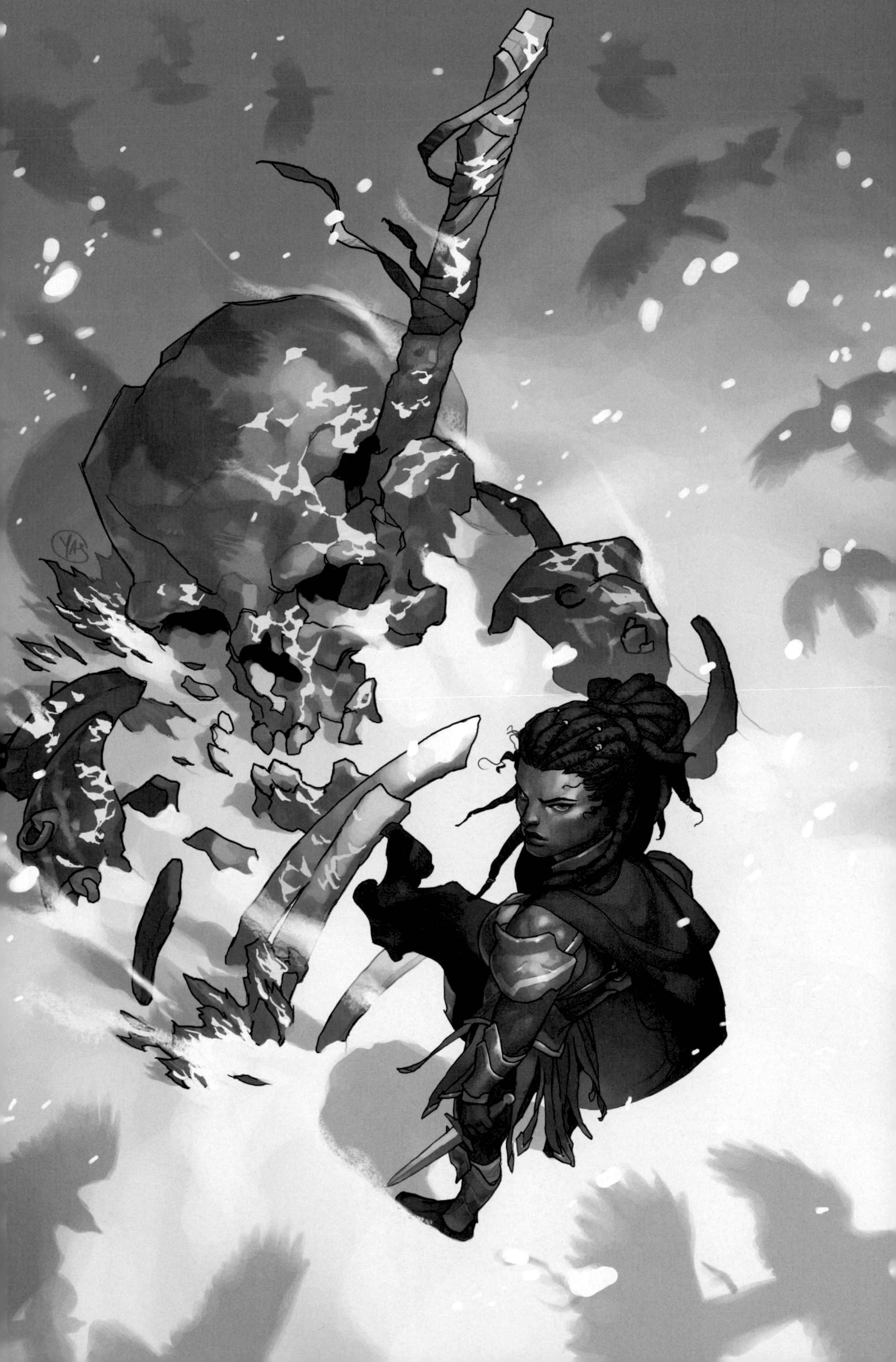

Variant cover art for issue #1 by Yasmine Putri

DRESSED TO KILL

Character designs by Ryan Benjamin

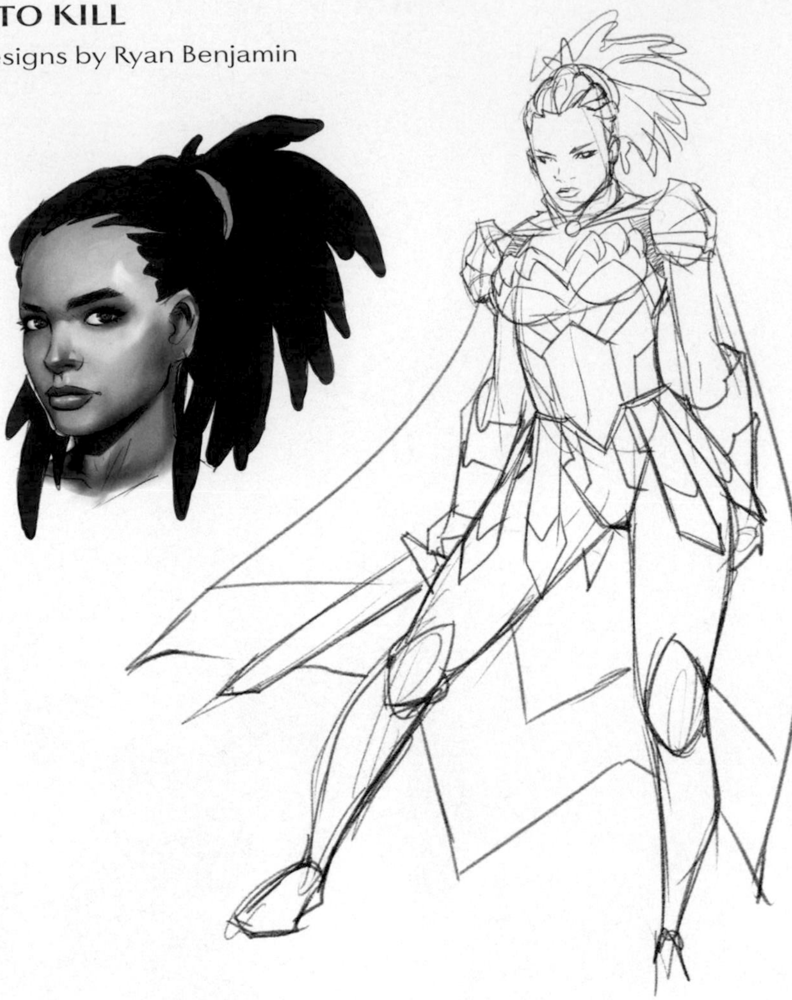

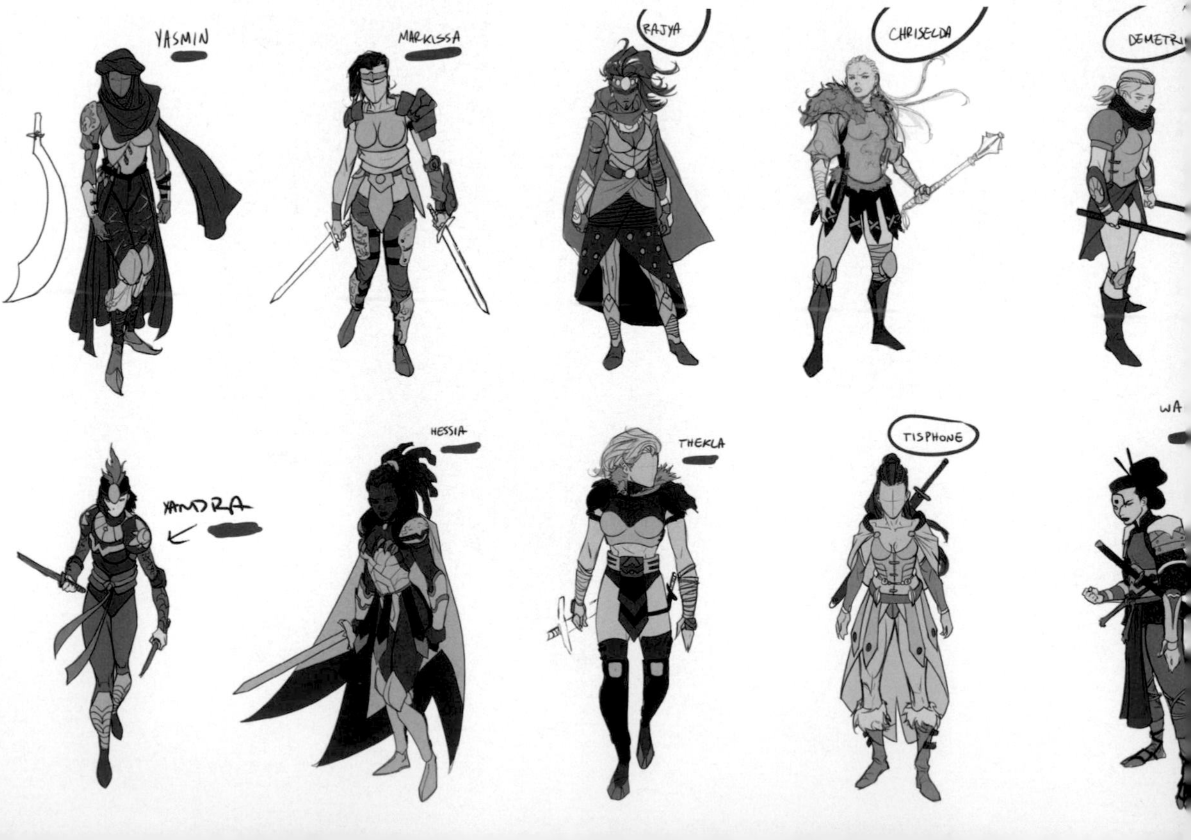
YASMIN
MARKISSA
RAJYA
CHRISELDA
YANDRA
HESSIA
THEKLA
TISPHONE

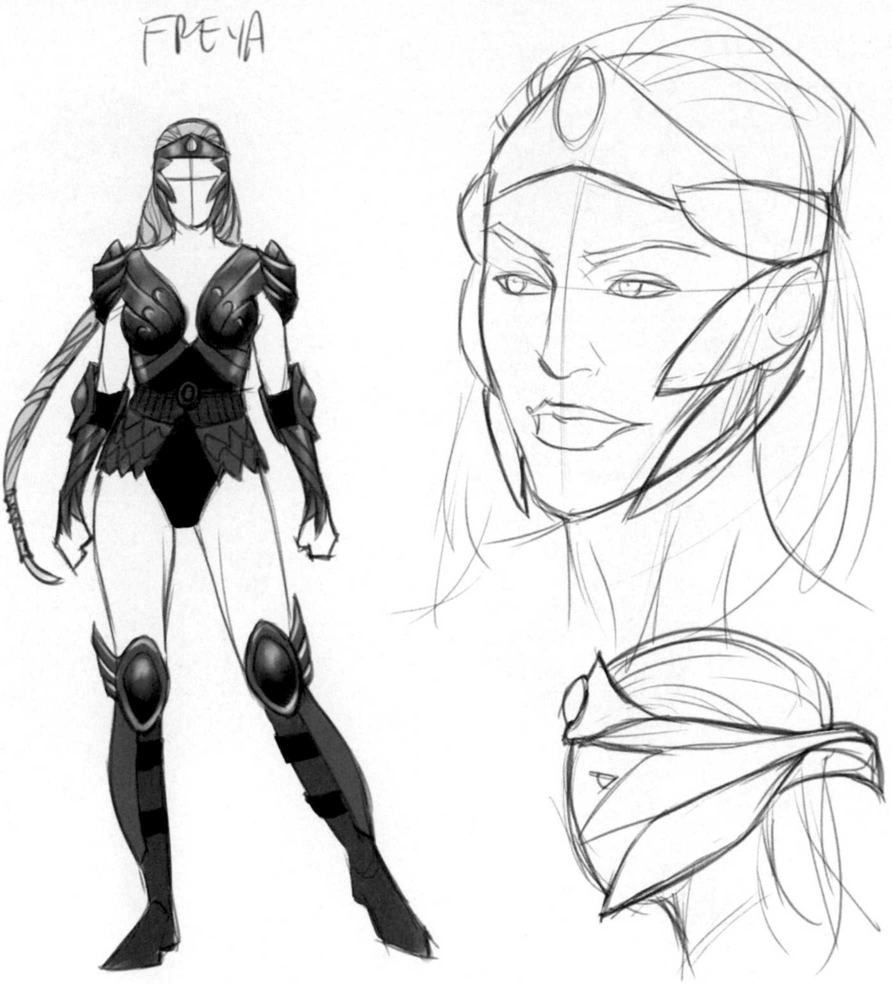
FREYA

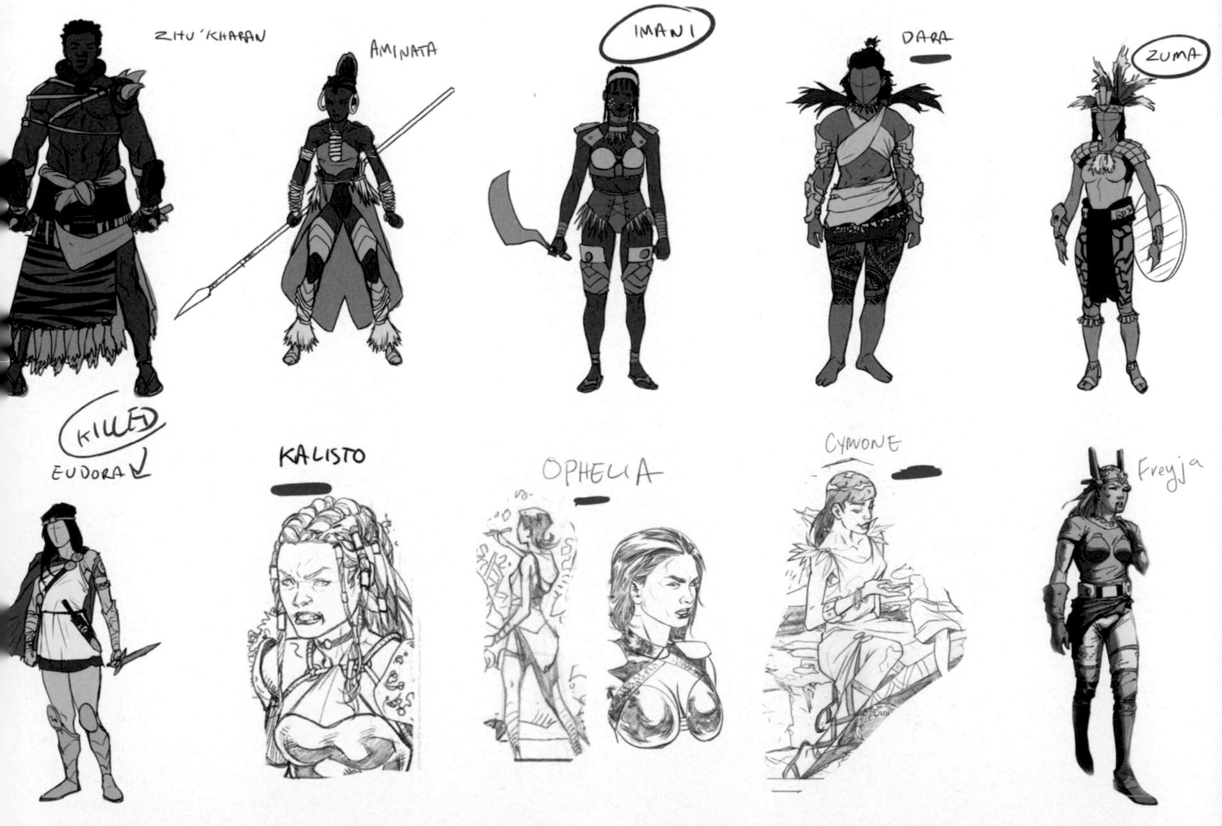
ZHU'KHARAN
AMINATA
IMANI
DARA
ZUMA
KILLED
EUDORA
KALISTO
OPHELIA
CYMONE
Freyja

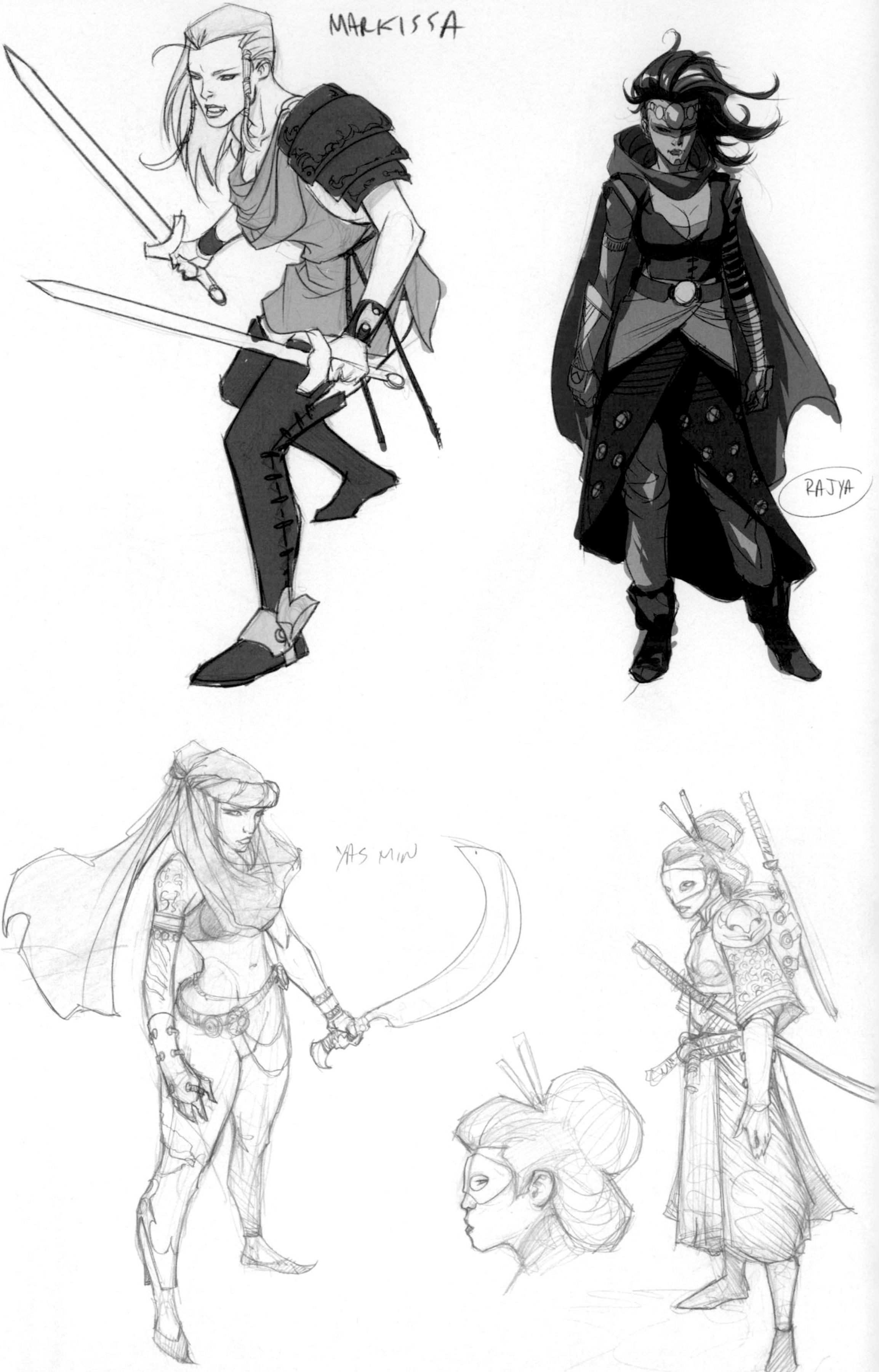
MARKISSA
RAJYA
YAS MIN

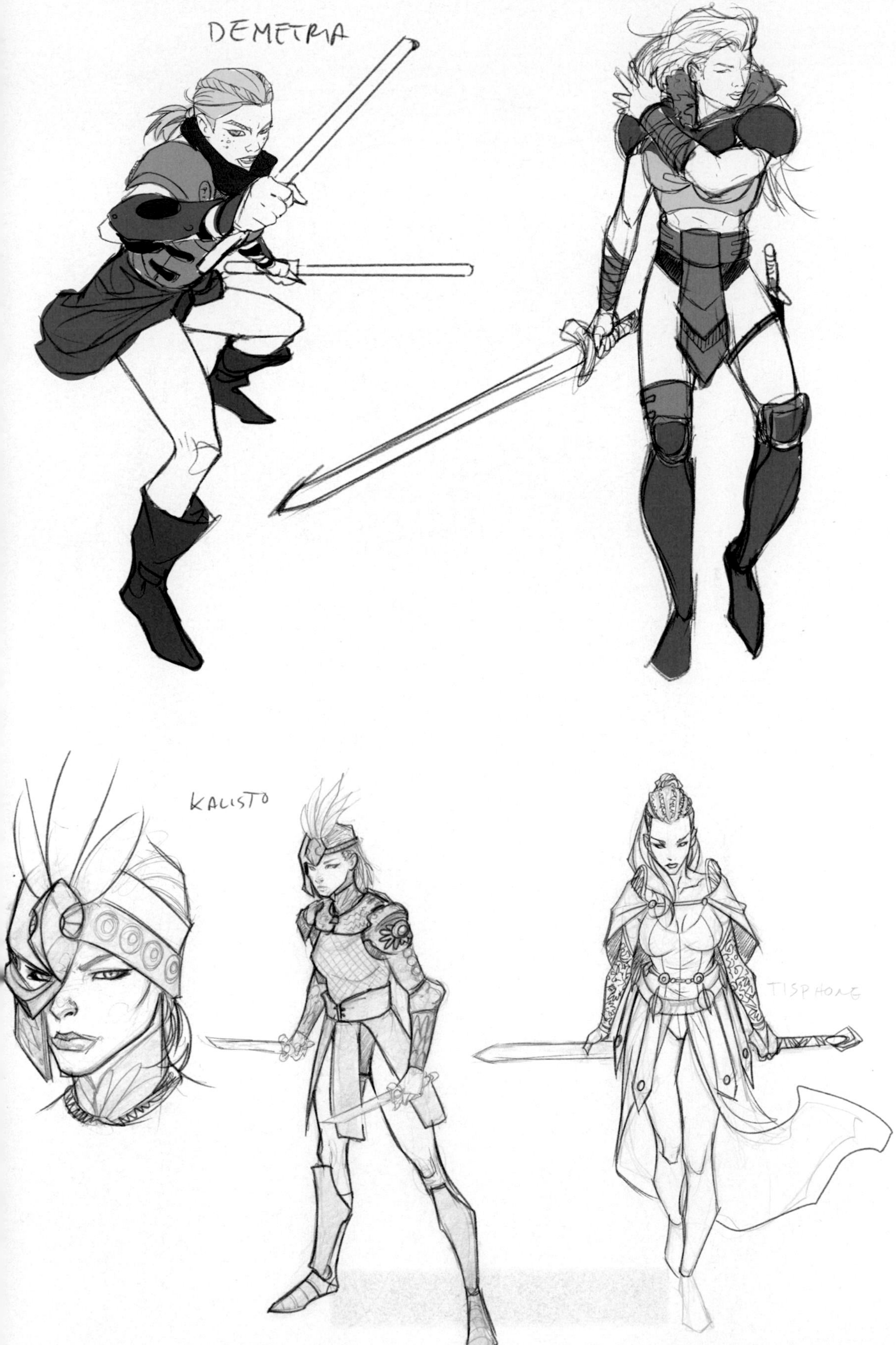

DEMETRIA
KALISTO
TISPHONE

Design for Thor's hammer by Jim Lee

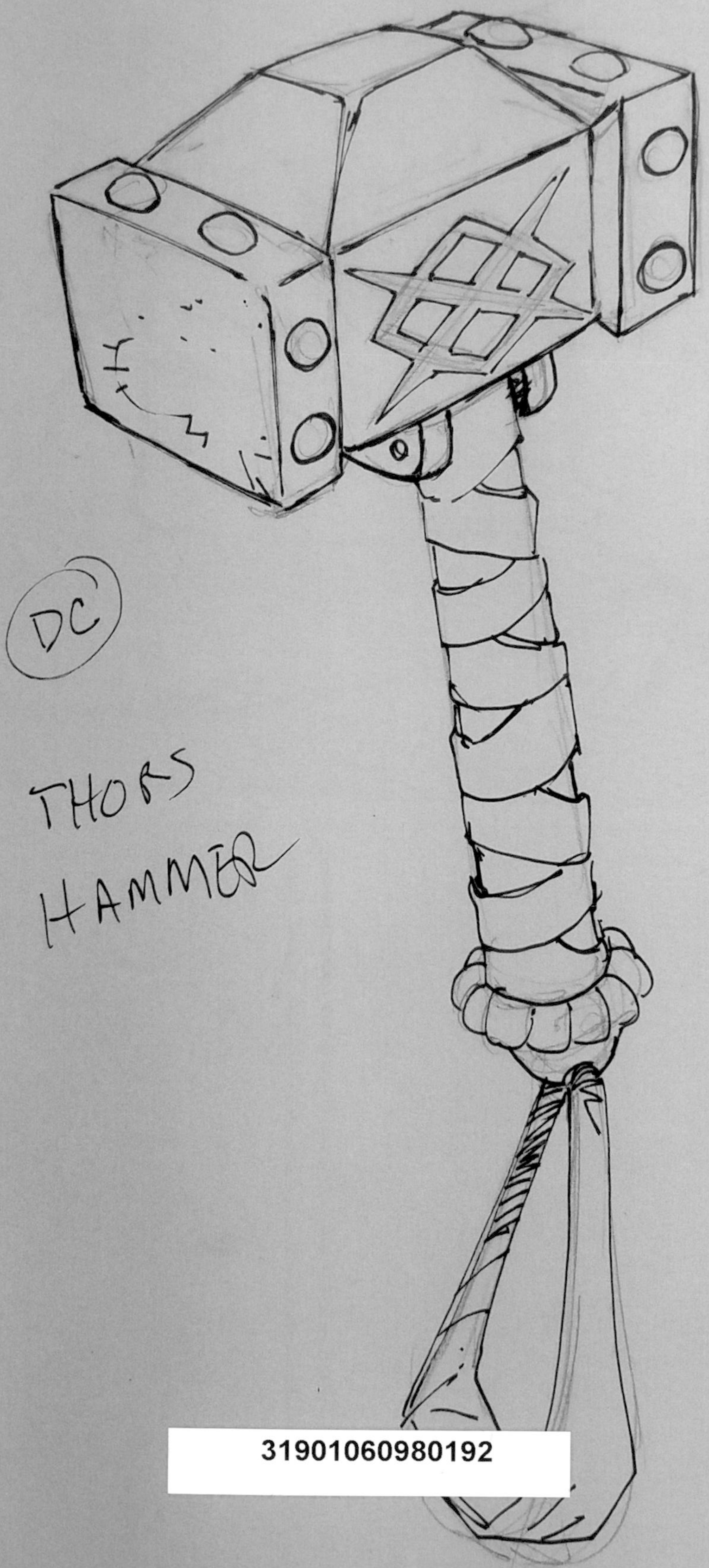
DC
THORS
HAMMER